THE MONARCH BUTTERFLY

THE MONARCH BUTTERFLY

BIOLOGY & CONSERVATION

Edited by

Karen S. Oberhauser

&

Michelle J. Solensky

COMSTOCK PUBLISHING ASSOCIATES, *a division of*

CORNELL UNIVERSITY PRESS

Ithaca & London

First published 2004 by Cornell University Press

Printed in the United States of America

Library of Congress Cataloging-in-Publication Data

The Monarch butterfly: biology and conservation / edited by Karen S. Oberhauser and Michelle J. Solensky.
p. cm.
Includes bibliographical references and index.
ISBN 0-8014-4188-9 (cloth : alk. paper)
1. Monarch butterfly. 2. Wildlife conservation. I. Oberhauser, Karen Suzanne. II. Solensky, Michelle J.
QL561.D3M66 2004
595.78′9—dc22

2004000884

Cornell University Press strives to use environmentally responsible suppliers and materials to the fullest extent possible in the publishing of its books. Such materials include vegetable-based, low-VOC inks and acid-free papers that are recycled, totally chlorine-free, or partly composed of nonwood fibers. For further information, visit our website at www.cornellpress.cornell.edu.

Cloth printing 10 9 8 7 6 5 4 3 2 1

Contents

Preface

Despite the fact that it is but one of over a million insect species in the world, no other nonpest insect has attracted as much attention as the monarch butterfly. Children study monarchs in school, citizens throughout North America track their migration and breeding, conservationists are concerned about the impacts of pesticides and habitat loss on monarchs, and citizens, government agencies, and conservation organizations try to alleviate these impacts. Scientists throughout the world study the monarch's mating behavior, interactions with milkweed and predators, responses to environmental change, and migration. Why all this attention? It is easy to understand why governments, scientists, and citizens are concerned about insect pests that consume human crops, spread disease, or represent a painful nuisance during backyard picnics or camping trips. It is also easy to understand our interest in beneficial insects that provide human food, like honeybees, or help to control pests, like a myriad of biological control agents. Such insects have large and measurable impacts on humans. Monarchs, however, do not. If monarchs became extinct tomorrow, it is likely that the impact on our material well-being would be negligible.

Part of our fascination with monarchs results from their spectacular and unique (among insects) migration, during which a single individual can traverse Canada, the United States, and Mexico. The concept that an organism with a mass 20% that of a penny can fly over 2000 miles from summer breeding grounds to overwintering sites in Mexico is mind-boggling, as are the aggregations of millions of butterflies seen at these sites, single-species groups that may be surpassed in number only by krill in waters surrounding Antarctica. In addition, their popularity and recognition make them excellent subjects for research and observation by students and other citizens. Monarchs are relatively easy to raise and observe in captivity; a surprising number of people remember discovering a monarch larva as a child and bringing it home to observe its transformation into a butterfly. This popularity also makes them the target of conservation concern. While human activities affect most of the organisms with which we share the earth, monarchs engender more than their share of public interest in this arena.

Perhaps it is their amazing biology, perhaps it is childhood memories, or perhaps the bold yellow, black, and white stripes on the larvae and the orange and black coloration on the adults, which warn other animals of danger and distastefulness, hold an unexplained attraction to the human psyche. In any case, this attraction and the resultant conservation and scientific interest have added a great deal to human knowledge of the natural world and to our concern about preserving it. This understanding and concern will serve us, and other organisms, well.

The discovery of the overwintering colonies of monarchs during the winter of 1975–1976 by Canadians Fred and Norah Urquhart and their colleagues Ken Brugger and Catalina Aguado triggered an outpouring of scientific interest. However, this species had already been the focus of important work on relationships between insects and their host plants, insect defenses from predation, mimicry, and overwintering biology. Much of this early work was carried out by Lincoln Brower and his students and colleagues, and Dr. Brower continues to be an important force in the research and conservation of monarchs.

There have been four international conferences on monarch biology and conservation: the Symposium on the Biology and Conservation of Monarch Butterflies (in Morelos, Mexico, 1981), the Second International Conference on the Monarch Butterfly (in Los Angeles, California, 1986), the North American Conference on the Monarch Butterfly (in Morelia, Michoacan, 1997), and the Monarch Population Dynamics Conference (in Lawrence, Kansas, 2001). Each emphasized the importance of international cooperation in monarch conservation. Since sound conservation and management policies require an understanding of the factors that affect the population dynamics of the species, participants in the Monarch Working Table at the Fifth Annual Meeting of the Trilateral Committee for Wildlife and Ecosystem Conservation and Management held on South Padre Island, Texas (February 2000), recommended a "continental diagnosis" that would pinpoint vulnerable monarch stages and locations. This diagnosis would synthesize existing information and identify what else needs to be known. The 2001 meeting and this book are direct results of the recommendations of the 2000 Trilateral Monarch Working Table and the start of a unique project—an attempt to understand the annual dynamics of a migratory insect with a continental distribution.

Presenters at the 2001 Monarch Population Dynamics Conference were invited to contribute chapters to this book, as were other monarch scientists. Because of the widespread interest of citizens and educators, the authors of the chapters that follow are an extremely diverse group. University scientists are joined by independent scientists, scientists working at institutions such as the National Parks Service, and high school teachers and students. These individuals are from the United States, Canada, Mexico, Australia, and the United Kingdom. Several chapters include input from citizen scientist projects—Journey North, the Monarch Larva Monitoring Project, and Monarch Watch—and represent the data collection efforts of thousands of citizens from the United States and Canada. This comprehensive representation of the current state of knowledge on all stages of the monarch's annual cycle could not have been met without such a diverse and knowledgeable group.

This book is divided into four parts. Part 1 emphasizes aspects of the breeding stage of monarchs' annual cycle; part 2 focuses on the migratory phase of this cycle; part 3 keys in on the dynamics of monarchs as they "hibernate" in densely populated sites in central Mexico and coastal California; and part 4 synthesizes current knowledge through integrating themes.

The conference that inspired this book was hosted by Monarch Watch (University of Kansas) in collaboration with Monarchs in the Classroom (University of Minnesota). It could not have transpired without additional support from the U.S. Fish and Wildlife Service, the National Fish and Wildlife Foundation, the University of Kansas (Office of the Provost, College of Liberal Arts and Sciences, and Natural History Museum and Biodiversity Research Center), the Monarch Butterfly Sanctuary Foundation, and the National Science Foundation. We thank all of these organizations. We also thank Jolene Lushine and Laura Molenaar for their expert editing.

Much of what is known about monarchs is the result of citizens who have volunteered in several monarch citizen science efforts throughout the past half-century. We thank participants in Dr. Fred Urquhart's tagging program, Journey North, Monarch Watch, the Monarch Larva Monitoring Project, the Monarch Monitoring Project (Cape May, N. J.), and Texas Monarch Watch for their important contributions. It is to these citizens that this book is dedicated.

PART I

Breeding Biology

1

Overview of Monarch Breeding Biology

Karen S. Oberhauser

Many people are attracted to the biology of monarchs by their spectacular migration and the unequaled phenomenon of millions of butterflies blanketing a few hectares of land in central Mexico. However, every adult that carries out this migration and joins millions of conspecifics in Mexico or thousands in California began its life as an egg on a milkweed plant and faced a myriad of environmental challenges as it developed. In addition, most generations of monarchs do not undergo the long-distance migrations to and from the overwintering sites. Preadult stages and the adult behaviors that produce them provide the subjects of this section: mating, egg laying, and the many challenges faced by eggs and larvae as they develop into adults.

EGGS AND LARVAE

Monarchs lay their eggs on milkweed plants; hence monarch biology is tied closely to milkweed biology. They utilize most of the over 100 North American species (Woodson 1954) in the milkweed family (Asclepiadaceae), the only group of plants that provide food for developing larvae. By laying eggs on the only plants their offspring can eat, females ensure that the larvae will have a ready supply of food on hatching.

Monarchs breed over a broad geographic and temporal range, and their numbers vary a great deal in space and time. Documenting variation in monarch egg and larva abundance is the topic of a citizen science effort reported in chapter 2 by Prysby and Oberhauser. In this project, volunteers throughout the breeding range have measured monarch densities for the past 6 years. Because densities of eggs and larvae are so much easier to quantify than those of the adults, researchers can use comparable methods in many areas to produce data that allow spatial and temporal comparisons.

It is difficult to tell just how many eggs each female butterfly lays during her life, but the average in the wild is probably 300 to 400. Captive monarch butterflies average about 700 eggs/female over 2 to 5 weeks of egg laying, with a record of 1179 eggs (Oberhauser 1997). Monarch eggs hatch about 4 days after they are laid, but the rate of development in this stage, like all other stages, is temperature dependent, with individuals in warmer environments developing more rapidly (Zalucki 1982).

Females have a limited amount of resources to allocate to egg production, and the proteins that are an important constituent of eggs must be either derived from nutrients ingested during the larval stage or obtained from males during mating (Boggs and Gilbert 1979, Oberhauser 1997). While an individual monarch egg weighs only about 0.460 mg, about 1/1000th the mass of an adult, females often lay more than their own mass in eggs throughout their lives. With this large an investment, there is likely to be a trade-off between the egg number and egg size. Oberhauser explores factors that affect monarch egg size in chapter 3. She found that larger females lay larger eggs, and that egg size decreases with female age.

Monarchs complete almost all of their growth during the larval stage. These insect "eating machines" take few breaks even to rest. They typically begin life by eating their eggshell, then move on to the milkweed leaves on which they were laid. The larval stage lasts from 9 to 14 days under normal summer temperatures. Larvae molt (shed their skin) as they grow, and the stages between larval molts are called instars. All monarchs go through five separate larval instars. From hatching to pupation, they increase their body mass about 2000 times (pers. observ.).

Monarch eggs and larvae have a slim chance of reaching adulthood; several previous studies documented mortality rates of over 90% during the egg and larval stages (Borkin 1982; Zalucki and Kitching 1982; Oberhauser et al. 2001). In chapter 2, Prysby and Oberhauser present additional data collected by citizen scientist volunteers on survival rates of eggs and larvae.

There are both abiotic and biotic sources of monarch mortality during the breeding season. Abiotic (nonliving) factors include environmental conditions such as adverse weather and pesticides. Biotic (living) factors that affect the survival of monarchs include natural enemies, and interactions with their milkweed hosts. Many monarchs in natural populations are killed by invertebrate predators that eat the monarchs themselves, or by parasitoids whose larvae develop in and eventually kill the monarch larvae. Diseases caused by bacteria, viruses, fungi, and other organisms are also significant sources of monarch mortality.

Chapters 4, 5, and 6 by Prysby, Rayor, and Calvert focus on invertebrate predators of monarchs. Prysby describes the overall impacts of natural enemies on monarch survival. In one experiment, she limited the access of predators to monarch eggs and larvae by constructing cages around milkweed plants. She found that excluding both terrestrial and aerial predators increased monarch survival. In another experiment, she found that monarch eggs were less likely to survive on plants on which ants had been observed. Finally, she found that over 14% of the monarchs that survive to late instar larval stages are killed by tachinid fly parasitoids. Rayor and Calvert focused on the effects of a single predator on monarch survival in their studies. Rayor (chapter 5) studied how predation by paper wasps is affected by larval size and the host plant species on which the larvae are feeding. She found that medium-sized larvae are most susceptible to paper wasp predation, and that the wasps generally preferred larvae that consumed milkweed host plants with lower levels of cardenolides. Since paper wasps are abundant throughout the entire monarch breeding range, Rayor concludes that they are likely to be a significant source of mortality. Calvert (chapter 6) used exclosures to study the impact of invasive fire ants on monarchs, and found that monarchs inside exclosures were much more likely to survive than those outside the structures. Despite the large amount of mortality from fire ants, Calvert suggests that pre–fire ant mortality may have been similarly high, since these invasive ants displaced native ants that also preyed on monarchs.

While the mortality described here appears to indicate that monarchs are helpless in the face of an onslaught of predators, monarchs have an effective chemical defense against many predators. They sequester cardenolides (also called cardiac glycosides) present in the milkweed (Brower and Moffit 1974). These compounds are poisonous to most vertebrates; hence monarchs face limited predation from frogs, lizards, mice, birds, and other animals with backbones. The insects described in the previous paragraph, as well as some bacteria and viruses, may be unharmed by the toxins or be able to overcome them. However, Rayor's finding that wasps are less likely to prey on monarchs consuming milkweed with high levels of cardenolides suggests that this defense is at least somewhat effective against invertebrate predators.

The benefits gained by monarchs from the sequestered cardenolides are not without cost. While cardenolides help monarchs in their defense against predators, these compounds are actually produced by milkweed plants as a chemical defense against herbivores. In addition, the plants produce a sticky substance called latex; this is the source of the name "milkweed." This substance also provides a mechanical defense against herbivores, whose mandibles may be glued together by the material or whose bodies may become mired in a drop of latex formed when the plant is injured. Several researchers have shown that monarch larvae are negatively affected by these defenses (Zalucki and Brower 1992; Malcolm and Zalucki 1996; Zalucki and Malcolm 1999; Zalucki et al. 2001). In chapter 7, Hoevenaar and Malcolm present a study of how defenses in *Asclepias curassavica* and *A. incarnata* milkweed plants affect the behavior of monarch larvae. Surprisingly, there were no differences in the monarch response to these two species, which vary in cardenolide content and latex volume, and Hoevenaar and Malcolm conclude that monarchs are well-adapted specialists that can handle the defenses in these two species without negative impacts on their performance.

Monarchs require specific abiotic conditions to survive. Eggs do not hatch in very dry conditions. Very hot weather also causes mortality; several studies have shown that temperatures above approximately 35°C (95°F) can be lethal to all stages (Zalucki 1982; Malcolm et al. 1987). Likewise, extended periods in which temperatures are below freezing can kill monarchs, although this has been best studied in overwintering adults (Anderson and Brower 1993, 1996; Brower et al., this volume). Threats due to very hot or very cold temperatures are magnified during the breeding season, since monarchs are indirectly affected by conditions that affect the health and survival of milkweed. Freezing temperatures and extremely dry conditions can be especially damaging to milkweed, and thus to monarchs.

PUPAE

During the pupal stage, the transformation to the adult stage is completed in a process that takes about 9 to 15 days under normal summer temperatures. From the outside, few of these changes are apparent until the final day, when the black, orange, and white wing patterns of the adults are visible through the pupal covering. This results from the development of the scale pigmentation at the very end of the pupal stage. However, most of the physiological and morphological changes that produce an adult monarch actually begin to occur within the larva. The wings and other adult organs develop from tiny clusters of cells already present in the larva, and by the time it pupates, the monarch has already begun the major changes to the adult form. As it forms the pupa, the antennae, proboscis, wings, and legs move to the surface just inside the exoskeleton, and the most notable changes that occur after this involve a major reorganization of the flight muscles in the thorax. Sperm also mature during the pupal stage, although eggs do not mature until after adult eclosion.

The ecology of monarch (or any other lepidopteran) pupae is not well studied, and unfortunately, this book does not add to our knowledge of pupal ecology. This is probably at least partially due to the fact that it is extremely difficult to find monarch pupae in the wild; their green color provides effective camouflage in a green world, and they appear to seek sheltered spots to undergo this transformation. Important issues remain to be studied: how larvae choose sites for pupation, how far they travel seeking these sites, what habitat characteristics are important in promoting pupal survival, and how much mortality from different sources occurs during this stage.

ADULTS

The primary goal during the adult stage is to reproduce—to mate and lay the eggs that will become the next generation. Adults in summer generations live from 2 to 5 weeks, while those that migrate may live up to 9 months. This difference is due to the fact that overwintering monarchs are not reproductive and can thus funnel more energy into survival. In addition, the cool conditions in the hibernation sites slow their metabolism, allowing them to live longer.

Summer-generation monarchs first mate when they are 3 to 8 days old (Oberhauser and Hampton 1995), and females begin laying eggs immediately after their first mating. Monarchs that overwinter do not lay eggs until spring (although they may mate before this). Both sexes can mate several times during their lives (e.g., Oberhauser 1989), and the ability of male monarchs to force unwilling females to copulate makes them unique among the Lepidoptera (Oberhauser 1989; Van Hook 1993; Frey et al. 1998). Since male reproductive success in most animals depends on the number of females with which they are able to copulate (Bateman 1948), determining the factors that affect male mating success is a major focus of many behavioral ecologists. Solensky and Oberhauser (chapter 8) discuss factors that affect the mating success of male monarchs. They found that mating success is a heritable trait; males that mate more often than other males tend to have sons that mate more often. Since males attempt to mate with many more females than they actually successfully copulate with, Solensky and Oberhauser tested whether males that mated more often simply tried to mate with more females, or whether they were more likely to be successful during any given mating attempt. They found that the latter was true; something about some males makes their mating attempts more likely to end in success. The characteristics that result in more frequent success remain unidentified.

Since there is a delay between adult emergence and egg laying and because monarch adults reproduce over a relatively long time period, maximizing reproductive success also requires being able to survive predators, environmental extremes, and other sources of mortality. Adult survival during the breeding season is another understudied area of monarch biology, despite its importance to monarch population dynamics. Important research topics that remain to be addressed include the effects of nectar availability and quality, the distances that females will fly to find milkweed host plants, the degree to which breeding monarchs remain in one area or move, and the effects of abiotic conditions on adult survival.

HUMAN-INDUCED MORTALITY DURING THE BREEDING SEASON

Humans often change the environment in ways that may kill monarchs. The most important source of human-caused mortality is loss of habitat, especially the destruction of milkweed and nectar sources. Some people consider milkweed a noxious weed and often destroy it. In addition, herbicides used to kill plants in agricultural fields, near roadsides, and in gardens may harm milkweed and nectar sources and may also kill monarchs directly. Monarchs can also be exposed to insecticides used to control pests in agricultural fields, forests, and gardens. Many people worry that the use of insecticides to combat mosquito-borne diseases like the West Nile virus will kill monarchs and other beneficial insects.

A potential source of monarch mortality that has received a great deal of attention recently is corn genetically modified to contain *Bacillus thuringiensis* (Bt) toxin (Losey et al. 1999; Jesse and Obrycki 2000; Oberhauser et al. 2001; Sears et al. 2001; Brower 2001). This corn produces a protein that is toxic to lepidopteran larvae and effective against the European corn borer, an important agricultural pest. However, the wind-dispersed pollen produced by Bt corn also carries the toxin. The toxicity of the pollen produced by different genetically modified corn varieties varies significantly, and the varieties now on the market have lower levels of toxin than some of the earlier varieties (Hellmich et al. 2001; Sears et al. 2001). If pollen with high levels of Bt is blown onto plants growing in or near cornfields, it could pose a threat to nontarget Lepidoptera that consume these plants. Most researchers who have assessed the risks of this technology isolated corn pollen from other material shed by the plant (particularly the pollen-bearing anthers) (Hellmich et al. 2001; Sears et al. 2001). Jesse and Obrycki (chapter 9) describe what happened when larvae were exposed to Bt corn pollen and anthers naturally deposited on milkweed plants within a cornfield. They found a consistent trend of lower survival in Bt fields than non-Bt fields. While this finding was not statistically significant (there is a 10% chance that their findings could have been due to random variation, versus the 5% generally taken to mean statistical significance), it clearly indicates that there is a good chance that the blanket conclusion that Bt corn poses *no* risks to monarchs (Sears et al. 2001) should be revisited.

References

Anderson, J. B., and L. P. Brower. 1993. Cold-hardiness in the annual cycle of the monarch butterfly. In S. B. Malcolm and M. P. Zalucki, eds., Biology and conservation of the monarch butterfly, pp. 157–64. Los Angeles: Natural History Museum of Los Angeles County.

Anderson, J. B., and L. P. Brower. 1996. Freeze-protection of overwintering monarch butterflies in Mexico: critical role of the forest as a blanket and an umbrella. Ecol. Entomol. 21:107–16.

Bateman, A. 1948. Intra-sexual selection in *Drosophila*. Heredity 2:349–68.

Boggs, C. L., and L. Gilbert. 1979. Male contribution to egg production in butterflies: evidence for transfer of nutrients at mating. Science 206:83–84.

Borkin, S. S. 1982. Notes on shifting distribution patterns and survival of immature *Danaus plexippus* (Lepidoptera: Danaidae) on the food plant *Asclepias syriaca*. Gt. Lakes Entomol. 15:199–207.

Brower, L. P. 2001. Canary in the cornfield. Orion 20:32–41.

Brower, L. P., and C. M. Moffit. 1974. Palatability dynamics of cardenolides in the monarch butterfly. Nature 249:280–83.

Frey, D., K. L. H. Leong, E. Peffer, R. K. Smidt, and K. S. Oberhauser. 1998. Mating patterns of overwintering monarch butterflies (*Danaus plexippus* [L.]) in California. J. Lepid. Soc. 52:84–97.

Hellmich, R. L., B. D. Siegfried, M. K. Sears, D. E. Stanley-Horn, M. J. Daniels, H. R. Mattila, T. Spencer, K. G. Bidne, and L. C. Lewis. 2001. Monarch larvae sensitivity to *Bacillus thuringiensis*-purified proteins and pollen. Proc. Natl. Acad. Sci. USA 98:11925–30.

Jesse, L. C. H., and J. J. Obrycki. 2000. Field deposition of Bt transgenic corn pollen: lethal effects on the monarch butterfly. Oecologia 125:241–48.

Losey, J. E., L. S. Rayor, and M. E. Carter. 1999. Transgenic pollen harms monarch larvae. Nature 399:214.

Malcolm, S. B., B. J. Cockrell, and L. P. Brower. 1987. Monarch butterfly voltinism: effects of temperature constraints at different latitudes. Oikos 49:77–82.

Malcolm, S. B., and M. P. Zalucki. 1996. Milkweed latex and cardenolide induction may resolve the lethal plant defense paradox. Entomol. Exp. Appl. 80:193–96.

Oberhauser, K. S. 1989. Effects of spermatophores on male and female monarch butterfly reproductive success. Behav. Ecol. Sociobiol. 25:237–46.

Oberhauser, K. S. 1997. Fecundity and egg mass of monarch butterflies: effects of age, female size and mating history. Funct. Ecol. 11:166–75.

Oberhauser, K. S., and R. Hampton. 1995. Relationship between mating and oogenesis in monarch butterflies. J. Insect Behav. 8:701–13.

Oberhauser, K. S., M. D. Prysby, H. R. Mattila, D. E. Stanley-Horn, M. K. Sears, G. Dively, E. Olson, J. M. Pleasants, W. F. Lam, and R. L. Hellmich. 2001. Temporal and spatial overlap between monarch larvae and corn pollen. Proc. Natl. Acad. Sci. USA 98:11913–18.

Sears, M. K., R. L. Hellmich, D. E. Stanley-Horn, K. S. Oberhauser, J. M. Pleasants, H. R. Mattila, B. D. Siegfried, and G. P. Dively. 2001. Impact of Bt corn pollen on monarch butterfly populations: a risk assessment. Proc. Natl. Acad. Sci. USA 98:11937–42.

Van Hook, T. 1993. Non-random mating in monarch butterflies overwintering in Mexico. In S. B. Malcolm and M. P. Zalucki, eds., Biology and conservation of the monarch butterfly, pp. 49–60. Los Angeles: Natural History Museum of Los Angeles County.

Woodson, R. E. 1954. The North American species of *Asclepia* L. Ann. Mo. Bot. Gard. 41:1–211.

Zalucki, M. P. 1982. Temperature and rate of development in two species of *Danaus*, *D. plexippus* and *D. chrysippus*. J. Aust. Entomol. Soc. 21:241–46.

Zalucki, M. P., and L. P. Brower. 1992. Survival of first instar larvae of *Danaus plexippus* L. in relation to cardiac glycoside and latex content of *Asclepias humistrata*. Chemoecology 3:81–93.

Zalucki, M. P., L. P. Brower, and A. M. Alfonso. 2001. Detrimental effects of latex and cardiac glycosides on survival and growth of first instar *Danaus plexippus* feeding on the sandhill milkweed *Asclepias humistrata*. Ecol. Entomol. 26:212–24.

Zalucki, M. P., and R. L. Kitching. 1982. Dynamics of Oriposition in *Danaus plexippus* (Insecta: Lepidoptera) on milkweed, *Asclepias spp.* J. Zool., Lond. 198:103–16.

Zalucki, M. P., and S. B. Malcolm. 1999. Plant latex and first-instar monarch larval growth and survival on three North American milkweed species. J. Chem. Ecol. 25:1827–42.

2

Temporal and Geographic Variation in Monarch Densities: Citizen Scientists Document Monarch Population Patterns

Michelle D. Prysby and Karen S. Oberhauser

INTRODUCTION

Few long-term records of insect populations exist, especially for nonpest species (Varley et al. 1974; Price 1984). Long-term data on abundance can help us better understand the ecology of insect populations and the impact of global climate change, pollution, habitat destruction, and other anthropogenic factors on them (e.g., Ehrlich and Murphy 1987; Pollard and Yates 1993). Monarch butterflies are especially interesting candidates for long-term population studies because of their continent-wide distribution, multiple overlapping generations, and annual long-distance migration. In addition, such studies will help us to understand the effects of anthropogenic practices such as pesticide use and habitat destruction, to identify and understand sources of variation in monarch abundance, and to identify regions or habitats of special importance to the production and recruitment of monarchs. Participants in the 1997 North American Conference on the Monarch Butterfly identified several research priorities to address these needs, including monitoring the distribution and abundance of monarchs, studying environmental effects on their distribution and abundance, and studying sources of mortality during all monarch life stages (United States Fish and Wildlife Service 1999).

Several programs monitor adult monarch populations. The North American Butterfly Association's annual Fourth of July Butterfly Count monitors summer populations (Swengel 1995); the Monarch Monitoring Project at Cape May Point, New Jersey, and Texas Monarch Watch monitor the size and timing of autumn monarch migrations (Walton and Brower 1996; Calvert and Wagner 1999); the Journey North program monitors the timing of the spring migration (Donnelly 1999; Howard and Davis, this volume); and researchers in Mexico monitor the size of the overwintering monarch colonies (García-Serrano and Alvarez 1999; García-Serrano et al., this volume). Missing in this array of programs is a study of monarch egg and larval populations. By monitoring immature stages, we can measure the temporal and spatial variation in monarch reproduction and learn more about how monarchs use the available habitat. We can also compare population statistics on immature stages to those estimated for summer, fall, and winter adult populations to identify how population size at one stage affects that at later stages.

Relevant monarch biology

The breeding range of the eastern migratory population (the focus of this study) extends from the southern United States to southern Canada and from the Atlantic Seaboard to the Rocky Mountains. The range is limited by the range of the monarch's host plants, which are all in the Asclepiadaceae family and primarily in the genus *Asclepias* (Lynch and Martin 1993). Each spring, the migratory generation returns to the southern United States from central Mexico and lays eggs. Successive generations recolonize the rest of the summer breeding range (Cockrell et al. 1993; Malcolm et al. 1993; Howard and Davis, this volume). Monarchs appear to vacate the southern United States for much of the summer, probably owing to high temperatures and host plant dieback (Malcolm et al. 1987; Calvert 1999). There is some evidence for more fall breeding in the southern United States (see Results), but it is unknown whether these reproductive butterflies are migrants returning from the north or butterflies that have remained in the south for the summer by utilizing nonnative *Asclepias curassavica* plants, or whether these fall offspring join the southern migration (Calvert 1999).

Monarchs have five larval instars. Under typical spring temperatures at 45° north latitude, development can require more than 60 days, compared to fewer than 30 days under summer conditions (Cockrell et al. 1993).

Interannual and geographic variation in monarch abundance

There is considerable evidence for yearly variations in monarch abundance throughout the annual cycle (Swengel 1990, 1995; García-Serrano and others 1999, this volume; Monarch Monitoring Project 2002). Possible causes include variation in abiotic factors (temperature, humidity, precipitation, and storm events), natural enemy abundance, host plant availability or quality, and human activities such as pesticide use and habitat destruction. Both the Fourth of July Butterfly Count data and the Cape May data illustrate a large drop in the number of monarchs between 1991 and 1992, and Swengel (1995) and Walton and Brower (1996) implicate abiotic factors in this decline. Zalucki and Rochester (1999) modeled the effects of climate on annual abundance of monarchs in Australia, finding that monarch abundance theoretically could vary among years by as much as 500%, due solely to weather-related abiotic factors.

Similarly, counts of adult monarch butterflies indicate a geographic variation in abundance. Counts appear to be lower in the eastern United States than in the Midwest (Malcolm et al. 1993; Swengel 1995; Calvert and Wagner 1999). Malcolm and coauthors (1993) argue that most monarchs migrate north through Texas and continue on to the Midwest and Great Lakes region, while a smaller number continue to the Northeast region. In addition, Wassenaar and Hobson (1998) used stable isotope analysis to identify the natal origins of monarchs at the Mexican overwintering sites, and found that 50% of these butterflies originated in the midwestern United States.

Variation in monarch phenology and within-year abundance patterns

There is general agreement that monarchs produce three generations in the northern part of their range. This estimate is supported by models that consider the number of day-degrees achieved for various sites (Malcolm et al. 1987) and by empirical evidence (Borkin 1982).

Both Cockrell and coworkers (1993) and Journey North (2002a) show significant variation among years in the onset of monarch reproduction in the Upper Midwest. Journey North data indicate that the dates of monarch arrival in Minnesota and Wisconsin can vary by several weeks, and that 1997 was a particularly late year (Journey North 2002b). This variation is expected, since the arrival of monarchs in the Upper Midwest depends on the timing of departure from the overwintering sites, the rate of development for the southern generations, and prevailing weather conditions along the migration routes, all of which may vary significantly among years. The end of reproduction, however, appears to be more consistent. By the last week in August, one third of wild-caught female monarchs in west-central Wisconsin and east-central Minnesota are in reproductive diapause, as are half of female monarchs emerging in outdoor cages during the last week of August (Goehring and Oberhauser 2002), presumably in response to changing daylength and temperature conditions. By the end of the second week in September, all wild-caught and emerging captive female monarchs are in diapause (Goehring and Oberhauser 2002).

Estimates of and variation in monarch survival

Monarchs experience high mortality rates in the early immature stages, following a typical type A survivorship curve (Zalucki and Kitching 1982). Four studies that reported mortality rates for naturally occurring monarchs produced similar mortality estimates. In Australia, Zalucki and Kitching (1982) observed 2% to 8% survival rates between the egg and fifth instar (L5) stages. In Wisconsin, Borkin (1982) estimated a 12% survival rate from egg to pupation. In Louisiana, Lynch and Martin (1993) observed a survival rate of 4% from egg to L5, and

Oberhauser and colleagues (2001) estimated approximately 5% to 10% survival rates from egg to L5 for sites throughout the breeding range. Zalucki and Kitching (1982), Lynch and Martin (1993), and Oberhauser and colleagues (2001) all found that most mortality occurred by the L3 stage. Little research exists on temporal, geographic, or habitat-based variation in mortality, although there is some evidence for increasing mortality with increasing size of milkweed patches (Zalucki and Kitching 1982).

The Monarch Larva Monitoring Project

The Monarch Larva Monitoring Project (MLMP) (Prysby and Oberhauser 1999) was designed to describe temporal and geographic variations in monarch egg and larval abundances, compare monarch production across different habitat types, and describe variations in monarch egg and larval survival. In order to gather data to describe these variations on a large scale, we relied on citizen science methods. The term "citizen science" refers to the involvement of nonscientists in scientific research. We used citizen science methods to allow us to obtain monarch population data over wide spatial and temporal scales and to promote public understanding of monarch ecology and conservation and of scientific research. Citizens have a long history of involvement with monarch research, beginning with Fred Urquhart's monarch tagging program in 1952 (Urquhart 1960) and continuing with programs such as Monarch Watch, Journey North, and Texas Monarch Watch. Since citizens have played a critical role in obtaining the knowledge that we have about monarch populations, their involvement should be incorporated into new monitoring projects whenever possible.

Here we describe MLMP methods and summarize the findings to date. These first in-depth analyses focus on phenological patterns in oviposition, and variations in abundance and survival. Data on parasitism rates are presented by Prysby (this volume).

METHODS

Volunteer recruitment and training

Volunteers were recruited via Monarch Watch (Monarch Watch 2002) and Journey North (Journey North 2002b) listservs, the Monarch Lab and MLMP websites (Monarch Lab 2002; Monarch Larva Monitoring Project 2002), word of mouth, and a network of cooperating nature centers. Many teacher-participants were part of the Monarch Monitoring Project, a program co-sponsored by Monarchs in the Classroom and the Science Museum of Minnesota and funded by the National Science Foundation.

Volunteers received hard copies of instructions or read them on our website, participated in 4- to 11-h workshops at nature centers, or were trained during the teacher Monarch Monitoring Project. Training workshops at nature centers were held in 1999 and 2000 in Tennessee, Vermont, and Wisconsin. In 2002, we instituted a series of 1.5-day train-the-trainer workshops for naturalists, with the first four presented in Minnesota, Vermont, North Carolina, and Texas. Naturalists then conducted their own 4- to 6-h sessions. Workshops consisted, at minimum, of a slide presentation on the biology and ecology of the monarch butterfly, a hands-on activity to learn to recognize its life cycle stages, practice with the monitoring protocol in the field, and a question-and-answer period.

We communicated with volunteers through e-mail, mailings, and the MLMP website. Mass communications included reminders to start monitoring and send in data, thank-you notes, informal questionnaires, and an annual newsletter. We also corresponded with individual volunteers in response to specific questions.

Scientist involvement

Scientists and field assistants from the University of Minnesota monarch lab group monitored a field site in west-central Wisconsin, using the same methods as the volunteer participants. In addition, three teams of collaborating scientists in Ontario, Iowa, and Maryland joined us in a more controlled study funded by the U.S. Department of Agriculture (USDA) to compare the abundance and survival of monarchs in cornfield, edge, and nonagricultural habitats (Oberhauser et al. 2001). The study used methods similar to those of the volunteer program with adaptations for agricultural habitats, and these results are included in the monitoring database.

Monitoring protocol

Each volunteer chose a site containing milkweed to monitor on a weekly basis. The number of milkweed ramets (individual stems that may be connected by roots to a larger plant), site size and type, and site location had no minimum requirements and varied greatly. Sites included small backyard gardens, railroad right-of-ways, abandoned fields and pastures, and restored prairies. Volunteers recorded the location, type, and dimensions of the site, and milkweed species and density. Those with small sites recorded the total number of milkweed ramets in the site along with the area of the site, and those with larger sites counted ramets in 15- to 100-m^2 plots along belt transects.

Volunteers estimated the monarch densities per ramet each week. They either examined all of the milkweed ramets in smaller sites or sampled a subset of ramets in larger sites. Participants who sampled a subset of ramets used haphazardly placed belt transects, thus avoiding the bias that could result from selecting ramets that might be more likely to have monarchs on them. They recorded the number of eggs and larvae (identified to instar) observed and the number of ramets examined. Larval instars were identified by head capsule size and tentacle length, following Oberhauser and Kuda (1997). Resulting data were summarized as number of monarch eggs and larvae per ramet.

Many volunteers monitored the characteristics of the milkweed ramets. They observed a random sample of ramets at evenly spaced intervals along a haphazardly placed transect, recording ramet height; presence or absence of buds, flowers, and seed pods; descriptions of any invertebrates observed on the ramet; leaf condition; and damage from herbivory or disease. Finally, they measured milkweed density within 1 m^2 of the focal ramet. They made the same measurements for all milkweed ramets with monarchs on them, thus providing records of the characteristics of "average" milkweed ramets and ramets with monarchs on them. These data have not been analyzed to date.

Approximately 10% of the volunteers collected fourth and fifth instar larvae found at the site and reared them to estimate rates of parasitism by flies and wasps. They recorded the date and larval stage at the time of collection and the outcome (healthy adult, parasitized by fly, parasitized by wasp, or died of unknown cause). The protocol directions included characteristics of common fly and wasp parasitoids, and volunteers only needed to identify the parasitoid to taxonomic order. Healthy butterflies and adult parasitoids were released back at the site whenever possible.

Many volunteers collected rainfall data at the site on at least a weekly basis. They also recorded the temperatures in full sun and shade when they monitored.

Data collection, management, and analysis

For the first 5 years of the project, volunteers returned data on paper forms or a spreadsheet template. We checked entered data against hard copies for validation and contacted volunteers when values seemed unusual. Data were managed in a Microsoft Access relational database. In 2002, volunteers used a web-based data entry format.

The presentation of phenological patterns in oviposition utilizes data from sites in the Upper Midwest, Northeast, and southern United States. We focused our statistical analyses of temporal and geographic variations in monarch abundance on the egg stage, since the lack of mobility of eggs makes this the best representation of monarch reproduction. We limited statistical analyses to sites in the Upper Midwest and Northeast regions because these regions comprise the vast majority of the available data. The Upper Midwest includes all sites in Minnesota, Wisconsin, Michigan, and Iowa. The Northeast includes U.S. sites east of the Great Lakes and north of the 40° latitude, as well as eastern Ontario and Quebec. Most analyses exclude agricultural fields and gardens. To analyze egg abundance, we used a generalized linear model developed in SAS with a binomial distribution and a logit link function (Agresti 2000; K. Barnes, pers. comm.). The response variable was the number of eggs observed per milkweed examined for the 1053 monitoring events that fit the criteria just described. Fixed-effects predictors included year, region (Upper Midwest or Northeast), latitude, and first, second, and third order year-by-week interactions to model the nonlinear peaks and valleys in oviposition. Site was included as a random effect. We included a repeated-measures component in the model to account for the fact that sites were monitored 1 to 20 times during each year. This analysis included data from only 1997 to 2000.

As an estimate of monarch survival, we used the ratio of the total number of fifth instars to the total number of eggs observed in each state, limiting the calculations to nonagricultural sites in the Upper Midwest and Northeast regions. Only sites with more than 10 monitoring events in a given year were included in this analysis.

RESULTS

Program results

An exact number of project participants is difficult to obtain, since many volunteers participated with their families or students. To date, over 300 volunteers have participated in the program. These participants include secondary and college students, teachers, naturalists, scientists, retirees, and people from other professions and backgrounds. Together, they have monitored a total of 264 sites during the first 6 years of the project, with 54 sites that have been monitored for 2 or more years. Each year, 29% to 67% of participants continue monitoring the following year.

Approximately 36% of sites were monitored by informal or formal educators who incorporated the project into learning activities. Teachers and students were excited to be participating in this "real science" endeavor. For example, Jane Borland, a high school teacher in Texas, has monitored with students since 1998. In 2000, she wrote:

> [We are] about to begin our third year of monarch larval monitoring. The first year, two students participated. As the Texas summer heat brought temperatures over 38°C each day, it became mandatory to monitor early in the morning, much to the dismay of sleepy teenagers. However, they were so interested in doing real scientific research that they made little fuss. To make things more challenging, we did not find a single egg or larva during the summer months. Each week, I reinforced the point that having data that showed no summer activity would one day be important to us. As fall migration season and cooler temperatures arrived, our enthusiasm was revitalized as we began to find eggs and larvae. There are currently eight dedicated students on our core research team. Once the students find their first eggs or larvae, they are hooked. . . . They are proud of their work and the fact that they are conducting valid scientific research. (J. Borland, pers. comm.)

Almost 90% of the data met the criteria for inclusion in the monarch abundance database by having at least one monitoring event in which the date, number of milkweeds examined, and number of monarch eggs and larvae observed were all clearly indicated. An additional 4% of sites returned only data on parasitism rates, and some participants returned data that lacked sufficient quantification for inclusion in either database. Table 2.1 summarizes the monitoring efforts, including only sites with data on monarch abundance. The sites are in 29 states and 2 Canadian provinces (figure 2.1), with most sites in the Upper Midwest.

Table 2.1. Summary of monitoring effort

Year	No. of sites	Average no. of weeks monitored (range)	Average no. of ramets examined/ week/site (range)	Upper Midwest	Northeast	Other locations
1997	18	10 (1–25)	184 (9–718)	61%	22%	17%
1998	17	10 (2–20)	122 (28–305)	76%	12%	12%
1999	35	11 (1–22)	96 (5–344)	60%	14%	26%
2000	41	12 (1–30)	122 (10–437)	59%	20%	21%
2001	21	11 (1–21)	127 (9–282)	76%	5%	19%
2002	69	9 (1–31)	74 (5–267)	41%	13%	46%

Note: All sites with data from at least 1 monitoring event are included. "Upper Midwest" includes sites in Minnesota, Wisconsin, Iowa, and Michigan. "Northeast" includes sites in Maine, New Hampshire, Vermont, Quebec, eastern Ontario, New York, Rhode Island, and Pennsylvania. Sites monitored as part of the USDA-funded research are not included.

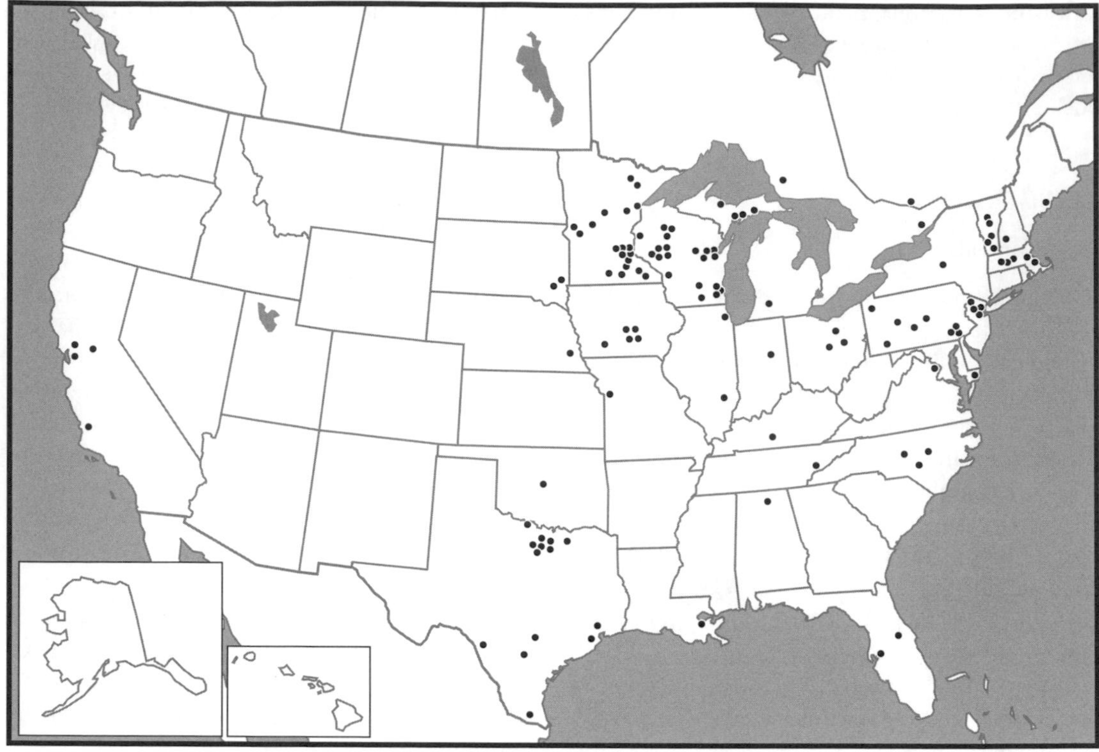

Figure 2.1. Location of sites for which we have data for at least 1 year.

Phenology and intra-annual patterns

Most observers in the Upper Midwest and Northeast monitored *Asclepias syriaca* (common milkweed). Observers in the southern United States monitored a wide variety of native species and the introduced *A. curassavica* (tropical milkweed).

Figure 2.2 shows egg densities over time for the Upper Midwest. Only data from 1997, 1998, 2000, and 2002 are illustrated to make the figure clearer; 1999 and 2001 values were quite similar to those in 2000. There tend to be two distinct peaks in egg densities, although the timing of the peaks varies among years. The first peak was earliest in 1998 and latest in 1997. The timing of the second peak in egg density is more consistent, occurring during the last half of July in all 4 years. This peak is wider than the first and probably represents overlapping generations (Borkin 1982). The end of breeding is more consistent across years; few eggs were observed after mid-August.

Figure 2.3 shows egg densities in Northeast sites. Only data from 2000 and 2002 are shown, as those are the only years in which more than two northeastern sites were monitored for most of the breeding season. There was not a clear pattern of peaks in egg abundance in 2000, and there was a much later first peak in 2002. Eggs were observed later in the season in the Northeast than in the Upper Midwest during both years.

Figure 2.4 illustrates monarch densities for representative sites in the southern part of the monarchs' breeding range in 2000. As expected, monarchs were observed earliest in Texas (figure 2.4a) and about 3 weeks later in southern Illinois (figure 2.4b). Both sites had few monarchs in midsummer but showed a late-summer or early-fall peak in abundance. The amount of fall breeding activity is especially striking

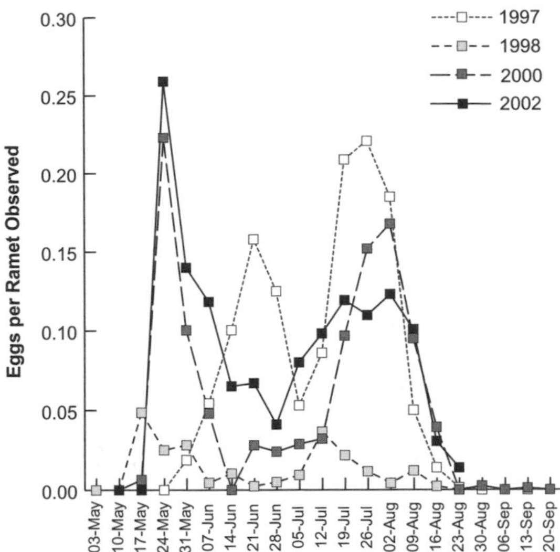

Figure 2.2. The number of eggs per milkweed observed over time in 4 years in the Upper Midwest. Points represent all of the eggs observed throughout the region in a given week divided by all of the plants observed. The x-axis shows the first day of the week during which sites were monitored.

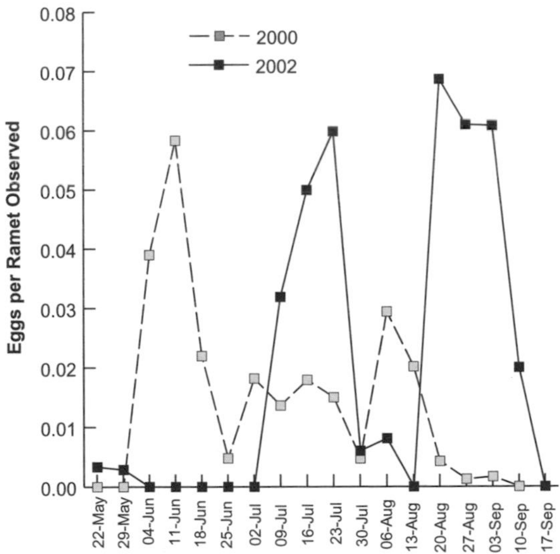

Figure 2.3. The number of eggs per milkweed observed in 2000 and 2002 in the Northeast. Points represent all of the eggs observed in the region in a given week divided by all of the plants observed. The x-axis shows the first day of the week during which sites were monitored.

for gardens planted with *A. curassavica*. For example, Borland found 678 monarch eggs over 5 weeks in a Texas garden with 130 *A. curassavica* plants (figure 2.4c).

Table 2.2. Egg density analysis: coefficients for region, latitude, and year

Effect	Coefficient	Standard error	*p* value
Region (Northeast)	−1.25	0.40	0.0017
Latitude	−0.09	0.10	0.3846
Year 1997	9.0741	5.0928	0.0751
Year 1998	3.4211	4.7499	0.4716
Year 1999	6.4826	4.6771	0.1661
Year 2000	6.5122	4.5994	0.1572

Note: The regression model included year, region, and latitude as fixed-effects predictors and site as a random effect. Repeated measures over weeks within a site were also included. The model included year*week, year*week^2, and year*week^3 to model the nonlinear relationship between egg densities and week. Year-by-week interactions and site all contributed significantly to the model.

Table 2.3. Egg density analysis: results of contrasts between years 1997 to 2000

Contrast	*df* (no./density)	F value	*p* value
1997 vs. 1998	1/968	4.28	0.0388
1997 vs. 1999	1/968	1.00	0.3175
1997 vs. 2000	1/968	1.06	0.3033
1998 vs. 1999	1/968	3.00	0.0834
1998 vs. 2000	1/968	3.64	0.0569
1999 vs. 2000	1/968	<0.00	0.9831

Note: There were significant contrasts among the years, with the probability of a milkweed plant having an egg significantly lower in 1998 than in any other year.

Temporal and geographic variation in egg densities

Tables 2.2 and 2.3 show the results of the regression analysis of the relationship between egg densities and temporal and geographic factors. Region had a significant effect, with per plant densities higher in the Upper Midwest than in the Northeast (figure 2.5). Egg density did not increase or decrease with increasing latitude (see table 2.2). There were significant contrasts among years, with egg densities significantly lower in 1998 than in other years ($p < 0.1$, see table 2.3).

Monarch survival

Figure 2.6 shows survival estimates in the upper midwestern sites. There are not strong differences in ratios among years, with means ranging from about 10% to 20%. These values are well within the range of survival observed in more controlled studies (Borkin 1982; Zalucki and Kitching 1982; Oberhauser et al. 2001).

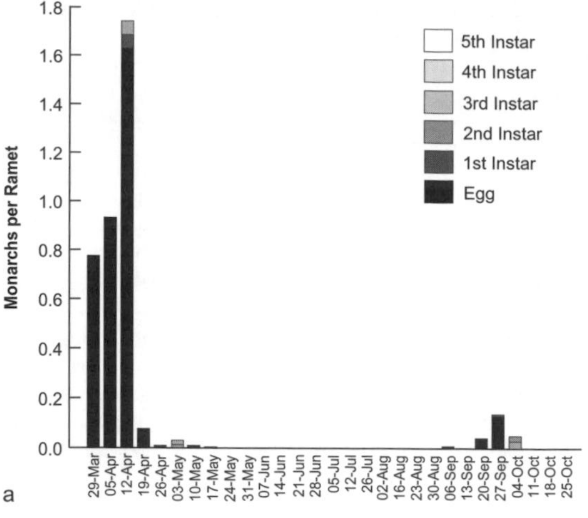

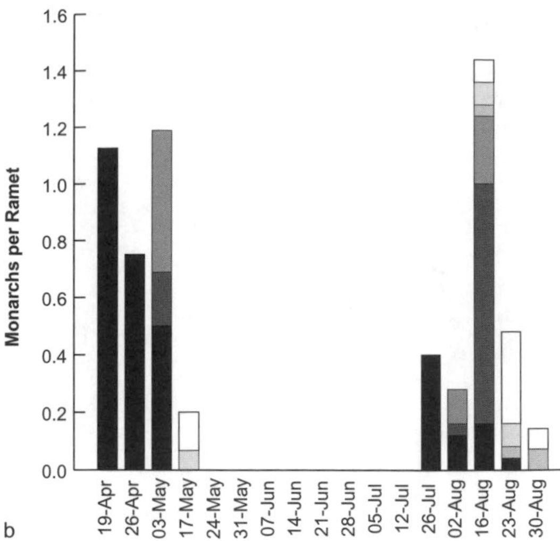

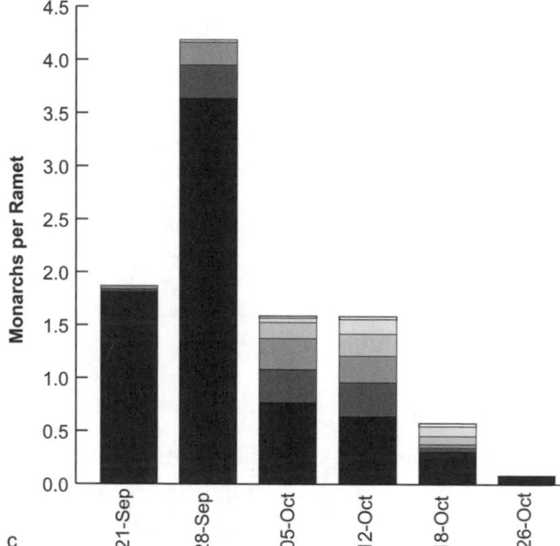

Figure 2.4. The number of monarch eggs and larvae per milkweed ramet for three sites in the southern and southeastern United States: (a) northern Texas in 2000, natural area with native milkweeds, data collected by Jane Borland and students of Lamar High School in Arlington; (b) southern Illinois 2000, garden planted with *Asclepias curassavica*, *A. incarnata*, and *A. tuberosa*, data collected by Kathy Phelps of Harrisburg; (c) northern Texas in 2000, garden planted with *A. curassavica*, data collected by Jane Borland and students of Lamar High School in Arlington. The x-axes show the actual date the site was monitored. The y-axes show the number of monarchs observed per milkweed ramet examined. Note that the axes vary among the graphs and that times between monitoring events at a given site often vary. Eggs and larval instars 1 through 5 are shown with differential shading.

DISCUSSION

Data validity

Data validity is an important issue for citizen science projects because of high observer variability, inconsistencies in observations, and other peculiarities of the method. Unfortunately, the structure of our study does not allow us to quantify the accuracy of volunteer-collected data. We have no way of knowing how the data ought to look because there have been no other studies in which monarch densities were measured over large spatial and temporal scales. We can, however, look at factors that might indicate how valid the data are.

Our first concern was the volunteers' ability to find monarch eggs and larvae. We know from our own monitoring that the total number of eggs per milkweed rarely exceeds 1, at least for the large, nonagricultural sites in the Upper Midwest. Nearly all volunteer observations were lower than 1 egg/milkweed. In addition, the phenological patterns in oviposition evident from the volunteer data are similar to those we have observed ourselves. If volunteers were greatly overestimating egg densities, perhaps by mistaking milkweed latex as monarch eggs, we would expect more observations exceeding 1 egg/milkweed and records of monarch eggs continuing into late August. Evaluating whether volun-

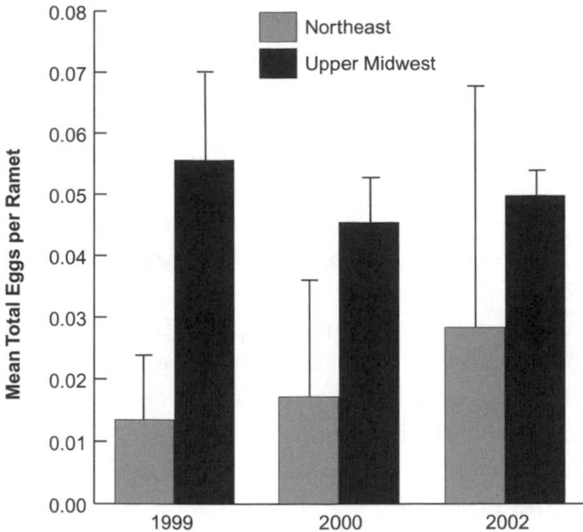

Figure 2.5. Mean total number of eggs observed per milkweed examined in 1999, 2000, and 2002, averaged across states in the Upper Midwest (Minnesota, Wisconsin, Michigan, and Iowa) and Northeast (1999—Vermont, Pennsylvania, and Quebec; 2000—New Hampshire, Vermont, New York, Pennsylvania, and southeastern Ontario; 2002—Vermont and Pennsylvania). Error bars show standard deviations.

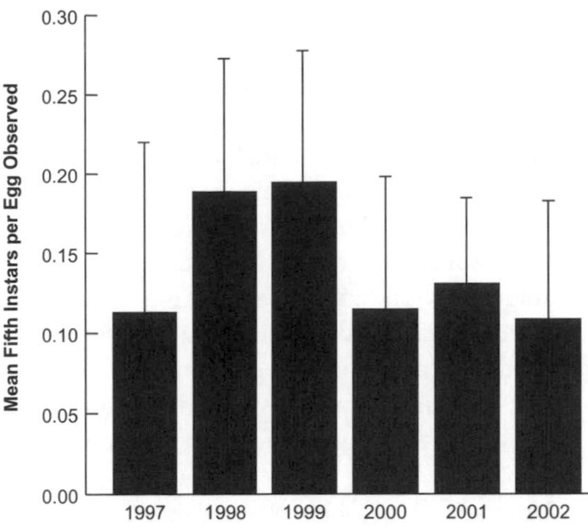

Figure 2.6. Mean ratios of fifth instars to eggs for upper midwestern sites, calculated by averaging state means within each year (state means are calculated by dividing the number of all of the eggs observed in the state in a given year by the number of all of the fifth instars observed in that year). Error bars show standard deviations.

teers are underestimating egg densities is more difficult. From our experience in training volunteers and watching them in the field, it seems that the less experience a volunteer has, the more careful he or she is when examining the milkweeds. In addition, the rough calculations of ratios of fifth instars to eggs suggest that volunteers locate most eggs. However, there were clearly exceptions, such as a few volunteers who reported more fifth instars than eggs. Our anecdotal observations suggest that volunteers are at least as accurate as the field assistants that we have hired to collect similar data. In fact, one of the data sets from our cooperating scientists' study (Oberhauser et al. 2001) had to be analyzed separately when we discovered that some of the field assistants did not distinguish first and second instar larvae correctly.

The dull color, small size, and cryptic behavior of first instars make this the most difficult stage to locate. In the absence of data on misidentification of larval instars, our analyses to date considered only fifth instars because the distinct characteristics of this stage make it the least likely to be overlooked or misidentified. Volunteers might overestimate the fifth instar densities because they can be seen from several meters away; volunteers observing a fifth instar from afar may be more likely to include that milkweed in their sampling. The fifth instar–egg ratios indicated that this is not a problem for most volunteers (see figure 2.6).

Phenological patterns

With three generations of monarchs predicted in the Upper Midwest (Borkin 1982; Zalucki 1982), one might expect to see three peaks in egg densities. However, differences in development time between the first and later generations result in just two peaks. The first generation, offspring of butterflies that were larvae in the southern United States earlier in the spring, can take up to 8 weeks to become adults owing to cool spring temperatures (Malcolm et al. 1987; Cockrell et al. 1993). The earlier spring migrants arrive, the longer the development time of the first northern generation (Cockrell et al. 1993). Thus, the time between the two peaks in egg densities varied from 5 weeks in 1997 (when monarchs arrived in the Upper Midwest later than average) to 8 weeks in 1998 (when monarchs arrived in the Upper Midwest earlier than average) (see figure 2.2). The second peak in egg densities represents the second and third northern generations of butterflies. These generations have a shorter development time, owing to warmer temperatures. Therefore, the eggs at the beginning of the second oviposition peak develop into mature adults that lay the eggs at the end of the peak.

The existence of several narrower peaks in the Northeast in 2000 (see figure 2.3) may be due to the fact that Northeast sites were located in two subregions, the Vermont/New Hampshire area and southern Ontario. The timing of monarch reproduction may be somewhat different in these two areas, leading to the appearance of several peaks when data from both areas are combined. In 2002, when there are clearer peaks, the only sites that had reported data at the time of analysis were in Vermont and Pennsylvania. Additional data will help to clarify this pattern.

Urquhart (1987) observed fall monarch reproduction in the southern United States, but there has been little research to describe its extent. Calvert (1999) suggests that some monarchs emerging in the fall disperse southward while laying eggs, similar to the northward spring migration. Observations of our volunteers in the southern states further quantify the amount and extent of this reproduction. Monarchs appear to achieve at least one additional generation in the South in late August and September.

Interannual variation in monarch abundance

Data on year-to-year differences in egg abundance allow us to look for relationships between egg and adult densities at different times of the year. Since our sample sizes are larger during the second peak in abundance (see figure 2.2), our discussion focuses on this peak and not the more variable and less reliable first peak. Reports to the Monarch Watch listserv related low numbers of migrating monarchs in 1998 (Taylor 1999), matching the egg densities that we observed that year. Comparisons with overwintering monarch populations are less clear. The colonies appear to have been several times larger in 1996–1997 than in subsequent years (García-Serrano et al., this volume), correlating with our high 1997 egg densities (see figure 2.2). Interestingly, breeding seasons for which high egg densities are evident in the MLMP data (such as 1997) are not consistently followed by large overwintering colonies; 1997–1998 was a relatively low-abundance year in the overwintering colonies (García-Serrano et al., this volume). This lack of correlation may be due to variations in adult survival rates during the migration or overwintering periods, and suggests that conditions faced during the overwintering or migration stages of the monarch's annual cycle may drive population dynamics more than conditions during the breeding stage. The year following a catastrophic storm in the overwintering colonies (2002; see Brower et al., this volume) has the second-lowest second peak (see figure 2.2), supporting this chain of cause and effect.

Monarchs arrived in the Upper Midwest earliest in 1998, the year that also had the lowest abundance. These two statistics may be unrelated, or they could reflect a biological relationship. Perhaps the slow development that results from early arrival and cool temperatures means that monarchs are exposed to more predation. Factors that resulted in earlier movement from the southern regions could also cause lower abundance.

Geographic variation in monarch abundances

Regional differences in egg densities support previous observations (Malcolm et al. 1993; Swengel 1995), with lower densities in the Northeast than the Upper Midwest. There are several possible explanations for this pattern. Malcolm and coauthors (1993) suggested that fewer monarchs migrate to the Northeast because of the barrier of the Appalachian Mountains. They found that the majority of adult monarchs captured in Pennsylvania and Massachusetts had fed on *A. humistrata* as larvae, a milkweed species restricted to the southeastern United States. This pattern suggests that the monarchs whose offspring colonize the northeastern region are a relatively small subset of the entire population that fly east from Texas and then lay eggs in the Southeast.

Biotic factors may also drive these patterns. Although the most common milkweed species in both regions is *A. syriaca*, the distribution and abundance of the host plant probably differ. For example, the overall area available for breeding may be larger in the Upper Midwest. A large portion of the Upper Midwest is farmland; Oberhauser and colleagues (2001) demonstrated that agricultural habitats are important contributors to the total monarch population in that region. More nonurban habitat in the Northeast is forest and contains less milkweed. Finally, the lower abundance of monarchs in the Northeast may be due to abiotic factors such as temperature, humidity, and cloud cover.

Monarch survival

Our estimates of monarch survival indicate that 10% to 20% of monarch eggs live to the fifth instar stage. Causes of mortality in eggs and early instar larvae may include predation, host plant defenses, and abiotic factors such as lethally high temperatures. We plan to use temperature records to develop models to estimate monarch survival more precisely, and utilize volunteers' observations of potential predators and milkweed condition to help identify causes of mortality.

CONCLUSIONS AND FUTURE OBJECTIVES

The MLMP has established a standardized methodology for monitoring monarch populations that can be used successfully by volunteers in a variety of habitats. We have organized a network of volunteers to monitor several regions of the United States and Canada, collecting data that document temporal and geographic differences in monarch abundance. Other aspects of the data—including female choice of oviposition plants and habitats, effects of landscape features, and sources of mortality—remain to be explored. The project will eventually provide a long-term data set that will allow continued contributions to our understanding of monarch distribution and abundance.

Acknowledgments

The dedication of over 300 volunteers has been the foundation of this research. Their work was not always easy; they persevered through mosquitoes, 38°C temperatures, and rain. We extend special appreciation to those volunteers who rarely found monarchs, yet remained dedicated to the project. Thanks also to the scientists and assistants who monitored in 2000 as part of the USDA research project. Kathie Barnes played an integral role in the statistical analyses and John Woodell, Ted Sands, and Brij Bhasin assisted with database queries. Sonia Altizer conducted the first weekly surveys of monarch egg and larval densities at our Wisconsin field site. Funding for training workshops and support materials was provided through a Joan DeWind Award from the Xerces Society and the National Science Foundation (NSF ESI-0104600). Monarchs in the Classroom (University of Minnesota) provided additional support for training and materials, as well as support for the website. The USDA provided funding for monitoring in 2000 by scientists in Iowa, Minnesota, Maryland, and Ontario. The National Science Foundation (NSF ESI-9731429) supported teacher involvement from 1998 to 2000. Patrice Morrow, Tony Murphy, Andy Davis, and John Obrycki provided comments on the manuscript. This research was completed to fulfill partially the requirements for a master's degree in Ecology, Evolution, and Behavior at the University of Minnesota.

References

Agresti, A. 2000. Random effects modeling of categorical response data. Sociol. Methodol. 30:27–80.

Borkin, S. S. 1982. Notes on shifting distribution patterns and survival of immature *Danaus plexippus* (Lepidoptera: Danaidae) on the food plant *Asclepias syriaca*. Gt. Lakes Entomol. 15:199–207.

Calvert, W. H. 1999. Patterns in the spatial and temporal use of Texas milkweeds (Asclepiadaceae) by the monarch butterfly (*Danaus plexippus* L.) during fall, 1996. J. Lepid. Soc. 53:37–44.

Calvert, W. H., and M. Wagner. 1999. Patterns in the monarch butterfly migration through Texas—1993 to 1995. In J. Hoth, L. Merino, K. Oberhauser, I. Pisantry, S. Price, and T. Wilkinson, eds., The 1997 North American Conference on the Monarch Butterfly, pp. 119–26. Montreal: Commission for Environmental Cooperation.

Cockrell, B. J., S. B. Malcolm, and L. P. Brower. 1993. Time, temperature, and latitudinal constraints on the annual recolonization of eastern North America by the monarch butterfly. In S. B. Malcolm and M. P. Zalucki, eds., Biology and conservation of the monarch butterfly, pp. 234–51. Los Angeles: Natural History Museum of Los Angeles County.

Donnelly, E. 1999. Journey North: tracking the migration over the Internet. In J. Hoth, L. Merino, K. Oberhauser, I. Pisantry, S. Price, and T. Wilkinson, eds., The 1997 North American Conference on the Monarch Butterfly, pp. 347–48. Montreal: Commission for Environmental Cooperation.

Ehrlich, P. R., and D. D. Murphy. 1987. Conservation lessons from long-term studies of checkerspot butterflies. Conserv. Biol. 1:122–31.

García-Serrano, E., and X. Mora Álvarez. 1999. Monitcro de las colonias de mariposa monarca en sus sitios de invernación en Mexico. In J. Hoth, L. Merino, K. Oberhauser, I. Pisantry, S. Price, and T. Wilkinson, eds., The 1997 North American Conference on the Monarch Butterfly, pp. 177–82. Montreal: Commission for Environmental Cooperation.

Goehring, L., and K. S. Oberhauser. 2002. Effects of photoperiod, temperature and host plant age on induction of reproductive diapause and development time in *Danaus plexippus*. Ecol. Entomol. 27:674–85.

Journey North. 2002a. Comparative migration maps. Journey North: monarch migration. http://www.learner.org/jnorth/tm/monarch/MigrationMaps.html. Accessed 30 April 2003.

Journey North. 2002b. Journey North archives. Journey North: monarch migration. http://www.learner.org/jnorth. Accessed 30 April 2003.

Lynch, S. P., and R. A. Martin. 1993. Milkweed host plant utilization and cardenolide sequestration by monarch butterflies in Louisiana and Texas. In S. B. Malcolm and M. P. Zalucki, eds., Biology and conservation of the monarch butterfly, pp. 107–23. Los Angeles: Natural History Museum of Los Angeles County.

Malcolm, S. B., B. J. Cockrell, and L. P. Brower. 1987. Monarch butterfly voltinism: effects of temperature constraints at different latitudes. Oikos 49:77–82.

Malcolm, S. B., B. J. Cockrell, and L. P. Brower. 1993. Spring recolonization of eastern North America by the monarch butterfly: successive brood or single sweep migration? In S. B. Malcolm and M. P. Zalucki, eds., Biology and conservation of the monarch butterfly, pp. 253–67. Los Angeles: Natural History Museum of Los Angeles County.

Monarch Lab. 2002. http://www.monarchlab.umn.edu. Accessed 30 April 2003.

Monarch Larva Monitoring Project. 2002. http://www.mlmp.org. Accessed 5 May 2002.

Monarch Monitoring Project. 2002. Monarch Monitoring Project: Cape May Point, N.J. http://www.concord.org/~dick/mon.html. Accessed 5 May 2002.

Monarch Watch. 2002. http://www.monarchwatch.org. Accessed 5 May 2002.

Oberhauser, K., and K. Kuda. 1997. A field guide to monarch caterpillars. Monarchs in the Classroom, University of Minnesota, St. Paul.

Oberhauser, K. S., M. D. Prysby, H. R. Mattila, D. E. Stanley-Horn, M. K. Sears, G. Dively, E. Olson, J. M. Pleasants, W. F. Lam, and R. L. Hellmich. 2001. Temporal and spatial overlap between monarch larvae and corn pollen: influence on risks imposed by Bt-corn. Proc. Natl. Acad. Sci. USA 98:11913–18.

Pollard, E., and T. J. Yates. 1993. Monitoring butterflies for ecology and conservation. London: Chapman and Hall.

Price, P. W. 1984. Insect ecology. 2d ed. New York: John Wiley and Sons.

Prysby, M. D., and K. S. Oberhauser. 1999. Large-scale monitoring of larval monarch populations and milkweed habitat in North America. In J. Hoth, L. Merino, K. Oberhauser, I. Pisantry, S. Price, and T. Wilkinson, eds., The 1997 North American Conference on the Monarch Butterfly, pp. 3379–83. Montreal: Commission for Environmental Cooperation.

Swengel, A. B. 1990. Monitoring butterfly populations using the Fourth of July Butterfly Count. Am. Midl. Nat. 124:395–406.

Swengel, A. B. 1995. Population fluctuations of the monarch (*Danaus plexippus*) in the 4th of July Butterfly Count 1977–1994. Am. Midl. Nat. 134:205–14.

Taylor, O. R. 1999. Monarch Watch 1998 season summary. University of Kansas Monarch Watch, Lawrence.

United States Fish and Wildlife Service. 1999. 1997 North American Conference on the Monarch Butterfly: roundtable discussions and priority actions. Washington, D.C.: United States Fish and Wildlife Service, Office of International Affairs.

Urquhart, F. 1960. The monarch butterfly, pp. 252–321. Toronto: University of Toronto Press.

Urquhart, F. 1987. The monarch butterfly: international traveler. Chicago: Nelson-Hall.

Varley, G. C., G. R. Gradwell, and M. P. Hassell. 1974. Insect population ecology: an analytical approach. Berkeley: University of California Press.

Walton, R. K., and L. P. Brower. 1996. Monitoring the fall migration of the monarch butterfly *Danaus plexippus* L. (Nymphalidae: Danainae) in eastern North America: 1991–1994. J. Lepid. Soc. 50:1–20.

Wassenaar, L. I., and K. A. Hobson. 1998. Natal origins of migratory monarch butterflies at wintering colonies in Mexico: new isotopic evidence. Proc. Natl. Acad. Sci. USA 95:15436–39.

Zalucki, M. P. 1982. Temperature and rate of development in *Danaus plexippus* L. and *D. chrysippus* L. (Lepidoptera: Nymphalidae). J. Aust. Entomol. Soc. 21:241–46.

Zalucki, M. P., and Kitching. 1982. Temporal and spatial variation of mortality in field populations of *Danaus plexippus* L. and *D. chrysippus* L. larvae (Lepidoptera: Nymphalidae). Oecologia 53:201–7.

Zalucki, M. P., and W. A. Rochester. 1999. Estimating the effect of climate on the distribution and abundance of *Danaus plexippus*: a tale of two continents. In J. Hoth, L. Merino, K. Oberhauser, I. Pisantry, S. Price, and T. Wilkinson, eds., The 1997 North American Conference on the Monarch Butterfly, pp. 151–63. Montreal: Commission for Environmental Cooperation.

3

Effects of Female Age, Female Mass, and Nutrients from Males on Monarch Egg Mass

Karen S. Oberhauser

INTRODUCTION

Reproductive success is determined not only by the quantity of offspring that individuals produce, but also by the quality of these offspring. It is often assumed that there is a trade-off between the size and fitness of offspring, and several studies have shown that their growth and survival are influenced by the resources allocated to eggs by their mothers (reviews in Fleming and Gross 1990 and Reznick 1991 [fish]; Kaplan 1991 [amphibians]; Fox 1994 [insects]). There is likely to be a negative correlation between the number and size of offspring, and thus egg size is likely to result from a balance between selection for large eggs and selection for large numbers of eggs. In many cases, the fitness consequences of egg size vary with environmental conditions, and large eggs are likely to be most advantageous in adverse environments (Janzen 1977; Braby 1994; Fox and Mousseau 1996; Fox et al. 1997; Fox 2000). However, several studies of offspring fitness and egg size in butterflies have shown no correlation between the two factors (Wiklund and Persson 1983; Karlsson and Wiklund 1984, 1985). It is possible that butterfly reproduction makes a correlation between egg size and offspring fitness unlikely. Newly hatched larvae are exposed to many kinds of mortality that may not be affected by variation in size, at least within the ranges of egg sizes that females can produce. Thus, female butterflies may maximize their reproductive success by laying as many eggs as possible, as long as these eggs are above a certain minimum size.

Research on lepidopteran egg mass has addressed the effects of interspecific and intraspecific differences in adult size, as well as female age. Wiklund and his collaborators found that egg mass increases with body size across several satyrid species (Wiklund and Karlsson 1984; Wiklund et al. 1987). However, there is not a consistent relationship between female size and egg mass across taxa; Jones and colleagues (1982) found a negative correlation in the cabbage white (*Pieris rapae*); Boggs (1986), a positive correlation in Mormon fritillaries (*Speyeria mormonia*); and Wiklund and Karlsson (1984), no correlation in 10 satyrid species. Egg mass decreases with female age in many species (Jones et al. 1982; Murphy et al. 1983; Wiklund and Persson 1983; Karlsson and Wiklund 1984, 1985; Wiklund and Karlsson 1984; Boggs 1986; Svärd and Wiklund 1988).

Across many groups of animals, egg size correlates with female body mass (Peters 1986). This relationship does not have to be a result of natural selection but could simply result from allometry, the scaling of body part size to overall size. Wiklund and colleagues (1987) argued that when fecundity is limited by the number of eggs females actually lay, owing to time constraints or the ability to find host plants, and not by the number they can physically produce, large females will lay larger eggs. This view does not imply that larger eggs are better, simply that egg size scales to female body size, often referred to as "nonadaptive scaling". It implies a neutral relationship between egg size and offspring fitness. When females can produce more eggs than they can

Table 3.1. Expected relationships between egg size, egg numbers, and egg size allometry

Relationship between egg size and offspring survival?	Is a trade-off expected between egg size and number of eggs that can be laid?	Degree of scaling of egg size to body size (allometry)
Weak (expected in butterflies	Yes, if fecundity is limited by the number of eggs produced.	Less: selection produces small eggs to maximize fecundity.
	No, if fecundity is limited by the number of eggs females can lay.	More: egg size doesn't affect fitness, so the only factor that affects egg size is female size (allometric scaling).

lay, there may not be a strong trade-off between egg size and egg number. However, when fecundity is limited by egg production, there will be a trade-off, resulting in selection on females to produce the smallest eggs possible, within limits posed by viability constraints. This could result in a weaker association between egg size and body size that is driven by natural selection. Since female monarchs do not seem to live long enough to lay all of the eggs they produce (Oberhauser 1997), a relationship between egg size and female body size in monarchs could support Wiklund and colleagues' (1987) argument of nonadaptive scaling (table 3.1).

Information on egg mass can also be used to assess the total investment that females make in their offspring, and the source of the nutrients they use to produce eggs. In monarchs, as in most other butterflies, females utilize materials transferred by males during mating in egg production. Sperm are transferred to females within a protein-rich spermatophore, and the spermatophore is digested by the female and used in both somatic and reproductive tissue (Boggs and Gilbert 1979). I previously showed that the number of eggs that females produce is affected by the amount of spermatophore nutrients received (Oberhauser 1989, 1997); here I report how female investment in offspring is affected by the amount of nutrients acquired from spermatophores.

METHODS

All monarchs used in this study were the offspring of wild-captured adults and were reared on fresh cuttings of *Asclepias syriaca* (common milkweed) under ambient Minnesota summer photoperiod and light conditions in a room with open windows. On the day after eclosion, I weighed adults to the nearest 0.01 mg and measured their forewings to the nearest 0.1 mm. Female mass and mean forewing length ranged from 288 to 624 mg and 43 to 55 mm, respectively, reflecting a wide range of sizes. Butterflies were kept in glassine envelopes and fed a 20% honey solution ad libitum every other day until they were ready to mate.

Females were allowed to mate with one or two males. Females were 5 to 10 days old at their first mating, and their mates were 5 to 11 days old and either unmated or recently mated. Recently mated males transfer much smaller spermatophores (about 7 mg) than virgin males (over 25 mg) (Oberhauser 1988). I used five different mating treatments in which the amount of spermatophore nutrients females received varied (Oberhauser 1988). Females (total $n = 47$) mated with either (a) two unmated males, receiving two large spermatophores (large-large treatment); (b) an unmated male followed by a mated male, receiving a large followed by small spermatophore (large-small treatment); (c) a mated male followed by an unmated male, receiving a small followed by large spermatophore (small-large treatment); (d) two mated males, receiving two small spermatophores (small-small treatment); or (e) one mated male, receiving one small spermatophore (small treatment). Thus, the total amount of spermatophore material received by females ranged from about 7 mg (delivered by one recently mated male) to over 50 mg (delivered by two unmated males). Intermating intervals ranged from 3 to 7 days, and females were kept in 0.7-m^3 cages with potted *A. curassavica* plants and fed daily until they died or stopped laying eggs. I counted the number of eggs laid by each female every day and weighed 10 eggs/female/day to the nearest 0.01 mg on a Mettler analytical balance. Since the balance was not sensitive enough to weigh individual eggs, I weighed batches of 5 eggs.

I used multiple regression analyses to test the effects of treatment, time, and female size on egg mass, and one-way analyses of variance to compare treatment means of total fecundity and total egg mass.

RESULTS

Egg mass

The mass of a single monarch egg ranged from 0.242 to 0.588 mg, with a mean mass of 0.460 mg. This mean equals approximately 1/1000th the mass of a female (about 480 mg).

Several factors affected egg mass. The most important factor was time; females tended to lay lighter eggs as they aged (figure 3.1). I used time since mating rather than absolute age as a predictor in this analysis, since eggs are formed within the female before mating. Thus, a female that doesn't mate until she is 10 days old will actually lay eggs that were manufactured when she was younger. The shape of the plot of egg mass on day of egg laying is concave, and using the log of time as a predictor significantly improved the regression over using untransformed data. When time was controlled, there was an effect of female mass on egg mass; larger females laid larger eggs (figure 3.2). In addition, females in the large-small and small spermatophore treatments laid smaller eggs than did other females (table 3.2).

Total reproductive effort

I measured female reproductive output in two ways: the number of eggs produced and the total egg mass produced. Egg mass was calculated by multiplying the average mass of the 10 eggs by the number of eggs laid by each female on each day of egg laying, and summing this over the female's egg-laying life span. Table 3.3 summarizes means for both of these measures in each mating treatment, and table 3.4 shows the results of a multiple regression of several predictors on total egg mass.

The total number of eggs produced by females ranged from 290 to 1179 (mean = 715). There was a treatment effect on total fecundity, with females that received a large first spermatophore tending to lay more eggs (see table 3.3), although only two treatments were significantly different from each other. The total egg mass laid by females ranged from 129 to 510 mg (mean = 323 mg). Again, females that received a larger first spermatophore tended to lay a greater total mass of eggs (see tables 3.3 and 3.4),

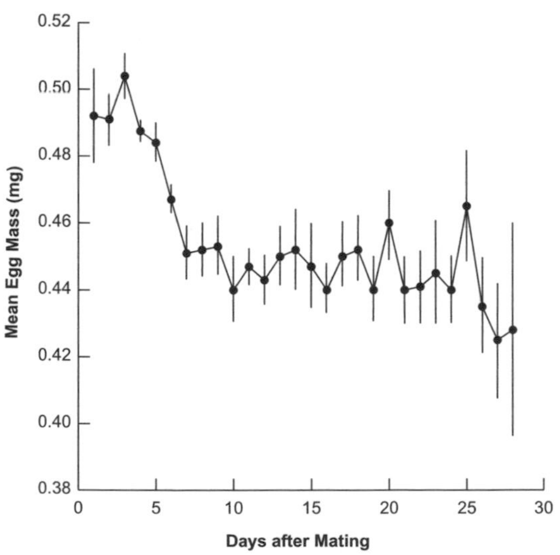

Figure 3.1. Egg mass over the period of egg laying. Bars represent one standard error. From Oberhauser 1997, reprinted with permission of Blackwell Publishing.

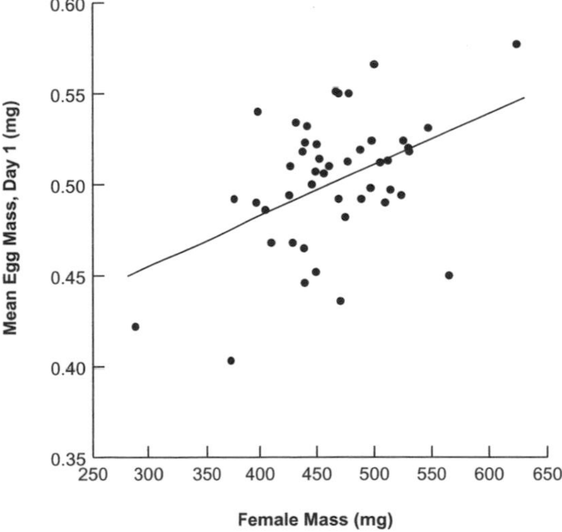

Figure 3.2. The mean mass of individual eggs laid by each female on the day after her first mating, as a function of female mass 24 h after eclosion.

Table 3.2. Significant predictors of egg mass

Predictor	Coefficient (SE)	t	p value
Constant	0.620 (0.221)	2.80	0.005
Log (time since first mating)	−0.280 (0.024)	−11.67	0.000
Female mass	0.036 (0.004)	8.44	0.000
Small spermatophore treatment	−0.0176 (0.005)	−3.53	0.000
Large-small spermatophore treatment	−0.0161 (0.004)	−4.13	0.000

Note: $n = 614$, adj. $R^2 = 0.231$. Time since first mating correlates with female age. There was no effect of interactions between treatments and time since first mating, or of first spermatophore size. SE, standard error.

Table 3.3. Lifetime fecundity means and total egg mass in the five mating treatments

Mating treatment	n	Mean fecundity	Total egg mass (mg)
a. Large-large	11	711[ab]	321[ab]
b. Large-small	9	936[a]	413[a]
c. Small-large	12	596[b]	275[b]
d. Small-small	9	700[ab]	317[ab]
e. Small	6	664[ab]	302[b]
Total or mean	47	715	323

Note: Mating treatments refer to the sizes of the two (or in the case of treatment e, one) spermatophores received from males. Means followed by the same letter are not significantly different at the 0.05 level of confidence (Tukey's least significant difference comparisons).

Table 3.4. Significant predictors of total egg mass

Predictor	Coefficient (SE)	t	p value
Constant	−84.12 (107.3)	−0.78	0.438
Egg-laying life span	8.471 (1.834)	4.62	0.000
Female mass at eclosion	0.5313 (0.2145)	2.48	0.018
Large first spermatophore	50.24 (24.07)	2.09	0.043

Note: $n = 44$, adj. $R^2 = 0.500$. SE, standard error.

although only the large-small, small-large, and small spermatophore treatments differed significantly. Female mass at eclosion and the total amount of time over which females laid eggs also affected total egg mass. Females that laid eggs over a longer period of time and those that weighed more at eclosion tended to lay a higher total mass of eggs (see table 3.4).

DISCUSSION

Even though individual eggs are small (weighing about 1/1000th as much as the female herself), female monarchs invest a large proportion of their mass in egg production. On average, females produce eggs that equal 70% of their initial body mass, with a range of 30% to 114%.

Female monarch butterflies lay smaller eggs as they age (see figure 3.1, table 3.2). Larger females tend to lay larger eggs (see table 3.2) and a greater total mass of eggs (see figure 3.2, table 3.4). While the amount of nutrients that females receive from male spermatophores affects their total egg mass, it does not appear to affect the mass of individual eggs. These results augment our understanding of how females utilize available nutrients for egg production. Since larger females tend to lay larger eggs, it appears that the nutrients that females consume as larvae affect egg mass. Nutrients that females receive from males do not affect egg mass in a predictable way; there were statistically significant negative effects of two mating treatments, but these treatments varied a great deal in the amount of spermatophore material received. In addition, as egg mass dropped most rapidly (days 3 to 7 of egg laying, see figure 3.1), most females are still obtaining nutrients from spermatophores (Oberhauser 1992).

In every case I have observed, female monarchs have eggs remaining in their ovaries at the end of their lives (Oberhauser 1997), suggesting that monarch fecundity is limited by female egg-laying life span, and not the total number of eggs produced. Thus, my finding that larger females lay larger eggs supports the hypothesis of Wiklund and colleagues (1987) that there will be nonadaptive scaling of egg size to body size when fecundity is limited by the number of eggs females can actually lay (see table 3.1). If there was strong correlation between egg mass and offspring fitness, all females should produce eggs of similar size. Wiklund and Karlsson (1984) suggested that females use a proportion of available reserves to produce eggs and as these reserves are depleted, females lay smaller eggs. My finding that egg mass decreases with female age supports this suggestion.

The arguments presented here assume that egg mass and offspring fitness are not correlated, as long as eggs are above some minimum size required for viability. This has not been tested in monarchs, and an important test of my conclusions would be to look for effects of egg mass on offspring fitness.

These findings have important implications for the population dynamics of monarchs. The fact that offspring number appears to be limited by the number of eggs females are able to lay, rather than produce, means that the density and quality of milkweed available will be an important determinant of population growth. If females spend more time searching for suitable oviposition sites, their realized fecundity will be decreased. Factors that result in an early departure from overwintering sites, such as lipid depletion and early mating (Oberhauser and Frey 1999), may result in less time for egg laying if females leave before milkweed is ready. The fact that female size influences egg numbers means that factors that affect one generation may have cascading effects into the next generation. Since adult size is determined during the larval stage, the quality and quantity of milkweed available to larvae will impact the number of eggs in the subsequent generation.

Acknowledgments

I thank De Cansler, Ann Feitl, Rachel Hampton, Brenda Jenson, and Christine Jessup for their help counting and weighing over 30,000 eggs. This study was funded by the National Science Foundation (DEB-9220829 and DEB-9442165).

References

Boggs, C. L. 1986. Reproductive strategies of female butterflies: variation in and constraints on fecundity. Ecol. Entomol. 11:7–15.

Boggs, C. L., and L. E. Gilbert. 1979. Male contribution to egg production in butterflies; evidence for transfer of nutrients at mating. Science 206:83–84.

Braby, M. F. 1994. The significance of egg size variation in butterflies in relation to host plant quality. Oikos 71:119–29.

Fleming, I. A., and M. T. Gross. 1990. Latitudinal clines: a trade-off between egg number and size in Pacific salmon. Ecology 71:1–11.

Fox, C. W. 1994. The influence of egg size on offspring performance in the seed beetle, *Callosobruchus maculates*. Oikos 71:321–25.

Fox, C. W. 2000. Natural selection on seed-beetle egg size in nature and the laboratory: variation among environments. Ecology 81:3029–35.

Fox, C. W., and T. A. Mousseau. 1996. Larval host plant affects the fitness consequences of egg size in the seed beetle *Stator limbatus*. Oecologia 107:541–48.

Fox, C. W., M. S. Thakar, and T. A. Mousseau. 1997. Egg size plasticity in a seed beetle: an adaptive maternal effect. Am. Nat. 149:149–63.

Janzen, D. 1977. Variation in seed size within a crop of a Costa Rican *Micuna andreana* (Leguminosae). Am. J. Bot. 64:347–49.

Jones, R. E., J. R. Hart, and G. D. Bull. 1982. Temperature, size and egg production in the cabbage butterfly (*Pieris rapae* L.). Aust. J. Zool. 30:223–32.

Kaplan, R. H. 1991. Developmental plasticity of egg size in response to competition in the cowpea weevil, *Callosobruchus maculates* (Coleoptera: Bruchidae). Oecologia 102:81–85.

Karlsson, B., and C. Wiklund. 1984. Egg weight variation and lack of correlation between egg weight and offspring fitness in the wall brown butterfly *Lasiommata megera*. Oikos 43:376–85.

Karlsson, B., and C. Wiklund. 1985. Egg weight variation in relation to egg mortality and starvation endurance of newly hatched larvae in some satyrid butterflies. Ecol. Entomol. 10:205–11.

Murphy, D. D., A. E. Launer, and P. R. Ehrlich. 1983. The role of adult feeding in egg production and population dynamics of the checkerspot butterfly *Euphydryas editha*. Oecologia 56:257–63.

Oberhauser, K. S. 1988. Male monarch butterfly spermatophore mass and mating strategies. Anim. Behav. 36:1384–88.

Oberhauser, K. S. 1989. Effects of spermatophores on male and female monarch butterfly reproductive success. Behav. Ecol. Sociobiol. 25:237–46.

Oberhauser, K. S. 1992. Rate of ejaculate breakdown and intermating intervals in monarch butterflies. Behav. Ecol. Sociobiol. 31:367–73.

Oberhauser, K. S. 1997. Fecundity and egg mass of monarch butterflies: effects of age, female size and mating history. Funct. Ecol. 11:166–75.

Oberhauser, K. S., and D. Frey. 1999. Coercive mating by overwintering male monarch butterflies. In J. Hoth, L. Merino, K. Oberhauser, I. Pisanty, S. Price, and T. Wilkinson, eds., The 1997 North American Conference on the Monarch Butterfly, pp. 67–78. Montreal: Commission for Environmental Cooperation.

Peters, R. H. 1986. The ecological implications of body size. Cambridge, U.K.: Cambridge University Press.

Reznick, D. N. 1991. Maternal effects in fish life histories. In E. C. Dudley, ed., The unity of evolutionary biology. Vol. 2, pp. 78–93. Portland, Ore.: Dioscorides.

Svärd, L., and C. Wiklund. 1988. Fecundity, egg weight, and longevity in relation to multiple matings in females of the monarch butterfly. Behav. Ecol. Sociobiol. 23:39–43.

Wiklund, C., and B. Karlsson. 1984. Egg size variation in satyrid butterflies: adaptive vs. historical "Bauplan", and mechanistic explanations. Oikos 43:391–400.

Wiklund, C., B. Karlsson, and J. Forsberg. 1987. Adaptive versus constraint explanations for egg-to-body size relationships in two butterfly families. Am. Nat. 130:828–38.

Wiklund, C., and A. Persson. 1983. Fecundity, and the relation of egg weight variation to offspring fitness in the speckled wood butterfly *Pararge aegeria*, or why don't female butterflies lay more eggs? Oikos 40:53–63.

4

Natural Enemies and Survival of Monarch Eggs and Larvae

Michelle D. Prysby

INTRODUCTION

Natural enemies are important to many Lepidoptera species. They can alter larval foraging behavior (Montllor and Bernays 1994), adult oviposition behavior (Bernays and Chapman 1994), and population dynamics (Dempster 1984; Haukioja 1994). They can also mitigate the effects of lepidopterans on their host plants (Montllor and Bernays 1994) and have been implicated in the evolution of host plant specificity in some species (Bernays and Graham 1988; Montllor and Bernays 1994).

A commonly held view states that monarchs are protected from natural enemies by their sequestration of cardenolide toxins from their milkweed host plants, and much research has utilized this assumption. For example, Rawlins and Lederhouse (1981) suggested that this chemical defense, along with larval warning coloration, allows monarch larvae to spend significant amounts of time basking in direct sunlight. Additional examples include studies of mimicry (e.g., Cohen 1985) and natural history (e.g., Urquhart 1960).

However, monarchs do have natural enemies and their effects are not negligible, at least on the adult stage. In Mexican overwintering sites, avian predation results in mortality rates of at least 9% (Calvert et al. 1979; Brower and Calvert 1985), and mice are estimated to kill about 5% of the monarchs in a given overwintering colony (Brower et al. 1985; Glendinning et al. 1988). Avian predators also consume monarch adults at the Californian overwintering sites (Sakai 1994). Wasps are the only invertebrate predator so far observed to attack overwintering adult monarchs (Leong et al. 1990). Additional observations have been made of natural enemies of adult monarchs during the breeding season. A few observations of bird predators exist (Smithers 1973; McIsaac 1991), but in most cases it is unknown whether these birds are significant predators of monarchs or naïve birds tasting a monarch for the first time. There are also several records of invertebrate predators feeding on adult monarchs, including spiders, mantids, and dragonflies (Smithers 1973; White and Sexton 1989).

Despite this research focus on predators of adults, natural enemies are likely to have a more significant impact on monarch eggs and larvae. Monarchs suffer significant mortality in these stages, with less than 12% surviving to the fifth instar (Borkin 1982; Oberhauser et al. 2001). Predators and parasitoids are important factors influencing survival and population dynamics in many other insect herbivore systems (Haukioja 1994) and are likely to be important sources of mortality in monarchs as well (Borkin 1982). Only a handful of studies, however, have investigated the specific effects of predators and parasitoids on immature monarchs.

Anecdotal field observations of monarch eggs and larvae cite ants, various Hemiptera species, coccinelids, cockroaches, spiders, wasps, lacewing larvae, and red velvet mites as monarch predators (Smithers 1973; Borkin 1982; Zalucki and Kitching 1982; pers. observ.). However, quantification of the importance of these predators is inconsistent or lacking, with a few exceptions. Calvert (1996, 1999, this volume) describes introduced fire ants (*Solenop-*

sis invicta Buren) as a major predator of monarch eggs and larvae in Texas, and suggests that the presence of fire ants severely limits the monarch population in that area. In a study of variation in monarch densities during the spring in Louisiana and Texas, Lynch and Martin (1993) frequently observed predation of monarch larvae by both crab spiders and ants. They found only weak correlations between the presence of monarchs and the presence of spiders or ants on milkweed, but still suggested that spiders and ants together could be a major mortality factor for monarchs in that region. Finally, Zalucki and Brower (1992) observed no effect of predator exclosures on monarch survival to the second instar, and concluded that host plant characteristics are a larger determinant of monarch survival through the early stages than are natural enemies.

Though generally thought to be more effective on vertebrates (Brower 1984), the sequestered cardenolides may deter some invertebrate predators. Berenbaum and Miliczky (1984) demonstrated that cardenolide-containing milkweed bugs were distasteful to mantid predators. Malcolm (1989) observed that the consumption of cardenolide-containing milkweed aphids by spiders resulted in a disruption of the spiders' web building and a reduction in the capture rate of future prey. Finally, Rayor (this volume) found that wasps that consume monarchs fed on either *Asclepias tuberosa* or *A. curassavica* (high-cardenolide milkweed species) developed more slowly than those that consumed a prey species without cardenolides.

Monarch parasitoids include 12 species of tachinid flies and at least 1 species of brachonid wasp (Arnaud 1978). Records of tachinid fly parasitism in North American monarch populations cite varying rates of parasitism, ranging from 1% in southern Ontario (Urquhart 1960) to 11.5% in Wisconsin (Borkin 1982) to 43% in Texas and Louisiana (Lynch and Martin 1993). The rate is much higher for Australian monarchs, reaching up to 100%, particularly in the fall (Smithers 1973; Zalucki 1981). Similarly high rates (70% to 98%) of parasitism exist in breeding populations of monarchs in central Mexico (E. Montesinos, pers. comm.). Parasitism rates of up to 42% were observed in Hawaiian monarchs. In the case of the Hawaiian monarchs, the parasitoid was *Lespesia archippivora*, a biocontrol agent introduced to control armyworms (Etchegaray and Nishida 1975a, 1975b).

Given that the studies on invertebrate predators of immature monarchs are few, largely qualitative, and conflicting, the goal of my research was to investigate the overall importance of invertebrate predators and parasitoids on monarch eggs and larvae. I sought to answer three specific research questions: (1) Are natural enemies in general, and invertebrate predators specifically, a significant source of mortality in natural monarch populations? (2) What are the specific effects of ant predators on natural monarch populations? (3) What is the extent of tachinid fly parasitism in natural monarch populations, and how does it vary geographically and temporally? I used two field experiments to study predators and estimated parasitism rates. I gathered additional data on parasitism rates as part of the Monarch Larva Monitoring Project (Prysby and Oberhauser, this volume).

METHODS

Effects of aerial and terrestrial predators on monarch survival

In June of 1998, I compared the survival of monarchs exposed to and those protected from predators. I focused on the egg and early instar stages. In an old field habitat in west-central Wisconsin, I chose 20 triplets of milkweed ramets, with the 3 plants within 2 m of each other. I made an effort to choose triplets of similar size and condition; otherwise choices were made haphazardly. I cut back the surrounding vegetation to a distance of approximately 0.25 m to ensure that no other plants were touching the ramets, and removed all invertebrates from them. I randomly assigned each ramet in a triplet to one of three treatments: exclusion of aerial and terrestrial predators, exclusion of terrestrial predators only, or control (no exclosure). Aerial predators included those likely to approach a ramet from the air, such as wasps, while terrestrial predators were those that crawled up the stem, such as ants. Exclosure treatment ramets had Insect Trap Coating paste (Tanglefoot Company, Grand Rapids, Michigan) applied to an 8 to 10-cm area of the stem, above the ground but below the lowest set of leaves. The "aerial and terrestrial" treatment ramets also had tomato cages covered in bridal veil placed over them. The cages were approximately 1 m tall and cone-shaped. I placed heavy chain over the bottom of the bridal veil to hold it down to the ground.

On 24 June, I collected eggs from lab-reared monarch butterflies. The eggs were laid on potted *A. curassavica* plants (tropical milkweed). Following the methods of Zalucki and Brower (1992), on 25 June I punched eggs out of the *A. curassavica* leaves using standard-sized hole punches, creating small leaf disks, each with 1 egg attached. Four eggs on leaf disks were glued to each milkweed ramet using milkweed latex from nonexperimental ramets. One disk was attached to the upper side of each of the four uppermost open leaves on each milkweed ramet.

Each morning for the following 7 mornings, I examined the plants and recorded the status of the monarch as alive, missing (monarch not located), or dead (monarch located but dead or nonviable). I also noted any other invertebrates found inside the cages or on the ramets.

Effects of ant and aphid presence on monarch survival

I conducted a pilot experiment in 1998 to see whether *Formica montana*, the dominant ant species at the field site, would attack monarch eggs. I glued one leaf disk with an egg to leaves on eight milkweed ramets on which *F. montana* individuals were tending aphids and to eight ramets without ants. I observed the ants' behavior and egg status on all ramets for several hours. I returned to the site after 48 h and recorded the status of any eggs that survived the initial observation period.

On 18 July 1999, I collected eggs from lab-reared female monarch butterflies on potted *A. curassavica* plants. The following day, I walked five belt transects across the same field site as used in the 1998 experiment. For every milkweed occurring along the belt transect, I recorded the presence or absence of ants and aphids. I then glued leaf disks, each with 1 egg, to 20 ramets in each of three categories: ants and aphids present, aphids only present, or clean (no ants or aphids). I assigned ramet categories on the basis of ant and aphid presence at the time when the eggs were first attached; the presence of ants and aphids on a ramet varied over the course of the 5-day experiment. I attached 1 egg/ramet to the underside of a leaf on the first or second open tier of leaves, mimicking the typical natural location of monarch eggs on *Asclepias syriaca* (common milkweed).

I included the aphids-only category because the presence of *F. montana* on milkweed ramets is highly associated with the presence of aphids (see Results) and because *F. montana* is a known aphid-tending species (Henderson and Jeanne 1992). I predicted that aphid presence would affect monarch survival indirectly, since ramets with aphids would be likely to attract ants.

On each day for the following 5 days, I monitored the ramets and recorded the status of each monarch (alive, dead, or missing), the stage of the monarch if present, the status of the leaf disk (present or absent), and the presence or absence of ants and aphids. On the final day of the experiment, I recorded the actual number of ants on each ramet, and a categorical estimate of the number of aphids (0, 1 to 10, 10 to 100, 100 to 1000, more than 1000).

Tachinid fly parasitism

During each week in the summer of 1999 and 2000, I recorded the presence of monarchs on a large sample of milkweed ramets (more than 100 ramets) (Prysby and Oberhauser, this volume). All fourth or fifth instar larvae were collected and reared to adults in the laboratory. Each larva was later scored as being a healthy butterfly, parasitized by tachinid flies, infected with the protozoan parasite *Ophryocystis elektroscirrha*, or dead from another cause. The flies were identified to family only, except for three voucher specimens that were sent to the U.S. Department of Agriculture (USDA) Systematic Entomology Laboratory for species identification. In 1999, I collected larvae from the same Wisconsin site where I did the predation experiments. In 2000, larvae were collected at five cornfields, field edges, and nonagricultural sites as part of a larger study of monarch phenology (Oberhauser et al. 2001). In addition, volunteers with the Monarch Larva Monitoring Project (Prysby and Oberhauser, this volume) collected and reared fourth and fifth instars and recorded outcomes.

Statistical analyses

For both experiments, I used logistic regression (LR) analyses to test the effects of each predictor on the probability of monarch survival. I used backward elimination to select the simplest possible model for explaining the variation in monarch survival (Trexler and Travis 1993; Agresti 1996). I followed a similar procedure to identify differences among treatments by combining two treatments into a single factor and comparing the resulting model to the model with all treatments as separate factors (Agresti 1996; S. Weisberg, pers. comm.). For the predator exclusion experiment, I included a blocking factor for the 20 different triplets of plants. I used the Arc program for all analyses (Cook and Weisberg 1999).

RESULTS

Effects of aerial and terrestrial predators on monarch survival

Overall monarch survival rate over 7 days was 18% (44/240), but it varied significantly among the three predator exclosure treatments (figure 4.1). Most monarchs died in the egg stage. Table 4.1 summarizes the analysis of factors that affected survival. Probability of monarch survival depended both on plant treatment and on plant triplet, the blocking factor. Of the nonsurviving monarchs, 11% were observed dead and 89% were missing. For the analyses, missing monarchs were assumed to be nonsurvivors, since eggs or very small larvae would be unlikely to survive if removed from the milkweed plant (Zalucki and Kitching 1982). Three eggs and one larva recorded as dead were killed accidentally, and these individuals were excluded from the regression analyses. Most surviving monarchs were first instars at the end of the 7 days.

To investigate differences among the three treatments, I ran stepwise simplifications of the regression model, setting two treatments equal to each other and checking for significant effects of the simplification using likelihood-ratio tests (table 4.1). All the treatments are significantly different from each other, but the differences between the control and exclosure treatments are much greater than the difference between the two exclosure treatments ($p < 0.001$ vs. $p = 0.032$).

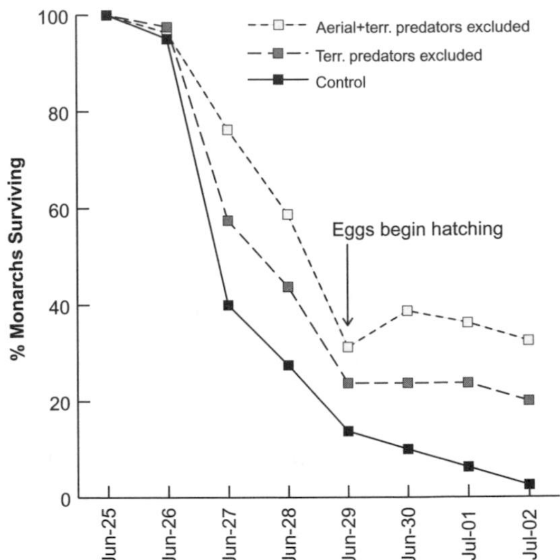

Figure 4.1. Monarch survival rate over time for three predator exclosure treatments. Each treatment group initially had 80 monarch eggs. Survival declined the most during the egg stage and leveled off after the eggs began hatching. The statistical analysis shown in table 4.1 considers only the final survival percentages at the end of the experiment.

Table 4.1. Significant predictors of monarch survival in the predator exclosure experiment

Predictor(s) tested	Deviance	*df*	ΔDeviance	Δ*df*	*p* value
Full model	47.37	38			
Ramet treatment	81.08	40	33.71	2	<0.0001
Block	81.54	57	34.17	19	0.0176
Terrestrial only vs. aerial and terrestrial	51.97	39	4.60	1	0.0320
Control vs. terrestrial only	62.37	39	14.99	1	0.0001
Control vs. aerial and terrestrial	80.90	39	33.52	1	<0.0001

Note: The full analysis of deviance likelihood ratio model has a blocking factor (representing the 20 ramet triplets) and a treatment factor with three categories (control, terrestrial predators excluded, aerial and terrestrial predators excluded). Each row shows the significance of including that predictor in the model or, in the case of the comparisons among treatment categories, the significance of the difference between a pair of categories. In each row, "Deviance" is the model deviance when the predictor is excluded from the model or the categories are combined, and "ΔDeviance" is the change in deviance when compared to the full model that has the predictor included or the categories separated. A significant *p* value indicates that the model simplification causes a significant change in model deviance. Both block and ramet treatment are significant, and all three treatment categories are significantly different from each other.

Neither the cages nor the adhesive were 100% effective. Invertebrates other than the monarchs were found on at least one occasion inside 11 of the 20 cages excluding aerial predators and on 8 of the 20 ramets excluding only terrestrial predators. Nine of these observations were of potential or known monarch predators, mainly ants and mites, and most occurred after two episodes of storms and high winds (on 26 and 27 June) that knocked over the cages and some of the ramets. In comparison, 14 of the 20 control ramets had invertebrates on them during the experimental period; 11 of these had ants.

Effects of ant and aphid presence on monarch survival

Of the 8 monarch eggs attached to milkweed ramets with *F. montana* present, ants removed all 8 within 90 min during the pilot study. Of the 8 eggs attached to ramets without *F. montana*, all survived at least 90 min, but 7 were missing 2 days later.

Table 4.2 shows the number of milkweed ramets observed with ants and aphids in the survey performed on day 1 of the experiment. Ant presence on milkweed ramets is significantly associated with aphid presence ($\chi^2 = 90.1$, $df = 1$, $p < 0.0001$). The dominant ant (more than 80% of those observed) was identified as *F. montana* (Emery) (identified by D. R. Smith, Systematic Entomology Laboratory, Agricultural Research Service, USDA).

Table 4.3 shows the numbers of ramets from the three initial treatment groups according to the five categories of aphid abundance at the end of the experiment. When comparing the aphids-only category to the ants and aphids category, there is an association between category and number of aphids ($r = 0.30$, $M^2 = 3.54$, $df = 1$, $p = 0.06$). Ramets with ants tended to have higher densities of aphids than did those without ants. In addition, ramets that had only aphids at the beginning of the experiment tended to have fewer ants on the last day than did ramets that had ants and aphids ($T = 1.95$, $df = 34$, $p = 0.06$).

The overall monarch survival rate on the 60 ramets over the 6 days was 23% (14/60), with only 5% of the monarchs on ramets with both ants and aphids on day 1 surviving (1/20) (figure 4.2). Most mortality for the ants and aphids category group occurred within 24 h (and thus on the eggs) of the start of the experiment. Probability of monarch survival depended on treatment (LR test = 6.92, $df = 57$, $p = 0.0314$).

Table 4.2. Milkweed ramets with ants or aphids

	Aphids present	Aphids absent	Totals
Ants present	73	9	82
Ants absent	45	130	175
Totals	118	139	257

Note: Number of ramets with ants or aphids, as measured on 19 July 1999, the first day of the experiment. Ant presence is significantly associated with aphid presence ($\chi^2 = 90.1$, $df = 1$, $p < 0.0001$).

Table 4.3. Ramet totals

Initial treatment group	Aphid abundance at end of experiment				
	0	1–10	10–100	100–1000	>1000
Control (clean)	15	4	0	0	0
Ants and aphids	1	2	6	9	2
Aphids only	3	7	7	3	0

Note: Number of ramets from each initial treatment group in five categories of aphid abundance, as measured on 24 July 1999 (final day of the experiment). There is a weak association between treatment group (ants and aphids or aphids only) and the categorical measurement of aphid number ($r = 0.30$, $M^2 = 3.54$, $df = 1$, $p = 0.06$).

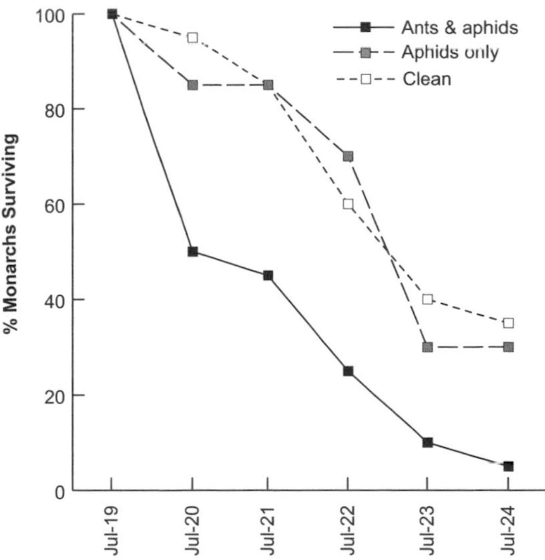

Figure 4.2. Monarch survival rate over time on milkweed ramets with aphids only, aphids and ants, and neither aphids nor ants (clean). Each category initially had 20 monarch eggs. Survival rates on clean ramets and ramets with aphids only are similar, and both are higher than the survival rate of monarchs on ramets with ants and aphids.

Table 4.4. Effects of ant and aphid presence on monarch survival

Model	Deviance	*df*	ΔDeviance	Δ*df*	*p* value
Full model	58.27	57			
Aphids only vs. ants and aphids	63.00	58	4.72	1	0.0298
Clean vs. ants and aphids	64.47	58	6.20	1	0.0128
Clean vs. aphids only	58.39	58	0.11	1	0.7356

Note: The full analysis of deviance likelihood ratio model has one predictor, plant category, with three levels (clean, only aphids present, ants and aphids present). Each row shows the significance of differences among the three categories. In each row, "Deviance" is the model deviance when the two categories are merged, and "ΔDeviance" is the change in deviance when compared to the full model that has the categories separated. A significant *p* value indicates that the model simplification causes a significant change in model deviance. The presence of ants and aphids together significantly affects the probability of monarch survival, while aphid presence alone does not affect monarch survival.

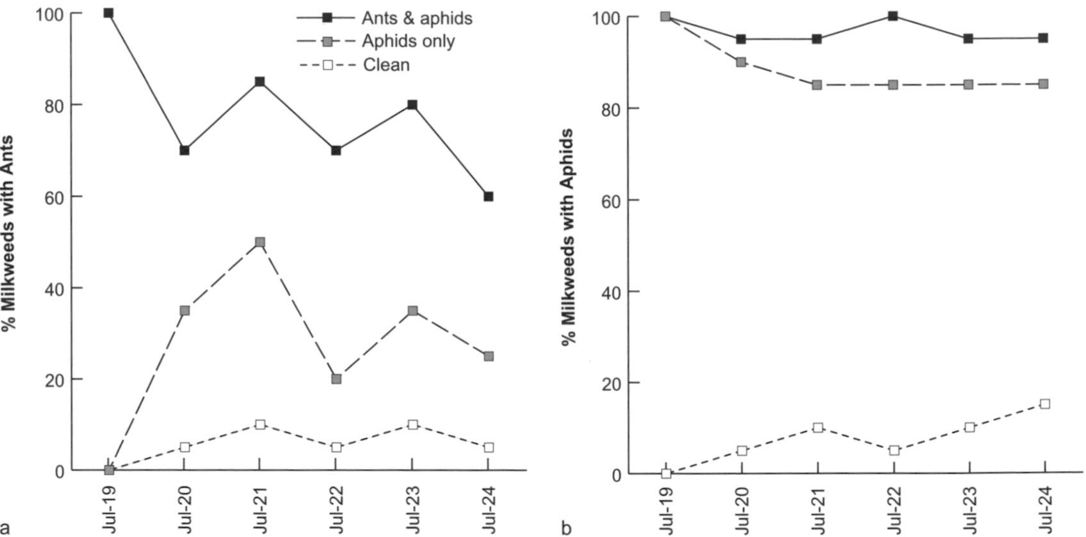

Figure 4.3. Percentage of milkweed ramets (out of 20) in the three initial categories with (a) ants present and (b) aphids present. Plant categories were assigned on the basis of ant and aphid presence on the first day of the experiment, so that all of the rametsin the ants and aphids category had both ants and aphids on day 1, although they did not all continue to have both throughout the experiment. Similarly, no ramets in the clean category had ants or aphids on day 1, but some ramets were subsequently colonized.

Table 4.4 shows the results of comparisons of the three treatment categories. The clean and aphids-only categories are both significantly different from the ants and aphids category, but not from each other. Therefore, ant presence reduces the probability of monarch survival, but aphid presence has no effect.

Because both ants and aphids are mobile, the experimental plants did not necessarily remain in their initial categories throughout the experiment. There was fluctuation in the number of plants with ants and aphids on them for the three initial categories (figure 4.3).

Parasitism rate observations

In 1999, 15% of the fourth and fifth instar monarch larvae collected were parasitized by tachinids; the rate was 23% in 2000 (figure 4.4). Three of the tachinid flies were identified as *L. archippivora* (Riley) (identified by N. E. Woodley, Systematic Entomology Laboratory, Agricultural Research Service, USDA). The other flies were similar in phenotype but were not identified to species. In 1999 and 2000, I observed hyperparasitoids in a total of four of the tachinid fly individuals and these were identified as *Perilampus hyalinus*

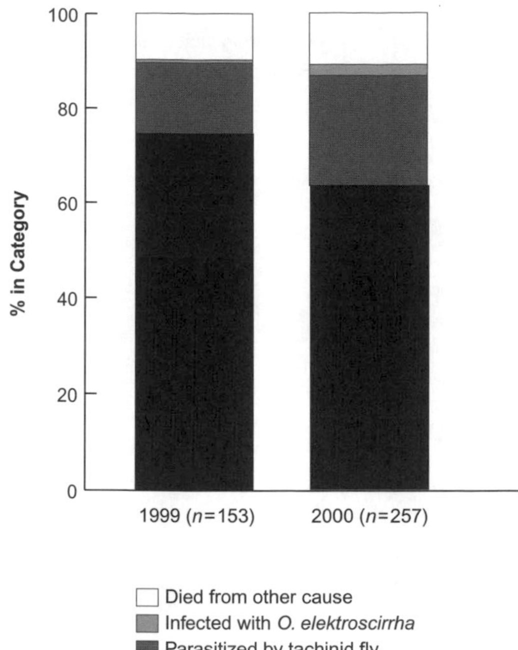

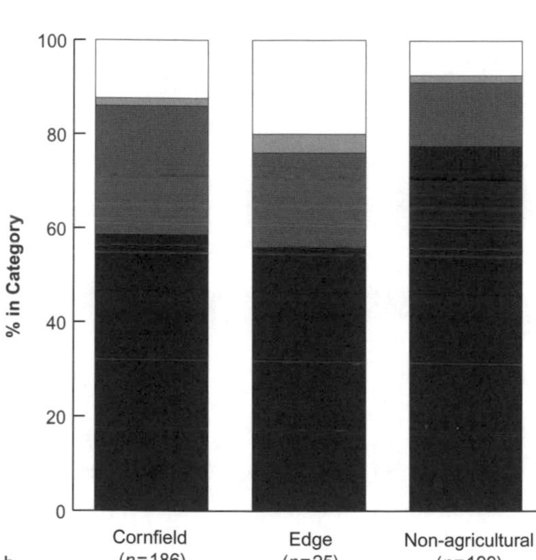

Figure 4.4. Percentage of larvae collected resulting in four outcomes: healthy adults, parasitized by tachinid flies, infected with *Ophryocystis elektroscirrha*, or died from another cause (including bacterial and viral diseases). All larvae were fourth or fifth instars when collected. Figure 4.4a shows the results divided by year; figure 4.4b shows the results divided by habitat.

(Say), though this group is now under revision (identified by E. E. Grissell, Systematic Entomology Laboratory, Agricultural Research Service, USDA). Approximately 10% of larvae collected each year died of other causes, including viral and bacterial diseases, developmental problems, and accidental deaths. A small percentage of larvae collected (0.6% in 1999, 2% in 2000) were infected with the protozoan parasite *O. elektroscirrha*. All monarchs with *O. elektroscirrha* were highly infected, with more than 1000 spores/cm^2 (Altizer and Oberhauser 2000).

A chi-square test showed no association between year and parasitism outcome ($\chi^2 = 6.68$, $df = 4$, $p > 0.10$), so I combined the data from both years to analyze the association between habitat type and outcome (figure 4.4), which was significant ($\chi^2 = 19.91$, $df = 6$, $p < 0.005$). More larvae than expected from the cornfields were parasitized, and more larvae than expected from the nonagricultural habitats were healthy.

Figure 4.5 shows parasitism rates for additional sites monitored by Monarch Larva Monitoring Project volunteers. Parasitism rates varied from 0% to 55%. Species were not identified.

DISCUSSION

Effects of aerial and terrestrial predators on monarch survival

The results of the predator exclosure experiment clearly show an increase in monarch survival when terrestrial (nonflying) invertebrates are excluded. Potential predators observed on the milkweed ramets during the experiment included ants, spiders, and red velvet mites, with ants the most common (observed on half of the control ramets at some point during the experiment).

Most of the mortality difference between the control and exclosure treatments occurred within the first 48 h of the experiment, though the differences in mortality widened slightly near the end of the 7-day experimental period. Monarchs on ramets excluding terrestrial predators suffered almost no mortality after eggs began hatching, while those on control ramets suffered mortality during the larval stage. Odds of survival were significantly higher for monarchs on ramets excluding both aerial and terrestrial predators than for those on ramets excluding only terrestrial predators. However, it is difficult to distinguish these differences from a cage effect. Monarchs in the cages were more protected from the elements, particularly during the two large storms that occurred during the experiment, and were probably less likely to fall off of the milkweeds.

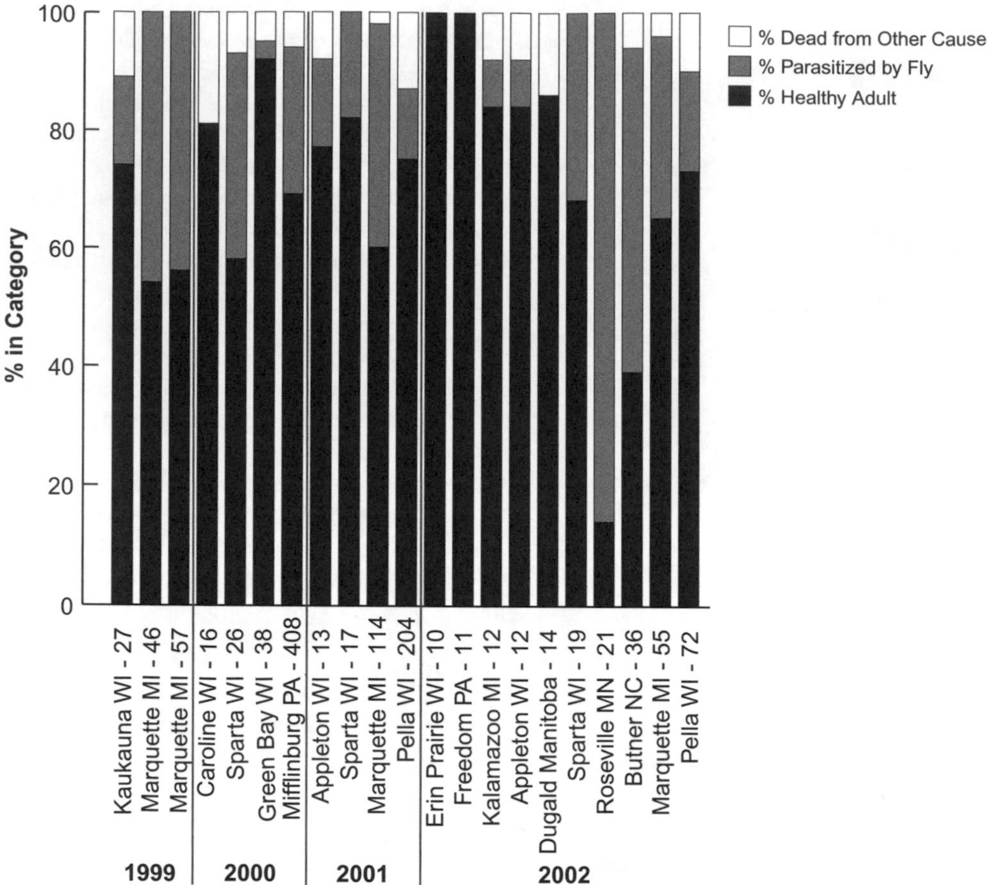

Figure 4.5. Percentage of larvae collected that were parasitized, not parasitized, or dead from another cause. Data from all Monarch Larva Monitoring Project (MLMP) sites with more than 10 larvae collected are shown. MLMP volunteers did not measure infection by *O. elektroscirrha*. Data are from 2000, unless otherwise noted. The Mifflinburg, Pennsylvania, site includes parasitism by both tachinid flies and an unknown hymenopteran.

Overall, 65% of the monarchs on the ramets excluding aerial and terrestrial predators were missing or dead at the end of the experiment. Some of this mortality could be due to experimental error or natural sources of mortality other than predators. Experimental errors include predators within exclosures, ineffectiveness of the latex glue technique (causing eggs to desiccate or be lost), accidental removal of eggs or larvae by observers, and larvae mired in the Insect Trap Coating paste. The latter two sources of experimental error are the only sources that can be directly quantified; together, they account for 3 of the 52 nonsurviving monarchs on the ramets excluding aerial and terrestrial predators. Natural mortality sources other than predators include larvae mired in the milkweed latex, larvae killed by the toxic cardenolides in the milkweed, eggs washed off of the plant in the rainstorms, larvae wandering off of the plant, and infertile eggs that did not hatch. I did not observe any larvae mired in the latex, and larvae are unlikely to be killed by the low cardenolide concentrations in *A. syriaca* (Malcolm and Zalucki 1996). Eggs usually withstand rain events, but most monarch eggs are laid on the undersides of leaves and are perhaps more protected than the eggs in this study (pers. observ.). The percentage of infertile eggs produced by female monarchs is variable, but can be as high as 55% for some females (M. Solensky, pers. comm.).

While it is clear that predator exclosures lead to higher survival rates, more studies are needed to further quantify the effects of predation in natural monarch populations. Data on how these effects vary temporally, spatially, and among different immature stages would provide a useful complement to this study. To reduce experimental error, future studies using the hole-punched leaf disk technique should use either older eggs that will hatch sooner or a stronger adhesive to reduce the likelihood of eggs falling off the plants. Attaching the leaf disks to the undersides of the milkweed leaves, rather than the upper sides, may also reduce experimental error. In addition, more stable predator exclosures would prevent failure during storms.

Effects of ant predators on monarchs

Based on both field surveys of milkweed and the exclosure experiment, ants (particularly *F. montana)* appear to be a common potential monarch predator, at least in this field site. Ants were found on 30% of milkweed ramets sampled just prior to the experiment and were significantly associated with milkweed ramets colonized by aphids. Surveys in southern Wisconsin by Hendersen and Jeanne (1992) also indicate a significant presence of *F. montana* on *A. syriaca*, with up to 20% of the ramets harboring ants tending aphids. In addition, Hendersen and Jeanne (1992) found *F. montana* on *A. syriaca* from late May until late August, nearly the entire breeding season of monarchs in the Upper Midwest (Prysby and Oberhauser, this volume).

Survival was seven times higher for monarchs on the clean ramets and ramets with aphids only than on the ramets with both ants and aphids (35% vs. 5%). Half of the monarchs on the ramets with ants and aphids died or disappeared within the first 24 h of the experiment. This pattern is consistent with my pilot study observations, in which *F. montana* individuals found and destroyed monarch eggs within minutes. Mortality on the clean ramets was likely due either to ants or other predators foraging on those plants during the study or to leaf disks falling off of the ramets. The latter experimental error probably accounted for less mortality in this experiment than the 1998 exclosure experiment because there were no storms and I periodically reattached loose leaf disks during the study. One clean ramet appeared to have been eaten by a deer or other herbivore during the experiment, and that monarch was reported as dead, since it had been in the egg stage. The survival rate of the monarchs on the clean ramets was higher than the survival rate of the monarchs on the control plants in the 1998 experiment, and was approximately the same as the survival rate observed by Malcolm and Zalucki (1996) on *A. syriaca* over a similar time period.

Given that ant presence is so strongly associated with aphid presence, I had expected to see a lower survival rate on the aphids-only ramets than on the clean ramets. These two categories, however, had virtually the same results (see figure 4.2, table 4.4). There are two possible factors influencing this result. First, ramets in the aphids-only category tended to have fewer aphids than the ramets in the ants and aphids category (see table 4.3). When I set up the experiment, it was unusual to see ramets that had high numbers of aphids, but no ants. Aphid density is likely to influence ant density and foraging (Hendersen and Jeanne 1992). Future studies should examine the effect of aphid density as well as aphid presence on monarch survival. Second, ramets in the aphids-only category may have recruited fewer ants during the experiment than ramets in the ants and aphids category, as evidenced by the differences in ant numbers on the last day of the experiment. While I addressed only the effects of ant presence and not the effects of different ant densities in this experiment, there is likely to be a relationship between ant density and monarch survival.

Given the results of this field study, a more controlled field or lab study to investigate the effects of *F. montana* and other ant species on monarch survival and behavior would be worthwhile. Future studies could examine the effects of ant density, and monarch stage on monarch survival. Spatially explicit studies accounting for the distribution of ant mounds and milkweed ramets may also yield interesting results. Finally, given the severe impact ants can have on monarch survival, experiments on the female monarch's choice of location for oviposition are an important next step. At least one other butterfly avoids host plants with ants (Bernays and Chapman 1994), and similar studies in monarchs would broaden our understanding of how and why monarchs choose specific host plant individuals.

Extent of tachinid fly parasitism in natural monarch populations

The high rates of tachinid fly parasitism observed in both 1999 and 2000 and in multiple locations demonstrate that parasitoids are a very significant source of mortality in monarchs. The difference in parasitism rates among the three habitats surveyed is intriguing. One possible explanation is that *L.*

archippivora demonstrates a density dependence in relation to its monarch host; per ramet monarch densities were significantly higher in cornfields than in the nonagricultural habitats (Oberhauser et al. 2001). The pattern also could be related to the use of alternative hosts by *L. archippivora*. This tachinid species is a generalist, attacking 13 different Lepidoptera families (Etchegaray and Nishida 1975a). Differences in the densities of these alternative hosts in the different habitats may affect the pattern observed. Alternatively, the differences could be due to the behavior of individual flies. Perhaps hosts are easier to find in cornfield habitats, or some other aspect of that habitat attracts them, such as the density or array of the host plants. In Australia, Zalucki (1981) found that milkweed patch size strongly influenced rates of parasitism in monarchs by another tachinid species. Parasitism rates were highest for larger patches of milkweed and lowest on isolated single ramets.

There are not enough data at this point to look for temporal or geographic trends in tachinid fly parasitism in monarchs. However, there is considerable variation within just the Upper Midwest and Great Lakes region (see figure 4.4). Parasitism levels in the Upper Midwest appear to be lower than that observed in nonmigratory populations of monarchs in Mexico (E. Montesinos, pers. comm.).

SYNTHESIS

The results of these studies demonstrate that natural enemies are important to monarchs. Both predators and parasitoids can significantly lower monarch survival, and these effects can occur as early as the egg stage (in the case of ant predators) or as late as the fifth instar or pupa (in the case of tachinid fly parasitoids). Although monarch eggs do contain some cardenolide toxins (Brower 1984), these toxins do not appear to afford them much protection against invertebrate natural enemies.

While these studies lay a basic groundwork for studying natural enemies in the monarch system, they also open many new questions. For example, are natural enemies a regulating factor for monarch populations (Dempster 1984)? How does the effect of natural enemies compare to other factors, such as host plant quality and availability and abiotic factors, and how does this effect vary in space and time? Do synergistic or antagonistic effects exist between natural enemies and other ecological factors? Previous theoretical and empirical studies indicated that natural enemies, though an important mortality source, do not play a role in the regulation of lepidopteran populations because they are not adequately density dependent (Dempster 1984). The natural enemies studied here, *F. montana* and *L. archippivora*, are likely to be too polyphagous to act as density-dependent monarch population regulators, but this system certainly needs more study to arrive at a definitive conclusion. The answers to these questions are important both for monarch conservation and for improving our understanding of insect herbivore population growth.

Acknowledgments

I thank Elaine Dunham, Youa Yang, John Woodell, and Melody Ng for providing field assistance for the predation experiments; and Matt Curtis, Jolene Lushine, Christine Worrall, and the many teachers, students, and volunteers who collected larvae in both 1999 and 2000. The Bell Museum of Natural History provided Dayton Natural History funds to support my field studies in 1998 and 1999, and the U.S. Department of Agriculture provided funding for collecting larvae in 2000. Thanks to Don Alstad and Karen Oberhauser for my use of their property in Wisconsin, and to Stacey Halpern, Patrice Morrow, Elizabeth Goehring, Lincoln Brower, and Karen Oberhauser for providing comments on this manuscript. This research was completed to fulfill partially the requirements for a master's degree in ecology, evolution, and behavior at the University of Minnesota.

References

Agresti, A. 1996. An introduction to categorical data analysis. New York: John Wiley and Sons.

Altizer, S. M., K. S. Oberhauser, and L. P. Brower. 2000. Associations between host migration and the prevalence of a protozoan parasite in natural populations of adult monarch butterflies. Ecol. Entomol. 25:125–39.

Arnaud, P. H., Jr. 1978. A host-parasite catalog of North American Tachinidae (Diptera). U.S. Department of Agriculture Miscellaneous Publication No. 1319. Washington, D.C.: U.S. Department of Agriculture.

Berenbaum, M. R., and E. Miliczky. 1984. Mantids and milkweed bugs: efficacy of aposematic coloration against invertebrate predators. Am. Midl. Nat. 111:64–68.

Bernays, E. A., and R. F. Chapman. 1994. Host-plant selection by phytophagous insects. New York: Chapman and Hall.

Bernays, E. A., and M. Graham. 1988. On the evolution of host specificity in phytophagous arthropods. Ecology 69:886–92.

Borkin, S. S. 1982. Notes on shifting distribution patterns and survival of immature *Danaus plexippus* (Lepidoptera: Danaidae) on the food plant *Asclepias syriaca*. Gt. Lakes Entomol. 15:199–206.

Brower, L. P. 1984. Chemical defense in butterflies. In R. I. Vane-Wright and P. R. Ackery, eds., The biology of butterflies, pp. 109–34. Orlando, Fla.: Academic Press.

Brower, L. P., and W. H. Calvert. 1985. Foraging dynamics of bird predators on overwintering monarch butterflies in Mexico. Evolution 39:852–68.

Brower, L. P., B. E. Horner, M. A. Marty, C. M. Moffitt, and R. B. Villa. 1985. Mice (*Peromyscus maniculatus, P. spicilegus,* and *Microtus mexicanus*) as predators of overwintering monarch butterflies (*Danaus plexippus*) in Mexico. Biotropica 17:89–99.

Calvert, W. H. 1996. Fire ant predation on monarch larvae (Nymphalidae: Danainae) in a central Texas prairie. J. Lepid. Soc. 50:149–51.

Calvert, W. H. 1999. Patterns in the spatial and temporal use of Texas milkweeds (Asclepiadaceae) by the monarch butterfly (*Danaus plexippus* L.) during fall, 1996. J. Lepid. Soc. 53:37–44.

Calvert, W. H., L. E. Hedrick, and L. P. Brower. 1979. Mortality of the monarch butterfly (*Danaus plexippus* L.): avian predation at five overwintering sites in Mexico. Science 204:847–50.

Cohen, J. A. 1985. Differences and similarities in cardenolide contents of queen *Danaus chrysippus* and monarch butterflies *Danaus plexippus* in Florida USA and their ecological and evolutionary implications. J. Chem. Ecol. 11:85–104.

Cook, R. D., and S. Weisberg. 1999. Applied regression including computing and graphics. New York: John Wiley and Sons.

Dempster, J. P. 1984. The natural enemies of butterflies. In R. I. Vane-Wright and P. R. Ackery, eds., The biology of butterflies, pp. 97–104. Orlando, Fla.: Academic Press.

Etchegaray, J. B., and T. Nishida. 1975a. Reproductive activity, seasonal abundance and parasitism of the monarch butterfly, *Danaus plexippus* (Lepidoptera: Danaidae) in Hawaii. Proc. Hawaiian Entomol. Soc. 12:33–39.

Etchegaray, J. B., and T. Nishida. 1975b. Biology of *Lespesia archippivora* (Diptera: Tachinidae). Proc. Hawaiian Entomol. Soc. 12:41–49.

Glendinning, J. I., A. Alonso Mejia, and L. P. Brower. 1988. Behavioral and ecological interactions of foraging mice (*Peromyscus melanotis*) with overwintering monarch butterflies (*Danaus plexippus*) in Mexico. Oecologia 75:222–27.

Haukioja, E. 1994. Effects of food and predation on population dynamics. In N. E. Stamp and T. M. Casey, eds., Caterpillars: ecological and evolutionary constraints on foraging, pp. 425–47. New York: Chapman and Hall.

Henderson, G., and R. L. Jeanne. 1992. Population biology and foraging ecology of prairie ants in southern Wisconsin (Hymenoptera: Formicidae). J. Kansas Entomol. Soc. 65:16–29.

Leong, K., D. Frey, and C. Nagano. 1990. Wasp predation on overwintering monarch butterflies (Lepidoptera: Danaidae) in central California. Pan-Pac. Entomol. 66:326–28.

Lynch, S. P., and R. A. Martin. 1993. Milkweed host plant utilization and cardenolide sequestration by monarch butterflies in Louisiana and Texas. In S. B. Malcolm and M. P. Zalucki, eds., Biology and conservation of the monarch butterfly, pp. 107–23. Los Angeles: Los Angeles County Museum of Natural History.

Malcolm, S. B. 1989. Disruption of web structure and predatory behavior of a spider by plant-derived chemical defenses of an aposematic aphid. J. Chem. Ecol. 15:1699–716.

Malcolm, S. B., and M. P. Zalucki. 1996. Milkweed latex and cardenolide induction may resolve the lethal plant defence paradox. Entomol. Exp. Appl. 80:193–96.

McIsaac, H. P. 1991. The capture and release of a monarch butterfly (Nymphalidae: Danainae) by a barn swallow. J. Lepid. Soc. 45:62–63.

Montllor, C. B., and E. A. Bernays. 1994. Invertebrate predators and caterpillar foraging. In N. E. Stamp and T. M. Casey, eds., Caterpillars: ecological and evolutionary constraints on foraging, pp. 170–202. New York: Chapman and Hall.

Oberhauser, K. S., M. D. Prysby, H. R. Mattila, D. E. Stanley-Horn, M. K. Sears, G. Dively, E. Olson, J. M. Pleasants, W. F. Lam, and R. L. Hellmich. 2001. Temporal and spatial overlap between monarch larvae and corn pollen: influence on risks imposed by Bt-corn. Proc. Natl. Acad. Sci. USA 98:11913–18.

Rawlins, J. E., and R. C. Lederhouse. 1981. Developmental influences of thermal behavior on monarch caterpillars (*Danaus plexippus*): an adaptation for migration (Lepidoptera: Nymphalidae: Danainae). J. Kansas Entomol. Soc. 54:387–408.

Sakai, W. 1994. Avian predation on the monarch butterfly, *Danaus plexippus* (Nymphalidae: Danainae), at a California overwintering site. J. Lepid. Soc. 48:148–56.

Smithers, C. N. 1973. A note on natural enemies of *Danaus plexippus* (L.) (Lepidoptera: Nymphalidae) in Australia. Aust. Entomol. Mag. 1:37–40.

Trexler, J. C., and J. Travis. 1993. Nontraditional regression analyses. Ecology 74:1629–37.

Urquhart, F. 1960. The monarch butterfly. Toronto: University of Toronto Press.

White, D. S., and O. J. Sexton. 1989. The monarch butterfly (Lepidoptera: Danainae) as prey for the dragonfly *Hagenius brevistylus* (Odonata: Gomphidae). Entomol. News 100: 129–32.

Zalucki, M. P. 1981. Temporal and spatial variation of parasitism in *Danaus plexippus* (L.) (Lepidoptera: Nymphalidae: Danainae). Aust. Entomol. Mag. 8:3–8.

Zalucki, M. P., and L. P. Brower. 1992. Survival of first instar larvae of *Danaus plexippus* (Lepidoptera: Danainae) in relation to cardiac glycoside and latex content of *Asclepias humistrata* (Asclepiadaceae). Chemoecology 3:81–93.

Zalucki, M. P., and R. L. Kitching. 1982. Temporal and spatial variation of mortality in field populations of *Danaus plexippus* L. and *D. chrysippus* L. larvae (Lepidoptera: Nymphalidae). Oecologia 53:201–7.

5

Effects of Monarch Larval Host Plant Chemistry and Body Size on *Polistes* Wasp Predation

Linda S. Rayor

INTRODUCTION

Monarch larvae are specialists on milkweed (*Asclepias* spp.) host plants. Milkweeds produce cardenolides, which are bitter, toxic, and effective deterrents for many herbivores and predators that feed on those herbivores (Brower 1984). Cardenolide concentrations, specific array of cardenolides, and relative emetic potency vary significantly among different *Asclepias* species (Malcolm 1991; Martin et al. 1992). Monarch larvae sequester and concentrate the cardenolides from their host plants in their tissues, hemolymph, and epidermis. Although monarchs do not sequester cardenolides in direct proportion to the concentrations or array in the plants, there is a monotonic increase in cardenolides in monarchs relative to the concentrations in their host plants (Malcolm and Brower 1989). Larvae that feed on host plants with different cardenolide concentrations are assumed to vary in their palatability to predators (Brower 1984). Because *Asclepias* species with different concentrations of cardenolides in their leaves overlap in their distribution, predators would be expected to encounter monarch larvae that present a spectrum of palatability (Brower 1984). To test the hypothesis that a palatability spectrum exists, I examined the predatory behavior of paper wasps in response to monarch larvae raised on *Asclepias* species that varied in their cardenolide concentrations.

Wasp predation on lepidopteran larvae

Predatory wasps exert a major selective force on lepidopteran larvae (Montllor and Bernays 1993; Raveret Richter 2000). The social paper wasps (Vespidae: *Polistes* spp.) specialize on lepidopteran larvae, which they capture to feed to their developing carnivorous larvae. The wasps are generalist predators, capturing whatever larval prey is abundant and sufficiently palatable. Because the adults feed solely on nectar, their foraging behavior for prey is dictated by the nutritional requirements of their larvae (Raveret Richter 2000). Acceptance or rejection of prey depends on the palatability of plant chemical defenses sequestered in the tissues of the larva or present in its gut (Stamp and Bowers 1991; Stamp 1992). Wasp larvae need to be fed continuously for a period of several weeks prior to pupation, and as soon as the first generation of adult daughters emerges, each nest has multiple foragers searching continuously for prey to satisfy their larval siblings.

Paper wasps are abundant worldwide in both urban and rural areas (Carpenter 1991; Reeve 1991). Their distribution completely overlaps the breeding ranges of monarch butterflies throughout North America (Ackery and Vane-Wright 1984; Carpenter 1991) and Australia (Richards 1978; James 1993). Fertilized queens overwinter in a state of diapause. Depending on the wasp species and climatic conditions in temperate North America, the queens start building their nests in the spring or early summer (Reeve 1991). The nests contain larvae from early summer into the early autumn (Reeve 1991) and, depending on the species, may be composed of 20 to over 100 individuals by the end of the summer (Reeve 1991). *Polistes* nests are found on eaves of buildings, fence posts, mailboxes, or in vegetation—essentially any location sufficiently protected from the elements. Wasp nests are numerous, in close proximity to one another, and most of the available nest sites are occupied in suitable habitats (pers. observ.).

Paper wasps are efficient, intelligent, generalist predators capable of flying over vast areas to search for prey. They search plants for prey while hovering or walking on them (Raveret Richter and Jeanne 1991; Nannoni et al. 2001; pers. observ.) and are attracted to frass and herbivore-damaged plants (Cornelius 1993). Wasp search behavior is influenced by the structure of the larval host plant (Geitzenauer and Bernays 1996). However, paper wasps are large enough that they are rarely deterred by a plant morphology (waxy or hirsute leaves) that can inhibit the movement of smaller insect predators (Eigenbrode et al. 2000).

Polistes predation involves locating prey, attacking it by repeated biting (never stinging), processing it to a manageable size, and flying back to the nest with pieces of prey (Rabb and Lawson 1957; Raveret Richter and Jeanne 1991; pers. observ.). Wasps make orientation flights as they leave the site of a successful prey capture (Raveret Richter 2000). After dropping off the prey on the nest, the forager rapidly returns to the site, where she may have left behind pieces of the prey, or to another site where hunting has been successful. The wasps return again and again to successful predation sites, which may be tens to hundreds of meters from their nests (Rabb and Lawson 1957; pers. observ.). Although wasps do not recruit nest mates to prey, they are highly visual and alert to what other wasps are doing, and are attracted to prey inspection or processing by other individuals (Raveret Richter 1990; Raveret Richter and Tisch 1999).

Numerous anecdotal reports of paper wasp predation on monarch larvae are found on Internet discussion groups, and predatory wasps have been observed to kill substantial numbers of monarch larvae in cornfields (M. R. Berenbaum, pers. comm.). However, there are no published accounts of these behaviors. Monarch larvae have been reported to be (potentially or actually) preyed on by reduviid and pentatomid bugs, coccinellid and lacewing larvae, ants, spiders, and birds (Lynch and Martin 1993; Zalucki and Kitching 1982; Calvert 1996; James 2000; Stimson and Kasuya 2000; Prysby, this volume). Because the *Polistes* wasps do not remain on the plant with the prey, they may be missed more often than the other predators. Yet these relatively large wasps may be especially important sources of mortality for later instar larvae.

Here, I report studies in which I examined (1) whether *Polistes* wasps readily prey on monarch larvae, (2) whether cardenolide concentrations in host plants affect the number of monarch larvae that the wasps capture, (3) whether the wasps prefer alternative prey species without cardenolides, and (4) whether wasps preferentially attack and successfully kill monarch larvae of a particular size.

METHODS

My students and I collected paper wasps, *P. dominulus* (Vespidae: Polistinae), from the wild around Ithaca, New York, during late May and early June in the years 1995 to 1998, 1999, and 2000. We maintained them in nests composed of 10 to 20 cells with eggs or larvae and a single or double foundress. We enclosed the wasps and their nests in cardboard boxes (approximately 30 × 20 cm) with screened front panels, which we hung in rooms (5.8 × 2.7 m) in the Entomology Insectary Greenhouse on the Cornell University campus. After the wasps had accepted the boxes as new sites for their nests (about 3 days), we removed the screens to allow them free flight throughout their room. Each room contained 4 to 7 nests, depending on the numbers of active foragers. All adults were individually marked with colored enamel paint. Other than the initial foundresses, all subsequent wasps were reared entirely in the greenhouse and had foraging experience only with prey species provided to them.

To evaluate whether the wasp behavior was natural in the controlled greenhouse environment, I investigated prey choice and size preferences in free-living wasps on the Cornell campus in 2000. In the outdoor experiments, the behavior and choices of the wild wasps agreed in all details with what we observed in the controlled greenhouse environment.

I will present only size preference data from the outdoor experiments here.

Monarch colonies were started annually from an inbred colony kept at Cornell University (Hughes et al. 1993) and mixed with wild monarch adults or larvae obtained from Minnesota (most years) or Virginia (in 1999 only). We allowed adults to oviposit on host plants in breeding cages and raised subsequent larvae on the appropriate *Asclepias* species. For the behavioral choice experiments (below), wasps were given a choice between monarch larvae that were raised on *Asclepias* species with high (*A. curassavica*), medium (*A. syriaca*, *A. incarnata*), or low (*A. tuberosa*, *A. verticillata*) cardenolide concentrations. (Mean cardenolide value for *A. curassavica* = 1055, *A. syriaca* = 50, *A. incarnata* = 14, *A. tuberosa* = 3, and *A. verticillata* = 1 μg/0.1 g dry weight of leaf tissue [Malcolm 1991].) Monarchs do not sequester cardenolides in direct proportion to the concentrations found in the *Asclepias* host plant, but most effectively sequester from species with intermediate cardenolide concentrations (Malcolm and Brower 1989). For example, monarchs raised on *A. syriaca* can concentrate cardenolides to approximately 350 in μg/0.1 g of dry butterfly, far higher than in the plant (Malcolm and Brower 1989). Monarchs feeding on high-cardenolide plants maintain high levels in their tissues, while monarchs raised on low-cardenolide plants retain low levels in their tissues.

Experimental design: Cardenolide concentrations

I developed behavioral choice tests to evaluate whether the wasps discriminate among monarch larvae that vary in their cardenolide concentration. My students and I presented freely foraging wasps with a choice of live monarch larvae on plants, with the two types of larvae used in each test based on what they were raised on: *A. curassavica* versus *A. incarnata*, 21 hours, 1995; *A. curassavica* versus *Pieris napi* or *Trichoplusia ni*, 13 hours, 1996; *A. curassavica* versus *A. tuberosa*, 55 hours, and *A. curassavica* versus *A. verticillata*, 3 hours, 1998; *A. curassavica* versus *A. syriaca*, 29 hours, and *A. curassavica* versus *Junonia coenia*, 2 hours, 1999. We observed foragers in one or two 1-hour sessions daily and recorded detailed behavioral data using the Noldus Observer 3.0 behavioral software on Psion handheld computers. We made focal observations on 5 to 10 individually marked wasps simultaneously. Prey was available only during recording sessions. With this experimental design, it was possible to record how many prey each wasp killed, along with details of her prey handling for her entire foraging life. The data presented here reflect the total number of prey items returned to the nests by the wasps ([initial attacks + prey remains + finds (remains left by other wasps) + stolen prey] – [rejected + dropped prey] = total prey items returned to nest, sensu Rayor and Munson 2002). Only wasps that had 5 or more total prey items were included in the analyses.

At the beginning of each choice test, we placed 6 to 8 size-matched larvae of each type on separate, large, minimally herbivore-damaged *Asclepias* "presentation" plants. As they were killed, larvae of the appropriate type were replaced on plants to maintain equal numbers of each prey type during the test. Care was taken not to attract the attention of foraging wasps as the larvae were replaced, and larvae were placed somewhere on the plants other than where the previous larva had been killed. Groups of presentation plants were less than 1 m from each other. Presentation plants were exchanged and leaves rinsed between sessions to minimize visual or olfactory cues from larval hemolymph. We moved presentation plants once during and between sessions so wasps could not simply return to the same location where they had experienced previous foraging success. The larvae were presented on the same *Asclepias* host plant species on which they had developed unless noted otherwise.

Experimental design: Effect of monarch larva size

Palatability is not the only factor that may affect predation by wasps. To determine whether there is a size at which monarch larvae are at particular risk of predation, I compared predation on three size classes of larvae in outdoor experiments for 10 h. My students and I placed live large (late fourth through fifth instar), medium (late third through early fourth instar), and small (second through early third instar), monarch larvae on two large *A. curassavica* plants. Each plant contained three individuals of each size (9 larvae total), all raised on *A. curassavica*. We recorded the number of times a wasp encountered or killed larvae of each size class. In addition, for each size class we calculated a "risk factor" (= probability of encounter × probability of mortality ×

100 = [number of encounters within the size-class / total encounters] × [number of times killed / number of encounters within the size-class] × 100).

RESULTS AND DISCUSSION

Do wasps prey on monarch larvae?

Paper wasps consumed substantial numbers of monarch larvae in the controlled indoor experiments, and free-living wasps outdoors flew far from their nests to forage on plants containing the larvae. Well over 5000 monarch larvae were killed and eaten by wasps over the course of this study. Although there were statistical differences in how the wasps responded to monarchs raised on the five different *Asclepias* species, the wasps readily consumed substantial numbers of all of these monarchs (see below).

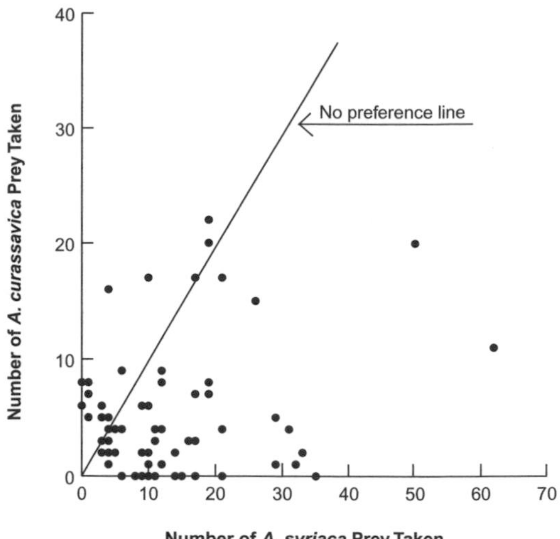

Figure 5.1. Wasp predation on monarch larvae reared on *Asclepias syriaca* and *A. curassavica.* Data points represent the total number of prey pieces of each type that 65 individual wasps took back to their nests. Data along the diagonal line indicate no preference for one prey type over the other; data above the diagonal line indicate a preference for *A. curassavica*–reared prey; data below the line indicate a preference for *A. syriaca*–reared prey. Because a number of wasps had the same attack patterns, some data points are superimposed over others. Only wasps that caught 5 or more total prey items were included in the Wilcoxon-signed rank test (WSRT) analysis or graphs. More pieces of *A. syriaca*– ($n = 871$) than *A. curassavica*– ($n = 363$) reared prey were brought to wasp nests.

Do wasps prefer larvae raised on milkweed plants with lower cardenolide concentrations?

The tendency of wasps to prefer monarchs reared on different *Asclepias* species was dependent on which two plants were compared. Figures 5.1 to 5.3 illustrate wasp preferences; in all cases the prey type predicted to be more palatable is on the x-axis, and the less palatable on the y-axis. Individual wasps captured significantly more *A. syriaca*–reared larvae than *A. curassavica*–reared larvae in behavioral choice tests (Wilcoxon-signed rank test [WSRT], $T = 1800$, $p < 0.0001$, wasp $n = 65$; figure 5.1), and significantly more *A. incarnata*– than *A. curassavica*–reared monarchs (WSRT, $T = 87.5$, $p < 0.002$, wasp $n = 13$, figure 5.2). Additionally, *A. verticillata*–reared monarchs were preferred over *A. curassavica*–reared monarchs (data not shown due to small total sample size for individual wasps: 52 *A. verticillata* prey, 33 *A. curassavica* prey, wasp $n = 17$, $\chi^2 = 4.24$, $p < 0.05$). For choices among monarch larvae raised on these four host plant species, individual wasps were significantly more likely to capture the lower-cardenolide, presumably more palatable larvae than the higher-cardenolide, less palatable larvae.

However, wasps were equally likely to capture monarchs raised on *A. tuberosa* (low cardenolide) and *A. curassavica* (high) (WSRT, $T = 842$, $p < 0.27$, $n = 48$ wasps, figure 5.3). Female monarchs rarely oviposit on *A. tuberosa* when other host plants are available (pers. observ.), and the growth rate of larvae on *A. tuberosa* is significantly slower than that of monarchs raised on other plants. *Asclepias tuberosa* is low in nitrogen, which may reduce the palatability or nutritional quality of monarchs reared on this plant species (L. P. Brower, pers. comm.).

It is possible that monarchs may entirely escape wasp predation if they are raised on *Asclepias* species with even higher cardenolide levels than those found in *A. curassavica* (1055 µg/0.1 g dry weight), such as *A. masonii* or *A. albicans* (7910 and 2845 µg/0.1 g dry weight, respectively [Malcolm 1991]), but I did not test monarchs raised on these plants. Wild and captive wasps readily consumed monarch larvae reared on *A. curassavica.*

Although there is evidence that the wasps discriminate between larvae raised on different host plants and that they tend to prefer larvae that have

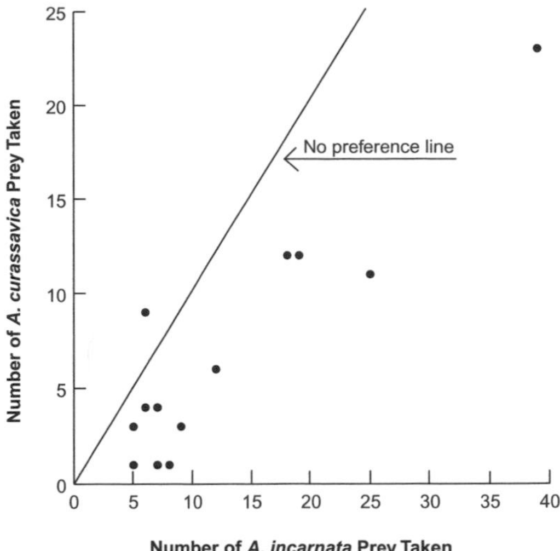

Figure 5.2. Wasp predation on monarch larvae reared on *A. incarnata* and *A. curassavica.* Data points represent the total number of prey pieces of each type that 13 individual wasps took back to their nests. Data above the diagonal line indicate a preference for *A. curassavica*–reared prey; data below the line indicate a preference for *A. incarnata*–reared prey. More pieces of *A. incarnata*– (n = 166) than *A. curassavica*– (*n* = 90) reared prey were brought to wasp nests.

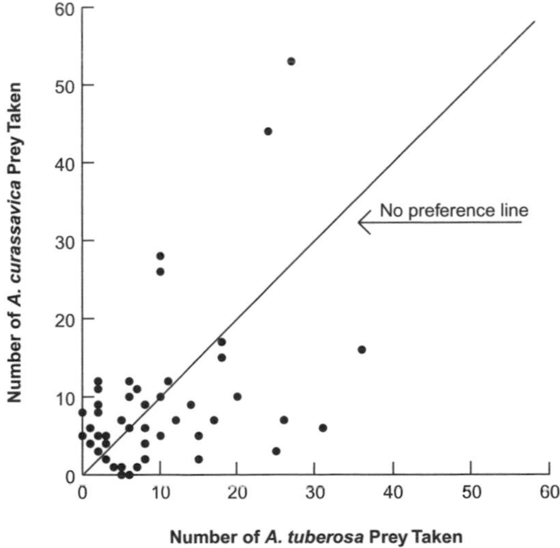

Figure 5.3. Wasp predation on monarch larvae reared on *A. tuberosa* and *A. curassavica.* Data points represent the total number of prey pieces of each type that 48 individual wasps took back to their nests. Data above the diagonal line indicate a preference for *A. curassavica*–reared prey; data below the line indicate a preference for *A. tuberosa*–reared prey. As many pieces of *A. curassavica*– (*n* = 465) as *A. tuberosa*– (*n* = 435) reared prey were brought to wasp nests.

sequestered lower cardenolide concentrations, the basis for the discrimination is not as tightly associated with cardenolide levels as I had predicted. There are likely to be other morphological, architectural, and nutritional factors associated with different *Asclepias* species that affect both monarch palatability and relative risk of wasp predation.

Contrary to my expectations, the most productive foragers, individuals with the most experience preying on monarchs, did *not* capture a greater percentage of palatable larvae than did wasps with less foraging experience. In all linear regressions between "total prey taken" and "percent palatable prey taken" for choice tests between monarchs raised on *A. curassavica* and on *A. tuberosa*, *A. syriaca*, or *A. incarnata*, less than 2% of the variation (all R^2 [adjusted] ≤2.1%, all F = not significant) was explained by greater experience with the prey.

Foraging wasps indicate dissatisfaction with prey by rejecting it entirely, wiping their mandibles frantically, or dropping the prey and then grooming their mouthparts and head persistently. Although some prey are totally rejected and left behind, wasps often resume processing what appears to be somewhat distasteful prey. As a part of the processing sequence with a diversity of lepidopteran larvae, wasps often remove guts that contain plant material. I have shown that *Polistes* wasps selectively remove the guts of *P. napi* that contain plant material from the crucifer *Erysimum*, which contains cardenolides, but do not remove the guts of conspecific larvae that fed on cabbage (pers. observ.). Wasps occasionally removed the guts of monarchs as they maxillated the prey into manageable balls for transport, but the removal of the guts did not appear to be deliberate (as it is for *Erysimum*-containing pierids). Gut removal was infrequent and not apparently in relation to cardenolide content in the larvae (pers. observ.). Because monarchs sequester chemical defenses throughout their bodies, removing the gut was not a sufficiently successful strategy to increase monarch palatability.

Do the wasps prefer species of larvae without cardenolides to monarch larvae?

When wasps were given a choice between highly palatable prey, such as the apparently succulent cabbage butterflies (Pieridae: *P. napi*) or cabbage looper moths (Noctuidae: *T. ni*) that had been raised on cabbage, they clearly preferred to capture the more palatable larvae over monarchs (WSRT, $T = 21$, wasp $n = 6$, $p = 0.02$). In these choice tests, although the wasps appeared to locate the brightly colored monarchs first, individual foragers rapidly switched to the more cryptic *P. rapae* and *T. ni* prey species. In contrast, when given a choice between monarch larvae and those of another unpalatable prey species, such as the buckeye butterfly (Nymphalidae: *J. coenia*), which contains highly unpalatable iridoid glycosides (Bowers 1984), the wasps preferred to take monarchs (WSRT, $T = 32.5$, wasp $n = 8$, $p < 0.025$). Thus, while monarch larvae are not necessarily the most palatable prey available to wasps, monarchs are highly acceptable to the generalist paper wasps and in some circumstances are considered significantly more palatable than the alternative prey species.

Do wasps preferentially attack monarch larvae of a particular size?

Wasps were attracted to large larvae first and tried to attack them (figure 5.4). But large larvae were difficult for most wasps to kill. The large larvae ignored the wasps, jerked their bodies, or dropped from the plant in 78 of 80 encounters. Most wasps simply gave up and hunted elsewhere. Only twice (less than 3%), after a prolonged battle, did wasps kill large monarch larvae. The risk factor for large monarchs is only 1.71.

Medium larvae were often sighted secondarily. But once encountered by the wasps, 67% ($n = 18/27$) were promptly killed (figure 5.4). Medium larvae have a risk factor of 15.38, an order of magnitude higher than that of the large larvae. Larvae in this size range are the preferred size of prey for most wasps (Rabb and Lawson 1957) and are clearly the most vulnerable to this relatively large invertebrate predator.

Small larvae were largely ignored by the wasps. Of the 117 total contacts between wasps and larvae in this experiment, only 10 involved small larvae (figure 5.4). Wasps generally killed small larvae once they were noticed, but such larvae were clearly smaller than the search image of most wasps. Small larvae have a risk factor of 6.84. While small monarchs are likely to be more vulnerable to smaller predators, such as coccinellids, chrysopids, and nabids (J. Losey, pers. comm.), at this size they are not at great risk from *Polistes* wasps. As monarch larvae grow, they bypass the risk of predation by smaller predators, but transiently increase their vulnerability to larger ones.

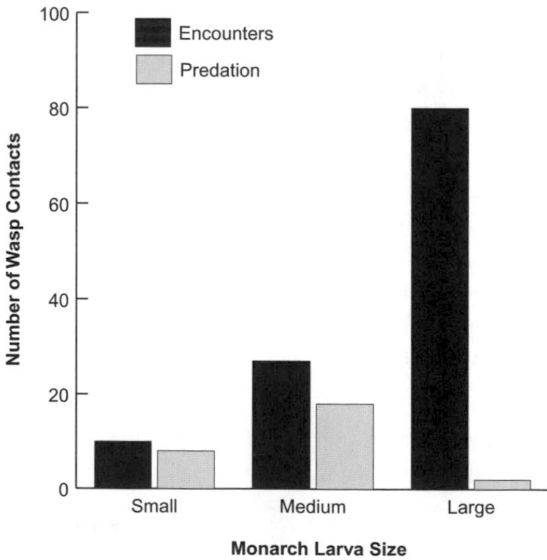

Figure 5.4. Monarch larva size affects both encounter rate and risk of predation by *Polistes* wasps.

CONCLUSION

Polistes wasps are likely to be a significant source of mortality to monarch larvae throughout their range. Regardless of the cardenolide concentrations found in the *Asclepias* species that monarch larvae are raised on, paper wasps find these monarch larvae to be acceptable prey. Overall, wasps prefer to take more larvae raised on species with a lower cardenolide concentration (*A. syriaca*, *A. incarnata*, *A. verticillata*), but cardenolide concentration is not the only factor affecting relative palatability (e.g., monarchs raised on *A. tuberosa* were less palatable than those raised on milkweed containing higher levels of cardenolide). Larvae that evade small invertebrate predators and reach medium sizes (from the late third through early fourth instar) are at the highest risk from *Polistes* wasps.

To a large extent, the effect of larval mortality due to predators has been underestimated in monarch population biology. Although monarch larval mortality is extremely high in field experiments (Zalucki and Kitching 1982; Prysby and Oberhauser, this volume; J. Losey, pers. comm.), most reports of predation focus on adults rather than larvae. Observing predation in the field can be difficult, and the predators' sublethal effects on larval behavior and growth can be subtle (Stamp and Bowers 1991). Future work on monarch larvae should further document the role of predation in monarch population biology.

Acknowledgments

This work could not have been done without the enthusiastic and able assistance of (then) undergraduate research assistants Jennifer Chow, Paul Latty, Jason Beckert, Lisa Taylor, Monica Lee, Steve Munson, Katrin Campbell, Larissa Mooney, Gavin Svenson, Lauren Cahoon, and Charlie Berk. Lincoln Brower, Alan Renwick, and Karen Oberhauser were constant sources of knowledge, experimental ideas, larvae, plants, and encouragement. Paul Feeny, Nancy Stamp, Cole Gilbert, and John Losey provided important suggestions in the development of various experiments. Patrick Hughes provided cabbage loopers as a backup diet during many summers. The research was supported by Cornell University; National Science Foundation grants (DEB-97 27547 and DEB-99 42154) to L. Rayor; Howard Hughes Undergraduate Research Fellowships to K. Campbell, L. Mooney, and P. Latty; Cornell University Minority Fund to P. Latty; and Cornell Honors Program to K. Campbell, L. Mooney, M. Lee, and S. Munson.

References

Ackery, P. R., and R. I. Vane-Wright. 1984. Milkweed butterflies: their cladistics and biology. Ithaca, N.Y.: Cornell University Press, Comstock Publishing.

Bowers, M. D. 1984. Iridoid glycosides and hostplant specificity in larvae of the buckeye butterfly, *Junonia coenia* (Nymphalidae). J. Chem. Ecol. 10:1567–77.

Brower, L. P. 1984. Chemical defense in butterflies. In R. I. Vane-Wright and P. R. Ackery, eds., The biology of butterflies, pp. 109–34. London: Academic Press.

Calvert, W. H. 1996. Fire ant predation on monarch larvae (Nymphalidae: Danainae) in a central Texas prairie. J. Lepid. Soc. 50:149–51.

Carpenter, J. 1991. Phylogenetic relationships and the origin of social behavior in the Vespidae. In K. G. Ross and R. W. Matthews, eds., The social biology of wasps, pp. 7–32. Ithaca, N.Y.: Cornell University Press, Comstock Publishing.

Cornelius, M. L. 1993. Influence of caterpillar-feeding damage on the foraging behavior of the paper wasp *Mischocyttarus flavitarsis* (Hymenoptera: Vespidae). J. Insect Behav. 6:771–81.

Eigenbrode, S. D., L. S. Rayor, J. Chow, and P. Latty. 2000. Effects of wax bloom variation in *Brassica oleracea* on foraging by a vespid wasp. Entomol. Exp. Appl. 97:161–66.

Geitzenauer, H. L., and E. A. Bernays. 1996. Plant effects on prey choice by a vespid wasp, *Polistes arizonensis*. Ecol. Entomol. 21:227–34.

Hughes, P. R., C. D. Radke, and J. A. Renwick. 1993. A simple, low-input method for continuous laboratory rearing of the monarch butterfly (Lepidoptera: Danaidae) for research. Am. Entomol. 39:109–11.

James, D. G. 1993. Migration biology of the monarch butterfly in Australia. In S. B. Malcolm and M. P. Zalucki, eds., Biology and conservation of the monarch butterfly, pp. 189–200. Los Angeles: Natural History Museum of Los Angeles County.

James, D. G. 2000. Feeding on larvae of *Danaus plexippus* (L.) (Lepidoptera: Nymphalidae) causes mortality in the assassin bug *Pristhesancus plagipennis* Walker (Hemiptera: Reduviidae). Aust. Entomol. 27:5–8.

Lynch, S. P., and R. A. Martin. 1993. Milkweed host plant utilization and cardenolide sequestration by monarch butterflies in Louisiana and Texas. In S. B. Malcolm and M. P. Zalucki, eds., Biology and conservation of the monarch butterfly, pp. 107–23. Los Angeles: Natural History Museum of Los Angeles County.

Malcolm, S. B. 1991. Cardenolide-mediated interactions between plants and herbivores. In G. A. Rosenthal and M. R. Berenbaum, eds., Herbivores: their interactions with secondary plant metabolites. 2nd ed. Vol. 1, pp. 251–96. San Diego: Academic Press.

Malcolm, S. B., and L. P. Brower. 1989. Evolutionary and ecological implications of cardenolide sequestration in the monarch butterfly. Experientia 45:284–95.

Martin, R. A., S. P. Lynch, L. P. Brawer, S. B. Malcolm, and T. Van Hook. 1992. Cardenolide content, emetic potency, and thin-layer chromatography profiles of monarch butterflies, and their larval host-plant milkweed, *Asclepias Humistrata*, in Florida. Chemoecology 3:1–13.

Montllor, C. B., and E. A. Bernays. 1993. Invertebrate predators and caterpillar foraging. In N. E. Stamp and T. M. Casey, eds., Caterpillars: ecological and evolutionary constraints on foraging, pp. 170–202. New York: Chapman and Hall.

Nannoni, A., R. Cervo, and S. Turillazzi. 2001. Foraging activity in European *Polistes* wasps (Hymenoptera: Vespidae). Boll. Soc. Entomol. Ital. 133:67–78.

Rabb, R. L., and F. R. Lawson. 1957. Some factors influencing the predation of *Polistes* wasps on the tobacco hornworm. J. Econ. Entomol. 50:778–84.

Raveret Richter, M. A. 1990. Hunting social wasp interactions: influence of prey size, arrival order, and wasp species. Ecology 71:1018–30.

Raveret Richter, M. 2000. Social wasp (Hymenoptera: Vespidae) foraging behavior. Annu. Rev. Entomol. 45:121–50.

Raveret Richter, M., and R. L. Jeanne. 1991. Hunting behaviour, prey capture and ant avoidance in the tropical social wasp *Polybia sericea* (Hymenoptera: Vespidae). Insectes Soc. 38:139–48.

Raveret Richter, M., and V. L. Tisch. 1999. Resource choice of social wasps: influence of presence, size and species of resident wasps. Insectes Soc. 46:131–36.

Rayor, L. S., and S. A. Munson. 2002. Larval feeding experience influences adult predator acceptance of chemically defended prey. Entomol. Exp. Appl. 104:193–201.

Reeve, H. K. 1991. Polistes. In K. G. Ross and R. W. Matthews, eds., The social biology of wasps, pp. 99–148. Ithaca, N.Y.: Cornell University Press, Comstock Publishing.

Richards, O. W. 1978. The Australian social wasps (Hymenoptera: Vespidae). Aust. J. Zool. 61:1–132.

Stamp, N. E. 1992. Relative susceptibility to predation of two species of caterpillar on plantain. Oecologia 92:124–29.

Stamp, N. E., and Bowers, M. D. 1991. Indirect effect on survivorship of caterpillars due to presence of invertebrate predators. Oecologia 88:325–30.

Stimson, J., and M. Kasuya. 2000. Decline in the frequency of the white morph of the monarch butterfly (*Danaus plexippus plexippus* L., Nymphalidae) on Oahu, Hawaii. J. Lepid Soc. 54:29–32.

Zalucki, M. P., and R. L. Kitching. 1982. Temporal and spatial variation of mortality in field populations of *Danaus plexippus* (L.) and *D. chrysippus* L. larvae (Lepidoptera: Nymphalidae). Oecologia 53:201–7.

6

The Effect of Fire Ants on Monarchs Breeding in Texas

William H. Calvert

INTRODUCTION

Circumstantial evidence suggests that the monarch butterfly populations of North America may be greatly reduced by fire ant (*Solenopsis invicta*) predation during the spring and fall in Texas (Calvert 1996) and possibly in other southern states. Further support for this thesis is derived from speculations about the remarkable recovery of the monarch population in the spring of 2001 (Taylor 2001). The previous winter, the monarch butterfly population was at an all-time low (García-Serrano et al., this volume). In a year's time, the population recovered and the fall 2001 population was among the highest in recent years (García-Serrano et al., this volume). Taylor attributes this recovery to a spring and summer drought in Texas during 2000 that suppressed the parasites and predators of monarchs (Anonymous 2001), of which the most effective are fire ants. The drought was followed by ample fall, winter, and spring rains that brought out abundant milkweeds in areas where there were few parasites and predators.

This chapter reports a study of the impact of fire ants on Texas spring monarch populations over 2 years. I assessed the impact of fire ants by excluding these predators from areas where milkweeds were present, and comparing reproductive success, as measured by the number of fifth instars produced, of areas within the exclosures to that outside the exclosures. The implication of fire ant predation on the spring population of monarchs in Texas for the monarch population in North America is discussed.

METHODS

I constructed exclosures designed to exclude fire ants at two locations near Austin, Texas: one at the Chandler Farm near Coupland (lat 30°28.84′N, long 97°19.17′W) and the other at the Masters' School (lat 30°16.71′N, long 97°31.48′W). These sites were chosen because milkweed was abundant and because the locations were on private property where they would not be disturbed when I was not present. The Chandler Farm had abundant *Asclepias oenotheroides*; the Masters' School had both *A. oenotheroides* and *A. asperula*. The distribution of these plants was extremely patchy and they were confined to plots of a quarter hectare or less. The areas with the most milkweeds had densities of approximately 20,000 milkweed stems/ha for both the Chandler Farm and the Masters' School.

During the first spring (1997), I constructed two exclosures at each site. These exclosures were 5-m-diameter cylinders made of 15.24-m-long × 0.41-m-high sheets of 30-gauge galvanized metal. The lower edge was buried approximately 0.15 m in the ground. Overlapping ends were fastened with screws affixed to a stake. Before fastening, chassis grease was applied between the overlapping ends. The sides were stabilized by driving rebar rods into the ground on either side of the sheet metal wall. To keep ants from coming over the top, chassis grease was smeared in an 8-cm-wide band around the inside rim of the metal exclosure. While ants were sometimes seen within the exclosures, at no time was an ant seen on the metal walls. It is unlikely that the ants entered the exclosures over the metal walls.

Initially, I used a shovel to remove fire ants from the interior space when they had gathered high in their mounds for warmth. After 2 weeks the mechanical removal method proved ineffective, and a short-lived carbamate pesticide (Sevin) was periodically applied to areas where I noticed fire ant activity and around the outside of the metal walls of the exclosures. Fire ants were not excluded from the interior space at all times (see table 6.3). By late April, the vegetation had grown so profusely that I could no longer trace the sources of fire ant trails within the exclosures, and I abandoned the effort to control them.

During the spring of 1998, there was little milkweed at the Chandler Farm, so I constructed three exclosures at the Masters' School site. On the basis of knowledge gained in 1997, I made improvements to augment the exclusion of fire ants from the exclosures. The outside periphery was left in the form of a shallow trench and filled to a depth of 5 cm with diatomaceous earth. Periodically the periphery was cleared of vegetation and spider webs that might offer a conduit over the trench for ants. The diatomaceous earth barrier was renewed after each rain and whenever the upper surface showed signs of caking. As in the previous spring, initial accumulations of fire ants were physically removed with a shovel. In addition, Orthene, an insecticide specifically designed to kill fire ants, was applied to the tunnels uncovered with a shovel and to any accumulations of fire ants observed during the experimental period. Orthene has an effective killing period of 4 months. In addition, I periodically soaked the periphery of the exclosures with a liquid insecticide, Home Defense. Both insecticides were applied whenever fire ants were found inside the exclosures.

I took care to keep the poisons away from potential host plants. However, there are several circumstances that will cause monarch larvae to abandon their feeding site, crawl about, and perhaps encounter the insecticide used in the interior of the exclosures. First, they will abandon a plant when all of its foliage is eaten. Normally larvae do not consume enough plant material from Texas milkweeds to cause total defoliation until the fifth or occasionally the fourth instar. In addition, fourth and fifth instars will drop off a plant when disturbed and must regain the foliar parts once the disturbance has passed. Finally, fifth instar larvae crawl away from the feeding site to find a spot in which to pupate.

Consumption of all of the leaf material in a cluster of host plants was rare, observed only once during the two-season experiment. To avoid counting them twice, I removed monarchs from the exclosure when they had reached fifth instar. Monarchs that drop from a host are assumed to crawl up a nearby host. Because of these factors, it is very unlikely that a monarch larva would crawl through an area in which insecticide had been applied.

I examined milkweeds for monarch eggs and larvae at the Chandler Farm and the Masters' School approximately every 4 days in 1997 commencing on 27 and 24 March at the two sites, respectively, and ending on 16 June. At the Masters' School in 1998, examination commenced on 1 April and was conducted approximately every 3.5 days until 16 May. I searched all milkweed stems within the exclosures and approximately equal numbers of stems outside within 30 m of the exclosures. Sample sizes varied during the season as the abundance of plants diminished. During late March and early April I sampled an average of 35 milkweeds outside and 41 inside the exclosures. At the end of the experiments, sample sizes fell to an average of 22 and 24 milkweeds outside and inside, respectively.

I determined the density of monarch immatures by recording the stem height of each plant, the number of eggs and larvae of each instar, the presence of potential predators, and the growth stage of the plant. The numbers of each immature stage were divided by the cumulative stem length of milkweeds examined outside and inside the exclosures to determine egg and larval stage densities per meter of plant stem examined.

On the dates when the stems were examined for eggs and larvae, baits were placed inside and outside the exclosures to determine the density of ants in the respective locations. To bait for ants, uncooked hot dog wieners were cut into quarters approximately 0.64 cm long and placed halfway down the barrel of 26 × 67-mm clear-plastic vials (see Porter et al. 1991). During the 1997 spring season, the vials were left in place for 30 to 90 min. During 1998, all baits were left in position for a standard 30 min. At the end of the collection period, they were gathered, quickly capped, labeled, and placed on ice. On return to Austin, they were placed in a freezer until the ants could be identified and counted. For each collection station, the number of ants was divided by the number of vials placed and the number of minutes that the vials were in position. Ants that came to the hot-dog baits were assumed to be potential predators of monarch butterflies.

RESULTS

The soils and vegetation zones differed between the sites. The Chandler Farm is located on the heavy clay soils of the Blackland Prairie approximately 60 km north of the Masters' School. The exclosures were placed in an unimproved pasture dominated by several species of grasses mixed with some herbs including the milkweed *A. oenotheroides*. In contrast, the Masters' School is located on sandy soils in the Post Oak Savannah. The area chosen for study was located partly above the drainage field of a septic system in a reclaimed field that featured a species-rich mixture of grasses and herbs. Both *A. asperula* and *A. oenotheroides* were abundant.

Oviposition was patchy at all locations and years. During the initial observation period, before the exclosures took effect on the fire ant populations, I expected egg densities to be the same inside and outside. They were not. Females laid nearly an egg per meter of stem more outside than inside the exclosures (mean $x - y = 0.95$, paired t test: $n = 38$, $t = 3.36$, $p = 0.002$). Diminished oviposition inside the exclosures suggests that the metal walls may have acted as a partial barrier to female monarchs searching for oviposition sites. The walls may have also acted as a barrier to searching aerial predators such as vespid wasps (Rayor, this volume), although this should augment the larval population inside.

Observations during 1997

Changes in the number of monarch eggs and larvae per meter of host stem at the Chandler Farm during the spring of 1997 show two basic patterns. After a small initial rise, probably due to an increase in the number of monarchs arriving into the area from Mexico, the number of eggs and larvae declined steadily throughout the spring from a high of 10.8 eggs/m of stem on 29 March to zero on 16 June outside the exclosure, and from a high of 4.9 on 29 March to zero on 26 April inside the exclosure (figure 6.1a). There was almost no higher instar development outside the exclosures. The most advanced instar observed outside the exclosures was a single fourth instar observed on 19 May. Development within the exclosures was comparatively high and showed a progression from early to late instars as the season advanced (figure 6.1 and tables 6.1 and 6.2).

At the Masters' School overall egg densities were greater outside the exclosure during the spring of 1997 (see table 6.1). Inside the exclosures, egg load on milkweeds declined from a high of 7.9 eggs/m of stem to zero on 26 April. A second but lesser egg-laying event began on 12 May, declined, and continued sporadically, until the experiment was terminated on 16 June (figure 6.1b). Outside the exclosure, oviposition closely followed that occurring inside. Egg laying began at a density of 6.1 eggs/m of stem, declined to zero on 26 April, increased again on 5 May, and declined until the termination of the experiment. On two dates during

Table 6.1. Comparing monarch production inside and outside the exclosures

Site	Treatment	Eggs	First	Second	Third	Fourth	Fifth	Meters of stem examined
Chandler, 1997	Outside	2.42	0.12	0.03	0.00	0.02	0.00	64.59
	Inside	0.94	0.10	0.08	0.10	0.13	0.26	62.55
Masters, 1997	Outside	1.40	0.06	0.02	0.01	0.00	0.01	143.10
	Inside	0.49	0.05	0.01	0.02	0.03	0.01	262.50
Masters, 1998	Outside	0.51	0.03	0.00	0.00	0.00	0.01	146.00
	Inside	0.43	0.05	0.04	0.05	0.07	0.07	254.90

Note: Data collected from two study sites in spring 1997 and 1998. The average numbers of monarchs in each life stage per meter of stem are shown.

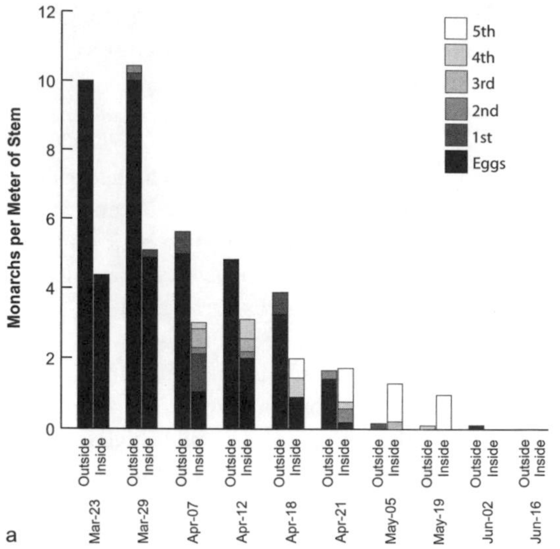

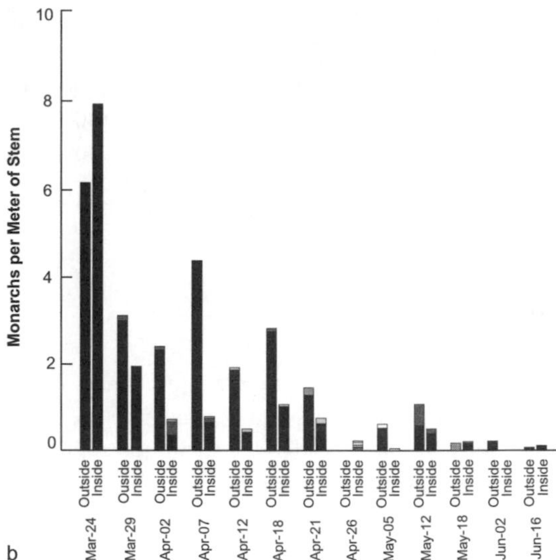

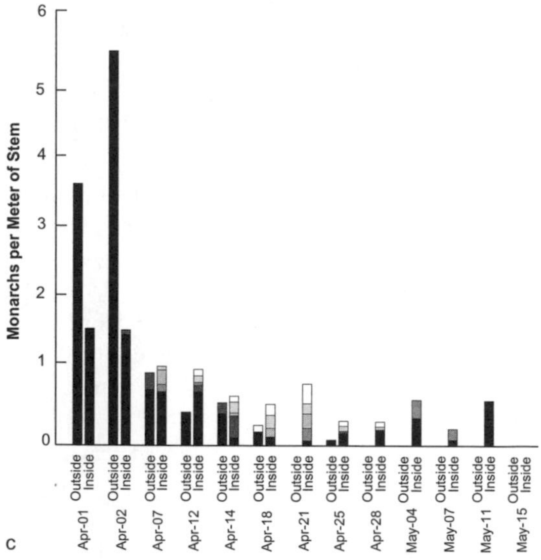

Figure 6.1. Eggs and larvae per meter of host plant stem at (a) the Chandler Farm during the spring of 1997, (b) the Masters' School during the spring of 1997, and (c) the Masters' School during the spring of 1998.

the resurgent period of laying (4 May to 16 June), no eggs were found. The difference between the two sites was in the amount of higher instar development. Chandler Farm produced a relatively large number of fifth instars per meter of stem (0.26) inside the exclosures and zero outside, whereas the Masters' School produced the same low number of fifth instars per meter of stem (0.01) inside and outside the exclosures (see table 6.1).

Observations during 1998

Monarch development at the Masters' School during the spring of 1998 was similar to the spring of 1997 at the Chandler Farm (see table 6.1). Oviposition outside the exclosures declined from a high of 5.4 eggs/m of stem on 2 April to zero on 21 April (figure 6.1c). No eggs were found outside the exclosures after 28 April. Egg laying inside the exclosures declined from a high of 1.6 eggs/m of stem on 1 April to zero on 15 May. A resurgence of laying was apparent inside the exclosures beginning about the end of April. Inside the exclosures more higher instars developed than outside (see table 6.1). No statistical differences were detected among sites and years for eggs laid inside the exclosures (analysis of variance: $n = 38$, F test 2.69, $p = 0.08$) or outside (analysis of variance: $n = 38$, F test 0.80, $p = 0.46$).

Table 6.2. Numbers of eggs and fifth instar larvae found inside and outside exclosures

	Outside			Inside		
	C97	M97	M98	C97	M97	M98
Eggs	156	200	74	59	129	109
Fifth instars	0	1	1	16	3	17
% Success	0	0.5	1.4	27	1.6	16

Note: Study sites include Chandler Farm in 1997 (C97) and Masters' School in 1997 (M97) and 1998 (M98). The percentage of success was calculated as follows: (the number of fifth instars / number of eggs) × 100. Since I wasn't tracking individual monarch survival, this estimate of success is approximate.

These trends of higher production inside the exclosures are also reflected in the numbers of fifth instar larvae found inside and outside the exclosures (see table 6.2). No larvae above fourth instar were found outside the exclosures at the Chandler Farm, while 16 were found inside. At the Masters' School in 1997, only 1 fifth instar was found outside the exclosures and 3 were found inside. In marked contrast, the following year 17 fifth instars were found inside the exclosures at Masters' School, while only 1 was found outside. As assessed by the presence of fifth instar larvae, reproductive success of monarchs was greater inside the exclosures than outside. Only at the Masters' School during the spring of 1997 was there virtually no difference.

Ant population density

Table 6.3 shows the density of fire ants inside and outside the exclosures for both years. The average of all dates shows that control of fire ants was better in 1998 than in 1997 and better at the Chandler Farm than the Masters' School in 1997. Perhaps more instructive are the averages for the four dates after the start date (table 6.3). The start date was excluded because control measures had not taken effect. These four dates were 29 March through 12 April, when monarchs were present as eggs or early instar larvae. These data show clearly that fire ant control within the exclosures was most effective during the beginning of the season.

DISCUSSION

Monarch population size in North America varies greatly each year (García-Serrano et al., this volume; Prysby and Oberhauser, this volume). Factors affecting that population size are likely to include weather, predators, parasites, and the abundance of host plant and nectar sources. This study shows that the spread through southern states of a very efficient, exotic predator, the imported fire ant (*Solenopsis invicta* Buren), may have affected monarch populations profoundly.

Table 6.3. Fire ant density inside and outside the exclosures

	C97	M97	M98
Overall average			
Outside	1.51	2.59	5.06
Inside	0.58	1.43	0.68
% Reduction	62	45	87
Initial average			
Outside	1.58	1.81	3.34
Inside	0.38	1.42	0.08
% Reduction	76	22	98

Note: Study sites include Chandler Farm in 1997 (C97) and the Masters' School in 1997 (M97) and 1998 (M98). The numbers of fire ants per vial per minute are shown. Percentage of reduction is a measure of the effectiveness of the exclosures and is defined as one minus the average number of ants/vial/min for all dates inside the exclosures divided by the average for outside the exclosures times 100. The overall average includes all dates (start date and dates after poison control was abandoned), and the initial average includes only the first four dates after the start date.

Fire ants arrived in Mobile, Alabama, from Brazil during the 1920s (Drees and Vinson 1993) and spread through much of the southern United States, an area where monarchs returning from Mexico are expected to lay eggs that will become the first spring generation (Malcolm et al. 1993), and where some monarchs laying eggs en route to Mexico in the fall produce an extra generation (Calvert 1999; Prysby and Oberhauser, this volume). Fire ants are especially prolific on Texas prairies where their colonies are polygynous (multiply queened; Porter et al. 1991) and may reach densities of 2000 mounds/ha (Drees and Vinson 1993). Fire ants specialize on arthropods (Porter and Savignano 1990) and have a reputation as voracious predators (Killion and Vinson 1995). Numerous anecdotal and published accounts document declines in arthropod populations as diverse as lone star ticks, chiggers, and cotton flea hoppers (Killion and Vinson 1995). In the vicinity of Austin, Texas, the abundance of lepidopterans has fallen to 50% of pre–fire ant levels (C. Durden, pers. comm.).

A preliminary study showed that fire ants are likely predators of monarch butterflies (Calvert 1996). During the spring of 1995, near Luling, Texas, a field of *A. oenotheroides* with a monarch egg density of 1250 eggs/ha failed to yield a single adult monarch. The same field contained a fire ant mound density of 1011/ha.

In this study, the reproductive success of monarchs, as measured by the relative numbers of fifth instars and eggs produced, is greater inside the exclosures than outside them (see table 6.2). At the Chandler Farm during the spring of 1997, estimated survival rates were 27% and 0% inside and outside the exclosures, respectively. At the Masters' School in 1998, estimated survival rates were 16% inside and 1.4% outside. Only at the Masters' School in the spring of 1997 was there any ambiguity about the effectiveness of the exclosures. During this season 1.6% and 0.5% were produced inside and outside the exclosures, respectively.

Fire ants were more abundant at the Masters' School than at the Chandler Farm (see table 6.3), and the control of them was not as effective in 1997 as it was in 1998. The combination of higher fire ant density at the Masters' School and less effective control of them during the first year of the study is the likely explanation for the lack of reproductive success at the Masters' School in 1997.

The heavy clay soils at the Chandler Farm were very different from the soil at the Masters' School, a sandy loam that had recently been disturbed during the construction of a septic system. This difference may account for the greater ability of fire ants to penetrate deeper into the soil and burrow under the exclosures at the Masters' School. The application of a diatomaceous earth barrier and the application of fire ant–specific pesticides in 1998 are the likely factors in bringing down the ant population inside the exclosures and the increase in monarch reproductive success that year.

The distribution of prairies in the Midwest and the pattern of the spring migration northward through Texas suggests that monarchs that breed on central Texas prairies and plains are the progenitors of monarchs that will breed in prairie states farther north (Malcolm et al. 1993). If the devastation of the population of monarchs oviposited near Luling, Texas, and the relative increase in reproductive success in relatively fire ant–free zones are indicative, the first spring generation reared within the fire ant zone must make only a small contribution to the monarch recolonization of prairies farther north. The generation laid by migrants passing through in the fall may be diminished for the same reasons. No evidence exists as yet for similar effects in areas farther east where fire ants are also abundant, but eastern fire ant colonies are mostly monogynous (single-queened) and are not as dense as those on the Texas prairies (Porter et al. 1991).

Inside the exclosures, the number of fifth instars exceeded the number of most lower instars in two of the three replicate groups (see table 6.1), a discrepancy that merits comment. I examined all plants carefully. I may have missed some first instar larvae, but second and higher stage instars are quite apparent. It is possible, but unlikely, that a small number of second through fourth instars were missed. Monarchs spend almost twice as much time in the fifth instar stage as in any other stage (Pulis et al. 2001), so second through fourth instar monarchs may have been undercounted because they were in these instar stages between sampling dates.

The production of fifth instar monarchs was 17.5 times greater inside the exclosures (see table 6.2). It is tempting to conclude that the population of monarchs in North America would be 17.5 times higher if there were no fire ants, but this argument is clearly fallacious. Fire ants have reduced other arthropod predators in their range, predators that would take a large toll on monarchs if they were not suppressed by the fire ants. Unfortunately, there are no comparable data from previous years. However, the low survival reported outside the fire ant range (Borkin 1982; Prysby and Oberhauser, this volume) suggests that these introduced predators may simply have replaced other native predators.

Acknowledgments

I wish to thank John Pruitt and Terry Masters of the Masters' School for Talented and Gifted Children for allowing access to the Masters' School study site and Charles Chandler for allowing access to the Chandler Farm. Phoebe Greisen, Kristen Smith, and Mark and Zach Knox helped construct the exclosures. Karen Oberhauser and Michelle Prysby made suggestions that greatly improved the manuscript. This research was supported by a grant from the National Geographic Society to William Calvert. I thank the society very much for their support.

References

Anonymous. 2001. Fire ant trails: news from the Texas imported fire ant research and management plan 4(5). Texas A&M University, College Stations, Texas.

Borkin, S. 1982. Notes on shifting distribution patterns and survival of immature *Danaus plexippus* (Lepidoptera: Danaidae) on the food plant *Asclepias syriaca.* Gt. Lakes Entomol. 15:199–206.

Calvert, W. H. 1996. Fire ant predation of monarch larvae (Nymphalidae: Danainae) in a central Texas prairie. J. Lepid. Soc. 50:149–51.

Calvert, W. H. 1999. Patterns in the spatial and temporal use of Texas milkweeds (Asclepiadaceae) by the monarch butterfly (*Danaus plexippus* L.) during fall, 1996. J. Lepid. Soc. 53:37–44.

Drees, B. M. 2001. News from the Texas imported fire ant research and management plan. Fire ant trails 4(1). Texas A&M University, College Station, Texas.

Drees, B. M., and S. B. Vinson. 1993. Fire ants and their management. Pamphlet B-1536. Texas Agricultural Extension Service, Texas A&M University, College Station, Texas.

Killion, M. J., and S. B. Vinson. 1995. Ants with attitudes. Wildl. Conserv. 98:51, 73.

Malcolm, S. B., B. J. Cockrell, and L. P. Brower. 1993. Spring recolonization of eastern North America by the monarch butterfly: successive brood or single sweep migration? In S. B. Malcolm and M. P. Zalucki, eds., Biology and conservation of the monarch butterfly, pp. 253–67. Los Angeles: Natural History Museum of Los Angeles County.

Porter, S. D., A. Bhatkar, R. Mulder, S. B. Vinson, and D. J. Clair. 1991. Distribution of polygyne fire ants (Hymenoptera: Formicidae) in Texas. J. Econ. Entomol. 84:866–74.

Porter, S. D., and D. A. Savignano. 1990. Invasion of polygyne fire ants decimates native ants and disrupts arthropod community. Ecology 71:2095–106.

Pulis, D., A. Schmitz, C. Steckling, M. Kometz, and R. Naber. 2001. Will not eating the chorion affect the growth of monarch larvae? Monarchs in the Classroom, University of Minnesota. http://www.monarchlab.umn.edu/research/GD/missheights.html. Accessed 27 March 2002.

Taylor, O. R. 2001. The great recovery of 2001. Monarch Watch. http://www.monarchwatch.org. Accessed 5 February 2002.

7

Effects of Milkweed Latex and Cardenolides on Foraging and Maintenance Behaviors of First Instar Monarch Larvae

Tammi Hoevenaar and Stephen B. Malcolm

INTRODUCTION

The rationale behind plant optimal defense theory is based on the interaction between plant investment in chemical defense and herbivore diet breadth (Feeny 1976; Rhoades and Cates 1976; Herms and Mattson 1992). Specialists with a narrow diet are predicted to be largely unaffected by the acute, toxic chemical defenses, but they are thought to be affected by chronic, digestibility-reducing defenses. Milkweed cardenolides have been cited as an example of acute chemical defenses; presumably monarch larvae are adapted specialists that are able to sequester and store cardenolides and glycosides from their milkweed hosts (Roeske et al. 1976; Malcolm and Brower 1989; Malcolm 1991, 1995; Nelson 1993). These sequestered cardenolides, which are both distasteful and toxic, are subsequently used by the adults for chemical defense against their natural enemies (Malcolm 1991, 1995).

Recent studies have shown that monarch larvae are negatively affected by the milky latex of their milkweed host plants (Zalucki et al. 1990; Zalucki and Brower 1992; Malcolm and Zalucki 1996; Zalucki and Malcolm 1999; Zalucki et al. 2001a, 2001b). There is also evidence that monarch larvae are negatively affected by the cardenolides in milkweeds (Zalucki et al. 1990). Malcolm and Zalucki (1996) and Zalucki and Malcolm (1999) report that partially severing the petiole of a leaf of the common milkweed, *Asclepias syriaca*, on which a monarch larva is feeding will cause that larva to grow faster than a larva that has been feeding on an unmanipulated *A. syriaca* leaf. This partial petiole-severing technique significantly reduces the leaf latex content (Zalucki and Malcolm 1999). However, it is still unclear how leaf latex negatively affects larval growth or whether leaf cardenolides play a role in this negative impact.

We addressed this question by observing the behavior of first instar monarch larvae on milkweed leaves with high or low constitutive cardenolide and high or low latex levels. We used swamp milkweed, *A. incarnata* L., which has low cardenolide content (Zalucki et al. 1990; Malcolm 1991, 1995), and *A. curassavica* L., which has high cardenolide content (Roeske et al. 1976; Malcolm and Brower 1989; Zalucki et al. 1990; Malcolm 1991, 1995). We also manipulated leaf latex levels by cutting through the laminar midrib of leaves to stop latex flow in the laticifers that enter the leaf through the petiole (Dussourd and Eisner 1987; Dussourd and Denno 1991; Dussourd 1993; Zalucki et al. 2001a).

METHODS

We purchased swamp milkweed, *A. incarnata*, from VanBochove's Greenhouse Direct in Kalamazoo, Michigan. We grew neotropical *A. curassavica* plants from seeds that originated from greenhouse plants grown at Michigan State University. All plants were between 4 and 12 months old at the initiation of observations and were grown in MetroMix 410 soilless medium. Despite the difference in constitutive cardenolide content and latex volume of these species (Malcolm 1995), their leaf morphologies and growth forms are similar. Both plant species are erect, short-lived perennials with smooth, entire, lanceolate leaves of equivalent leaf area (Woodson 1954). The same plants were tested for cardenolide content by J. W. Martel and S. B. Malcolm (pers. observ.), and the mean leaf cardenolide concentrations for herbivore-free control plants were found to be 1621 μg/g dry leaf for *A. curassavica* and 0 μg/g dry leaf for *A. incarnata*.

All plants on which larvae were introduced were growing in pots. They either were intact or had the midrib of all leaves severed near the base of the leaf. We also maintained an intact plant of each species without larvae. This generated a sample size of 32 total observations (2 plant spp. × 2 plant treatments × 8 larval replicates).

All experimental larvae were newly hatched neonates that we observed for 2-h periods throughout the duration of the first instar stage. We observed larvae in groups of 4 in an environmental chamber on a 16-h : 8-h (light-dark) and 28°C : 25°C (day-night) cycle at 70% humidity. Under these conditions, larvae completed the first instar stage in 48 h.

We collected eggs from wild-caught, mated females kept in screen cages containing potted plants of either *A. incarnata* or *A. curassavica* in the Western Michigan University (WMU) Plant Sciences Greenhouse. We collected eggs each morning by cutting them from leaves with a 5-mm-diameter hole punch. We placed each leaf disk on a water-moistened piece of filter paper in a plastic petri dish at room temperature. At the black head stage shortly before larval emergence, we moved the eggs to a 5°C cold cabinet to synchronize hatching. Additional eggs were provided by Monarch Watch.

For our experiments, we placed leaf disks with eggs that were about to hatch on the lower side of a leaf in the third pair of leaves from the top of each experimental plant. We glued leaf disks with a dab of latex (from a plant not used in the experiments) and left the eggs to hatch. As we placed eggs on experimental plants, we removed a leaf from each manipulated and control plant for an initial measure of leaf latex content. We measured latex from the midrib distal to the cut by blotting the midrib on preweighed and dried filter paper. We weighed the filter papers wet and then reweighed them once they had dried.

We observed and recorded all behaviors of newly emerged larvae for their first 2 h on the experimental plants. These observations were repeated for nine more 2-h observation periods, separated by a break of 3 h, until just before the larvae molted to the next instar. This resulted in 20 observation hours over a 48-h period.

When we completed each instar replicate, we collected all leaves that had been chewed from each experimental plant as well as a leaf from each intact control plant for a final measurement of leaf latex content. We recorded a digital image of all experimental and control leaves in the Biological Imaging Center so that we could measure leaf area consumed. We also obtained final live weights of larvae, then freeze-dried and reweighed them. Leaves from which latex samples were collected were also freeze-dried so that dry latex weights could be expressed per dry leaf weight.

RESULTS

Leaf latex

Wet weights of latex collected on filter paper from intact and severed leaf midribs at the start of larval observations (figure 7.1a) were not significantly different between *A. incarnata* and *A. curassavica* (analysis of variance [ANOVA] $F_{1,28} = 0.0008$, $p = 0.98$) or between plants used in either intact or severed treatments (ANOVA $F_{1,28} = 2.84$, $p = 0.10$). However, there were significant differences in wet weights of latex collected from leaf midribs at the end of larval observations (figure 7.1b). Significantly more latex was collected from leaves of *A. curassavica* than *A. incarnata* (ANOVA $F_{1,27} = 5.06$, $p = 0.03$) and significantly more latex was collected from intact leaves than leaves with a severed midrib (ANOVA $F_{1,27} = 10.42$, $p = 0.003$).

Larval weights

There were no significant differences between larval wet or dry masses on the two host plants (wet masses ANOVA $F_{1,56} = 1.94$, $p = 0.17$; dry masses ANOVA $F_{1,21} = 0.21$, $p = 0.65$) or on intact and severed leaves (wet masses ANOVA $F_{1,56} = 0.20$, $p = 0.66$; dry masses ANOVA $F_{1,21} = 0.01$, $p = 0.91$).

Larval feeding behaviors

Larval behaviors included feeding (chewing leaves and egg chorion), maintenance (resting, spinning silk, and cleaning frass), and moving (moving,

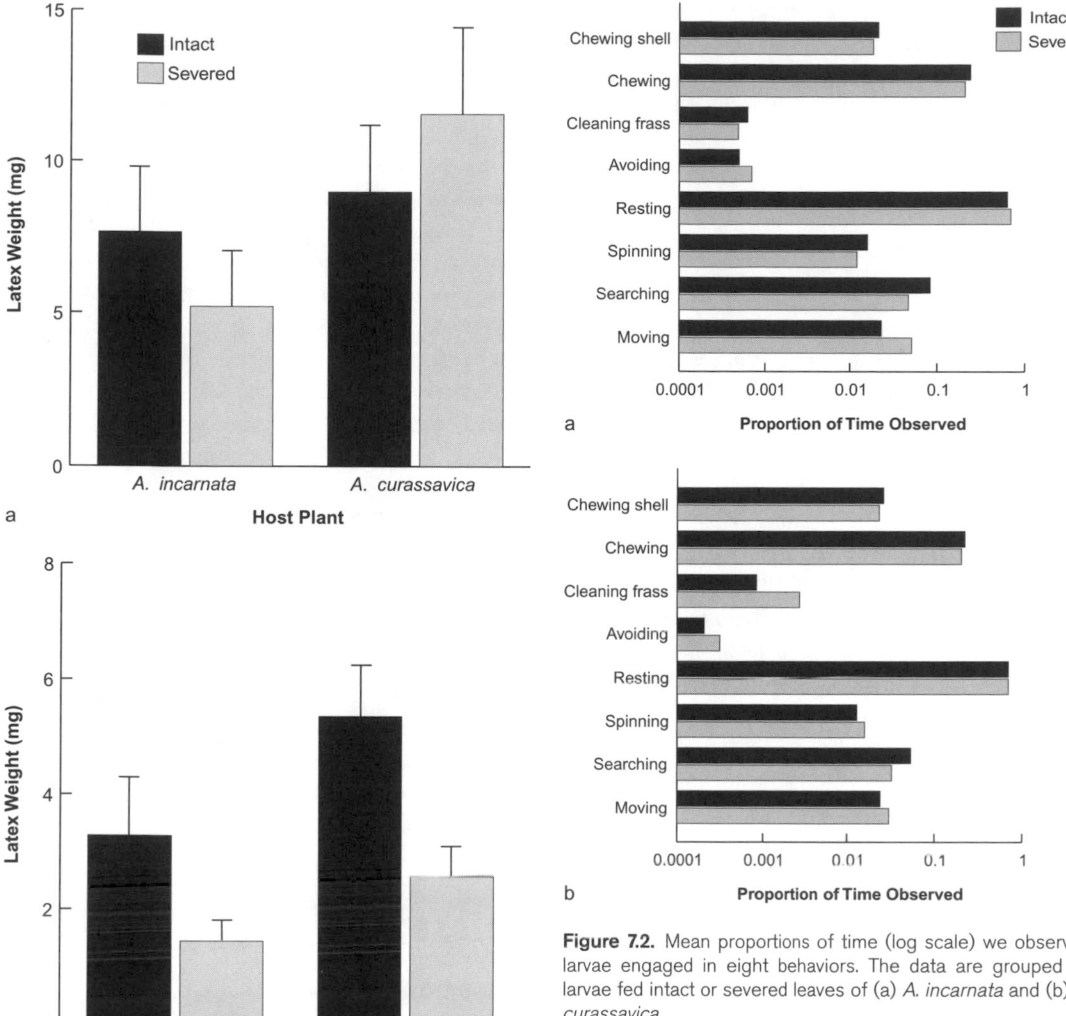

Figure 7.2. Mean proportions of time (log scale) we observed larvae engaged in eight behaviors. The data are grouped by larvae fed intact or severed leaves of (a) *A. incarnata* and (b) *A. curassavica.*

Figure 7.1. Mean wet weights (plus 1 standard error) of latex that was collected on filter paper from the distal section of the midrib, which had been cut near the base of the leaf adjacent to the petiole for *Asclepias incarnata* and *A. curassavica.* Values are given for the (a) initial latex content at the start of observations and (b) final latex content at the end of larval observations.

searching, and avoiding latex) behaviors (figure 7.2). Both searching and spinning silk behaviors involved the use of silk matrices spun onto leaf surfaces; we could distinguish between these because searching involved spinning silk with side-to-side head movements while moving forward. Spinning silk did not involve forward movement and produced a pad of silk as illustrated in Malcolm 1995. Larvae can avoid latex by falling from the leaf on a silk thread attached to the pad, and then climbing back to the leaf.

We ranked the proportion of time each larva spent on each behavior and averaged them across all plant treatments. Larvae spent most of their time resting, followed by chewing leaves; then searching, moving, and chewing the egg shell (three-way tie); spinning silk without moving; and lastly cleaning frass and avoiding latex (two-way tie). We compared ranks of time spent on each behavior between plant species and found no difference for intact (Mann-Whitney $U = 1484$, $p = 0.86$) or severed leaves (Mann-Whitney $U = 1400$, $p = 0.75$). Similarly we found no difference in larval behaviors between intact and severed leaves of either *A. incarnata* (Mann-Whitney $U = 1456$, $p = 0.99$) or *A. curassavica* (Mann-Whitney $U = 1306$, $p = 0.54$).

Data for proportions of time spent in each behavior by larvae in each plant and leaf treatment were distributed normally, and we compared these proportions by analyses of variance. We found no significant effects of leaf treatment (figure 7.2) on any behavior. Similarly, we found no significant effects of host plant species on any behavior.

DISCUSSION

Although we were able to disrupt the latex supply to leaves of both species by severing the midrib, this treatment had no effect on larval growth or feeding and maintenance behaviors. In fact our data are striking for the lack of any larval response to either leaf cardenolide or leaf latex. This argues that first instar larvae are well-adapted specialists on these two host plant species. Although *A. incarnata* and *A. curassavica* differ markedly in their constitutive cardenolide contents and latex characteristics (Malcolm 1995), first instar larvae performed equally well on either species. We explain this absence of a performance or behavior difference in two ways. First, *A. incarnata* and *A. curassavica* may be insignificant host plants of monarchs, with little selective pressure on monarchs to handle species-specific characteristics. Thus monarch larvae may perform equally poorly on the two plants. Alternatively, monarch larvae are well-adapted specialists that perform equally well on these two host plants by handling variable cardenolide and latex levels effectively.

Current evidence leads us to reject the second hypothesis; monarchs are affected by latex in other milkweed species, and there is a negative relationship between larval performance and cardenolide levels in other milkweeds. The growth rates of first instar larvae were significantly higher on severed leaves than intact leaves for six milkweed species (*A. erosa*, *A. eriocarpa*, *A. californica*, *A. humistrata*, *A. syriaca*, and *A. tuberosa*) but not on *A. incarnata*, *A. curassavica*, or A. *fruticosa* (Zalucki and Malcolm 1999; Zalucki et al. 1990, 2001a, 2001b). In comparison with other species, both *A. incarnata* and *A. curassavica* have relatively low latex levels, but *A. incarnata* has less latex than *A. curassavica* (Malcolm 1995; Zalucki et al. 2001b). However, this difference may not be great enough to cause measurable impacts on larval growth or survival.

We conclude that first instar monarch larvae are able to exploit leaves of the milkweeds *A. incarnata* and *A. curassavica* equally effectively or equally poorly despite their different cardenolide contents and differences in their latex contents. The possibility that neither of these milkweed species is important to migratory monarchs as larval food resources may preclude strong selection toward increased latex volumes. *Asclepia incarnata* occurs in wetlands throughout eastern North America (Woodson 1954) and *A. curassavica* is a neotropical annual that is grown as an ornamental but cannot tolerate winter conditions characteristic of the northern United States. Thus neither milkweed is likely to be an important host plant for monarch larvae.

Acknowledgments

We are grateful to Chris Jackson, WMU greenhouse manager, for extensive help with growing plants, maintaining monarchs, and monitoring environment chambers. Jennifer Lawson and Kate Lawton kindly helped with larval observations and data entry. We are also grateful for funding from the WMU Graduate Student Research and Creative Activities Support Fund and the Graduate College for a travel grant.

References

Dussourd, D. E. 1993. Foraging with finesse: caterpillar adaptations for circumventing plant defenses. In N. E. Stamp and T. M. Casey, eds., Caterpillars: ecological and evolutionary constraints on foraging, pp. 92–131. New York: Chapman and Hall.

Dussourd, D. E., and R. F. Denno. 1991. Deactivation of plant defense: correspondence between insect behavior and secretory canal architecture. Ecology 72:1383–96.

Dussourd, D. E., and T. Eisner. 1987. Vein-cutting behavior: insect counterploy to the latex defense of plants. Science 237:898–901.

Feeny, P. 1976. Plant apparency and chemical defense. Recent Adv. Phytochem. 10:1–40.

Herms, D. A., and W. J. Mattson. 1992. The dilemma of plants: to grow or defend. Q. Rev. Biol. 67:283–335.

Malcolm, S. B. 1991. Cardenolide-mediated interactions between plants and herbivores. In G. A. Rosenthal and M. R. Berenbaum, eds., Herbivores: their interactions with secondary plant metabolites. 2nd ed. Vol. 1, pp. 251–96. San Diego: Academic Press.

Malcolm, S. B. 1995. Milkweeds, monarch butterflies, and the ecological significance of cardenolides. Chemoecology 5/6: 101–17.

Malcolm, S. B., and L. P. Brower. 1989. Evolutionary and ecological implications of cardenolide sequestration in the monarch butterfly. Experientia 45:284–95.

Malcolm, S. B., and M. P. Zalucki. 1996. Milkweed latex and cardenolide induction may resolve the lethal plant defence paradox. Entomol. Exp. Appl. 80:193–96.

Nelson, C. J. 1993. Sequestration and storage of cardenolides and cardenolide glycosides by *Danaus plexippus plexippus* and *D. chrysippus petilia* with a review of some factors that influence sequestration. In S. B. Malcolm and M. P. Zalucki, eds., Biology and conservation of the monarch butterfly, pp. 91–106. Los Angeles: Natural History Museum of Los Angeles County.

Rhoades, D. F., and R. G. Cates. 1976. Toward a general theory of plant antiherbivore chemistry. Recent Adv. Phytochem. 10:168–213.

Roeske, C. N., J. N. Seiber, L. P. Brower, and C. M. Moffit. 1976. Milkweed cardenolides and their comparative processing by monarch butterflies. Recent Adv. Phytochem. 10:93–167.

Woodson, R. E., Jr. 1954. The North American species of *Asclepias* L. Ann. Mo. Bot. Gard. 41:1–211.

Zalucki, M. P., and L. P. Brower. 1992. Survival of the first instar larvae of *Danaus plexippus* (Lepidoptera: Danainae) in relation to cardiac glycoside and latex content of *Asclepias humistrata* (Asclepiadaceae). Chemoecology 3:81–93.

Zalucki, M. P., L. P. Brower, and A. Alonso-Mejía. 2001a. Detrimental effects of latex and cardiac glycosides on survival and growth of first-instar *Danaus plexippus* feeding on the sandhill milkweed *Asclepias humistrata*. Ecol. Entomol. 26:212–24.

Zalucki, M. P., L. P. Brower, and S. B. Malcolm. 1990. Oviposition by *Danaus plexippus* in relation to cardenolide content of three *Asclepias* species in the southeastern USA. Ecol. Entomol. 15:231–40.

Zalucki, M. P., and S. B. Malcolm. 1999. Plant latex and first instar monarch larval growth and survival on three North American milkweed species. J. Chem. Ecol. 25: 1827–42.

Zalucki, M. P., S. B. Malcolm, T. D. Paine, C. C. Hanlon, L. P. Brower, and A. R. Clarke. 2001b. It's the first bites that count: survival of first-instar monarchs on milkweeds. Aust. Ecol. 26:547–55.

8

Behavioral and Genetic Components of Male Mating Success in Monarchs

Michelle J. Solensky and Karen S. Oberhauser

INTRODUCTION

Female eggs are tens of thousands of times larger than male sperm (Walters 1988). This size differential sets the stage for conflict between the sexes by making female gametes a valuable resource for which males must compete (Bateman 1948; Andersson 1994). The number of gametes produced by each sex increases the inequality in parental investment. A female animal typically produces between a few hundred (e.g., humans [Walters 1988]) and a few thousand eggs (e.g., dragonflies [McVey 1988]) in her lifetime. Some female fish produce an amazing 5 million eggs in one season (e.g., cod [Daly and Wilson 1983]). But even these very fecund females pale in comparison to males, who can produce more than 300 million sperm in just one ejaculation (e.g., humans [Walters 1988]). Consequently, female reproductive success is typically limited by the number of eggs produced, while male success is limited by the number of females inseminated. Thus, males often exhibit greater variation in mating frequency than do females (e.g., Bateman 1948).

Variation in male mating frequency can result from genotypic and environmental differences, which can be manifested in male morphology, physiology, or behavior. Researchers have found correlations between male size and mating success in several taxa (e.g., insects [Simmons 1987; Gilburn et al. 1992; Brown et al. 1996; Iyengar et al. 2001], anurans [Howard 1988], and birds [Weatherhead et al. 1999]) and between mating success and other morphological traits (e.g., abdominal ventral process length in water striders, *Gerris odontogaster* [Arnqvist 1989], and forceps length in earwigs, *Forficula auricularia* [Tomkins and Simmons 1999]). Male behavior can also influence mating success. Male picture-winged flies (*Drosophila silvestris*) are more likely to mate when they spend more time courting and vibrating their wings (Boake and Konigsberg 1998). Physiology, especially the production of pheromones or accessory gland material, can influence male mating success (e.g., hydroxydanaidal production in *Utetheisa ornatrix* [Iyengar et al. 2001]). Watt and coworkers (1986) found that genetically controlled differences in the structure of a glycolytic enzyme, phosphoglucose isomerase, affected male mating frequency. Griffith and colleagues (1999) investigated the relative roles of genes and environment in male sexual ornamentation in house sparrows (*Passer domesticus*) and found that environmental variation was the main source of resemblance between fathers and sons, suggesting that both genes and environment can influence sexually selected traits.

Monarch courtship is unusual among the Lepidoptera in that males sometimes force females to copulate (Van Hook 1993; Oberhauser and Frey 1999) and appear not to use chemical courtship (Pliske 1975; Boppré 1993). Males initiate mating attempts by pursuing females in the air, often forcing them to the ground and engaging in a protracted ground struggle (Hill et al. 1976; Frey et al. 1998). The male probes the female with the tip of his abdomen while the female appears to resist. About 30% of mating attempts at overwintering sites end in copulation, so females are often able to avoid unwanted matings (Frey 1999; Oberhauser and Frey 1999). Both females and males often mate multiply during their lifetimes.

Monarch males vary greatly in their ability to achieve copulations. Oberhauser (1989) found that lifetime male mating frequency ranged from 0 to 11 copulations ($n = 47$), with half of the males mating fewer than three times and most males (95%) mating fewer than eight times. However, the source of this variation is not understood. Previous studies have failed to reveal correlations between male size or wing condition and male mating success (Falco 1998; Oberhauser and Frey 1999). We attempted to understand variation in male mating success by estimating the genetic and environmental components of male mating frequency and investigating the correlation between male behavioral traits and mating success.

METHODS

Obtaining adults

We reared parental adults from eggs laid by wild females from Texas, Alabama, and Minnesota in spring 1998 and 1999. Groups of eggs or larvae were collected from milkweed patches at least 2 km apart, resulting in a high probability that eggs from different milkweed patches were produced by different, unrelated females. On eclosion, adults were numbered and stored in glassine envelopes at room temperature. Adults were fed a solution of 20% honey-water once in the lab, and had constant access to sponges saturated with honey-water and cut flowers upon release into outdoor cages.

Assessing male mating success

To measure heritability, we need to quantify the trait under investigation. Our trait of interest was lifetime male mating frequency, but we needed to assign pairs for the mating design before the end of the males' lives. Therefore, we determined the number of days during a 10-day period on which each male secured a mate when given access to females. We used data collected in a previous study of lifetime mating frequency to assess the quality of this 10-day measure as a predictor of lifetime male mating success (Solensky 2003). Monarchs remain paired throughout the night so males can mate only once per day and all pairs can be recorded by checking the cage at dusk. We released an equal number of males and females (5 to 7 days old, typically 30 of each) into an outdoor cage ($1.8\,m^3$) and recorded mating activity. We then calculated the proportion of days during which each male had mated.

Estimating genetic component of male mating success

At the end of the 10-day assessment period, we selected 10 to 13 sires with mating frequencies that represented the observed distribution. We mated each sire to 3 or 4 unrelated virgin females, and reared 30 offspring from each cross. We then measured the mating success of several sons from each female. We tested 150 male offspring in 1998 (10 sires × 3 dams × 5 sons) and 208 male offspring in 1999 (13 sires × 4 dams × 4 sons).

Although the dams mated to each sire were not related to each other, each female had a sister mated to each of the other males. This resulted in not only full- and half-siblings among paternal groups, but also cousins between paternal groups. These modifications to the standard half-sib crossing design are not readily accommodated by many quantitative genetic analyses (e.g., parent-offspring regression and partitioning of variance using analysis of variance). We used restricted maximum likelihood estimation (REML) to estimate the additive genetic and environmental variance components. We calculated narrow-sense heritability, which is defined as the ratio of additive genetic variance to total phenotypic variance: $h^2 = V_A/V_P$. We also calculated the coefficient of additive genetic variation, which scales the additive genetic variance component by the trait mean ($cV_A = V_A^{1/2}/\bar{x}$) rather than by the total variance and may be a more informative measure of additive genetic variance than heritability (Kruuk et al. 2000). We analyzed differences in mating success between generations using logistic regression.

Measuring behavioral component of male mating success

We observed the mating behavior of parental males used in the study just described. For each mating attempt observed, we recorded the identity of the individuals involved, attempt duration, and whether the attempt resulted in copulation. We also measured the mating success of each focal male.

Table 8.1. Mating attempt predictions

Hypothesis	Attempt duration	Proportion of attempts with females	Frequency of attempts	Female resisting at end of attempt
Male persistence	**>**	=	≤	≥
Male is better able to identify females	=	**>**	≤	≥
Male tries more often	≤	=	**>**	≥
Male is better able to force	<	=	≤	**≥**
Female choice	<	=	≤	**>**

Note: Predictions for characteristics of mating attempts involving successful males *compared to* those involving less successful males. Boldface symbols distinguish between hypotheses.

Several hypotheses may explain variation in male mating success, and each makes predictions about how specific characteristics of mating attempts should vary (table 8.1).

1. Duration: If successful males struggle with females for longer on average than less successful males, this suggests that successful males are more persistent. All other hypotheses predict that successful males should have attempts of equal or shorter average duration than less successful males.
2. Proportion of attempts with females: Male monarchs in wild populations frequently attempt to mate with other males (25% to 30% of attempts at overwintering sites [Oberhauser and Frey 1999]). If successful males have a higher proportion of attempts with females, then successful males are better able to discriminate between males and females. All other hypotheses predict no difference in proportion of attempts with females.
3. Frequency of attempts: If some males mate more frequently because they initiate mating attempts more often, then successful males should have a higher frequency of attempts than less successful males. They may be generally more active but equal in other respects (same average attempt duration), or they may spend less time on each attempt but attempt more frequently (shorter average duration). All other hypotheses predict an equal or lower frequency of attempts, since they all predict that successful males are more likely to mate during a given attempt, and therefore less likely to have to engage in a large number of mating attempts.
4. Female resistance behavior: If some males are more successful because they are better able to force females to mate, mating attempts involving successful males should be more or equally as likely to end with females still resisting. Alternatively, if females assess male quality and accept mating with certain males more readily, they should be more likely to cease resistance during mating attempts with successful males. This last hypothesis is in a different category from the others in that male mating success is driven by both male and female traits rather than just by male traits.

We analyzed attempt duration using the base 10 log of duration in seconds, retaining only the first observation of each female to ensure that observations were independent of female identity (n = 143 attempts). For analysis of other behavioral variables we summarized the data by male identity, resulting in observations describing individual males (n = 51 males). Proportions were arcsine square root transformed to approximate a normal distribution, and data were analyzed using least-squares linear regression.

RESULTS

Assessment of male mating success

Male mating success in a 10-day period (from day 5 to day 14 after eclosion) is a good predictor of life-

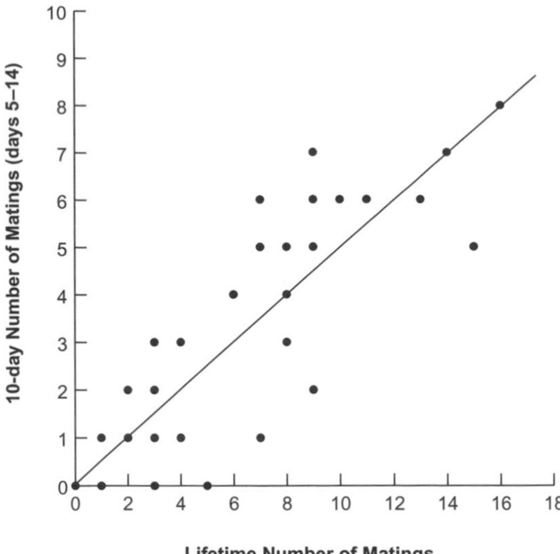

Figure 8.1. Correlation between lifetime mating success and mating success and mating success during a 10-day period for male monarchs.

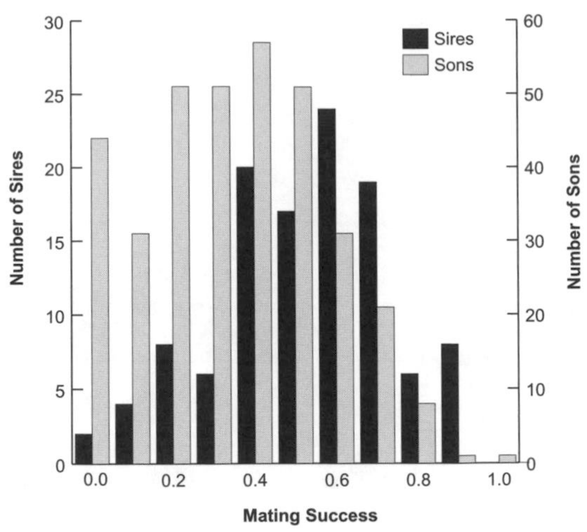

Figure 8.2. Frequency distribution of male mating success in the parental (sires) and the F_1 (sons) generation (1998 and 1999 combined).

time male mating frequency (n = 49, R^2 = 0.7638, p < 0.0001). Males mated from 0 to 16 times during their lifetimes, and from 0 to 8 times during the 10-day period from 5 to 14 days after eclosion (figure 8.1).

Genetic component of male mating success

The proportion of days that males mated ranged from 0 to 0.9 among sires and 0 to 1 among sons (figure 8.2). Males in the sire group mated more frequently than their offspring (p < 0.001, figure 8.3). We tested the sires in June and July and the male offspring in late August through early September, so the difference in mating frequency may be at least partially explained by warmer temperatures during the parental mating period (2.9°C higher mean temperature, table 8.2). There was a small but significant effect of year on male mating success, with males mating more frequently during the first year of the study (p < 0.001, figure 8.3).

We found significant additive genetic variance associated with male mating success (table 8.3). Although the additive genetic variance was nearly the same in both years, heritability estimates varied as a result of increased environmental variance in the second year compared with the first. The coefficient of additive genetic variance was nearly the same in both years.

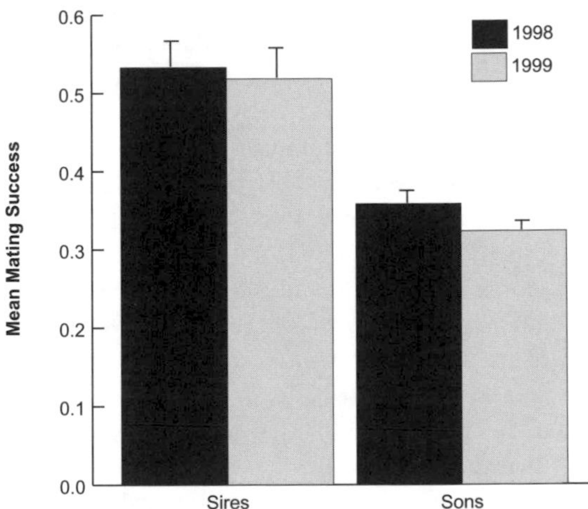

Figure 8.3. Effect of generation and year of study on male mating success (means are show +1 standard error).

Table 8.2. Mean temperature during the four periods of mating frequency observations

Year	Generation	Dates of observation	Mean temperature (°C) (standard error)
1998	Sires	10/7–19/7	24.6 (0.7)
1998	Sons	30/8–8/9	19.9 (0.8)
1999	Sires	23/6–7/7	23.1 (1.0)
1999	Sons	18/8–27/8	21.6 (0.6)

Table 8.3. Estimated variance components of male mating success and significance level of additive genetic variance

Year	V_A	V_A p value	V_E	V_P	h^2	$\bar{x}$	cV_A
1998	0.0261	0.007	0.0340	0.0601	0.434	0.358	45.1%
1999	0.0245	0.00005	0.0633	0.0878	0.279	0.323	48.4%

Note: V_A (additive genetic variance) + V_E (environmental variance) = V_P (total phenotypic variance); h^2 (heritability) = V_A/V_P; $\bar{x}$ = the mean proportion of days mated of all males in the offspring generation; and cV_A (coefficient of additive genetic variation) = $\sqrt{V_A}/\bar{x}$.

Behavioral component of male mating success

During 51.3h of observation, we recorded 442 mating attempts, 273 (62%) involving a male and a female. Of the male-female attempts, 85 (31%) ended in mating. Male wing length was not correlated with mating success ($n = 51$, $p = 0.94$). Average attempt duration was not correlated with male mating success ($n = 143$, $p = 0.47$, figure 8.4a). We found no significant correlation between mating success and the proportion of male-female attempts ($n = 51$, $p = 0.16$) or the frequency of attempts ($n = 51$, $p = 0.21$) (figure 8.4b,c). However, male mating success was positively correlated with the proportion of mating attempts that ended in copulation ($n = 51$, $p = 0.007$, figure 8.4d), meaning that successful males not only mate on a greater proportion of days (by definition) but also are more likely to be successful in any given attempt.

DISCUSSION

Genetic component of male mating success

Male mating success in monarchs is a heritable trait; there is a genetic component underlying a trait or suite of traits that influences male mating success. Environmental variation was higher than additive genetic variation in both years, so there is a substantial environmental component to male mating success. The additive genetic variance estimates were similar in both years of our study, but the environmental variance was higher in the second year than in the first, resulting in a lower heritability estimate in the second year. Because environmental variance is likely to be higher in the wild, heritability of this trait in wild populations is likely to be lower than this estimate. However, the response to selection depends only on the genetic variance, not on other variance components (Fisher 1958), so heritability is not as useful a measure as the coefficient of additive genetic variance when considering the evolution of a trait.

Behavioral and life history traits often have lower heritability estimates than do morphological or physiological traits (Mousseau and Roff 1987; Roff and Mousseau 1987), but more genetic variance (Houle 1998). For this reason, comparisons of heritability between behavioral traits are expected to be more meaningful than comparisons between behavioral and morphological or physiological traits. Our estimates of heritability of male mating success in monarchs ($h^2 = 0.43$ and 0.28) are comparable to heritability estimates of reproductive behaviors in other insect taxa (e.g., sperm competition success in bulb mites, *Rhizoglyphus robini*, $h^2 = 0.28$ [Radwan 1998]; female choice for male ultrasonic signals in pyralid moth, *Achroia grisella*, $h^2 = 0.21$ [Jang and Greenfield 2000]). Our estimates of the coefficient of variation (45.1% and 48.4%) are quite high in comparison with the estimated average of 10% for life history traits in general (Rowe and Houle 1996), and in comparison with behavioral traits specifically in other taxa (e.g., female choice for male ultrasonic signals in pyralid moth, *Achroia grisella*, cV_A = 18.26% [Jang and Greenfield 2000]; male breeding success in red deer, *Cervus elaphus*, cV_A = 23.94% [Kruuk et al. 2000]; urine marking in bank voles, *Clethrionomys glareolus*, cV_A = 25.47% [Horne and Ylonen 1998]).

Until recently, prevailing quantitative genetic models predicted little genetic variation in traits strongly tied to fitness owing to fixation of favored alleles by directional selection (Borgia 1979; Charlesworth 1987; Falconer 1989). However, sexually selected traits often do not fit these predictions (e.g., Mousseau and Roff 1987; Pomiankowski and Moller 1995; Kingsolver et al. 2001). Several hypotheses have been proposed to resolve this

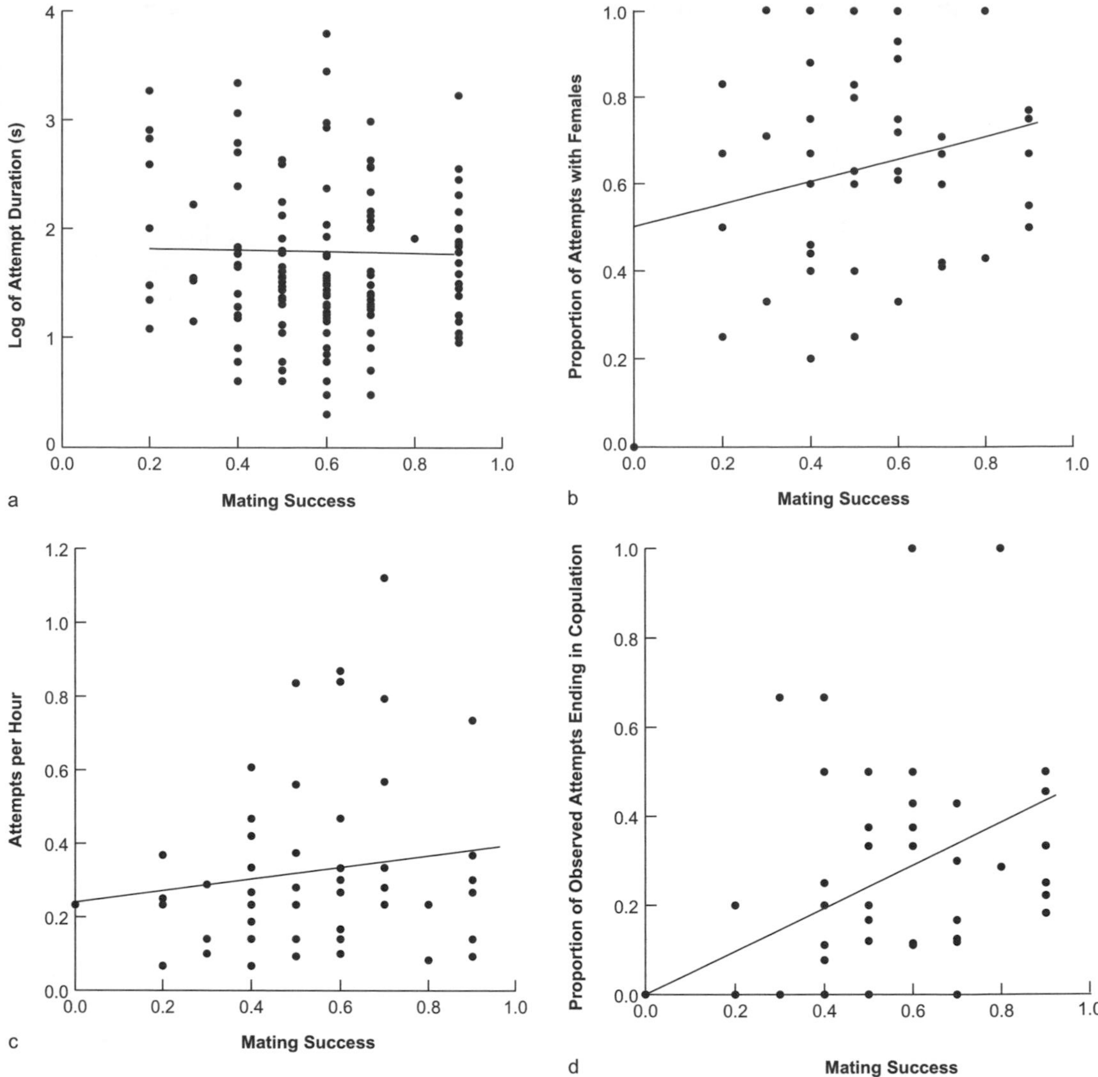

Figure 8.4. Correlations between mating success and (a) average attempt duration, (b) proportion of attempts with females, (c) frequency of attempts (measured as the number of mating attempts per hour of observation), and (d) proportion of attempts ending in copulation.

paradox (e.g., Houle 1998). Pomiankowski and Moller (1995) suggested that sexual selection favors extreme rather than mean values of traits, resulting in directional rather than stabilizing selection and consequently higher variance. Additive genetic variance can also be maintained in populations by spatial or temporal environmental heterogeneity (Schmidt et al. 2000; Wipking and Kurtz 2000). This may be especially relevant in monarchs since mating occurs in extremely variable environments; they mate not only in the overwintering colonies, in which densities can exceed 10 million monarchs/ha (e.g., Calvert, this volume; Brower et al., this volume), but also in midwestern prairies where densities are typically less than 50 monarchs/ha. Presumably, selection favors different male traits under such different circumstances.

Behavioral component of male mating success

Attempt duration was not correlated with male mating success, which is consistent with the hypotheses that successful males are better able to identify females or attempt to mate more frequently (see table 8.1). However, successful males were not more likely to attempt to mate with females than were less successful males, so there appeared to be no difference in their ability to discriminate between males and females in initiating mating attempts. Successful males were not observed in attempts more frequently than less successful males, so variation in male mating success is unlikely to be explained simply by differential effort. These data therefore fail to support any single hypothesis presented earlier. However, we found that successful males had not just a higher number of matings (by definition), but also a higher proportion of mating attempts that ended in copulation; they were thus more likely to be successful in any given attempt. This suggests that there is some, as yet undefined, male trait or traits that affect male mating frequency by making males with these traits more likely to succeed in individual mating attempts.

Our behavioral observations were not detailed enough to determine with confidence whether females were resisting at the end of attempts, but some males may be better able to force females or be more attractive to females. Moreover, some males may be successful because they are persistent while others are better able to force females or are more attractive to females. This combination predicts no correlation between male mating success and attempt duration since these competing hypotheses predict opposite trends.

Studying monarch behavior in captive populations

Monarchs were maintained at densities higher than typically found in summer breeding populations (5 to 50/ha), but lower than densities observed at some overwintering sites (10,000 to 50,000,000/ha [Tuskes and Brower 1978; Calvert, this volume; Brower, this volume]). Because monarchs are not uniformly distributed throughout overwintering sites, the density of monarchs in sunny patches of air, canopy, or ground may well exceed the density of monarchs used in this study (185,000/ha).

Although monarch mating behavior has traditionally been described as being initiated in the air (Pliske 1975; Hill et al. 1976), recent studies of overwintering populations in the western United States suggest that aerial captures occur infrequently. Leong (1995) observed that males often initiate mating attempts by pouncing on a stationary monarch in the tree canopy, and Falco (1998) found that this "pounce" method of capture was more likely to result in a mating attempt than an aerial pursuit. In cages, aerial pursuits are limited, but males do initiate mating attempts by pouncing on females resting on the sides of the cages.

Acknowledgments

We thank Frank Shaw for assistance with the analysis of genetic variance and Frank Shaw and Ruth Shaw for their advice in designing the genetic crosses. Betsy Chastain, Tiffany Miley, Amy Alstad, Cassie Clark, and Stephanie Friedland observed and recorded mating attempt data; they and Michelle Prysby, Athena Decker, Sonia Altizer, Elizabeth Larkin, and Youa Yang assisted with rearing larvae and processing adults for the genetic study. This research was supported financially by grants to M. Solensky from the Dayton and Wilkie Funds for Natural History, Bell Museum, University of Minnesota; by a doctoral dissertation fellowship to M. Solensky from the National Science Foundation; and by Monarchs in the Classroom, University of Minnesota.

References

Andersson, M. 1994. Sexual selection. Princeton: Princeton University Press.

Arnqvist, G. 1989. Sexual selection in a water strider: the function, mechanism of selection and heritability of a male grasping aparatus. Oikos 56:344–50.

Bateman, A. J. 1948. Intra-sexual selection in *Drosophila.* Heredity 2:349–68.

Boake, C. R. B., and L. Konigsberg. 1998. Inheritance of male courtship behavior, aggressive success, and body size in *Drosophila silvestris.* Evolution 52:1487–92.

Boppré, M. 1993. The American monarch: courtship and chemical communication of a peculiar danaine butterfly. In S. B. Malcolm and M. P. Zalucki, eds., Biology and conservation of the monarch butterfly, pp. 29–41. Los Angeles: Natural History Museum of Los Angeles County.

Borgia, G. 1979. Sexual selection and the evolution of mating systems. In M. S. Blum and N. A. Blum, eds., Sexual selection and reproductive competition in insects, pp. 19–80. New York: Academic Press.

Brown, W. D., J. Wideman, M. C. B. Andrade, A. C. Mason, and D. T. Gywnne. 1996. Female choice for an indicator of male size in the song of the black-horned tree cricket, *Oecanthus nigricornis* (Orthoptera: Gryllidae: Oecanthinae). Evolution 50:2400–11.

Charlesworth, B. 1987. The heritability of fitness. In J. W. Bradbury and M. Andersson, eds., Sexual selection, pp. 21–40. Chichester, U.K.: Wiley.

Daly, M., and M. Wilson. 1983. Sex, evolution and behavior. 2nd ed. Boston: Willard Grant Press.

Falco, L. R. 1998. Variation in male courtship behaviors of the monarch butterfly (*Danaus plexippus* L.) at central California overwintering sites. Master's thesis, California Polytechnic State University, San Luis Obispo.

Falconer, D. S. 1989. Introduction to quantitative genetics. 3rd ed. New York: John Wiley and Sons.

Fisher, R. A. 1958. The genetical theory of natural selection. 2nd ed. New York: Dover Press.

Frey, D. 1999. Resistance to mating by female monarch butterflies. In J. Hoth, L. Merino, K. Oberhauser, I. Pisantry, S. Price, and T. Wilkinson, eds., The 1997 North American Conference on the Monarch Butterfly, pp. 79–87. Montreal: Commission for Environmental Cooperation.

Frey, D., K. Leong, E. Peffer, R. Smidt, and K. Oberhauser. 1998. Mating patterns of overwintering monarch butterflies (*Danaus plexippus* L.) in California. J. Lepid. Soc. 52:84–97.

Gilburn, A. S., S. P. Foster, and T. H. Day. 1992. Female mating preference for large size in *Coelopa frigida*. Heredity 69:209–16.

Griffith, S. C., I. P. Owens, and T. Burke. 1999. Environmental determination of a sexually selected trait. Nature 400: 358–60.

Hill, H., A. Wenner, and P. Wells. 1976. Reproductive behavior in an overwintering aggregation of monarch butterflies. Am. Midl. Nat. 95:10–19.

Horne, T. J., and H. Ylonen. 1998. Heritabilities of dominance-related traits in male bank voles (*Clethrionomys glareolus*). Evolution 52:894–99.

Houle, D. 1998. How should we explain variation in the genetic variance of traits? Genetica 102/103:241–53.

Howard, R. D. 1988. Sexual selection on male body size and mating behaviour in American toads, *Bufo americanus*. Anim. Behav. 36:1796–808.

Iyengar, V. K., C. Rossini, and T. Eisner. 2001. Precopulatory assessment of male quality in an arctiid moth (*Utetheisa ornatrix*): hydroxydanaidal is the only criterion of choice. Behav. Ecol. Sociobiol. 49:283–88.

Jang, Y., and M. D. Greenfield. 2000. Quantitative genetics of female choice in an ultrasonic pyralid moth, *Achroia grisella*: variation and evolvability of preference along multiple dimensions of the male advertisement signal. Heredity 84:73–80.

Kingsolver, J. G., H. E. Hoekstra, J. M. Hoekstra, D. Berrigan, S. N. Vignieri, C. E. Hill, Hoang, P. Gibert, and P. Beerli. 2001. The strength of phenotypic selection in natural populations. Am. Nat. 157:245–61.

Kruuk, L. E. B., T. H. Clutton-Brock, J. Slate, J. M. Pemberton, S. Brotherstone, and F. E. Guinness. 2000. Heritability of fitness in a wild mammal population. Proc. Natl. Acad. Sci. USA 97:698–703.

Leong, K. L. H. 1995. Initiation of mating activity at the tree canopy level among overwintering monarch butterflies in California. Pan-Pac. Entomol. 71:66–68.

McVey, M. E. 1988. The opportunity for sexual selection in a territorial dragonfly, *Erythemis simplicicollis*. In T. H. Clutton-Brock, ed., Reproductive success: studies of individual variation in contrasting, pp. 344–62. Chicago: University of Chicago Press.

Mousseau, T. A., and D. A. Roff. 1987. Natural selection and the heritability of fitness components. Heredity 59:181–97.

Oberhauser, K. 1989. Effects of spermatophores on male and female monarch butterfly reproductive success. Behav. Ecol. Sociobiol. 25:237–346.

Oberhauser, K., and D. Frey. 1999. Coercive mating by overwintering male monarch butterflies. In J. Hoth, L. Merino, K. Oberhauser, I. Pisantry, S. Price, and T. Wilkinson, eds., The 1997 North American Conference on the Monarch Butterfly, pp. 79–87. Montreal: Commission for Environmental Cooperation.

Pliske, T. 1975. Courtship behavior of the monarch butterfly, *Danaus plexippus* L. Ann. Entomol. Soc. Am. 68:143–51.

Pomiankowski, A., and A. P. Moller. 1995. A resolution of the lek paradox. Proc. R. Soc. Lond. B 260:21–29.

Radwan, J. 1998. Heritability of sperm competition success in the bulb mite, *Rhizoglyphus robini*. J. Evol. Biol. 11:321–27.

Roff, D. A., and T. A. Mousseau. 1987. Quantitative genetics and fitness: lessons from *Drosophila*. Heredity 58:103–18.

Rowe, L., and D. Houle. 1996. The lek paradox and the capture of genetic variance by condition dependent traits. Proc. R. Soc. Lond. B 263:1415–21.

Schmidt, P. S., M. D. Bertness, and D. M. Rand. 2000. Environmental heterogeneity and balancing selection in the acorn barnacle *Semibalanus balanoides*. Proc. R. Soc. Lond. B 267:379–84.

Simmons, L. W. 1987. Heritability of a male character chosen by females of the field cricket, *Gryllus bimaculatus*. Behav. Ecol. Sociobiol. 21:129–33.

Solensky, M. 2003. Reproductive fitness in monarch butterflies, *Danaus plexippus*. Ph.D. thesis, University of Minnesota, St. Paul.

Tomkins, J. L., and L. W. Simmons. 1999. Heritability of size but not symmetry in a sexually selected trait chosen by female earwigs. Heredity 82:151–57.

Tuskes, P. M., and L. P. Brower. 1978. Overwintering ecology of the monarch butterfly, *Danaus plexippus* L., in California. Calif. Ecol. Entomol. 3:141–53.

Van Hook, T. 1993. Non-random mating in monarch butterflies overwintering in Mexico. In S. B. Malcolm and M. P. Zalucki, eds., Biology and conservation of the monarch butterfly, pp. 49–60. Los Angeles: Natural History Museum of Los Angeles County.

Walters, M. J. 1988. Courtship in the animal kingdom. New York: Doubleday.

Watt, W., P. A. Carter, and K. Donohue. 1986. Females' choice of "good genotypes" as mates is promoted by an insect mating system. Science 233:1187–90.

Weatherhead, P. J., K. W. Dufour, S. C. Lougheed, and C. G. Eckert. 1999. A test of the good-genes-as-heterozygosity hypothesis using red-winged blackbirds. Behav. Ecol. 10:619–25.

Wipking, W., and J. Kurtz. 2000. Genetic variability in the diapause response of the burnet moth *Zygaena trifolii* (Lepidoptera: Zygaenidae). J. Insect Physiol. 46:127–34.

9

Survival of Experimental Cohorts of Monarch Larvae following Exposure to Transgenic Bt Corn Pollen and Anthers

Laura C. H. Jesse and John J. Obrycki

INTRODUCTION

Recent data on the effects of transgenic *Bacillus thuringiensis* (Bt) corn pollen on larvae of the monarch butterfly and the black swallowtail, *Papilio polyxenes*, two butterfly species that occur on plants within and adjacent to cornfields in the midwestern United States, have been used by the U.S. Environmental Protection Agency (EPA) in a reassessment of regulatory decisions and the re-registration of transgenic Bt corn hybrids (EPA 2000; Wraight et al. 2000; Hellmich et al. 2001; Oberhauser et al. 2001; Pleasants et al. 2001; Sears et al. 2001; Stanley-Horn et al. 2001; Zangerl et al. 2001). This EPA reassessment was in response to the laboratory study by Losey and coworkers (1999) which demonstrated that monarch larvae ingested Bt corn pollen when they were placed on milkweed leaves covered with pollen and that consumption of this pollen caused increased mortality. Similarly, we found that monarch larvae suffer increased mortality when exposed to levels of Bt (Events Bt11 and 176) corn pollen and anther material from two types of transgenic corn, Bt11 and 176, they are likely to encounter in the field (Jesse and Obrycki 2000). Anthers, plant structures that release pollen, are typically shed during anthesis and contain higher levels of Bt toxins than the pollen itself (Jesse and Obrycki 2000; Hellmich et al. 2001).

Criticisms of our previous research (Jesse and Obrycki 2000) have pointed out that our pollen collection methods failed to exclude corn anthers, and that the presence of these anther parts influenced our results (Hellmich et al. 2001). We discussed the presence of anthers in our study and quantified the amount of nonpollen corn tissue in our samples (Jesse and Obrycki 2000). Bt toxin is expressed in anther tissue, although the exact level of the toxin relative to that in pollen is unknown (Jesse and Obrycki 2000). Monarch larvae exposed to pollen and anther parts from another type of transgenic Bt corn, MON810, experience increased mortality and reduced weight gain compared to larvae exposed to pollen alone (Hellmich et al. 2001).

As corn pollinates, the filament attaching the anthers to the tassel elongates and allows the anthers to hang freely from the plant to aid in the dispersal of pollen (Kiesselbach 1999). The anthers commonly fall off the tassel and land on surrounding vegetation and the soil. Because of the higher levels of toxin in anther tissue, this raises the question of whether monarch larvae feeding on *Asclepias syriaca* in cornfields are exposed to higher levels of Bt toxin than pollen densities alone would indicate.

Detailed field studies are needed to quantify the effect of naturally deposited Bt corn pollen and anthers on monarch larvae. The presence of anthers on milkweed leaves was noted by Hellmich and coauthors (2001), but the density of anthers was not quantified. In a summary of Bt corn nontarget effects (Sears et al. 2001), consideration of the presence and effects of anthers from Bt corn hybrids on milkweeds was ignored. However, corn pollen and anthers naturally occur on milkweed plants in cornfields, suggesting that anthers do not represent experimental contamination as suggested by Hellmich and coauthors (2001), but are a potential source of Bt toxin that needs to be considered.

The focus of the initial research examining the effects of Bt corn on monarchs was on pollen drift outside cornfields. This initial emphasis was appropriate because pollen disperses from the plant and may be ingested by lepidopterans feeding on noncorn host plants outside of fields (Losey et al. 1999; Jesse and Obrycki 2000; Hellmich et al. 2001; Stanley-Horn et al. 2001; Zangerl et al. 2001). However, milkweed plants are relatively common in cornfields (Hartzler and Buhler 2000), and monarch larvae developing on milkweeds in cornfields produce a significant proportion of the adult population in the midwestern United States (Oberhauser et al. 2001). Thus, research needs to focus on the within-field interaction between transgenic corn hybrids and monarch larvae; in this context, the deposition of anthers on milkweeds becomes an important consideration.

The objectives of this study were to quantify (1) the frequency of anther occurrence on milkweed plants within cornfields, and (2) the effect of Bt corn pollen and anthers on cohorts of monarch larvae placed on caged *A. syriaca* within Bt and non-Bt cornfields.

MATERIALS AND METHODS

Field survey 2000

We conducted a survey of naturally occurring monarchs on *A. syriaca* at three field sites with Bt (transgenic corn type Event MON810) and non-Bt corn plots separated by less than 3.2 km. Each cornfield had a minimum of 20 *A. syriaca* ramets growing within the first ten rows of corn, and at least 100 *A. syriaca* ramets growing within a 600-m transect in the roadside parallel to the cornfield. We surveyed each field site weekly from 3 to 28 July for eggs and larvae. At two of the field sites, *A. syriaca* ramets growing within 0.5 m of the first row of corn and between the first and tenth rows of corn on which we found eggs or larvae were also examined for anther presence during anthesis (12 or 14 July). In addition, we conducted a systematic survey of every fifth *A. syriaca* within corn rows for monarch life stages.

Experimental monarch cohort study 2000

Results from the study conducted during 2000 were published in the article by Stanley-Horn and coauthors (2001). We include a brief description of the methods here, to serve as a basis for comparison with the 2001 cohort study. Three 1-acre (0.4-ha) sites at Iowa State University research farms (Burkey, Bruner, and Johnson Farms) in Story County, Iowa, were planted as paired plots of approximately 0.5 acre (0.2 ha) of Bt corn (N4640Bt, Northrup King, Event Bt11) and 0.5 acre (0.2 ha) of non-Bt corn (N4640, NK).

We transplanted *A. syriaca* plants to three locations at each field site: 2 m from the edge of the cornfield, at the edge of the cornfield, and in the cornfield 4.6 m from the edge. We placed 6 plants at each location for each corn hybrid, resulting in 36 transplanted plants at each site (18/hybrid). Approximately 7 days after the start of anthesis, we placed five first instar monarchs on each *A. syriaca* plant. We recorded the number and life stage of monarch larvae every 24 h for 7 days, and then every 48 h for another 7 days.

Experimental monarch cohort study 2001

Three 1-acre (0.4-ha) fields at Iowa State University research farms (Burkey, Bruner, and Agronomy Farms) in Story County, Iowa, were planted on 29 May as paired plots of approximately 0.5 acre (0.2 ha) of Bt corn (N67-T4, Northrup King, Event Bt11) and 0.5 acre (0.2 ha) of non-Bt corn (N59-Q9, NK). Thirty-two to 44 rows of each hybrid were planted at each field site. The same pairs of corn hybrids were used in 2000 and 2001.

We transplanted *A. syriaca* plants (5 to 50 cm tall) to field sites between 9 July and 13 July. Plants were watered frequently until roots were established. We planted 3 plants approximately 3 m apart in the eighth, thirteenth, and eighteenth rows of corn, and 2 plants in the twenty-third row of each hybrid.

Anthesis began on about 30 July in all fields. We placed tomato cage frames in the ground over 2 of the 3 *A. syriaca* plants in the eighth, thirteenth, and eighteenth rows, and over both *A. syriaca* plants in the twenty-third row on 1 and 2 August, leaving 3 plants uncaged within each corn hybrid at each farm. We placed a cylindrical mesh cage (0.45 m high × 0.25 m diameter, NO-SEE-UM netting, Balsom Hercules Group, Providence, R.I.) around each tomato cage and folded it down to the ground to allow pollen and anthers to be naturally deposited on the *A. syriaca* plant. We raised the mesh cages around the tomato frames to exclude predators on the day first instar monarchs were placed on the plant.

Between 5 and 7 August, we placed 3 first instar monarchs on each *A. syriaca* plant at the Burkey and Agronomy Farms. On 4 August, we placed 2 first instar monarchs on 4 plants in the Bt corn plot at the Bruner Farm (1 plant was left uncaged) and on 6 plants in the non-Bt corn (2 plants were left uncaged). The total number of caged larvae placed in Bt fields was 48, and in non-Bt fields was 50. The total number of uncaged larvae placed in Bt fields was 17, and in non-Bt fields was 16. We recorded the number and life stage of each monarch larva every 24 h until pupation. If an entire *A. syriaca* plant was consumed, larvae were moved onto another plant in the same field plot that did not have larvae on it, or moved into the laboratory and reared at 21°C and fed *A. syriaca* leaves free of pollen and anthers daily until pupation. Twenty-four hours after pupation, we weighed each chrysalis. Twenty-four hours after eclosion, adults were placed in envelopes and frozen. Adults were dried at 30°C for 24 h and then at approximately 23°C for 1 week, and weighed on a Mettler AE100 balance (Jesse and Obrycki 2000). We measured the right forewing lengths from the white spot at the base of the wing to the apex (Donham and Taylor 2000).

On 15 August, we removed one 0.79-cm^2 leaf sample with a No. 6 cork borer from a middle leaf of each *A. syriaca* plant in each plot. We counted pollen grains under a dissecting scope to assess pollen densities (Jesse and Obrycki 2000). We counted the number of anthers deposited on each plant by visually examining the entire plant in the field.

Data analysis

We analyzed survival curves for the uncaged larvae in the 2000 and 2001 experimental cohort study using LIFETEST (SAS 8.0) (results for 2000 presented in Stanley-Horn et al. 2001). Because of the tendency of monarch larvae to move off *A. syriaca* plants when molting (Borkin 1982), we observed larvae reappearing on later sampling dates. These reappearing larvae were added to the previous sample count.

We analyzed the number of surviving larvae in the 2001 experimental cohort study using a macro called GLIMMIX, which uses a mixed model analysis with both fixed and random effects on binomial data (alive or dead). The corn hybrid (Bt or non-Bt) was a fixed effect. The random effects were field location, *A. syriaca* plant, and the monarch larvae.

We analyzed pupal and adult weights and wing lengths of individuals that had been exposed to Bt and non-Bt anthers and pollen in the 2001 experimental cohort using PROC GLM (SAS 8.0).

RESULTS

Field survey 2000

We observed monarchs (eggs or larvae) on 21 of 35 *A. syriaca* plants examined in the two Bt cornfields on 12 or 14 July; one or more anthers were observed on 18 of these plants (table 9.1). We examined an additional 14 plants within the Bt cornfields with no monarchs as part of a systematic survey of every fifth *A. syriaca* plant. At least one anther was observed on 10 of these 14 plants.

Table 9.1. Survey of monarchs on milkweed with anthers in Bt and non-Bt cornfields

	Bt cornfields		Non-Bt cornfields	
	No. of plants examined	Plants with anthers	No. of plants examined	Plants with anthers
Plants with monarchs				
12 July	14	79%	6	100%
14 July	7	100%	4	75%
Plants without monarchs				
12 July	5	80%	12	92%
14 July	9	67%	4	75%

Note: The number of *A. syriaca* plants with at least one corn anther observed during a survey for monarch life stages in 2000. On 12 July, we sampled a Bt cornfield planted with Asgrow 730Bt and a non-Bt cornfield planted with Asgrow 730. On 14 July, we sampled a Bt cornfield planted with Pioneer 35N05 and a non-Bt cornfield planted with Garst Hybrids.

We observed monarchs on 10 plants growing in the non-Bt cornfields on 12 or 14 July. At least one anther was deposited on 9 of them (table 9.1). Of the additional 16 *A. syriaca* plants examined in the systematic survey of plants with no monarchs, one or more anthers were found on 14 plants.

Experimental cohort study: Uncaged *A. syriaca* 2000 and 2001

Results from the 2000 uncaged experimental cohort study have been published in the article by Stanley-Horn and coauthors (2001). Briefly, the results showed that the survival curves for monarch larvae on uncaged *A. syriaca* plants in 2000 were similar for monarch larvae in the Bt cornfields compared to larvae in the non-Bt cornfields (log-rank $p = 0.84$, Wilcoxon-signed rank test [WSRT] $p = 0.72$) (figure 9.1). The survival curves for uncaged cohorts of monarch larvae were similar for larvae in the Bt cornfield in 2000 and 2001 (log-rank $p = 0.60$, WSRT $p = 0.85$). The survival curves for larvae in the non-Bt cornfield in 2000 and 2001 were similar at the beginning and end of the sampling period, but survival from day 4 to 10 was higher in 2001 ($p = 0.32$, log-rank $p = 0.01$) (figure 9.1).

Experimental cohort study: Caged *A. syriaca* 2001

We observed a trend of higher survival to the adult stage among monarch larvae exposed to non-Bt corn pollen and anthers (56%) compared to survival of larvae in the Bt cornfields (23%). Of the 48 larvae exposed to Bt corn pollen and anthers, 11 survived to adulthood, while 28 of 50 larvae exposed to non-Bt corn pollen and anthers survived to adulthood, a 33% increase in survival. An initial decline in survival we observed during the first day was likely due to larval wandering and predation (figure 9.2). No predators were observed in field cages after the first 4 days. After 7 days in the cornfields, we observed no additional mortality in the larvae in the non-Bt cornfields, whereas mortality in the Bt cornfields continued to occur until day 22 (figure 9.2). The difference in the survival of monarch larvae in the Bt cornfield compared to the non-Bt cornfield was not significant at the 0.05 level ($F = 8.5$, $df = 1, 2$, $p = 0.10$). Larvae from the non-Bt cornfield pupated between days 12 and 18, and those from the Bt fields pupated between days 13 and 17 and on day 21.

Masses of pupae from larvae reared in the Bt and non-Bt cornfields were similar (Bt: 1.2 ± 0.05 g, $n = 11$; non-Bt: 1.1 ± 0.03 g, $n = 29$; $F = 1.13$, $df = 1$,

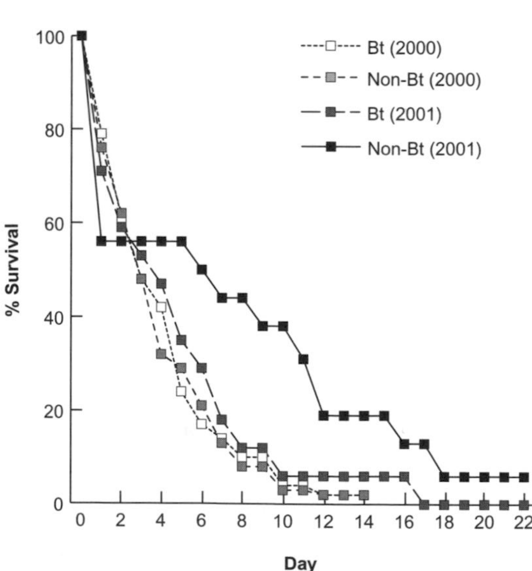

Figure 9.1. Survival rates for experimental cohorts of monarch larvae placed on uncaged *Asclepias syriaca* in Bt and non-Bt cornfields in 2000 and 2001. Data from 2000 reported in Stanley-Horn et al. 2001.

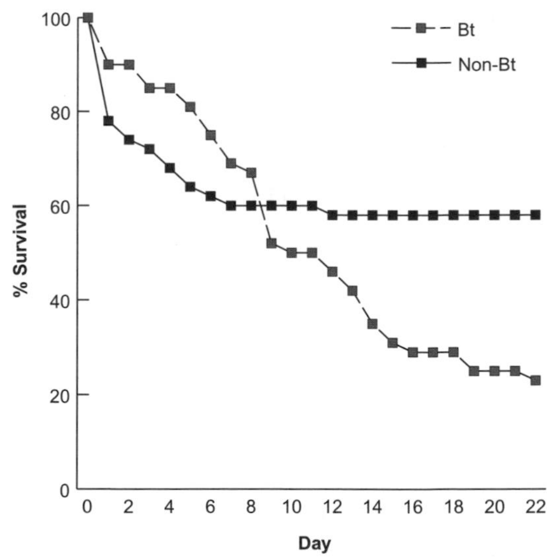

Figure 9.2. Survival rates for an experimental cohort of monarch larvae on caged *A. syriaca* plants, which minimized predation, in Bt and non-Bt cornfields. Larvae in the non-Bt cornfield entered the pupal stage on days 12 to 18, larvae in the Bt cornfield entered the pupal stage on days 13 to 17 and day 21. Pupae are included in the percentage surviving.

Table 9.2. Percentage of *A. syriaca* with anthers in Bt and non-Bt cornfields

Farm	Bt cornfield			Non-Bt cornfield		
	Pollen	Anthers	Plants with anthers	Pollen	Anthers	Plants with anthers
BU	154 ± 23 (64–253) *n* = 7	23 ± 9 (0–68) *n* = 7	86%	154 ± 59 (28–306) *n* = 4	10 ± 8 (0–19) *n* = 5	80%
BR	111 ± 51 (32–260) *n* = 4	10 ± 7 (1–30) *n* = 4	100%	47 ± 13 (9–82) *n* = 6	17 ± 4 (3–28) *n* = 6	100%
AG	175 ± 22 (114–299) *n* = 8	45 ± 12 (2–104) *n* = 9	100%	60 ± 8 (18–109) *n* = 9	16 ± 4 (0–34) *n* = 9	89%

Note: The average number of pollen grains/cm^2 ± standard error (range), the average number of anthers/plant ± standard error (range), and the percentage of *A. syriaca* plants with anthers within Bt and non-Bt cornfields in 2001. We sampled fields at Burkey Farm (BU), Bruner Farm (BR), and Agronomy Farm (AG), Iowa State University research farms near Ames.

38, $p = 0.29$). Average wing lengths were also similar (Bt: 5.0 ± 0.06 cm, $n = 8$; non-Bt: 4.9 ± 0.05 cm, $n = 28$; $F = 2.09$, $df = 1, 37$, $p = 0.16$), as were dry masses of adults (Bt: 0.18 ± 0.01 g, $n = 8$; non-Bt: 0.16 ± 0.01 g, $n = 28$; $F = 1.48$, $df = 1, 37$, $p = 0.23$). No sublethal effects of Bt corn tissue consumption were observed.

Pollen densities on milkweed leaves within Bt cornfields ranged from 52 to 315 pollen grains/cm^2, with an average of 240 ± 28 pollen grains/cm^2 ($n = 20$) (table 9.2). Anther densities on the *A. syriaca* plants in the Bt cornfields ranged from 0 to 104 anthers/plant (mean = 30 ± 7 anthers/plant, $n = 20$). Pollen densities within the non-Bt cornfields ranged from 39 to 490 pollen grains/cm^2 (mean = 121 ± 24 pollen grains/cm^2, $n = 19$, table 9.2). Anther densities on the *A. syriaca* plants in the non-Bt cornfields ranged from 0 to 34 anthers/plant (mean = 15 ± 2 anthers/plant, $n = 20$, table 9.2).

DISCUSSION

Quantification of anthers on milkweeds in cornfields

In the 2000 survey of naturally occurring milkweed plants we observed at least one anther on 84% of the plants. In 2001 anthers were present on 93% of the milkweed plants transplanted into cornfields, with densities ranging from 0 to 104 anthers/plant. Anthers are much larger (approximately 5 mm) than pollen grains (approximately 0.09 mm, or 90 µm), and there are a limited number of anthers on each corn tassel. However, anthers have higher levels of the Bt toxin than pollen does, which, combined with their larger size, makes it difficult to calculate the amount of Bt toxin on *A. syriaca* from both anthers and pollen. Anthers adhered to *A. syriaca* with moisture from rain and dew, and therefore were eaten by larger monarch instars (pers. observ.).

Our results demonstrate that monarch larvae feeding on milkweed plants within Bt cornfields will be exposed to anthers expressing the Bt toxin. Studies are needed to determine stage-specific consumption rates of anthers by monarch larvae (Hileman 2001). Laboratory bioassays using Bt corn pollen and anthers that have been sifted through mesh screens (which break anthers into smaller pieces) have documented a higher mortality of first instars compared to mortality from exposure to only Bt pollen (Hellmich et al. 2001). As with pollen, the densities of anthers on nontarget host plants outside of cornfields would likely decline rapidly from field edges (Jesse and Obrycki 2000; Pleasants et al. 2001; Zangerl et al. 2001).

Survival of experimental cohorts of monarch larvae in Bt and non-Bt fields

In 2000, we observed similar rates of mortality of monarch larvae on uncaged *A. syriaca* plants in Bt and non-Bt cornfields (data reported in Stanley-Horn et al. 2001). Data from experimental cohorts of monarch larvae placed in Bt and non-Bt cornfields in New York showed similar patterns of mortality (Stanley-Horn et al. 2001). In an Illinois cornfield Zangerl and coworkers (2001) observed over 120 arthropods, many predaceous, occurring on 24 *A. syriaca* plants over a 5-day study period. In our 2000 field survey of 331 *A. syriaca* plants with monarchs, aphids infested 9% of the plants, and predaceous arthropods were observed on 15% of the plants (Jesse 2001). These studies in Illinois (Zangerl et al. 2001) and Iowa (Jesse 2001) and those reported by Prysby (this volume) suggest that predation is a significant mortality factor of young monarch larvae. Life table analysis shows high levels of monarch mortality (92% to 98% from eggs to late instars), which may conceal an additional mortality factor (Zalucki and Kitching 1982; Jesse and Obrycki 2003), making experimental exclusion of mortality from predation important in any field assessment of the effect of Bt corn tissues on monarch survival (Carey 1993).

In the 2001 experimental cohort study, we minimized predation through mechanical exclusion to quantify mortality due to exposure to Bt corn pollen and anthers. We observed a trend toward higher rates of mortality of larvae in Bt cornfields. This trend was observed even though the number of degrees of freedom (1, 2) was relatively low. These observations differ from those of Stanley-Horn and coworkers (2001), who also caged monarch larvae on *A. syriaca* plants in Event Bt11 cornfields to minimize predation, and reported no increase in mortality. In their caged studies, first or third instars remained in the field for only 5 days and were primarily second or fourth instars, respectively, when returned to the laboratory. As a result of this relatively short field exposure, in most cases only one larval stage was exposed to Bt corn pollen and anthers (Stanley-Horn et al. 2001). In our study, monarch larvae remained in the field until the *A. syriaca* plants were consumed. Larvae brought into the laboratory and fed clean *A. syriaca* leaves were fourth and fifth instars (with the exception of one third instar) that had been in the field for 8 to 18 days. Two factors may contribute to the lack of a Bt corn effect observed by Stanley-Horn and coworkers (2001): (1) first instars placed in the field may not have consumed anthers because of the relatively large size of this plant tissue, and (2) third instars were probably large enough to consume anthers, but if the effect of Bt toxin is cumulative, the field exposure time (5 days) may have been too short to cause measurably higher mortality.

Spatial overlap of monarch larvae and Bt corn tissues within cornfields

Initial concern about the effects of Bt corn on monarch larvae was dismissed by some because it was assumed that agricultural fields were milkweed free due to weed suppression techniques, thus limiting monarch exposure to Bt corn pollen (Shelton and Roush 1999). However, public and regulatory concerns about the potential risks of Bt corn pollen for monarchs have resulted in further investigations, which determined that milkweeds occur within and near cornfields (Hartzler and Buhler 2000), monarchs utilize milkweeds in the cornfields (Jesse 2001; Oberhauser et al. 2001), and phenological overlap exists between corn anthesis and susceptible larval stages (Oberhauser et al. 2001).

The occurrence of immature stages of monarchs on *A. syriaca* plants in cornfields, cornfield edges, soybean fields, forage crop fields, and nonagricultural land was determined at several sites in North America (Oberhauser et al. 2001). Immature monarchs were present in all habitats throughout the summer; the temporal overlap between the peak of the immature migratory generation of monarchs and corn pollination ranged from 15% in Iowa to 62% in Ontario (Oberhauser et al. 2001). Nonagricultural habitats in Ontario produced approximately 100 times more monarchs than did cornfields on a per area basis; nonagricultural habitats were 2 times more productive in Minnesota and Wisconsin and 4 times more productive in Iowa (Oberhauser et al. 2001). However, the proportion of agricultural land is so high compared to the total land area in these states that Oberhauser and colleagues (2001) estimated that 73 (Minnesota and Wisconsin) and 43 (Iowa) times more monarchs are being produced from milkweeds in cornfields than in nonagricultural land. These results indicate that increases in within-field mortality of monarch larvae due to the deposition of transgenic Bt anthers and pollen on *A. syriaca* could harm monarch populations (Oberhauser et al. 2001).

The initial focus on the potential effects of Bt corn on monarch butterflies was on the potential for pollen drift outside of fields. A number of studies examined the deposition of pollen on plants at gradients from field edges (Jesse and Obrycki 2000; Pleasants et al. 2001; Zangerl et al. 2001). In these out-of-field pollen drift studies, a focus on the concentration of Bt toxin in pollen would be appropriate (Hellmich et al. 2001). However, given that milkweeds are relatively abundant in cornfields (Hartzler and Buhler 2000), and in the Midwest, cornfields are a major source of adult monarchs (Oberhauser et al. 2001), within-field aspects of the interaction between Bt corn and monarchs need to be examined.

The present study demonstrates that anthers from Bt corn plants are deposited frequently on milkweed plants. Our previous study, which examined within-field and edge effects of the anthers and pollen from Bt corn, showed significant increases in the mortality of monarch larvae exposed to these plant tissues (Jesse and Obrycki 2000). In this study, we have documented trends toward increased mortality caused by exposure to Bt corn tissue of monarch larvae that were caged to exclude mortality due to predation. Multiple biotic factors (i.e., predation and Bt toxin) are likely interacting to cause the mortality of monarch larvae in Bt cornfields.

Acknowledgments

The Leopold Center for Sustainable Agriculture, Ames, Iowa, and the U.S. Department of Agriculture Monarch/Bt Corn grant program provided funds for this research. Laura Jesse was supported by an EPA STAR Fellowship. We would also like to thank Mark Anderson, Barb Benjerdes, Susan Chapman, Lindsay Clark, Kristen Nonnecke, John Ohlfest, and Neil Stensland for their assistance. This is Journal Paper No. J-19646 of the Iowa Agriculture and Home Economics Experiment Station, Ames, Iowa, Project No. 3437 and supported by Hatch Act and State of Iowa funds.

References

Borkin, S. S. 1982. Notes on shifting distribution patterns and survival of immature *Danaus plexippus* (Lepidoptera: Danaidae) on the food plant *Asclepias syriaca*. Gt. Lakes Entomol. 15:199–206.

Carey, J. R. 1993. Applied demography for biologists. New York: Oxford University Press.

Donham, P., and O. R. Taylor. 2000. In the classroom, research projects: Size and mass. Monarch Watch. http://monarchwatch.org/class/studproj/mass.htm. Accessed 2 June 2003.

EPA (Environmental Protection Agency). 2000. Bt corn data call-in 15/12/99. Office of Pesticide Programs: US Environmental Protection Agency. http://www.epa.gov/pesticides/biopesticides/otherdocs/bt_dci.htm. Accessed 6 March 2001.

Hartzler, R. G., and D. D. Buhler. 2000. Occurrence of common milkweed (*Asclepias syriaca*) in cropland and adjacent areas. Crop Prot. 19:363–66.

Hellmich, R. L., B. D. Siegfried, M. K. Sears, D. E. Stanley-Horn, M. J. Daniels, H. R. Mattila, T. Spencer, K. G. Bidne, and L. C. Lewis. 2001. Monarch larvae sensitivity to *Bacillus thuringiensis*-purified proteins and pollen. Proc. Natl. Acad. Sci. USA 98:11925–30.

Hileman, B. 2001. Engineered corn poses small risk. Chem. Eng. News 79:11.

Jesse, L. C. H. 2001. The effects of Bt corn pollen on two non-target lepidopteran species, *Danaus plexippus* (Lepidoptera: Danaidae) and *Euchatias egle* (Lepidoptera: Arctiidae). Master's thesis, Iowa State University, Ames.

Jesse, L. C. H., and J. J. Obrycki. 2000. Field deposition of Bt transgenic corn pollen: lethal effects on the monarch butterfly. Oecologia 125:241–48.

Jesse, L. C. H., and J. J. Obrycki. 2003. Occurence of *Danaus plexippus* L. (Lepidoptera: Danaidae) on milkweeds (*Asclepias syriaca*) in transgenic Bt corn agroecosystems. Ag., Eco., & Enviro. In Press.

Kiesselbach, T. A. 1999. The structure and reproduction of corn. 50th anniversary ed. Cold Spring Harbor, N.Y.: Cold Spring Harbor Laboratory Press.

Losey, J. E., L. S. Rayor, and M. E. Carter. 1999. Transgenic pollen harms monarch larvae. Nature 399:214.

Oberhauser, K. S., M. D. Prysby, H. R. Mattila, D. E. Stanley-Horn, M. K. Sears, G. Dively, E. Olson, J. M. Pleasants, W. F. Lam, and R. L. Hellmich. 2001. Temporal and spatial overlap between monarch larvae and corn pollen. Proc. Natl. Acad. Sci. USA 98:11913–18.

Pleasants, J. M., R. L. Hellmich, G. P. Dively, M. K. Sears, D. E. Stanley-Horn, H. R. Mattila, J. E. Foster, T. L. Clark, and G. D. Jones. 2001. Corn pollen deposited on milkweeds in and near cornfields. Proc. Natl. Acad. Sci. USA 98:11919–24.

Sears, M. K., R. L. Hellmich, D. E. Stanley-Horn, K. S. Oberhauser, J. M. Pleasants, H. R. Mattila, B. D. Siegfried, and G. P. Dively. 2001. Impact of Bt corn pollen on monarch butterfly populations: a risk assessment. Proc. Natl. Acad. Sci. USA 98:11937–42.

Shelton, A. M., and R. T. Roush. 1999. False reports and the ears of men. Nat. Biotechnol. 17:832.

Stanley-Horn, D. E., G. P. Dively, R. L. Hellmich, H. R. Mattila, M. K. Sears, R. Rose, L. C. H. Jesse, J. E. Losey, J. J. Obrycki, and L. Lewis. 2001. Assessing the impact of Cry1Ab-expressing corn pollen on monarch butterfly larvae in field studies. Proc. Natl. Acad. Sci. USA 98:11931–6.

Wraight, C. L., A. R. Zangerl, M. J. Carroll, and M. R. Berenbaum. 2000. Absence of toxicity of *Bacillus thuringiensis* pollen to black swallowtails under field conditions. Proc. Natl. Acad. Sci. USA 97:7700–3.

Zalucki, M. P., and R. L. Kitching. 1982. Dynamics of oviposition in *Danaus plexippus* (Insecta: Lepidoptera) on milkweed, *Asclepias spp.* J. Zool. Lond. 198:103–16.

Zangerl, A. R., D. McKenna, C. L. Wraight, M. Carroll, P. Ficarello, R. Warner, and M. R. Berenbaum. 2001. Effects of exposure to event 176 *Bacillus thuringiensis* corn pollen on monarch and black swallowtail caterpillars under field conditions. Proc. Natl. Acad. Sci. USA 98:11908–12.

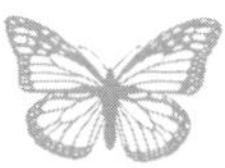

PART II

Migration Biology

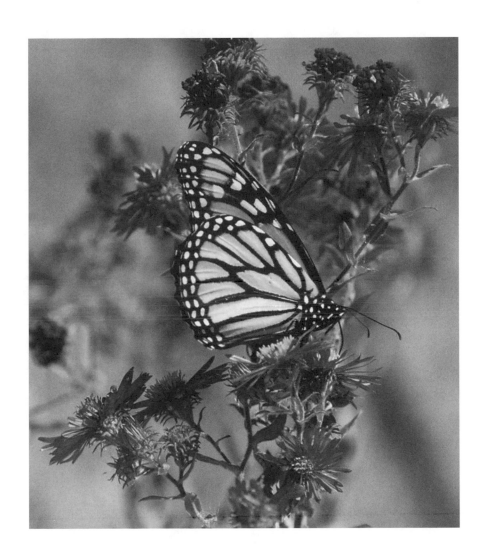

10

Overview of Monarch Migration

Michelle J. Solensky

Unlike most temperate insects, monarch butterflies cannot survive a long cold winter. Every fall, North American monarchs fly south to spend the winter at roosting sites. In the spring, these overwintering monarchs fly north toward their breeding range. The monarch is the only butterfly to make such a long, two-way migration, flying up to 4830 kilometers (3000 miles) in the fall to reach their winter destination (Urquhart and Urquhart 1978). Monarchs that live east of the Rocky Mountains generally fly to overwintering sites in the mountains of central Mexico, while monarchs west of the Rocky Mountains typically overwinter along the California coast (figure 10.1a). Recent field work suggests that some western monarchs move south and southeast out of the inland northwest and Great Basin, entering the Mexican state of Sonora from Arizona. The number and winter destination of these monarchs have not yet been determined (Pyle 2000; Brower and Pyle, in press). It has been proposed that this western North American population is not truly migratory but rather represents an annual expansion and contraction of the range of California monarchs (Wenner and Harris 1993). That is, these monarchs may be year-round residents of California whose offspring are able to spread to surrounding states during the mild summer weather but are forced to return to California or perish when the inhospitable northern winters return. This issue is still being debated and offers great potential (and substantial challenges) for study by West Coast residents.

In Australia, monarchs sometimes exhibit seasonal movement, but they move from inland to coastal areas in a north to northeasterly direction during the fall and winter (James 1993). Because the most spectacular monarch migrations (in terms of distance and numbers of migrants) occur in the eastern North American population, much of the research on monarch migration has focused on this population. Amazingly, these butterflies fly from their summer breeding range, which spans more than 100 million ha, to winter roosts that cover less than 20 ha, often to the exact same trees, year after year. Since the discovery of these winter roosts in Mexico by the scientific community in 1975 (Urquhart 1976), researchers have struggled to understand the cues that cause monarchs to begin their migration, the mechanisms they use to orient and find the overwintering sites, and the patterns of fall and spring flight.

INITIATION OF FALL MIGRATORY BEHAVIOR

Spring and summer monarchs become reproductive within a few days of eclosion. Late-summer and early-fall monarchs emerge in reproductive diapause, which is a state of suspended reproductive development. Diapause is controlled by neural and hormonal changes triggered by environmental factors signaling the onset of unfavorable conditions. Goehring and Oberhauser (2002) found that decreasing daylength, fluctuating temperatures, and senescing host plants each caused an increase in the proportion of monarchs that emerged in reproductive diapause, but the strongest response occurred among monarchs exposed to all three cues. Making use of more than one cue to assess current and near future habitat suitability could be a more optimal strategy for organisms in unpredictable environments.

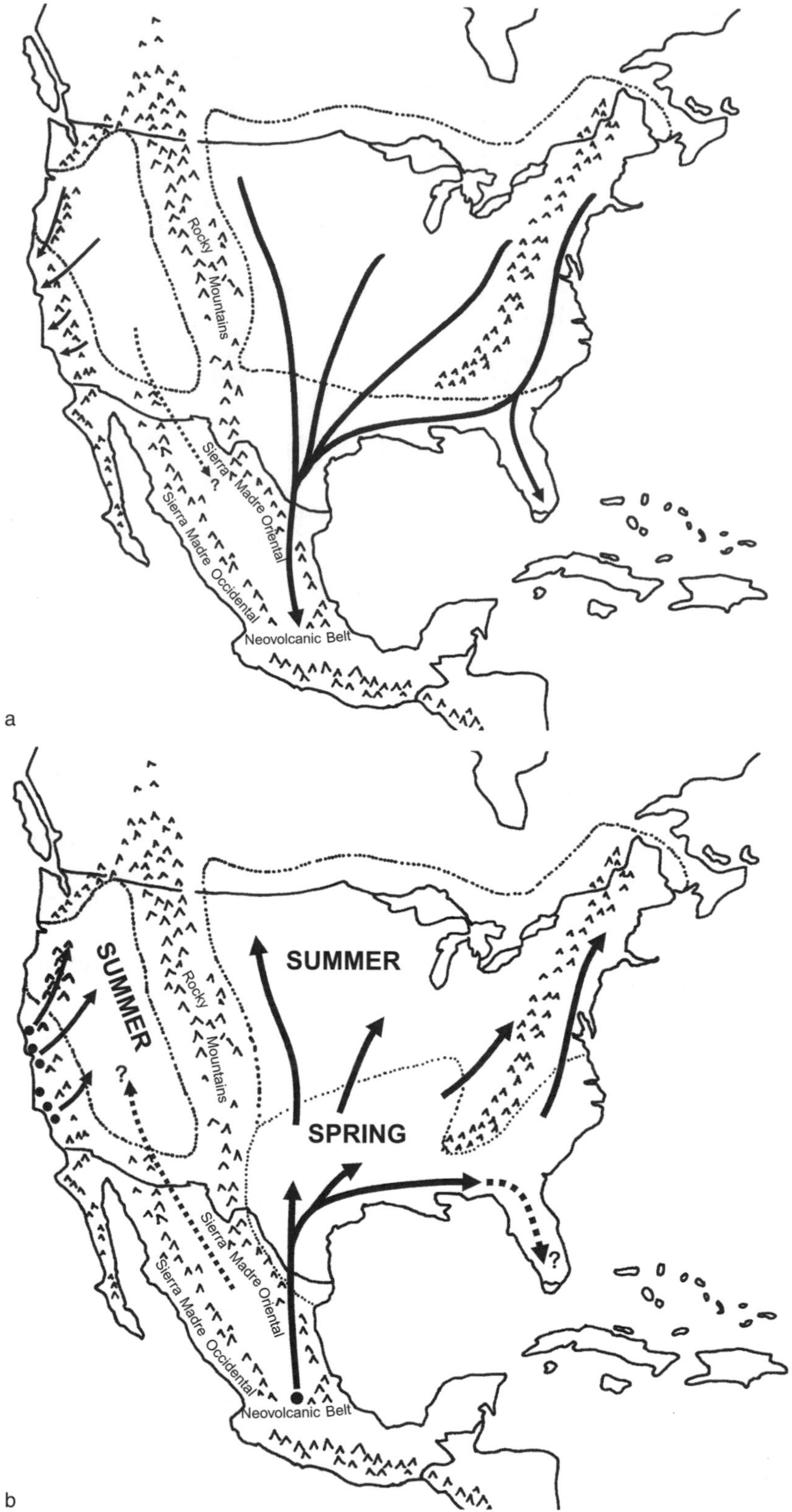

Figure 10.1. The (a) fall and (b) spring and summer migratory routes of North American monarchs. Dashed lines indicate hypothetical movement.

For many years, scientists have suspected that reproductive diapause and migratory behavior in monarchs are coupled. Perez and Taylor (chapter 11) tested this assumption by collecting fall migrants and exposing them to summer daylengths and temperatures. These manipulated butterflies exhibited reproductive behavior but continued to show migratory directionality in flight. These authors argue that while reproductive diapause can be readily reversed in fall migrants, migratory behavior is resistant to changes in environmental conditions. This hypothesis is supported by Borland and colleagues (chapter 13), who compared the reproductive status of monarchs collected in the northern and southern United States during the fall migration. More monarchs had mated in the South than in the North, which is consistent with the peak in egg and larva abundance typically observed in southern states during September and early October (Prysby and Oberhauser, this volume). Borland and colleagues also report a pattern of scale loss and wing damage that is consistent with increased mating activity in early migrants in the South.

ORIENTATION MECHANISMS

Orientation is not well understood in insects. In monarchs, orientation is especially mysterious. How do millions of monarchs start their southbound journey from all over eastern and central North America and end up in a very small area in the mountains of central Mexico? We know that they do not learn the route, since only about every fifth generation of monarchs makes the long migration to and from Mexico. Therefore, monarchs must rely on instincts to find overwintering sites. Other animals use celestial cues (the sun, moon, or stars), the earth's magnetic field, landmarks (mountain ranges or bodies of water), polarized light, infrared energy perception, or some combination of these cues. Calvert and Wagner (1999) proposed that mountain ranges and river valleys might be used by monarchs to orient during their migration, but celestial cues and the earth's magnetic field have been studied the most.

Since monarchs migrate during the day, the sun is the celestial cue most likely to be useful in pointing the way to the overwintering sites. Kanz (1977) and Schmidt-Koenig (1985, 1993) suggested that monarchs use the angle of the sun along the horizon in combination with an internal body clock to maintain a southwesterly flight path, and Mouritsen and Frost (2002) confirmed this hypothesis. Because monarchs often migrate on cloudy days, this sun compass must be combined with the use of some other cue. Scientists have suggested that monarchs may use a magnetic compass to orient, as has been demonstrated in some migratory birds (Wiltschko and Wiltschko 1972; Emlen et al. 1976). However, Mouritsen and Frost (2002) showed that migratory monarchs exhibited randomly oriented flight when presented with only magnetic field cues and did not respond to magnetic field shifts, suggesting that monarchs do not use the earth's magnetic field to orient during migration. They suggest that monarchs may use polarized light patterns, which penetrate cloud cover, to orient on cloudy days.

PATTERNS OF FALL MIGRATION

The fall migratory route of the eastern North American population is perhaps the most well-studied aspect of monarch biology (Brower 1977, 1985, 1995; Urquhart and Urquhart 1978; Monarch Watch 2001). The first large-scale study of the fall monarch migration began in 1937 when Dr. Fred Urquhart recruited volunteers to tag monarchs (Urquhart and Urquhart 1978). In the fall of 1992, a new volunteer-based tagging program was established by Monarch Watch (2001) to continue the study of fall migratory routes. These tagging programs have revealed much information about the patterns and timing of the fall monarch migration. More recently, Wassenaar and Hobson (1998) used stable isotopes to estimate the origin of monarchs overwintering in central Mexico. They found that about half of the monarchs collected from 13 overwintering sites had migrated from the midwestern United States, with smaller numbers originating from the northeastern United States and Canada. While tagging reveals patterns of individual fall migrants, stable isotope studies show promise for revealing population-level migratory patterns.

Long before scientists discovered the winter destination of migratory monarchs, they were aware of ephemeral aggregations of monarchs in the fall throughout the United States and Canada. Like migratory birds, monarchs make frequent stops during their migration. Monarchs form roosts at night and during inclement weather; these roosts range in size from a few dozen to a few thousand individuals. Scientists know very little about where and when monarchs stop during their migration. Davis and Garland (chapter 12) used methods from ornithological studies to investigate factors influencing monarch stopover decisions. They showed how monarch tags can be used not only to provide traditional information on routes of travel, but also for examining aspects of stopover behavior. They found that monarchs commonly stayed at the roosting site for at least 2 days, but that wind condition had only a small effect on the numbers of roosting monarchs. They suggest that the physical condition of monarchs may influence their decision to stop migrating, as they found that damaged monarchs were more numerous at roosting sites during favorable wind directions when they otherwise should have been migrating. Based on evidence from studies of avian migration, Davis and Garland propose that energy reserves may also influence the migration and stopover decisions of these butterflies, with monarchs staying longer at stopover sites when their lipid reserves are small. Borland and colleagues (chapter 13) investigate the relationships between body condition and migration by comparing the body size and reproductive status of monarchs collected in the northern and southern United States and early and late in the migration. Their results support the idea that energy reserves may influence monarch migration; monarchs collected in the South were heavier than those captured in the North, suggesting that nectaring along the migratory path results in weight gain and increased energy reserve. These results agree with those of Gibo and McCurdy (1993). We have much to learn about basic migration patterns and strategies in monarchs. Orientation mechanisms have gained much attention from researchers, but few studies have addressed stopover ecology or the characteristics of monarchs that increase migratory success. These two chapters make important contributions to these fields of studies, but emphasize that many questions remain unanswered, making this a fruitful area for future research.

INITIATION AND PATTERNS OF SPRING MIGRATION

Malcolm and colleagues (1993) and Cockrell and others (1993) reported the dates for the first sightings of eggs, larvae, and the larval host plants of adult monarchs arriving at different latitudes in eastern North America. These articles established the general pattern of spring movement and demonstrated that recolonization of the northern ranges of the breeding habitat occurs over two generations (figure 10.1b). The monarchs that overwinter in Mexico fly north to repopulate the southern half of the United States, and their offspring complete the journey to the northern United States and southern Canada.

Spring migratory routes are considerably more difficult to identify and study than fall routes because in the spring monarchs are dispersed and consequently are far less noticeable than the fall migrants that form spectacular roosts. Scientists have come to rely on citizens to help them gather information about spring monarch migration, in a partnership called "citizen science." Journey North was established in 1991 with two goals in mind: to improve science and math education and to study several species of migratory animals. This program involves schoolchildren from every U.S. state and seven Canadian provinces. These students report their first sightings of monarch butterflies every spring. Through these reports, we can learn about when and where monarchs travel as they migrate north in the spring. Howard and Davis (chapter 14) describe the patterns of spring migration and monarch abundance based on data collected by Journey North participants over a 6-year period from 1997 to 2002. They found a striking regularity of the migratory pattern from year to year, although the average arrival date at different latitudes and the duration of migration did vary between years. They suggest that this annual variation may stem from differences in environmental conditions or in the timing of milkweed emergence, and plan to investigate these potential causes using additional data collected by Journey North participants. This is the first published account of data from this incredibly successful citizen science program, and it attests to the value of collaboration between citizens and research scientists.

References

Brower, L. P. 1977. Monarch migration. Nat. Hist. 84:41–53.

Brower, L. P. 1985. New perspectives on the migration biology of the monarch butterfly, *Danaus plexippus* L. In M. A.

Rankin, ed., Migration: mechanisms and adaptive significance, pp. 748–85. Contributions in Marine Science, Vol. 27 Suppl. Port Aransas, Texas: Marine Science Institute, University of Texas at Austin.

Brower, L. P. 1995. Understanding and misunderstanding the migration of the monarch butterfly (Nymphalidae) in North America: 1857–1995. J. Lepid. Soc. 49:304–85.

Brower, L. P., and R. M. Pyle. In press. Interchange of migratory monarchs between Mexico and Western United States, and the importance of floral corridors to the fall and spring migrations. In G. Nabhan, ed., Migratory pollinators and their corridors. Tuscon: University of Arizona Press.

Calvert, W. H., and M. Wagner. 1999. Patterns in the monarch butterfly migration through Texas—1993 to 1995. In J. Hoth, L. Merino, K. Oberhauser, I. Pisantry, S. Price, and T. Wilkinson, eds., The 1997 North American Conference on the Monarch Butterfly, pp. 119–25. Montreal: Commission for Environmental Cooperation.

Cockrell, B. J., S. B. Malcolm, and L. P. Brower. 1993. Time, temperature and latitudinal constraints on the annual recolonization of eastern North America by the monarch butterfly. In S. B. Malcolm and M. P. Zalucki, eds., Biology and conservation of the monarch butterfly, pp. 233–51. Los Angeles: Natural History Museum of Los Angeles County.

Emlen, S. T., W. Wiltschko, N. Demong, R. Wiltschko, and S. Bergman. 1976. Magnetic direction finding in migratory indigo buntings. Science 193:505–8.

Gibo, D. L., and J. A. McCurdy. 1993. Lipid accumulation by migrating monarch butterflies (*Danaus plexippus* L.). Can. J. Zool. 71:76–82.

Goehring, L., and K. S. Oberhauser. 2002. Effects of photoperiod, temperature and host plant age on induction of reproductive diapause and development time in *Danaus plexippus*. Ecol. Entomol. 27:674–85.

James, D. G. 1993. Migration biology of the monarch butterfly in Australia. In S. B. Malcolm and M. P. Zalucki, eds., Biology and conservation of the monarch butterfly, pp. 189–200. Los Angeles: Natural History Museum of Los Angeles County.

Kanz, J. E. 1977. The orientation of migrant and non-migrant monarch butterflies, *Danaus plexippus* (L.). Psyche 84:120–41.

Malcolm, S. B., B. J. Cockrell, and L. P. Brower. 1993. Spring recolonization of eastern North America by the monarch butterfly: successive brood or single sweep migration? In S. B. Malcolm and M. P. Zalucki, eds., Biology and conservation of the monarch butterfly, pp. 253–67. Los Angeles: Natural History Museum of Los Angeles County.

Monarch Watch. 2001. Monarch watch migration and tagging. www.monarchwatch.org/tagmig/index.htm. Accessed 21 January 2003.

Mouritsen, H., and B. J. Frost. 2002. Virtual migration in tethered flying monarch butterflies reveals their orientation mechanisms. Proc. Natl. Acad. Sci. USA 99:10162–66.

Pyle, R. M. 2000. Chasing monarchs: migrating with the butterflies of passage. Boston: Houghton Mifflin.

Schmidt-Koenig, K. 1985. Migration strategies of monarch butterflies. In M. A. Rankin, ed., Migration: mechanisms and adaptive significance, pp. 786–98. Contributions in Marine Science, Vol. 27 Suppl. Port Aransas, Texas: Marine Science Institute, University of Texas at Austin.

Schmidt-Koenig, K. 1993. Orientation of autumn migration in the monarch butterfly. In S. B. Malcolm and M. P. Zalucki, eds., Biology and conservation of the monarch butterfly, pp. 275–83. Los Angeles: Natural History Museum of Los Angeles County.

Urquhart, F. A. 1976. Found at last; the monarch's winter home. Nat. Geogr. Mag. 150:161–73.

Urquhart, F. A., and N. R. Urquhart 1978. Autumnal migration routes of the eastern population of the monarch butterfly (*Danaus p. plexippus* L.; Danaidae; Lepidoptera) in North America to the overwintering site in the Neovolcanic Plateau of Mexico. Can. J. Zool. 56:1759–64.

Wassenaar, L. I., and K. A. Hobson. 1998. Natal origins of migratory monarch butterflies at wintering colonies in Mexico: new isotopic evidence. Proc. Natl. Acad. Sci. USA 95:15436–39.

Wenner, A. M., and A. M. Harris. 1993. Do California monarchs undergo long-distance directed migration? In S. B. Malcolm and M. P. Zalucki, eds., Biology and conservation of the monarch butterfly, pp. 275–83. Los Angeles: Natural History Museum of Los Angeles County.

Wiltschko, W., and R. Wiltschko. 1972. Magnetic compass of European robins. Science 176:62–64.

11

Monarch Butterflies' Migratory Behavior Persists despite Changes in Environmental Conditions

Sandra M. Perez and Orley R. Taylor

INTRODUCTION

Monarch butterflies in eastern North America are known for their extensive southbound migration in the fall. During this time, their range contracts severely from its spring and summer area to a much smaller area in the mountains of central Mexico's Transvolcanic Belt. The contraction of the range occurs as a result of active movement (migration) of adult monarchs to the overwintering sites in central Mexico.

Several generations each year develop, breed, and die in their summer grounds throughout the United States and southern Canada. Important environmental cues set the overwintering generation apart by initiating a change in reproductive condition and migratory state.

After eclosion, the ovaries and testes of spring and summer generations become mature in 3 to 7 days (Zalucki 1982; Oberhauser and Hampton 1995; Goehring and Oberhauser 1999, 2002). In contrast, monarch migrants, like most migrating insects, largely remain in an extended pre-reproductive state referred to as "diapause" (Dingle 1972; Herman 1981; Goehring and Oberhauser 2002). Reproductive diapause entails a delay in the physiological maturation of the butterfly's reproductive organs and the onset of reproductive behaviors such as mating and oviposition. Reproductive diapause is seen exclusively in monarchs that eclose in late summer and early fall, and is a response to environmental conditions associated with fall (e.g., decreasing photoperiod, fluctuating temperatures, increasing host plant age [Goehring and Oberhauser 1999, 2002]). It occurs in the same individuals that perform the long-distance migration to Mexico. The migratory condition is characterized most notably by flight behavior; as a group, monarchs observed in the fall show strong directional preferences for the south and southwest (Kanz 1977; Schmidt-Koenig 1985; this chapter). This behavior contrasts with that of reproductive summer monarchs, which show a random distribution in flight direction (Kanz 1977; this chapter). Directionality in flight behavior, therefore, is used here as the functional definition of being in migratory condition.

Reproductive diapause can be interrupted. The animals can be returned to normal reproductive behavior by extending the photoperiod and increasing temperatures (pers. observ.). Whether migratory condition can also be interrupted by a similar manipulation of environmental conditions has remained unanswered. In this study we changed the environmental conditions of the adults to reverse the diapause state and tested for changes in migratory condition.

METHODS

We conducted these experiments during August and September of 1997 and 1998. All monarchs tested were collected from the field while either foraging on flowers during the day or clustering in trees at night. None of the experimental subjects were reared in a lab.

For purposes of comparison, we conducted two experimental control treatments. Control I (nonmigratory control) entailed collecting monarch adults in Lawrence, Kansas, during August 1997, 2 to 4 weeks before migratory behavior becomes apparent in local monarchs. These butterflies were held in outdoor screen cages ($3\,m^3$) set up over cultivated fields of milkweed plants (*Asclepias curassavica*). During their outdoor captivity, butterflies fed on nectar from the milkweed flowers from one to several days before testing. The other comparison group, control II (migratory control), was collected in mid-September from nighttime clusters of migratory monarchs along the Kansas River near Lawrence, Kansas. Butterflies for control II were also housed in the outdoor screen cages from one to several days until testing.

Experiment I monarchs were collected with those for control II, but then held in indoor cages and fed on artificial nectar (Perez et al. 1999). To reverse the reproductive diapause condition common for migratory monarchs, we held them under an extended photoperiod (14-h light : 10-h dark) and higher temperatures (approximately 25°C) more typical of summer conditions. We monitored these butterflies at the end of each day and set aside each copulating pair. Once butterflies were observed *in copula* (3 to 8 days), we presumed that at least the male and possibly the female were out of diapause and tested the pair the next day. Flight directionality was tested outdoors under normal autumn conditions.

Our second experiment was conducted in order to compensate for the problem of having to release the subjects outdoors under autumn conditions, since our results (see below) could have been due to a physiological mechanism that could not be reversed or to the butterflies simply "reading" the local fall conditions. Ideally, we would artificially induce the migratory behavior in the lab, reverse the diapause, and then test for directionality under summertime conditions. Unfortunately, because no one has yet induced the migratory condition in the lab, we were unable to create migrants when and where we wanted them. Instead, we used monarchs that had been naturally induced to migrate in the North and shipped them south to summertime conditions for diapause reversal and directionality testing. Experiment II butterflies were collected from Madison, Wisconsin, as the migration was beginning in late August 1998. They were then shipped south overnight to Austin, Texas, through which monarchs normally pass in the late September and early October. In other words, the monarchs were advanced over 1600 km southward and 4 to 5 weeks temporally for this experiment. In Austin, they were held in an outdoor screen cage and fed artificial nectar for 6 to 7 days. Daytime temperatures during captivity rose to 30°C to 35°C in the afternoons. Whether these conditions caused a reversal of the diapause condition such as that seen in experiment I monarchs is uncertain. Our expectation was that their reproductive status would change and that the butterflies now being released free of all indications of autumn would not show directional flight. They were tested 6 to 7 days after transportation to Austin, since this was the amount of time needed to reverse diapause in most experiment I butterflies.

All of the subjects were tested in the same manner. We released them individually on sponges attached to the center of cardboard "launch pads" in an open field. Their tarsal claws hooked into the sponges, preventing them from being blown off the launch pads before they were flight ready. Releases occurred under mostly sunny conditions. Prior to release, butterflies were cooled (0°C to 4°C) to prevent an undirected escape response. Once a subject warmed up enough to leave its launch pad and begin directed flight, we followed it for approximately 1 to 5 min. When the subject's flight was steady for a minimum of 5 s, we recorded horizontal body orientation (or heading), which is the direction in which the butterfly's head points in flight. Using handheld compasses, we made direction measurements to the nearest 5° and made the appropriate declination adjustments for each site. All data were subsequently analyzed using circular statistics (Zar 1974). We used the Raleigh test of uniformity to determine whether groups showed significant directionality or random distributions. The length (r) of the mean vector (μ) was used to indicate the strength of the directionality, and the Watson-Williams F test to compare mean directions of different groups. We used $p < 0.01$ to indicate statistical significance.

RESULTS

Monarchs in control I (a nonmigratory group collected in early August) showed no directionality (figure 11.1, table 11.1). Those in control II (a

Table 11.1. Directional response of experimental monarchs

Group	Presumed reproductive state	Release conditions	n	Raleigh test of uniformity (p)	Mean direction	Observed migratory condition
Control I	Reproductive	Summer	71	>0.06	Random	Nonmigratory
Control II	Diapause	Fall	77	<0.01	SW (238°)	Migratory
Experiment I	Diapause to reproductive	Fall	76	<0.01	SSW (214°)	Migratory
Experiment II	Diapause to reproductive	Summer	29	<0.01	SW (257°)	Migratory

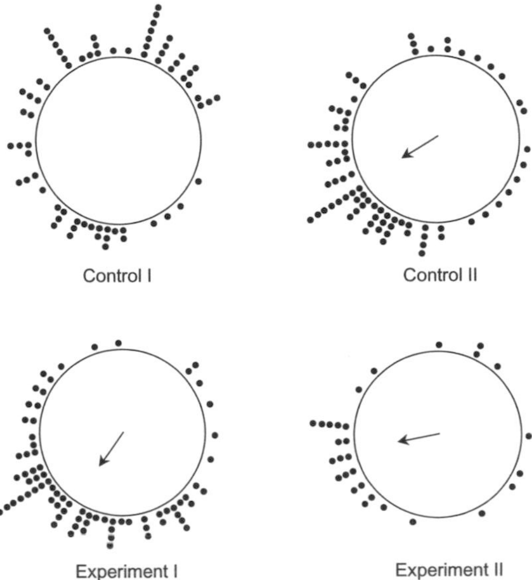

Figure 11.1. Nonmigratory monarchs (control I) show a random orientation, whereas migratory monarchs (control II) show significant directionality. Migratory behavior stays constant despite changes in the conditions of captivity (experiment I) and the conditions of release (experiment II).

migratory group collected in mid-September and then held outdoors in Kansas) showed directional flight to the southwest (figure 11.1, table 11.1). Experiment I butterflies, collected in migratory condition but experimentally manipulated to reverse diapause, continued to show migratory behavior as demonstrated by the groups' significant directionality toward the southwest (figure 11.1, table 11.1). These results were no different when the females were compared with the males (Watson-Williams $F = 1.34$, $p = 0.25$), which is important because we were certain only of the diapause reversal for the males.

In experiment II, monarchs that were advanced ahead of the normal migratory conditions to an area where no monarchs were migrating yet, and that were presumably taken out of diapause, continued to show significant directionality toward the southwest (figure 11.1, table 11.1). Although experiment II butterflies flew in a slightly different direction than experiment I butterflies (Watson-Williams $F = 7.73$, $p = 0.01$), the results are not significantly different from the control II results (Watson-William $F = 1.53$, $p = 0.22$).

DISCUSSION

The migratory state, which includes directional flight, of monarchs appears to be resistant to environmental changes. Once the migratory behavior has been induced, they continue to show directional flight in spite of changes in reproductive physiology or the seasonal time and place of their release. It appears that once triggered, the migratory condition stays "on" until the monarchs arrive at their overwintering destination. Although it is probably the case that most, if not all, monarchs are in a nonreproductive state at the time the migration is initiated (Goehring and Oberhauser 1999, 2002), our results suggest that reproductive diapause is not a necessary condition for the butterflies that migrate in the fall.

The resistance of migratory behavior to environmental change contrasts with reproductive diapause, which can be reversed by changing the ambient temperature and photoperiod to which the monarchs are exposed. Indeed, the independence of diapause and migration is indicated by the slow reversal of diapause beginning in February at the overwintering sites (Van Hook 1993; Goehring and Oberhauser, this volume). Monarchs begin to mate at the overwintering colonies in the middle of February and are reproductive as they move north, with the females laying eggs on newly emerged spring milkweeds as they migrate north-northeast through Mexico and the southern United States from late February through April.

The factors that induce migratory behavior and reproductive diapause appear to be different, but causal relationships are only partly understood. There is evidence that migratory behavior is associated with a change in sun angle (the angle of the sun above the horizon at noon) in the fall and the spring (O. R. Taylor and D. L. Gibo, pers. comm.). Although the passage of the migration through each latitude is correlated with sun angles ranging from 56° to 47° in the fall, migratory behavior appears to be induced by conditions or environmental cues that occur before the declining sun angle reaches 56° in the fall. The nature of these conditions and how they are perceived is unknown. Goehring and Oberhauser (1999, 2002) have proposed that diapause is induced by a combination of conditions that include host plant quality, the rate of change of daylength, and the difference between daytime and nighttime temperatures. A difficulty with this interpretation is that the rate of change of daylength in the prediapause period declines from north to south. For monarchs to be responding to rates of daylength changes, they would be responding to different rates at different latitudes. James (1982, 1993) suggested that diapause in Australian monarchs can be induced in the adult stage by increasing the difference between daytime and nighttime temperatures in the early fall. Regardless of what factors trigger the diapause, it is apparent that the diapause condition can be reversed more easily than the migratory state by changing environmental conditions.

The results of this study suggest several lines of research. One task will be to identify the environmental triggers of the migration. Another will be to identify the cues at the overwintering sites that cause the end of the southbound movements. Factors that initiate the remigration of the overwintering monarchs also need to be defined. These studies and others will lead ultimately to identification of the genes that are turned on and off to allow the extraordinary seasonal migration of monarchs and possibly many other insects.

Acknowledgments

We wish to thank Randy Korb, Rick Campbell, Bill Calvert, and Karen Oberhauser. Support for this study was provided by a National Science Foundation Starter Grant to S. Perez, Monarch Watch, and the College of Science of the University of Texas at El Paso.

References

Dingle, H. 1972. Migration strategies of insects. Science 4028:1327–35.

Goehring, L., and K. Oberhauser. 1999. Environmental induction of reproductive diapause in *Danaus plexippus.* In J. Hoth, L. Merino, K. Oberhauser, I. Pisantry, S. Price, and T. Wilkinson, eds., The 1997 North American Conference on the Monarch Butterfly, pp. 89–100. Montreal: Commission for Environmental Cooperation.

Goehring, L., and K. Oberhauser. 2002. Effects of photoperiod, temperature and host plant age on induction of reproductive diapause and development time in *Danaus plexippus.* Ecol. Entomol. 27:674–85.

Herman, W. S. 1981. Studies on the adult reproductive diapause of the monarch butterfly, *Danaus plexippus.* Biol. Bull. 160:89–106.

James, D. G. 1982. Ovarian dormancy in *Danaus plexippus* (L.) (Lepidoptera Nymphalidae)—oligopause not diapause. J. Aust. Entomol. Soc. 21:31–35.

James, D. G. 1993. Migration biology of monarchs in Australia. In S. B. Malcolm and M. P. Zalucki, eds., Biology and conservation of the monarch butterfly, pp. 189–200. Los Angeles: Natural History Museum of Los Angeles County.

Kanz, J. E. 1977. The orientation of migrant and non-migrant monarch butterflies, *Danaus plexippus* (L.). Psyche 84:120–41.

Oberhauser, K. S., and R. Hampton. 1995. The relationship between mating and oogenesis in monarch butterflies (Lepidoptera: Danainae). J. Insect Behav. 8:701–13.

Perez, S. M., O. R. Taylor, and R. Jander. 1999. Testing monarch butterfly orientation in the field during the autumn migration. In J. Hoth, L. Merino, K. Oberhauser, I. Pisantry, S. Price, and T. Wilkinson, eds., The 1997 North American Conference on the Monarch Butterfly, pp. 127–32. Montreal: Commission for Environmental Cooperation.

Schmidt-Koenig, K. 1985. Migration strategies of monarch butterflies. In M. A. Rankin, ed., Migration: mechanisms and adaptive significance, pp. 786–98. Contributions in Marine Science, Vol. 27 Suppl. Port Aransas, Texas: Marine Science Institute, University of Texas at Austin.

Van Hook, T. 1993. Non-random mating in monarch butterflies overwintering in Mexico. In S. B. Malcolm and M. P. Zalucki, eds., Biology and conservation of the monarch butterfly, pp. 49–60. Los Angeles: Natural History Museum of Los Angeles County.

Zalucki, M. P. 1982. Temperature and rate of development in *Danaus plexippus* L. and *D. chrysippus* L. (Lepidoptera: Nymphalidae). J. Aust. Entomol. Soc. 21:241–46.

Zar, J. H. 1974. Biostatistical analysis, pp. 615–59. 3rd ed. Upper Saddle River, N.J.: Prentice Hall.

12

Stopover Ecology of Monarchs in Coastal Virginia: Using Ornithological Techniques to Study Monarch Migration

Andrew K. Davis and Mark S. Garland

INTRODUCTION

The general migration strategy of monarch butterflies in eastern North America has been well documented and studied (e.g., Brower 1995, 1996; Knight et al. 1999), and their overwintering destination is widely known and has itself been the subject of study (Calvert et al. 1983, 1986; Brower and Calvert 1985). There are also many large-scale, long-term monarch migration monitoring projects, such as Monarch Watch (Taylor 1997), Texas Monarch Watch (Texas Monarch Watch 2002), the Monarch Monitoring Project in Cape May, New Jersey (Walton and Brower 1996), and Journey North (Howard and Davis, this volume). These projects focus on mapping migration routes and documenting seasonal and spatial distribution along the migration pathways. Here, we introduce a new area of research in monarch migration, that of stopover ecology.

Monarchs, like most landbird migrants, must make frequent stops during their migration. Where and for how long birds choose to stop during migration is not random, and it may not be for monarchs as well. Researchers refer to sites at which birds stop as "stopover sites," and to this area of research as "stopover ecology." It is widely accepted that stopover sites represent crucial links between avian breeding and wintering areas, and that suitable sites are necessary for successful migrations (Hutto 1998); birds can rest, avoid predators, forage, and refuel their energy supply (fat stores) at these sites. We suggest that monarchs must face similar needs during migration.

Typically, a researcher studying avian stopover ecology traps birds at areas where they accumulate, individually marks them with numbered leg bands, and makes behavioral observations while the birds are present. Birds rarely stay more than a few days at most sites, so there is usually a constant turnover of individuals. The same should be true for areas where monarchs tend to concentrate each fall.

Determining what constitutes suitable stopover sites for birds involves comparing stopover durations over numerous sites and differing habitats within the migration route (e.g., Davis 2001; Schaub et al. 2001). It is commonly assumed that migrating birds do not stay long in an unsuitable site (Morris 1996); areas where birds routinely stay longer than a day are considered suitable sites. To determine stopover durations, birds must be captured at least twice (e.g., Latta and Brown 1999).

Wing tags for monarchs are easily acquired and used by many butterfly enthusiasts and professional researchers. The main goal of tagging efforts thus far has been to determine migration routes (Taylor 1997), speed of travel (Garland and Davis 2002), and recovery rates in Mexico (Taylor 1997). Here, we used wing tags to determine how long monarchs stop at our site in the same way that ornithologists use leg bands.

Radar counts of birds have been compared to weather variables in many studies (Richardson 1972, 1978, 1990). This research has shown that the most important weather variables influencing the number of landbird migrants in the air are wind direction and speed. In addition, wind conditions influence the numbers and condition of birds that become grounded at stopover sites (Davis 1999). It is clear that monarch flight strategies are influenced by wind conditions (Gibo and Pallett 1979; Schmidt-Koenig 1985). Because of this, wind conditions also affect the counts of migrating monarchs utilizing specific flight strategies (Davis and Garland 2002); monarchs fly close to the ground when they encounter headwinds and soar high during tailwinds. Furthermore, monarchs tagged during favorable wind conditions travel faster than those tagged during unfavorable winds (Garland and Davis 2002). Thus, wind clearly influences the migratory flight of monarchs. However, there is little published information on how wind conditions influence monarchs' stopover decisions.

Our research documents some general aspects of the stopover ecology of monarchs at a known monarch concentration site in coastal Virginia. Specifically, we attempted to determine (1) the number of days monarchs commonly spend at the site; (2) whether there are sex-related differences in stopover durations; (3) the influence of wind conditions on stopover decisions; (4) the influence of wind conditions on stopover duration; and (5) whether the decision to stop is related to the physical condition of the monarchs. We discuss the implications of our results for monarch taggers and explain how they can incorporate our methods into existing programs.

METHODS

Study site

We studied the stopover ecology of monarchs on the southern tip of the Delmarva Peninsula (the outer barrier of the Delaware Bay in Virginia) at the Coastal Virginia Wildlife Observatory (CVWO; in Kiptopeke State Park 5 km from the end of the peninsula), the Eastern Shore of Virginia National Wildlife Refuge (ESVNWR; 1 km from the end of the peninsula), as well as in surrounding areas within a 5-km radius. Further detail of the study site is provided elsewhere (Garland and Davis 2002). We had previously found that large numbers of monarchs migrate through this area each fall and concentrate at the southern tip of the peninsula, allowing large amounts of data collection in a single season.

Field methods

To document the temporal distribution of monarch migration, we used a point-count technique common in studies of migrating raptors. During the fall of 2000 we counted all monarchs seen from the CVWO hawkwatching platform in Kiptopeke State Park. The platform is approximately 5 m above ground, with good visibility in a 360° radius. CVWO employs a hawkwatcher to count migrating raptors from this platform during the fall, and this individual counted any monarchs seen during the raptor count. The daily counting period was divided into three segments—from 1 h after sunrise until 10:00 AM, from 10:30 AM to 1:00 PM, and from 1:30 to 4:00 PM. We considered the total number of monarchs seen from the hawkwatch platform to be indicative of the number of monarchs actively migrating through our study area.

At the end of every day we counted all monarchs at a known accumulation site located near the hawkwatching site. The site is a 1-ha area located at the extreme southern tip of the Delmarva Peninsula that is owned and protected by the ESVNWR. This point of land represents one of the last places where monarchs can stop and rest before crossing the Delaware Bay. We had found previously that monarchs tended to concentrate in this area, roosting in two to three specific trees each fall (Garland and Davis 2002). We visited this site daily just before dusk for approximately 20 min, or on some occasions the next morning just after sunrise, since monarchs do not fly at night (Brower 1995). On each visit, we recorded the number of monarchs seen roosting in the area or flying in the vicinity of the roost trees (or estimated when numbers were larger than 100). Thus, this method targeted monarchs that had stopped migrating at the end of each day.

We also captured and tagged monarchs (using Monarch Watch tags) at specific sites within the CVWO and ESVNWR between 7 September and 28 October. The capture effort varied throughout the study, owing to weather, the number of people capturing or tagging, or other logistic reasons. We recorded the sex of each butterfly and any wing damage. We considered monarchs with damaged wings as those with tears (in either wing) greater than one third the total length of the forewing or holes or pieces missing from either forewing. When we captured a previously tagged individual, we recorded the date and time in order to calculate stopover durations.

The stopover duration of bird migrants is usually calculated by subtracting the date of initial capture from that of the final capture (e.g., Morris et al. 1996; Yong et al. 1998). We modified this by adding 1 day to the result. This addition was necessary since some individuals were recaptured later on the same day they were initially captured, and subtracting the two would have resulted in a stopover of "0 days." Thus, a stopover duration of 2 days indicates that the monarch was present at the site on at least 2 consecutive days. Since we cannot be sure that we captured individuals on the date of their arrival or that the last recapture was on the date of their departure, this method is a conservative estimate of stopover duration (Morris 1996; Morris et al. 1996; Yong et al. 1998). We used a Student *t* test to test for sex-related differences in the average stopover duration of monarchs at our site.

Wind data

We obtained wind data (direction and speed) from a weather station located on the eastern side of the peninsula approximately 100 km north of our site. Wind data were recorded daily at heights ranging from 13 to 1000 m. Wind conditions at this location are similar to those at our site (Garland and Davis 2002). Based on these data, we categorized each day of our study as having overall favorable or unfavorable wind directions and light or strong wind speeds. We assumed that for monarchs heading south-southwest along the Atlantic coast, favorable wind directions included winds from the north, northeast, or north-northeast. All other directions were considered unfavorable. We defined wind speeds under 25 km/h as light and those over 25 km/h as strong.

Data analysis

To determine the relationship between numbers of migrating versus roosting monarchs, we compared the daily numbers of monarchs counted from the hawkwatch platform to the daily numbers of grounded individuals (i.e., counted at the roosting site) with a Pearson correlation test that used the ranks of the actual numbers. We tested for wind effects on the numbers of migrating and roosting monarchs using Kruskal-Wallis (KW) analyses of variance (ANOVAs). The Kruskal-Wallis ANOVA was appropriate for this test (and most of our additional tests) as it is less sensitive to small and variable sample sizes. For this and other tests involving wind conditions, we only used data from days in which 5 or more monarchs were seen during the hawkwatch and roost counts combined.

We tested whether the proportion of monarchs that were recaptured varied with wind conditions. For this test, we calculated the proportion of individuals out of the total number captured each day that we later recaptured. We then tested whether this proportion was affected by the wind conditions in which monarchs were first captured using a Kruskal-Wallis ANOVA on the log-transformed proportions. For this test we pooled light and strong unfavorable directions since there were fewer than 3 days with unfavorable light conditions with captured monarchs. We tested for sex-related differences in the duration of stopover with a Student *t* test.

Finally, we tested for an effect of wind condition on the proportion of monarchs with damaged wings using a Kruskal-Wallis ANOVA. Again we used the log-transformed proportion of individuals with wing damage and pooled strong and light winds in unfavorable directions.

In all tests, significance was accepted when $p < 0.05$. When $p < 0.1$, the result was considered marginally significant.

RESULTS

A total of 1033 monarchs were counted from the hawkwatch platform and 1243 at the roost site during September and October. The bulk of the movement was during October (figure 12.1). Daily numbers of monarchs seen flying from the hawkwatch platform were weakly correlated with the number of roosting monarchs (figure 12.2). In general, on days when large numbers of monarchs migrated, large numbers also roosted at the end of the peninsula. However, on some days large numbers migrated and did not stop, while on other days large numbers of monarchs were counted at the roost but few were seen migrating.

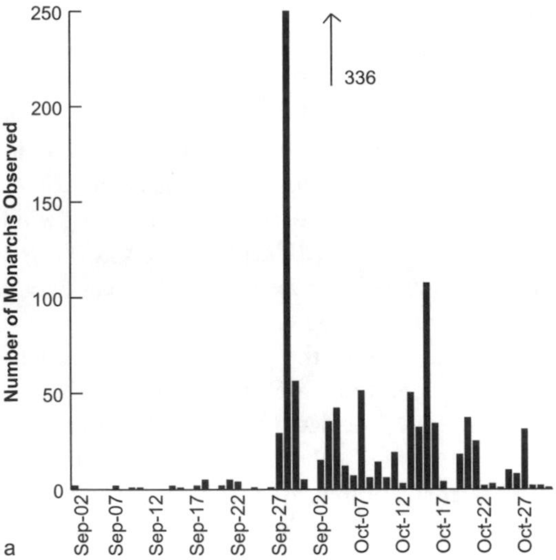

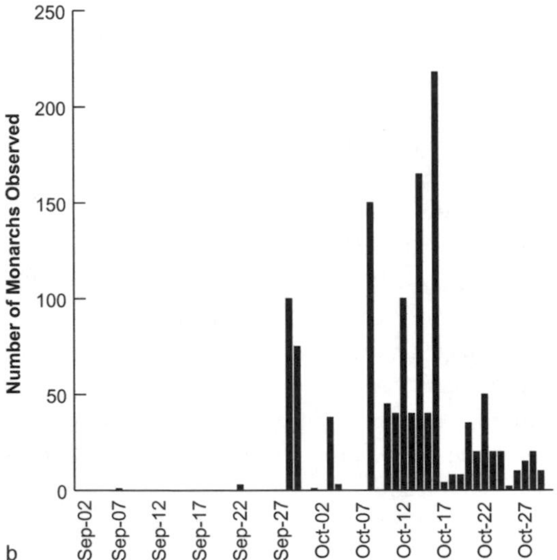

Figure 12.1. Temporal distribution of monarchs in coastal Virginia during the 2000 migration period, as documented by (a) the count from the hawkwatch platform and (b) counts made at the roosting site. The total daily numbers of monarchs seen are presented.

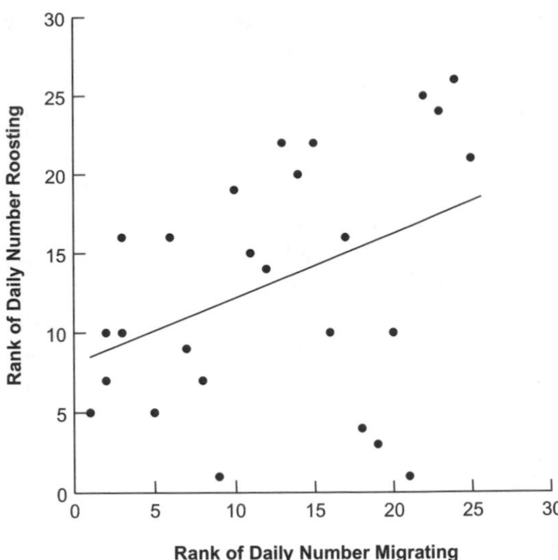

Figure 12.2. Ranks of daily numbers of roosting versus migrating monarchs.

Table 12.1. Tagging summary

Date in 2000	Wind direction	Wind speed (km/h)	Total no. tagged	% Later recaptured
27 Sept	N	26.6	14	0.0
28 Sept	N	15.8	95	1.1
29 Sept	NE	24.1	39	0.0
2 Oct	NNE	39.9	17	0.0
3 Oct	WNW	33.7	11	18.2
7 Oct	N	43.3	41	7.3
10 Oct	W	40.5	37	16.2
11 Oct	NW	35.9	59	1.7
12 Oct	N	20.7	49	4.1
13 Oct	N	25.1	49	4.1
14 Oct	NW	17.3	27	0.0
15 Oct	NW	27.2	24	4.2
16 Oct	NE	6.2	23	0.0
17 Oct	ENE	36.5	16	6.3
19 Oct	NW	34.7	14	7.1
20 Oct	NNE	11.5	37	8.1
21 Oct	SW	25.1	27	0.0
22 Oct	NE	32.8	10	0.0
23 Oct	ENE	29.4	7	14.3
25 Oct	NNE	17.0	9	0.0
26 Oct	SE	13.0	14	7.1
27 Oct	NE	32.2	33	6.1
28 Oct	NW	46.4	13	0.0

Note: Table displays when more than 6 monarchs are tagged, and the associated wind conditions during 2000.

We captured a total of 688 monarchs (46% females) on 36 days from 7 September to 30 October. Most of these captures were in late September and throughout October. We later recaptured 27 (3.9%) of these (table 12.1). Most monarchs stayed 2 days at our site, and few stayed longer than 4 days (figure 12.3). No sex-related differences in the average stopover length were found (t test, $n = 26$, $p = 0.987$).

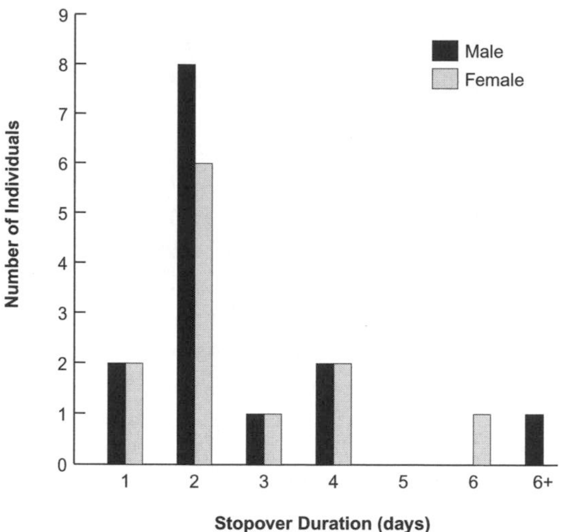

Figure 12.3. Frequency distribution of stopover duration for males and females during 2000. We calculated stopover duration as the date of final capture minus the date of initial capture plus 1.

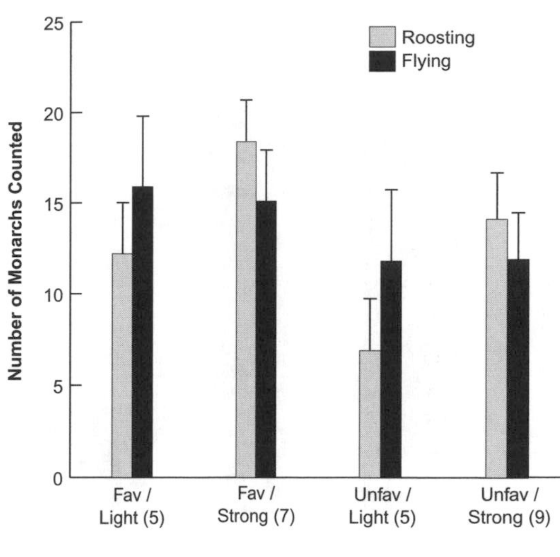

Figure 12.4. Total numbers of migrating monarchs counted from the hawkwatch platform (flying) and grounded monarchs counted at the roost site (roosting) during all wind conditions. The numbers of days in each wind condition category (favorable or unfavorable directions, light or strong wind speeds) are shown in parentheses. Only data from the main migration period (28 September to 28 October) were used. Days when fewer than 5 monarchs were seen (from the hawkwatch and roost counts combined) are excluded.

Effect of wind

The total number of days for which we could record wind conditions was fewer than 30 (we did not include days on which we observed fewer than 5 monarchs). When we categorized the days according to favorable or unfavorable wind directions and light or strong winds, our sample sizes for each treatment were further reduced. Thus the results of our tests involving wind conditions must be interpreted cautiously.

We found a marginally significant effect of wind condition on the numbers of roosting monarchs (KW statistic = 6.79, $df = 3$, $p = 0.079$; figure 12.4), but no effect on the numbers of migrating monarchs (KW statistic = 1.435, $df = 3$, $p = 0.697$). The average proportion of monarchs that were later recaptured was highest when monarchs were tagged during unfavorable wind directions. When wind conditions were favorable (light winds from the north or northeast), the fewest monarchs were later recaptured (figure 12.5), but this result was not statistically significant (KW statistic = 2.55, $df = 2$, $p = 0.279$).

The overall proportion of monarchs with damaged wings was 4.8%. During favorable wind conditions (light winds from the north), the average proportion of monarchs with damaged wings was 4.6% (figure 12.6). During favorable directions and strong winds, the average was 5.2%. During

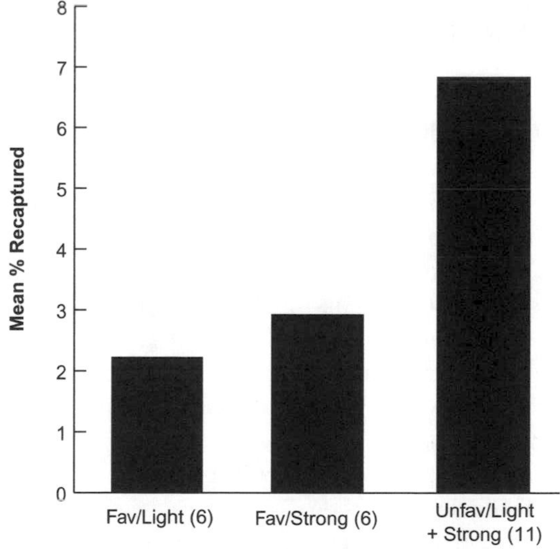

Figure 12.5. Average percentage of monarchs that were recaptured after the initial tagging, during all wind conditions. The numbers of days in each wind condition category (favorable or unfavorable directions, light or strong wind speeds) are shown in parentheses. Days when fewer than 5 monarchs were seen (from the hawkwatch and roost counts combined) are excluded.

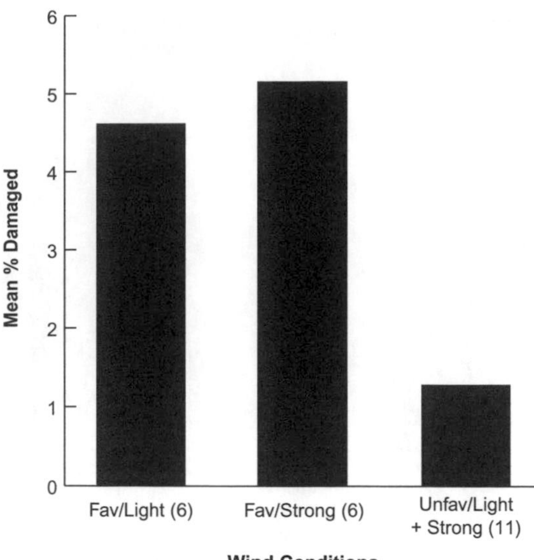

Figure 12.6. Percentage of monarchs with damaged wings captured during each wind condition. The numbers of days in each wind condition category (favorable or unfavorable directions, light or strong wind speeds) are shown in parentheses. Days when fewer than 5 monarchs were captured are excluded.

unfavorable directions and both light and strong winds, only 1.3% of monarchs had damaged wings. These differences were not statistically significant (KW statistic = 1.993, $df = 2$, $p = 0.369$).

DISCUSSION

In this study we adapted techniques used to study bird migration and applied them to the study of stopover ecology in monarchs. This enabled us to provide the first information on this important topic. We monitored the temporal distribution of monarch migration using a point-count method from a hawkwatch platform; temporal distribution has previously only been documented with a driving census (Walton and Brower 1996). We collected information on factors causing monarchs to stop migrating by monitoring a nearby roost site. Finally, by tagging and recapturing monarchs, we could document how long monarchs commonly stop at our site during migration and address factors potentially causing them to stop.

That we only recaptured 27 individuals (3.9%) of the 688 total tagged is not surprising. Ornithologists studying landbird stopover commonly recapture less than 5% of their total captures (e.g., Moore et al. 1990; Morris et al. 1996; Davis 2001). This means, however, that sites where large numbers of monarchs can be captured and multiple years of tagging are necessary to calculate reliable estimates of stopover duration at any given site. The median stopover duration for monarchs at our site in coastal Virginia was 2 days during the 2000 migration season (see figure 12.3), but this result is difficult to interpret since the lack of similar studies in this area of research precludes us from comparing our result to others. Thus it is not known if this duration is a long stopover or a short one. It is generally accepted that long stopovers indicate high-quality sites for landbirds (e.g., Davis 2001), and monarchs may be no different. Nor do we know if this 2-day stopover is indicative of a normal year. More research will provide insight into these questions.

Many of our analyses on the effects of wind conditions on aspects of stopovers did not show significant trends, although there was a marginally significant effect of wind conditions on the numbers of roosting monarchs. However, this could be attributed to the small sample sizes for the tests. Since we could only test for the effect of wind conditions when there were actually monarchs at our site, and since monarchs passed through our site in such a short time, we were left with fewer than 30 days with monarch and wind data for our tests. Researchers who wish to conduct similar studies should monitor for several years in order to collect sufficient data.

One factor that may influence stopover decisions is a monarch's condition. Although the result was not statistically significant, damaged monarchs may have been most numerous during favorable wind directions. When conditions are favorable for active migration, we expect most monarchs to be migrating. Those that we captured on the ground included a considerable number of damaged individuals, indicating that they could not fly or somehow required more time on the ground.

Other factors may cause monarchs to stop migrating or prolong their stopovers. Given the similarities between monarch and bird migrations, we can draw some insight into these possible factors from stopover research on landbirds. It is generally accepted that landbirds stop migrating and set down to forage when their fat supplies are low (Morris 1996). Further, birds stay longer at a stopover site when their fat stores are small than when they are large (e.g., Yong and Moore 1993). Additional research could determine whether monarchs also make stopover decisions based on energy supplies.

It is also generally accepted among ornithologists that landbirds make stopover decisions based on the suitability of the site (Hutto 1998; Latta and Brown 1999; Gellin and Morris 2001). It is not known what constitutes a quality habitat for monarchs' stopover, but nectar sources, roost sites, shelter, or the presence of other monarchs could be important. Further, the presence of many monarchs at a site during migration does not indicate that the site has suitable habitat. Ornithologists have long recognized that the density of individual birds in any habitat is not indicative of its suitability (Van Horne 1983). This is one of the primary reasons why stopover lengths must be compared among several sites to determine the importance of each site during migration.

The stopover ecology of monarchs is a research area that requires more attention by scientists and monarch taggers. Certain annual staging areas have been documented in northern areas, although they have been described as overnight roosting locations rather than stopover sites (Urquhart and Urquhart 1979). However, areas where monarchs roost during migration should also be considered stopover sites, since monarchs interrupt their migration, become grounded for short periods, and subsequently utilize resources (i.e., roost trees, possibly nectar sources) at these sites. These factors are all typical of avian stopovers. The degree to which roosting sites and stopover sites are related is unknown.

It is our hope that these findings will encourage further studies of stopover ecology, an important but little-studied aspect of the monarchs' annual cycle of migration, overwintering, and breeding. The techniques we used in this study were simple and noninvasive and could be easily incorporated into existing monarch or tagging programs. To make meaningful comparisons between geographic locations, results using methods similar to ours from many locations must become available. We need to know where, when, and why monarchs choose to stop during migration. Many scientists and volunteers currently tag monarchs each fall; our results demonstrate that they could easily provide information other than migratory routes to and recovery rates at the overwintering sites. Monitoring the movement and presence of monarchs at specific sites on a daily, standardized basis, and keeping track of associated environmental conditions can increase our knowledge of migration dynamics.

Acknowledgments

Paige Cunningham, Sue Rice, Brian Sullivan, Stephanie Mason, Lynn Davidson, Hal Wierenga, George Armistead, Harry Armistead, and Liz Armistead assisted with this study. We thank the staff of the ESVNWR for granting access to the roost. We also thank Clem Pruitt, of the Chesapeake Bay Bridge Tunnel, for allowing access to Bridge Tunnel property. Calvin Brennan, the CVWO hawkwatcher in 2000, counted monarchs for us. Sonia Altizer provided comments on an early draft of the manuscript. Logistical support was provided by the CVWO. Financial support was through a U.S. Fish and Wildlife Service research grant to M. Garland.

References

Brower, L. P. 1995. Understanding and misunderstanding the migration of the monarch butterfly (Nymphalidae) in North America: 1857–1995. J. Lepid. Soc. 49:304–85.

Brower, L. P. 1996. Monarch butterfly orientation: missing pieces of a magnificent puzzle. J. Exp. Biol. 199:93–103.

Brower, L. P., and W. H. Calvert. 1985. Foraging dynamics of bird predators on overwintering monarch butterflies in Mexico. Evolution 39:852–68.

Calvert, W. H., M. B. Hyatt, and N. P. M. Villasenor. 1986. The effects of understory vegetation on the survival of overwintering monarch butterflies (*Danaus plexippus* L.) in Mexico. Acta Zool. Mex. 18:1–17.

Calvert, W. H., W. Zuchowski, and L. P. Brower. 1983. The effect of rain, snow and freezing temperatures on overwintering monarch butterflies in Mexico. Biotropica 15:42–47.

Davis, A. K. 1999. The stopover ecology of landbirds on Bon Portage Island, Nova Scotia. Master's thesis, Acadia University, Wolfville, Nova Scotia, Canada.

Davis, A. K. 2001. Blackpoll warbler (*Dendroica striata*) fat deposition in southern Nova Scotia during autumn migration. Northeast. Nat. 8:149–62.

Davis, A. K., and M. S. Garland. 2002. An evaluation of three methods of counting migrating monarch butterflies in varying wind conditions. Southeast. Nat. 1:55–68.

Garland, M. S., and A. K. Davis. 2002. An examination of monarch butterfly (*Danaus plexippus*) autumn migration in coastal Virginia. Am. Midl. Nat. 147:170–74.

Gellin, C. E., and S. R. Morris. 2001. Patterns of movement during passerine migration on an island stopover site. Northeast. Nat. 8:253–66.

Gibo, D. L., and M. J. Pallett. 1979. Soaring flight of monarch butterflies, *Danaus plexippus* (Lepidoptera: Danaidae), during the late summer migration in southern Ontario. Can. J. Zool. 57:1393–401.

Hutto, R. L. 1998. On the importance of stopover sites to migrating birds. Auk 115:823–25.

Knight, A. L., L. P. Brower, and E. H. Williams. 1999. Spring remigration of the monarch butterfly, *Danaus plexippus* (Lepidoptera: Nymphalidae) in north-central Florida: estimating population parameters using mark-recapture. Biol. J. Linn. Soc. 68:531–56.

Latta, S. C., and C. Brown. 1999. Autumn stopover ecology of the blackpoll warbler (*Dendroica striata*) in thorn scrub forest of the Dominican Republic. Can. J. Zool. 77:1147–56.

Moore, F. R., P. Kerlinger, and T. R. Simons. 1990. Stopover on a Gulf Coast barrier island by spring trans-gulf migrants. Wilson Bull. 102:487–500.

Morris, S. R. 1996. Mass loss and probability of stopover by migrant warblers during spring and fall migration. J. Field Ornithol. 67:456–62.

Morris, S. R., D. W. Holmes, and M. E. Richmond. 1996. A ten-year study of the stopover patterns of migratory passerines during fall migration on Appledore Island, Maine. Condor 98:395–409.

Richardson, W. J. 1972. Autumn migration and weather in eastern Canada: a radar study. Am. Birds 26:10–17.

Richardson, W. J. 1978. Timing and amount of bird migration in relation to weather: a review. Oikos 30:224–72.

Richardson, W. J. 1990. Timing of bird migration in relation to weather: updated review. In E. Gwinner, ed., Bird migration, pp. 78–101. Berlin: Springer-Verlag.

Schaub, M., R. Pradel, L. Jenni, and J.-D. Lebreton. 2001. Migrating birds stop over longer than usually thought: an improved capture-recapture analysis. Ecology 82:852–59.

Schmidt-Koenig, K. 1985. Migration strategies of monarch butterflies. In M. A. Rankin, ed., Migration: mechanisms and adaptive significance, pp. 786–98. Contributions to Marine Science, Vol. 27 Suppl. Port Aransas, Texas: Marine Science Institute, University of Texas at Austin.

Taylor, O. R. 1997. Monarch Watch: education, conservation and research. In J. Hoth, L. Merino, K. Oberhauser, I. Pisantry, S. Price, and T. Wilkinson, eds., The 1997 North American Conference on the Monarch Butterfly, pp. 355–60. Montreal: Commission for Environmental Cooperation.

Texas Monarch Watch. 2002. Texas Monarch Watch. http://www.tpwd.state.tx.us/nature/education/tracker/monarch/. Accessed 26 March 2002.

Urquhart, F. A., and N. R. Urquhart. 1979. Breeding areas and overnight roosting locations in the northern range of the monarch butterfly (*Danaus plexippus plexippus*) with a summary of associated migratory routes. Can. Field Nat. 93:41–47.

Van Horne, B. 1983. Density as a misleading indicator of habitat quality. J. Wildl. Manag. 47:893–901.

Walton, R. K., and L. P. Brower. 1996. Monitoring the fall migration of the monarch butterfly *Danaus plexippus* L. (Nymphalidae: Danainae) in eastern North America: 1991–1994. J. Lepid. Soc. 50:1–20.

Yong, W., D. M. Finch, F. R. Moore, and J. F. Kelly. 1998. Stopover ecology and habitat use of migratory wilson's warblers. Auk 115:829–42.

Yong, W., and F. R. Moore. 1993. Relation between migratory activity and energetic condition among thrushes (Turdinae) following passage across the Gulf of Mexico. Condor 95:934–43.

13

Characteristics of Fall Migratory Monarch Butterflies, *Danaus plexippus*, in Minnesota and Texas

Jane Borland, Carol C. Johnson, Thomas William Crumpton III, Markisha Thomas, Sonia M. Altizer, and Karen S. Oberhauser

INTRODUCTION

The monarch butterfly is well known for its annual late-summer and fall migration from the United States and Canada to Mexico, which can cover more than 3000 km (Urquhart and Urquhart 1976). During their fall migration, monarchs nectar on a variety of flowering plants, roost in trees at night, and ride air currents driven by the changing weather patterns. Traveling at speeds up to 50 km/h and altitudes that may exceed 1 km (Gibo 1986), monarchs fly southwest from breeding grounds in the northeastern quarter of the United States and southeastern Canada. Several southbound migratory routes east of the Rocky Mountains converge in central Texas before continuing to the overwintering sites in Mexico (Brower 1996; Calvert and Wagner 1999; Rogg et al. 1999).

It has been generally accepted that southbound monarchs in the fall are in a state of delayed reproductive development called "diapause," a phase of sexual inactivity triggered by late-summer photoperiod and temperature conditions (e.g., Brower 1985, 1995). In Minnesota, these changes occur in late August (Goehring and Oberhauser 2002). However, in many parts of the southern United States, eggs and larvae are observed after a period of absence during the summer months, indicating that breeding monarchs are present during the fall migration (Calvert 1999; Prysby and Oberhauser, this volume). Since there is little or no reproduction this far south during the summer (Prysby and Oberhauser, this volume), it is most likely that these breeding monarchs come from elsewhere, presumably from northern breeding grounds. However, their origin and reproductive history are not known (Calvert 1999).

Here, we report on the physical characteristics of monarchs at different times and locations along the migratory route. Comparing these characteristics will increase our understanding of the migratory process in monarchs, providing information on the phenomenon of fall reproduction, possible effects of size and wing condition on migratory success, and effects of flight on wing condition and mass.

METHODS

We examined fall migratory butterflies over a 6-week period at the beginning and end of their migratory path through the central United States over 4 successive years, assessing their size (mass and wing length), wing condition, and female reproductive status. Monarchs were sampled opportunistically in Minnesota, Wisconsin, and Texas during August, September, and October in 1998 to 2001. Northern monarchs were sampled in late August and early September within 100 km of St. Paul, Minnesota, and represent the early phase of the fall migration. Southern monarchs were sampled from September through November in North Central Texas, the Texas Hill Country, and South Texas. Most monarchs were netted while in flight or as they nectared on flowers. We captured a total of 2081

Table 13.1. Sampling locations and dates

State	Date	*n*	Proportion male	Location
Minnesota	20/8/98	11	0.73	Wayzata, Hennepin County
Minnesota	21/8/98	79	0.72	Cannon Falls, Goodhue County
Texas	3/9–6/10/98	12	0.60	Arlington, Tarrant County
Texas	20/9/98	8	0.89	Colorado Bend State Park, San Saba County
Texas	9/10/98	11	0.64	Mo Ranch, Kerr County
Texas	11/10/98	80	0.69	Selah Ranch, Blanco County
Texas	12–13/10/98	74	0.54	Garner State Park, Uvalde County
Texas	25/10/98	14	0.79	Castroville, Medina County
Texas	23/11/98	5	0.40	San Antonio, Bexar County
Minnesota	4/9/99	276	0.39	Cannon Falls, Goodhue County
Texas	2/10/99	73	0.45	Garner State Park, Uvalde County
Texas	3/10/99	173	0.64	Colorado Bend State Park, San Saba County
Texas	10/10/99	88	0.44	Selah Ranch, Blanco County
Wisconsin	25/8/00	22	0.73	St. Croix County
Minnesota	4/9/00	61	0.00	Cannon Falls, Goodhue County
Texas	13/9–9/10/00	184	0.48	Arlington, Tarrant County
Texas	10/10–2/11/00	211	0.61	Arlington, Tarrant County
Texas	13/10/00	81	0.48	Selah Ranch, Blanco County
Wisconsin	19/8/01	80	0.45	St. Croix County
Texas	16/8–10/10/01	178	0.72	Arlington, Tarrant County
Texas	13-30/10/01	94	0.73	Arlington, Tarrant County
Texas	14/10–24/11/01	229	0.47	San Antonio, Bexar County

butterflies over the 4 years of the study. Specific locations, dates of capture, and sample sizes are shown in table 13.1.

For each monarch captured, we recorded the sex, forewing length from the point of attachment to the most distal tip, and wet mass. Butterflies were either weighed in the field using a Mettler balance or brought back to the classroom or lab in glassine envelopes and measured within 6 h if not held on ice, or 24 h if held on ice. We assessed wing condition (Monarch Lab 2002) on a scale of 1 (newly emerged, pristine wings) to 5 (extreme scale wear). Wing damage was recorded as the number of wings that were tattered, broken, or missing pieces, and ranged from 0 (no wings damaged) to 4 (all wings damaged). Wing damage, while often correlated with wing condition, reflects specific events that cause wing tatter and is probably a measure of the frequency of events such as mating struggles, encounters with predators, or windy weather. Parasite infection by *Ophryocystis elektroscirrha* was determined by counting the number of abdominal spore prints on over 1000 of the butterflies (following Altizer and Oberhauser 1999) and rating it on a scale of 0 (no spores) to 5 (1000 spores or more). Finally, we assessed the mating status of females by palpating their lower abdomens to detect spermatophores (following Van Hook 1999). We did not check our assessments of mating status with dissections, since we did not have permission to use destructive sampling at the locations of most of our collections. Previous assessments have indicated that our palpation techniques are 85% to 95% accurate, with most errors occurring in the direction of categorizing females as unmated when they actually contain a small spermatophore (pers. observ.).

We used regression models to determine the predictor variables that were most important in explaining variation in the continuous variables of wing length and mass, testing the effects of year, state, date of collection, and sex. To assess the effects of date of capture on the ordinal variables of wing damage and wing condition, we used the nonparametric Spearman rank correlation. We used Kruskal-Wallis (KW) analysis of variance (ANOVA) to compare ordinal variables (wing damage and wing condition), and parametric ANOVA models to compare continuous variables (size measurements) from butterflies in difference categories.

RESULTS

Size

Wing length tended to decrease with date of capture, when butterflies from both ends of the migratory path or only within Texas are compared (table 13.2). This effect can be visualized by comparing wing lengths of individuals captured in the northern states with those captured in Texas (figure 13.1a). Individuals tended to be smaller in 1999 (table 13.2) and larger in 1998 and 2000 (table 13.2), and males were larger than females (table 13.2, figure 13.1a).

Monarch mass also varied with date and location of capture. Mass tended to increase with time of capture, when butterflies from both ends of the migratory path or only within Texas are compared (table 13.3); individuals of both sexes captured in Texas tended to be heavier than those captured in Minnesota and Wisconsin, and males were heavier than females (see figure 13.1b). Butterflies in 1998 tended to be lightest and those in 1999 tended to be heaviest (see table 13.3), the opposite of what is expected based on wing length.

Wing condition and damage

We assessed the effects of date on wing condition (scale loss) separately for the two sexes, since females are darker than males and tend to be scored higher for scale loss (pers. observ.). There was a significant positive correlation between wing condition and date when butterflies from both ends of the U.S. migratory path were compared (table 13.4), indicating that the amount of scale loss increased over time. However, there was not a significant relationship between date and condition when butterflies captured only in Texas were included in the analysis (table 13.4). Mated females tended to be more worn than those that had not mated, although this effect was not significant at the 0.05 level of confidence (mean wing condition for mated and unmated females = 2.41 and 2.19, respectively, KW statistic = 3.56, $p = 0.0591$).

Table 13.2. Analysis of factors related to wing length

Variable	Coefficient (standard error)	t value	p value
All butterflies[a]			
Constant	57.31 (0.773)	74.16	<0.001
Male	0.351 (0.115)	3.02	0.002
Date	–0.020 (0.003)	7.16	<0.001
1999	–0.369 (0.126)	–2.93	0.003
Texas butterflies only[b]			
Constant	57.8 (1.42)	40.8	<0.001
Male	0.277 (0.137)	2.02	0.043
Data	–0.023 (0.005)	–4.58	<0.001
1998	0.875 (0.208)	4.20	<0.001
2000	0.674 (0.152)	4.43	<0.001

[a] Cases included = 2059, $R^2 = 0.029$.
[b] Cases included = 1539, $R^2 = 0.035$.

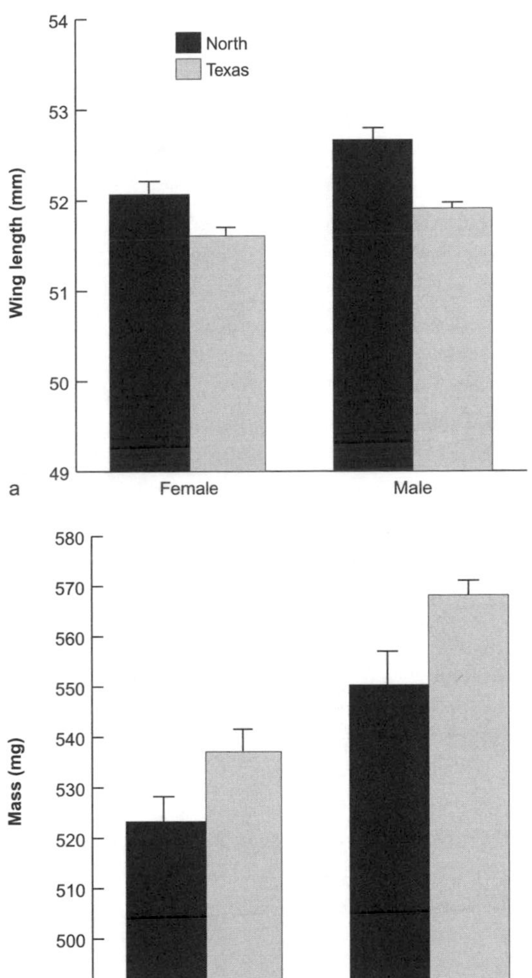

Figure 13.1. Effects of collection location and gender on monarch (a) wing length and (b) mass. Northern butterflies were captured in Minnesota and Wisconsin in August or early September, and Texas butterflies in September or October. Error bars show 1 standard deviation. For analysis of significant effects, see tables 13.2 and 13.3.

We also compared the number of damaged wings separately for males and females, since mating attempts may affect the likelihood of wing damage differently in the two sexes. For both sexes, the number of damaged wings increased with time when all butterflies were compared (table 13.4). However, when northern butterflies were excluded from the sample, the number of damaged wings decreased significantly with time for both sexes (table 13.4). On average, females had fewer damaged wings than males (mean values for males and females = 0.68 and 0.47, respectively, KW statistic = 27.41, $p < 0.001$). Mated females had more damaged wings than virgins (figure 13.2).

Wing length did not vary significantly among wing damage or condition categories for either sex. However, there was a significant association between mass and wing condition in both sexes, such that individuals with poorer wing condition tended to be lighter (figure 13.3).

Table 13.3. Analysis of factors related to mass

Variable	Coefficient (standard error)	t value	p value
All butterflies[a]			
Constant	−643.2 (53.61)	−12.00	<0.001
Male	29.03 (4.16)	6.98	<0.001
Date	0.777 (0.103)	7.55	<0.001
1998	−63.01 (6.39)	−9.86	<0.001
1999	28.65 (4.71)	6.08	<0.001
Wing length	18.62 (0.800)	23.28	<0.001
Texas butterflies only[b]			
Constant	−733.1 (76.68)	−9.56	<0.001
Male	28.57 (5.07)	5.63	<0.001
Date	1.01 (0.187)	5.38	<0.001
1998	−77.01 (7.93)	−9.71	<0.001
1999	51.26 (6.04)	8.48	<0.001
Wing length	19.05 (0.947)	20.12	<0.001

[a] Cases included = 2005, $R^2 = 0.275$.
[b] Cases included = 1487, $R^2 = 0.285$.

Sex ratios and reproductive status

Sex ratios of our collections showed a high degree of variation (see table 13.1). Some samples were highly male biased, while others were female biased (including one 2000 Minnesota sample in which all of 61 butterflies were females).

Overall, 13.6% of the females that we collected had mated, as determined by nondestructive abdominal palpation. The proportion of females

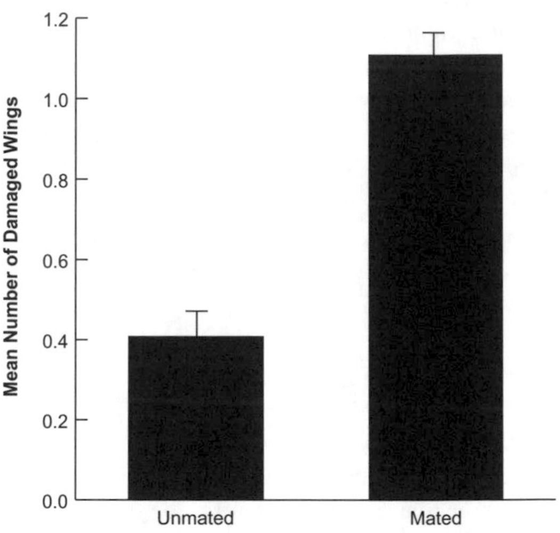

Figure 13.2. Mean number of damaged wings on mated and unmated females for all years in all locations. Although means are shown, the distribution was very skewed toward low numbers of damaged wings, and the statistical analysis utilized the nonparametric Kruskal-Wallis (KW) analysis of variance (ANOVA) (KW statistic = 33.55, $p < 0.001$). Sample sizes are 746 and 119 for unmated and mated females, respectively. Error bars show 1 standard error.

Table 13.4. Spearman rank correlations between date of capture and wing condition

Variable	Sex	Sample	Correlation coefficient (with date of capture)	p value
Scale loss	Male	All	0.068	0.027
	Female	All	0.135	<0.001
	Male	Texas only	−0.013	0.708
	Female	Texas only	0.031	0.439
No. of damaged wings	Male	All	0.082	0.007
	Female	All	0.127	<0.001
	Male	Texas only	−0.130	<0.001
	Female	Texas only	−0.155	<0.001

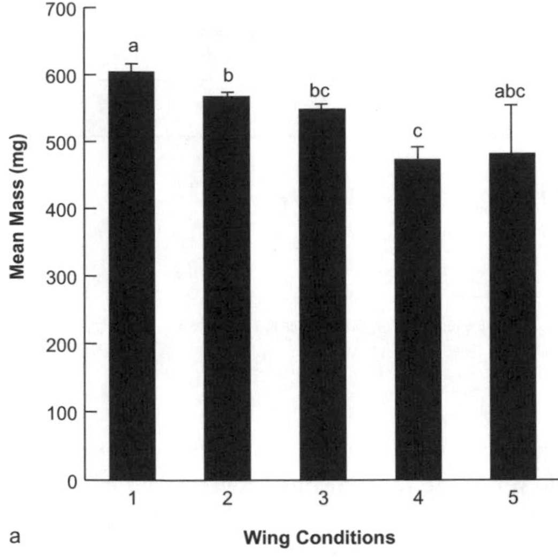

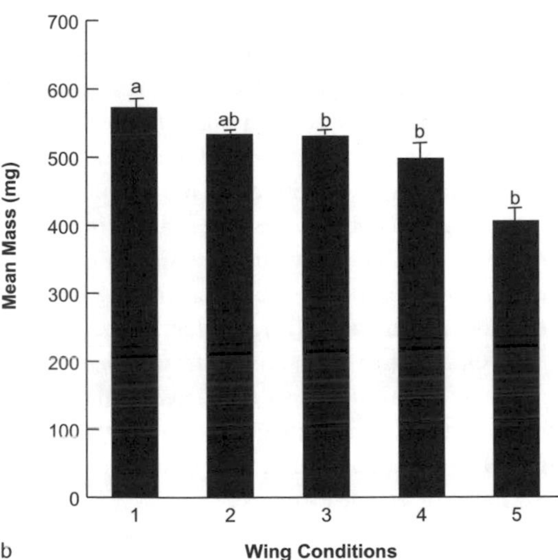

Figure 13.3. Mean masses for (a) males and (b) females in all five wing condition categories. Data were analyzed using one-way ANOVA (males $F = 12.55$, $df = 4, 1011$, $p < 0.001$; female $F = 5.62$, $df = 4, 886$, $p < 0.001$). Columns with the same letters above them are statistically indistinguishable (Tukey's test). Sample sizes were less than 10 in category 5 for both sexes, resulting in a lack of statistical power to distinguish masses of butterflies in this category from others.

with spermatophores did not vary among years ($\chi^2 = 4.69$, $df = 3$, $p = 0.196$). However, date and location of collection had significant effects on the likelihood that a female had mated. Seven (3.0%) of 235 females collected in Minnesota and Wisconsin had mated, while 113 (17.5%) of 645 had mated in Texas. This difference is significant ($\chi^2 = 30.92$, $df = 1$, $p < 0.001$). When only Texas females were included in a

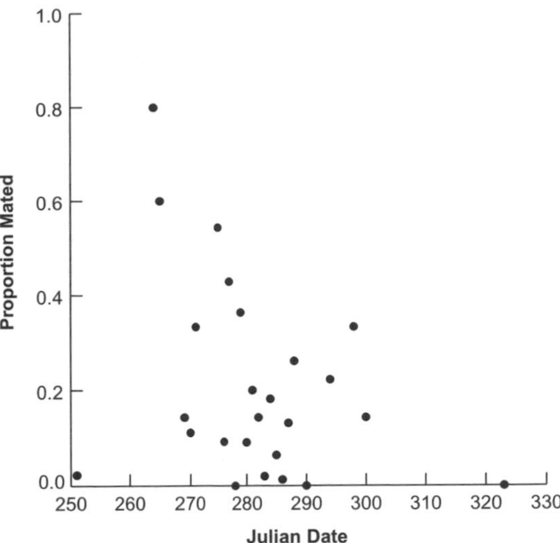

Figure 13.4. The proportion of females that were mated across all years (as determined by nondestructive abdominal palpation) as a function of date of capture in Texas. Julian date 250 = 11 September. Only dates on which 5 or more females were sampled are shown.

Kruskal-Wallis ANOVA, virgins had significantly later dates of collection (mean Julian dates for virgin and mated females = 280 and 278 [7 and 5 October], respectively, KW statistic = 9.9, $p = 0.002$). The latter effect is illustrated in figure 13.4, which shows the proportion of females mated versus date of collection in Texas.

Spore load

Ophryocystis elektroscirrha infection levels were consistently low (table 13.5). Of the 1046 butterflies sampled across the 4 years, only 12 (1.14%) were infected at levels 3 to 5. These levels are commonly thought to represent infections received during the larval stages, while levels 1 and 2 are thought to represent the transfer of spores from adult to adult during mating, contact in roosting sites, or handling (Altizer and Oberhauser 1999).

DISCUSSION

Reproductive status

Analysis of the variation in many characteristics of monarch butterflies along the migratory path can add to our understanding of their population

Table 13.5. *Ophryocystis elektroscirrha* infection levels

State and year	*n*	Spore load					
		0	1	2	3	4	5
Minnesota/Wisconsin 1998	80	100%					
Texas 1998	189	98.4% (186)	0.5% (1)			1.1% (2)	
Texas 1999	280	100%					
Texas 2000	384	91.9% (353)	4.7% (18)	1.3% (5)	0.5% (2)	1.3% (5)	0.3% (1)
Texas 2001	113	98.2% (111)				0.9% (1)	0.9% (1)

Note: Butterflies were not tested for spore loads in Minnesota and Wisconsin in 1999 to 2001. Parentheses show the number in each category. Spore load is according to the scale described in text.

dynamics. Our most striking finding was that a large proportion of females captured in Texas each fall had mated (over 17%), unlike those collected in Minnesota and Wisconsin (3%). The low frequency of mating in northern fall populations is similar to that found previously (Pliske 1973; Brower 1985; Goehring and Oberhauser 2002), and is very different from the situation during the summer, when most females have mated (Goehring and Oberhauser 2002; pers. observ.). A peak in egg and larva abundance in Texas during September and early October (Prysby 2001; Prysby and Oberhauser, this volume) suggests that female mating status was reflective of their reproductive status; they were not in diapause. Since monarchs are absent from most of the southern United States throughout much of the summer (Calvert 1999; Prysby and Oberhauser, this volume), these reproductive females must have come from elsewhere. They could have broken diapause to reproduce, or they may not have been in diapause as they migrated south. Our finding that females at the beginning of the migratory path were almost all unmated suggests the former, but we would need similar data from locations along the migratory route to completely understand the dynamics of fall reproduction. Most female monarchs captured in Texas had not mated, indicating that there is variation in the response of individuals to environmental conditions; investigating the reasons for this variation could provide another fruitful avenue for further study.

Wing condition

We found greater scale loss and wing damage among Texas migrants than in northern samples, suggesting that these two locations represent different points on the migratory pathway, as expected. However, the relationship between date of capture and wing status was not consistent. Early Texas migrants tended to have more wing damage than late Texas migrants (see table 13.4), but wing condition within Texas did not vary with date of capture. Scale loss patterns suggest that there is a continual stream of similarly aged migrants into the state, but that there may be behavioral differences between early and late arrivals, with early arrivals more likely to have engaged in behaviors that resulted in tattered or torn wings. Since early migrants are more likely to be reproductive, it is possible that mating or other behaviors associated with reproduction cause wing tatter (Oberhauser 1989; Frey 1999; Oberhauser and Frey 1999). Our finding that mated females have more damaged wings than unmated females (see figure 13.3b) supports this explanation, although we only have correlative evidence.

Size

Our finding that females are smaller is a consistent pattern in monarchs (e.g., Oberhauser and Frey 1999; Monarch Lab 2002). The significant differences in wing length and mass between states are interesting, particularly because they are in opposite directions (northern individuals had longer wings but were lighter, see tables 13.2 and 13.3). We interpret these results with caution. Mass is expected to vary with recent feeding and resting history, and since many of our samples consisted of large collections at the same place and time (see table 13.1), conclusions about the effects of date or location on mass would need to be supported with additional data. Brower (1985) and Gibo and McCurdy (1993) reported that monarchs may gain lipid mass as they make their southern trip, and our comparison between northern and southern collections corroborates their finding. The increase in mass over time in Texas may be due to the fact that more butterflies collected later were in reproductive diapause, and thus not channeling resources to reproduction.

Different researchers measured butterflies collected in the North and the South, and the finding that butterflies collected in the North had longer wings could possibly be due to the confounding of observers with location. If the effect is real, it would suggest that smaller individuals are better able to make the migratory flight, contrary to previous suggestions that larger individuals are more successful migrants (Masters et al. 1988; Arango 1996; Van Hook 1996; Alonso-Mejia et al. 1997). The decrease in wing length over time within Texas is less likely to be due to observer effects, since the same people measured the butterflies. It is possible that late arrivals are compromised during their larval development and sacrifice wing length to rapid development or lipid storage. The year-to-year variation in both monarch mass and wing length warrants further study. We do not have explanations for this variation, and the limited number of years covered by our study makes explorations of environmental differences pure speculation at this point. In addition, the large collections at the same place and time may have influenced the patterns we observed, and accurate comparisons would require a more consistent sampling pattern than our opportunistic methods.

The negative relationship between mass and the degree of wing scale loss (see figure 13.3) suggests that smaller butterflies were more likely to engage in behaviors that caused scale loss. More research on the relationship between size and activity would help to address this issue. This relationship has also been observed in the overwintering colonies (K. S. Oberhauser, pers. observ.) and could result if smaller butterflies travel more slowly, nectar more often, or spend more time flying in search of flowers, and thus incur more scale loss as they migrate.

CONCLUSION

Comparisons of the characteristics of monarchs from different states and phases of fall migration are rare, and there is much to be learned from long-term monitoring of adult conditions. Associations between characteristics and environmental conditions could provide fruitful research directions, and we are continuing to collect these data to look for such associations.

Acknowledgments

We would like to thank William Calvert, Michelle Solensky, Liz Goehring, and other members of the Monarch Monitoring Science Museum of Minnesota/Monarchs in the Classroom project, the Lamar High School and John Jay High School research teams, and David Astin and his Wayzata High School students in Minnesota for their help designing and carrying out this project. Michelle Solensky and Liz Goehring made useful suggestions for improving the manuscript. Research was supported by the National Science Foundation (ESI 9731429), Monarchs in the Classroom at the University of Minnesota, and a National Science Foundation Presidential Award of Excellence in Mathematics and Science Teaching to J. Borland.

References

Alonso-Mejía, A., E. Rendón Salinas, E. Montesiños-Patino, and L. P. Brower. 1997. Use of lipid reserves by monarch butterflies overwintering in Mexico: implications for conservation. Ecol. Appl. 7:934–47.

Altizer, S. M., and K. S. Oberhauser. 1999. Effects of the protozoan parasite *Ophryocystis elektroscirrha* on the fitness of monarch butterflies (*Danaus plexippus*). J. Invertebr. Pathol. 74:76–88.

Arango, N. V. 1996. Stabilizing selection in migratory butterflies: a comparative study of queen and monarch butterflies. Master's thesis, University of Florida, Gainesville.

Brower, L. P. 1985. New perspectives on the migration biology of the monarch butterfly, *Danaus plexippus* L. In M. A. Rankin, ed., Migration: mechanisms and adaptive significance, pp. 748–85. Contributions in Marine Science, Vol. 27. Suppl. Port Aransas, Texas: Marine Science Institute, University of Texas at Austin.

Brower, L. P. 1995. Understanding and misunderstanding the migration of the monarch butterfly (Nymphalidae) in North America. J. Lepid. Soc. 49:304–85.

Brower, L. P. 1996. Monarch butterfly orientation: missing pieces of a magnificent puzzle. J. Exp. Biol. 199:93–103.

Calvert, W. H. 1999. Patterns in the spatial and temporal use of Texas milkweeds (Asclepiadaceae) by the monarch butterfly (*Danaus plexippus* L.) during fall, 1996. J. Lepid. Soc. 53:37–44.

Calvert, W. H., and M. Wagner. 1999. Patterns in the monarch butterfly migration through Texas—1993 to 1995. In J. Hoth, L. Merino, K. Oberhauser, I. Pisantry, S. Price, and T.

Wilkinson, eds., The 1997 North American Conference on the Monarch Butterfly, pp. 119–26. Montreal: Commission for Environmental Cooperation.

Frey, D. 1999. Resistance to mating by female monarch butterflies. In J. Hoth, L. Merino, K. Oberhauser, I. Pisantry, S. Price, and T. Wilkinson, eds., The 1997 North American Conference on the Monarch Butterfly, pp. 79–87. Montreal: Commission for Environmental Cooperation.

Gibo, D. L. 1986. Flight strategies of migrating monarch butterflies (*Danaus plexippus* L.) in southern Ontario. In W. Danthanarayana, ed., Insect flight: dispersal and migration, pp. 172–84. Berlin: Springer-Verlag.

Gibo, D. L., and J. A. McCurdy. 1993. Lipid accumulation by migrating monarch butterflies (*Danaus plexippus* L.). Can. J. Zool. 71:76–82.

Goehring, L., and K. S. Oberhauser. 2002. Effects of photoperiod, temperature and host plant age on induction of reproductive diapause and development time in *Danaus plexippus*. Ecol. Entomol. 27:674–85.

Masters, A. R., S. B. Malcolm, and L. P. Brower. 1988. Monarch butterfly (*Danaus plexippus*) thermoregulation behavior and adaptations for overwintering in Mexico. Ecology 69:458–67.

Monarch Lab. 2002. Monarchs in the Classroom. Updated March 2002. Research topics: Vital statistics. http://www.monarchlab.umn.edu/research/VS/vs.html. Accessed 15 April 2002.

Oberhauser, K. S. 1989. Effects of spermatophores on male and female monarch butterfly reproductive success. Behav. Ecol. Sociobiol. 25:237–46.

Oberhauser, K. S., and D. Frey. 1999. Coerced mating in monarch butterflies. In J. Hoth, L. Merino, K. Oberhauser, I. Pisantry, S. Price, and T. Wilkinson, eds., The 1997 North American Conference on the Monarch Butterfly, pp. 67–78. Montreal: Commission for Environmental Cooperation.

Pliske, T. E. 1973. Factors determining mating frequencies in some New World butterflies and skippers. Ann. Entomol. Soc. Am. 66:164–69.

Prysby, M. D. 2001. Temporal and geographical variation in monarch egg and larval densities (*Danaus plexippus*): an ecological application of citizen science. Master's thesis, University of Minnesota, St. Paul.

Rogg, K. A., O. R. Taylor, and D. L. Gibo. 1999. Mark and recapture during the monarch migration: a preliminary analysis. In J. Hoth, L. Merino, K. Oberhauser, I. Pisantry, S. Price, and T. Wilkinson, eds., The 1997 North American Conference on the Monarch Butterfly, pp. 133–38. Montreal: Commission for Environmental Cooperation.

Urquhart, F. A., and N. R. Urquhart. 1976. The overwintering site of the eastern population of the monarch butterfly (*Danaus p. plexippus*; Danaidae) in southern Mexico. J. Lepid. Soc. 30:153–58.

Van Hook, T. 1996. Monarch butterfly mating ecology at a Mexican overwintering site: proximate causes of non-random mating. Ph.D. thesis, University of Florida, Gainesville.

Van Hook, T. 1999. The use of bursa copulatrix dissection and abdominal palpation to assess female monarch butterfly mating status. In J. Hoth, L. Merino, K. Oberhauser, I. Pisantry, S. Price, and T. Wilkinson, eds., The 1997 North American Conference on the Monarch Butterfly, pp. 101–11. Montreal: Commission for Environmental Cooperation.

14

Documenting the Spring Movements of Monarch Butterflies with Journey North, a Citizen Science Program

Elizabeth Howard and Andrew K. Davis

INTRODUCTION

Although the overwintering location of the eastern North American population of the monarch butterfly in central Mexico has been known to the scientific community since 1976 (Urquhart 1976), scientists have only begun to understand how the annual spring recolonization of eastern North America proceeds. It had previously been thought that overwintering monarchs continued their northward spring migration until they reached their summer destinations, laying eggs along the way. This had been termed the "single sweep hypothesis" (Malcolm et al. 1993). This hypothesis has since been replaced by the "successive brood hypothesis," which argues that the majority of overwintering monarchs only migrate northward in the spring to the southern United States, laying eggs along the way. Their offspring then complete the journey northward to the upper reaches of the monarchs' breeding range (Cockrell et al. 1993; Malcolm et al. 1993).

Cockrell and colleagues (1993) provided the most comprehensive, large-scale documentation of the spring migration of eastern monarchs thus far. By surveying for immature stages of monarchs on milkweed transects at 62 locations and latitudes during the spring migration, they estimated the dates at which the eggs were laid, and thus documented the temporal and spatial distribution of ovipositing (migrant) females. However, one drawback to this method of quantifying migration is that dates of oviposition may not necessarily reflect the true timing of arrival of migrants to an area, since females may not oviposit on the date of arrival. It is possible that after arriving at a location, females may require a period of time to find milkweed plants on which to lay their eggs. Further, this method assumes that females oviposit equally along the migration route, while in actuality many external factors other than the urge to oviposit may cause a female to stop migrating. During fall migration, monarchs can be forced to land because of wind conditions unfavorable for migration (Davis and Garland, this volume). Such conditions must also influence migrating adults in the spring as well. Moreover, milkweed emergence rates and quality can vary spatially, and females may not choose to oviposit at all places they stop. Thus, a more direct way to document the spatial and temporal patterns of spring migration is to observe the arrival of adult butterflies to locations throughout the migration range. Until now, this has not been possible, as this task would require large numbers of observers operating simultaneously throughout the migratory pathways.

The timing of spring migration is unlikely to be the same each year since many aspects of the life history of monarchs show an annual variation, as do biotic and abiotic factors affecting their habitat in springtime. Breeding populations fluctuate annually (Swengel 1995; Prybsy and Oberhauser, this volume), which leads to corresponding fluctuations in the numbers of fall migrants (Brower 1995; Walton and Brower 1996). Further, the temporal distribution of fall migration varies each year (Walton and Brower 1996). Annual variation may also exist in the proportion of monarchs that successfully complete the fall migration to Mexico (Garland and Davis 2002). This, in turn, leads to an annual variation in the numbers of overwintering monarchs, as reflected in yearly measurements of the area of the overwintering colonies (García-Serrano et al., this volume). Finally, owing to predation at the overwintering colonies (Brower and Calvert 1985) and catastrophic weather events (Calvert et al. 1983; Brower et al., this volume), the numbers of monarchs that survive through the spring will also vary. Thus, the number of monarchs that migrate each spring is expected to fluctuate between years. Coupled with this, North America's climatic and weather patterns vary widely each spring during the northward migration of the overwintering generation, the development of the first spring generation, and its subsequent migration, all of which affect the pace of the spring migration (Zalucki and Rochester, this volume; Feddema et al., this volume). There is little published documentation of an annual variation in any aspect of the spring migration of monarchs, although Cockrell and colleagues (1993) briefly noted a yearly variation in spring oviposition dates at several latitudes in their 3-year study.

Aside from the study by Cockrell and colleagues (1993), much of our knowledge on the patterns of spring migration of the eastern monarch population is based on short-term studies carried out at specific sites along the migration pathways (e.g., Riley 1993; Knight et al. 1999). Although these studies are necessary to examine key aspects of the spring migration in detail, long-term, wide-scale quantitative programs are needed to gain a fuller understanding of it (Brower 1995). Long-term programs that quantify the fall migration at specific sites along the migration route have been established (Walton and Brower 1996; Garland and Davis 2002; Davis and Garland 2002), but more wide-scale programs are needed for the fall migration as well (Brower 1995).

Citizen science programs allow for large-scale and simultaneous data collection, by having individuals from the public observe and record data on natural events and then submit their data to a central repository for analysis. The Cornell Lab of Ornithology, a pioneer of citizen science programs for the study of birds, runs several backyard bird-watching programs. The data collected in these programs have already allowed Cornell scientists to document and study, among other things, the spatial variation in the winter abundance of birds (Wells et al. 1998), and the spread of a novel disease in house finches (*Carpodacus mexicanus*) across most of eastern North America (Dhondt et al. 1998; Hartup et al. 1998; Hochachka and Dhondt 2000; Dhondt et al. 2001; Hartup et al. 2001). These studies attest to the power and scope of citizen science.

Three large-scale citizen science programs focused on monarch butterflies have been established. In the Monarch Larva Monitoring Project, volunteers collect data on the spatial and temporal abundance of monarch eggs and larvae (Prysby and Oberhauser 1999; this volume). Monarch Watch is a volunteer-based organization that tracks the fall migration by distributing numbered monarch tags and collecting and disseminating the resulting capture-recovery data (Monarch Watch 2002). These programs provide important information on aspects of breeding biology and fall migration, respectively.

Journey North (Journey North 2002) is a citizen science program that documents the spring migration of monarchs. It was established in 1994 to fill a crucial gap in our knowledge of the spring movements. In this Internet-based program, volunteers across North America watch for migrating adult monarchs in the spring and record the date and location of the first monarch seen. The data are then entered on-line and collated and stored by Journey North. Participants can view on-line maps of all sightings on the Journey North website and follow the northward migration of monarchs each spring.

The Journey North program has been described only once in the scientific literature (Donnelly 1999), and no results of the program have been presented to date. Here, we provide a more complete overview of the program. We show what Journey North has revealed about the spatial patterns of spring migration, and how consistent the patterns are from year to year. Next, we address several questions that remain unanswered about the spring migration. In particular, we use the Journey North data to test for annual variation in the timing of spring migration at four different latitudes, as well as variation in the duration of the migration.

METHODS

The Journey North program

Journey North is funded by Annenberg/Corporation for Public Broadcasting, a project within the Corporation for Public Broadcasting whose mission is to use media and telecommunications to advance excellent teaching in America's schools. As such, the project's most important purpose is to engage students in grades K through 12 in a global study of wildlife migration and seasonal change. Using the Internet, students share their field observations with classmates across North America.

The Journey North monarch program begins in February each year. Everyone who contributes observations to Journey North must register on-line. Registration is free, but participants must provide their e-mail address for quality control purposes. Participants are asked to watch for monarchs as they go about their daily activities throughout the spring and summer months. While they are encouraged to standardize their observation methods (set aside a time of day, survey the same location, etc.), the data accepted by Journey North are not limited to those collected by standardized methods.

When the participants observe a monarch for the first time in the spring, they record this observation at the Journey North website. On the website, participants enter the monarch sighting date, the nearest town, their state or province, latitude and longitude (if known), their e-mail address, their names or their teaches' names, and any other comments. Besides dates of first adults, participants can also record sightings of overwintering monarchs and the dates they first observe milkweed, their first monarch egg, first monarch larvae, and any other related monarch observations.

Beginning in February each year, Journey North publishes weekly monarch migration updates (a map of monarch sightings) based on the sightings received from participants up to that point (figure 14.1). The updates are distributed by e-mail to all participating sites and posted to the Journey North website. The updates begin when monarchs are still at the Mexican overwintering sites, about 6 weeks before the migration usually enters Texas.

In addition to Journey North's own on-line observation network, the project actively seeks contributions of sightings from outside sources. These include butterfly listservs, nature center contacts, and individual contacts. Staff personnel enter these sightings into the Journey North database. Latitude and longitude can be entered by participants, but because observers often do not have this information readily available, the Journey North database appends latitude and longitude coordinates overnight, using the "nearest town" as a geographic reference. These coordinates are obtained from the U.S. zip code database for U.S. sightings. Canadian and Mexican latitude and longitude coordinates are entered manually. All data are currently stored online where they can be viewed by the public.

A great deal of personalized communication takes place between Journey North staff and the observation network. All sightings reported to the database are reviewed on a daily basis. The comments are read and the observer is contacted if there is a need for clarification. Great care is taken to assess the validity of observations, particularly when they are unusual. Sightings by schoolchildren are reported by their teachers, not students, and teachers play an important role in validating observations before submitting them. Journey North personnel remove questionable observations from the database.

As adult monarch sightings are reported each year and the locations and dates are updated on the on-line migration maps, one thing becomes evident about the timing and distribution of the spring migration. As the migration expands into a particular area, multiple sightings are usually reported on the same day, and in some cases within hours of each other, particularly in areas where many observers are located. Thus, we are confident that the participants accurately record the wave of arriving monarchs. However, in some cases sightings of migrating monarchs by two or more different citizens in the same location are separated by over 1 week. In these cases, the second observer's "first monarch sighting" was not the actual date of first arrival to the area, as reported by the first observer. This is one drawback to the Journey North program, since it cannot be known whether the observer saw one of the actual first monarchs in the area. However, these cases represent roughly 5% of the data for each year (pers. observ.); thus the analyses reported in this chapter should not be largely affected.

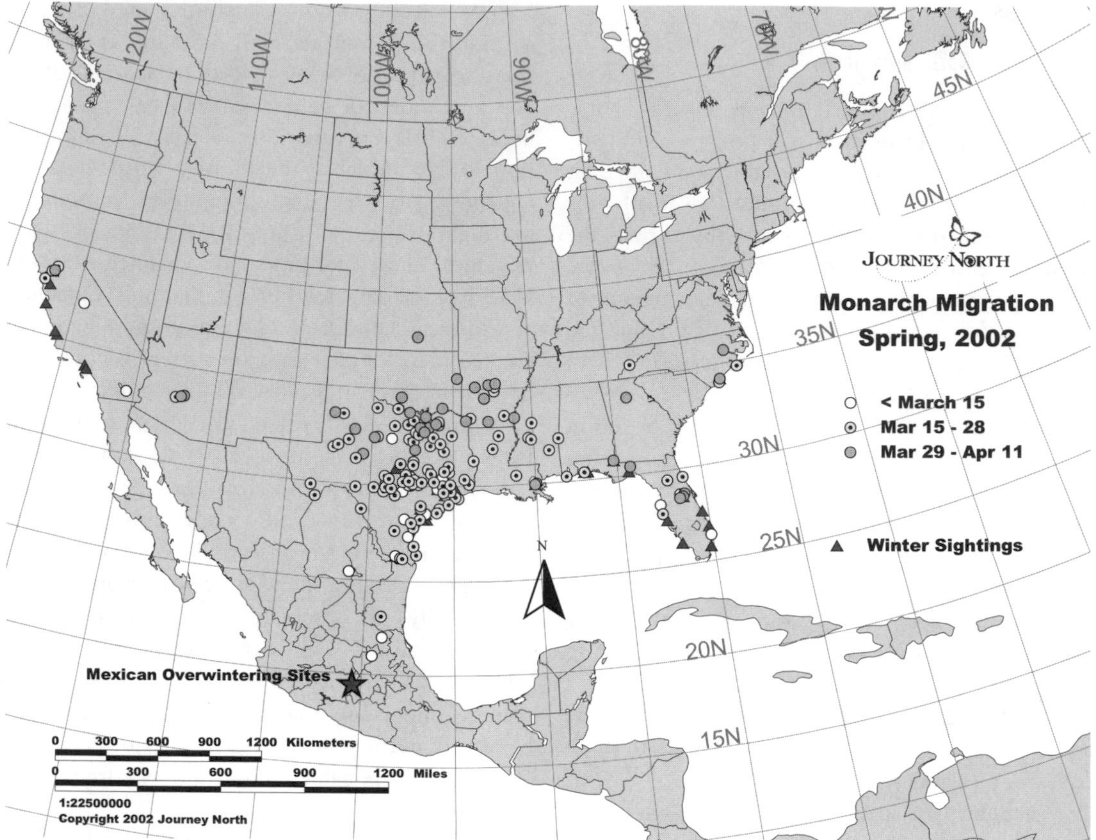

Figure 14.1. Sample map of spring monarch migration (2002) presented on the Journey North website, produced by data from participants.

Patterns of spring migration

Early in each spring migration, a considerable number of monarchs are sighted in the southeastern states before they are spotted at middle latitudes (pers. observ.). We investigated this pattern to determine whether it holds true in all years by determining the first monarch sighting for each state or province (within the range of the eastern population) in each of the 6 years, and then ranked these dates. We calculated the mean rank for each state over the 6 years, and then ranked these means to derive an overall "occupation order" of each state or province. We used these annual ranks to determine whether the order of state or province occupation is consistent among years, by performing Pearson correlations of the ranks between all year-to-year combinations.

Annual variation in migration timing

Sightings of overwintering adult monarchs are reported to Journey North each year. These sightings are usually in January or February, and occur mostly below 30° north latitude (pers. observ.). However, occasionally sightings of overwintering monarchs (in January and February) at or near 30° are reported. To ensure that these sightings did not confound our analyses of the spring migration, we only used sightings after 1 March. This resulted in little loss of data.

We used the Journey North data from 1997 to 2002 to determine whether annual variation exists in either the timing or the duration of the spring migration. To test for variation in timing among years, we first standardized the dates of the Journey North sightings across all years by transforming all dates into Julian dates (the number of days since 1 January). Since we were interested in the differences in timing at low, middle, and upper latitudes, we divided the sightings into four groupings, based on the latitude at which they were made. To simplify the groupings, we rounded all latitudes in the data set to whole numbers. For example, 36.7° north became 37° north. This resulted in sightings (Julian dates) of spring monarchs at 30° to 34°, 35° to 39°, 40° to 44°, and 45° north latitude and above for each year (see figure 14.1). We then performed separate one-way analyses of variance on the sighting dates in each of these four latitude groups between years to assess annual variation in the spring migration timing.

Annual variation in migration duration

To calculate travel time, one needs a starting point location, an end point location, and a measure of the time taken to go between the two. Here we assume the "end point" is a sighting of monarchs in the northern sections of the breeding range. Since we were interested in knowing how long it takes the population to reach the northernmost breeding areas, and whether this duration varies among years, we assume that sightings above 45° north latitude represent expansion of the population into the northernmost breeding range.

We define the "start date" of migration as the median date on which monarchs reached 30° north latitude in a given year (see figure 14.1). We used the median date rather than the mean date as it is less sensitive to extreme values (which exist at the lower latitudes). As such, the date of "migration initiation" in this case does not represent the date monarchs depart their overwintering colonies. Rather, it is the date monarchs begin to travel across the lower 48 states. Thus we calculated the median date of observations at 30° north (after rounding all latitudes to whole numbers) for each year (table 14.1). With these six annual start dates at 30° north latitude as the "start point," we then calculated the time (measured in days) taken to expand into the northernmost breeding range (45° and above) for each of the sightings at 45° and higher. We then performed a one-way analysis of variance on these "duration values" to assess annual variation in the average duration of migration.

Table 14.1. Average monarch arrival to 30° north latitude

Year	*N*	Mean date	Median date	Range (days)
1997	25	17 March	17 March	36
1998	25	26 March	21 March	73
1999	26	22 March	21 March	39
2000	26	13 March	12 March	26
2001	42	26 March	24 March	67
2002	74	18 March	17 March	27
Overall	218	19 March	17 March	73

Note: Based on Journey North data.

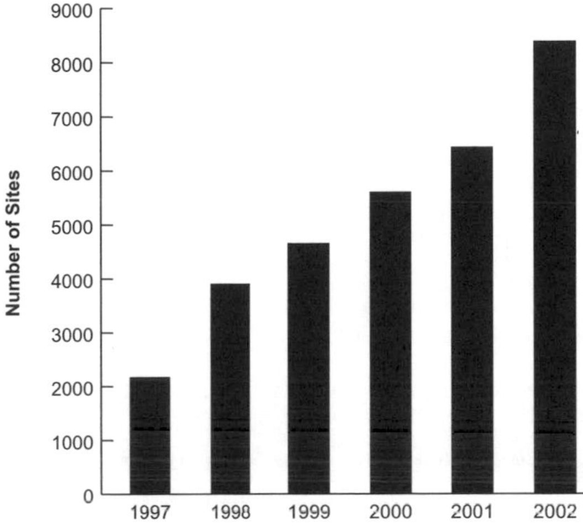

Figure 14.2. The number of registered monarch observation sites in North America from 1997 to 2002.

RESULTS AND DISCUSSION

Journey North participants

From 1997 to 2002, the number of participants submitting observations of spring monarchs has grown steadily each year, from 2171 in 1997 to 8380 registered sites in 2002 (figure 14.2). Based on questionnaires distributed in 2000 and 2001, we determined the setting in which Journey North was used during those years (figure 14.3). Although Journey North targets students, only 63% of the participants in 2000 and 2001 were students. Elementary students made up the bulk of the student participants. A large portion of the participants (21%) were families or individuals.

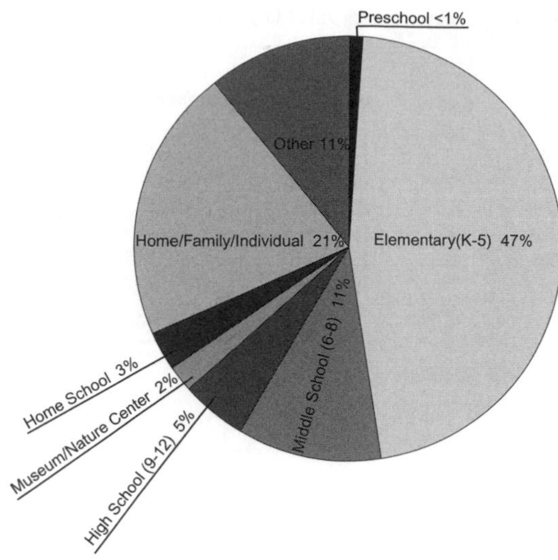

Figure 14.3. The occupation or setting in which participants used Journey North during 2000 and 2001.

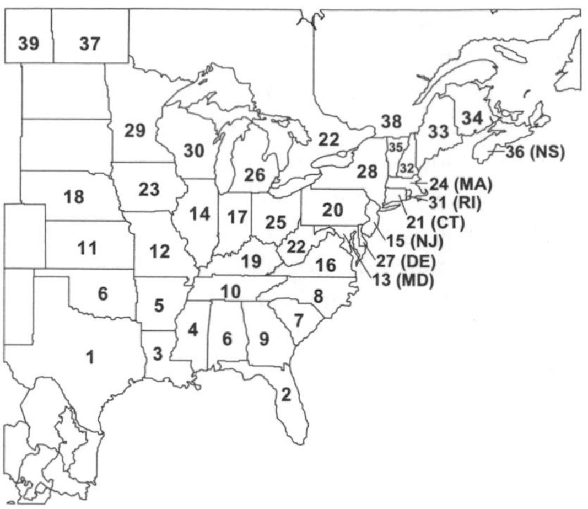

Figure 14.4. Average order of occupation of each state or province by monarchs during spring migration, based on first sightings of monarchs reported to Journey North. The ranks of the 6-year average of first arrival dates to each state or province are shown. Sightings before 1 March are excluded.

Patterns of spring migration

Once migrating monarchs reach the United States, the first state occupied is nearly always Texas, followed usually by either Florida or Louisiana (table 14.2, figure 14.4), although the Florida sightings may have been of monarchs originating in that state. Mississippi is usually next, followed by Arkansas and Oklahoma. It is not known whether monarchs are able to safely and regularly cross the Gulf of Mexico during migration as birds do (e.g., Gauthreaux 1999), although it is generally thought that they do not (Brower 1995). If this is true, then the sightings of early monarchs in the southeast, before sightings to the north, indicates that once the monarchs pass through Texas, some of them make an eastward movement across the southeastern states, before spreading across more northern latitudes. The migration then presses northward (probably composed mostly of second-generation monarchs) across a broad front, finally reaching the Canadian provinces, which are always last (figure 14.4). The order of state or province occupation was highly correlated between all year-to-year combinations (table 14.3), indicating that there is little variation in this overall pattern of spatial occupation during migration.

Annual variation in migration timing and duration

There was significant annual variation in migration timing at all latitude groupings (p = 0.009, 0.000, 0.020, and 0.000 for groupings 30° to 34°, 35° to 39°, 40° to 44°, and 45° and above, respectively; table 14.4, figure 14.5). Further, there was significant annual variation in the calculated migration durations ($df = 353$, $F = 27.16$, $p < 0.001$; figure 14.6). The time needed by the population (which includes returning and newly emerged adults) to reach the upper portions of their breeding areas ranged from 88.1 days in 1997 to 64.8 days in 2001. Interestingly, the longest calculated spring migration (1997) immediately followed the largest overwintering population recorded thus far, while the shortest migration (2001) immediately followed one of the lowest overwintering populations to date (García-Serrano et al., this volume). However, this trend may not be consistent in all years. In 2002, a severe storm caused a much-publicized population crash in the overwintering population, leaving very low numbers left to remigrate in the following spring (Brower et al., this volume). During this year, the migration duration was the second longest of all 6 years of the Journey North data. Furthermore, despite the low numbers of adults in 2002, the timing of the start of the spring migration that year appeared to be similar to that for most other years. In fact the only aspect of

Table 14.2. Arrival ranking

State/province	1997	1998	1999	2000	2001	2002	Mean rank	Overall rank
TX	1	1	1	1	1	2	1.2	1
FL	1	3	3	5	2	1	2.5	2
LA	3	2	2	2	3	5	2.8	3
MS	5	6	4	3	4	3	4.2	4
AR	5	5	5	7	6	6	5.7	5
OK	8	4	7	6	7	10	7.0	6
AL	4	10	8	4	8	8	7.0	6
SC	10	14	6	9	8	6	8.8	7
NC	7	10	12	10	11	4	9.0	8
GA	11	8	17	8	5	12	10.2	9
TN	8	16	9	12	10	9	10.7	10
KS	17	9	9	13	15	11	12.3	11
MO	12	12	12	15	17	13	13.5	12
MD	20	19	12	11	16	17	15.8	13
IL	15	13	12	19	23	15	16.2	14
NJ	17	17	18	13	23	13	16.8	15
VA	15	20	20	15	13	20	17.2	16
IN	25	7	21	24	12	26	19.2	17
NE	27	15	16	20	19	19	19.3	18
KY	13	39		21	13	16	20.4	19
PA	21	25	22	32	28	17	24.2	20
CT	22	33	28	17	23	23	24.3	21
WV	19	30	31	22	22		24.8	22
ON	28	29	11	33	26	22	24.8	22
IA	30	31	25	25	18	21	25.0	23
MA	13	22	31	29	32	28	25.8	24
OH	26	33	19	25	28	25	26.0	25
MI	32	18	24	30	26	28	26.3	26
DE	24	32		18	28	31	26.6	27
NY	29	27	23	28	20	33	26.7	28
MN	31	23	25	27	33	26	27.5	29
WI	34	21	27	31	31	24	28.0	30
RI	23		35	22	36		29.0	31
NH	38	28	29	34	20	30	29.8	32
ME	39	23	37	35	33	34	33.5	33
NB		26	34	39	37		34.0	34
VT		35	30	36	35	35	34.2	35
NS	33	37	31	38			34.8	36
MB	35		38	36	38	31	35.6	37
PQ	36	37	35	40	39		37.4	38
SK	36	36	39		40		37.8	39

Note: Ranks of U.S. states and Canadian provinces by the first arrival dates of monarchs in each year. Average of ranks from all 5 years is also shown. Sightings before 1 March are excluded. States or provinces from which less than 4 years of data were collected are excluded. Some states or provinces were tied with others in the same year.

migration in 2002 that appeared different from other years was the late arrival of monarchs to the northern latitudes (see table 14.4, figure 14.5), and this appeared to be due to a colder than average spring in these areas (pers. observ.). Thus, it seems that the monarch population size has little to do with spring migration timing.

The reasons, in part, for the long migration duration in 1997 and the short duration in 2001 can be seen in figure 14.5. In 1997 monarchs reached 30° north latitude early and the upper latitudes (45° and higher) very late in the season, causing a long migration duration for that year. In 2001, however, they reached 30° later, resulting in a short migration duration. Interestingly, in all years except 1997 monarchs seemed to reach the upper two latitude bands close to the same date, regardless of how early or late the migration began. Arrival to the middle

Table 14.3. Correlation matrix

	1997	1998	1999	2000	2001	2002
1997	1.0 $n = 39$	0.717 $n = 37$	0.825 $n = 37$	0.903 $n = 38$	0.818 $n = 38$	0.888 $n = 33$
1998		1.0 $n = 39$	0.820 $n = 37$	0.770 $n = 38$	0.764 $n = 38$	0.718 $n = 33$
1999			1.0 $n = 39$	0.854 $n = 38$	0.877 $n = 38$	0.898 $n = 31$
2000				1.0 $n = 39$	0.879 $n = 39$	0.867 $n = 33$
2001					1.0 $n = 39$	0.818 $n = 33$

Note: For each year combination, the order of state or province occupation (rank of first-sighting dates) is correlated. Pearson correlation coefficients and sample sizes are shown. *P* values for all correlations were less than 0.001.

Table 14.4. Latitudinal progression of monarch migration

North latitude	1997	1998	1999	2000	2001	2002	Overall average	Oviposition date
30°–34°	23 Mar (2.8) $n = 60$	3 Apr (5.4) $n = 65$	25 Mar (3.4) $n = 59$	20 Mar (2.6) $n = 67$	30 Mar (3.1) $n = 99$	25 Mar (2.8) $n = 190$	26 Mar (1.5) $n = 541$	1 Apr (3.3) $n = 26$
35°–39°	14 Apr (2.7) $n = 111$	25 Apr (5.0) $n = 66$	16 Apr (3.5) $n = 84$	13 Apr (2.7) $n = 115$	1 May (4.5) $n = 98$	24 Apr (5.4) $n = 101$	20 Apr (1.7) $n = 575$	24 Apr (8.0) $n = 10$
40°–44°	15 May (4.1) $n = 109$	20 May (3.4) $n = 122$	21 May (2.9) $n = 127$	16 May (2.4) $n = 171$	19 May (2.0) $n = 214$	1 Jun (3.2) $n = 192$	21 May (1.2) $n = 935$	24 May (5.6) $n = 15$
45°+	11 Jun (4.9) $n = 48$	24 May (4.4) $n = 51$	25 May (2.1) $n = 64$	23 May (3.8) $n = 45$	25 May (2.6) $n = 80$	2 Jun (3.3) $n = 71$	28 May (1.5) $n = 359$	

Note: Based on all Journey North spring sightings from 1997 to 2002. Average dates are shown with ±95% confidence intervals and sample sizes. Significant annual variation in arrival dates was found with each latitude group. Oviposition date was calculated from data presented in Cockrell et al. 1993.

latitudes (35° to 39°) is approximately 20 days following arrival to the lower (30° to 34°) ones, no matter how early or late the migration is (see figure 14.5), suggesting a constant rate of travel by monarchs throughout the lower latitudes. This implies that when the migration starts late, the arrival to the middle latitudes is also late. In addition, it suggests that the primary factor influencing the timing of arrival to the lower and middle latitudes may be the date migration started from the overwintering areas.

Arrival to the 40° to 44° latitudes is usually 1 month after arrival to the 35° to 39° latitudes (see figure 14.5). This longer interval between latitudes probably occurs because these monarchs represent the offspring of the overwintering adults. Moreover, the time needed by these butterflies to reach the last latitude level is usually very short (1 week or less, except in 1997).

Dates of arrival to each of the latitude categories did not correspond with previous information based on larval censuses. Cockrell and colleagues (1993) provided the dates of first oviposition at several latitudes in 1985 and 1986 (only one data point was presented for 1987 and consequently was not included in their article). If we categorize their published data according to our latitude groupings, we can derive average dates of oviposition for comparison with our average dates of arrival. The average

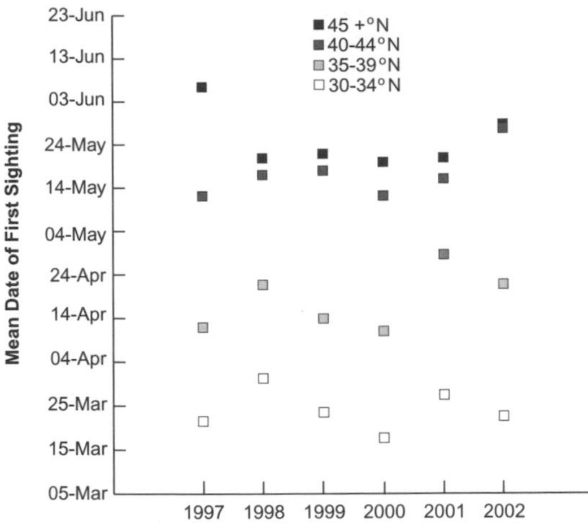

Figure 14.5. Annual variation in monarch arrival to each latitude group. Mean dates of first sightings are presented.

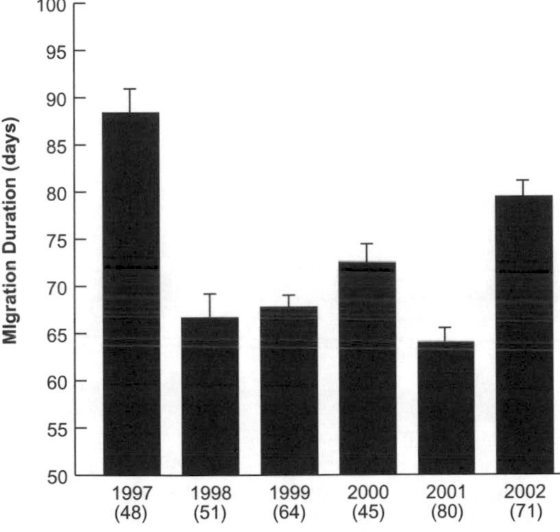

Figure 14.6. Average duration of migration (time needed to reach the upper breeding range), for years 1997 through 2002. Sample sizes for each year are indicated in parentheses. Standard error bars are shown with each average.

date of first oviposition at the 30° to 34° group was 1 April (n = 26, 95% confidence interval [CI] = 3.3 days), for the 35° to 39° group was 24 April (n = 10, 95% CI = 8.0 days), and for the 40° to 44° group was 24 May (n = 15, 95% CI = 5.6 days) (see table 14.4). We did not calculate an average date for the 45° and higher group since most of their sites in that group were censused in a different year. Each of these oviposition dates is 5 or more days later than our average dates of arrival to the same latitudes. Since their oviposition data were collected more than a decade prior to our data, detailed comparisons of the two data sets would not be meaningful. However, the data suggest that oviposition occurs later than monarch arrival to an area.

Annual variation in the timing of spring migration has not been previously documented in the scientific literature. That we found a yearly variation in the timing and duration of the spring migration could imply that at least in some years, environmental factors have a significant influence. In the fall monarchs travel faster when they migrate with tailwinds than with headwinds (Garland and Davis 2002), and also tend not to fly during unfavorable wind conditions (Schmidt-Koenig 1985; Davis and Garland 2002; Davis and Garland, this volume). It is not known if monarchs respond similarly to such weather conditions in the spring.

Alternatively, since female monarchs oviposit on emerging milkweeds as they migrate in the spring (Brower 1995), it may be that they are limited by the timing of milkweed emergence each year, which is also affected by environmental conditions. In one study in Louisiana, the arrival of spring migrant monarchs was closely synchronized with the availability of suitable milkweed host species (Riley 1993). Journey North data, along with corresponding large-scale environmental data, could elucidate whether this holds true across the breeding range. Further, owing to the geographic variation in spring climate (i.e., coastal areas tend to be warmer than inland areas), longitudinal variation may exist in the timing of milkweed emergence. This may lead to a corresponding longitudinal variation in spring migration and may explain the early eastward progression across southeastern states.

It is not known which, if either, of the above possibilities is more important in controlling the timing of spring migration, but we are currently using Journey North data to address this question. That these issues can be examined at all is due to the long-term and large-scale nature of the Journey North program. These results provide an example of how citizen participation in data collection can add greatly to our understanding of monarch butterflies.

Acknowledgments

This study is the result of thousands of volunteer participants who submitted their observations faithfully every year. We thank all who participated, and continue to participate, in the program. We also thank members of the Journey North staff: Beth Allen, Julie Brophy, Jane Duden, Laura Erickson, Wei-Hsin Fu, Joel Halvorson, Mary Hosier, Daphne Karypis, and Ed Piou. Invaluable assistance was provided by Lincoln Brower from the project's inception in 1994, and by Bill Calvert, Karen Oberhauser, and Chip Taylor, who also helped guide scientific direction over the years. Mike Quinn of Texas Monarch Watch and Chip Taylor of Monarch Watch contributed supplementary migration data from their two programs. Sonia Altizer and Lincoln Brower provided helpful advice on various aspects of this manuscript. Funding for Journey North is provided entirely by Annenberg/Corporation for Public Broadcasting. Additional funding was provided by the National Fish and Wildlife Foundation from 1995 to 1998.

References

Brower, L. P. 1995. Understanding and misunderstanding the migration of the monarch butterfly (Nymphalidae) in North America: 1857–1995. J. Lepid. Soc. 49:304–85.

Brower, L. P., and W. H. Calvert. 1985. Foraging dynamics of bird predators on overwintering monarch butterflies in Mexico. Evolution 39:852–68.

Calvert, W. H., W. Zuchowski, and L. P. Brower. 1983. The effect of rain, snow and freezing temperatures on overwintering monarch butterflies in Mexico. Biotropica 15:42–47.

Cockrell, B. J., S. B. Malcolm, and L. P. Brower. 1993. Time, temperature, and latitudinal constraints on the annual recolonization of eastern North America by the monarch butterfly. In S. B. Malcolm and M. P. Zalucki, eds., Biology and conservation of the monarch butterfly, pp. 233–51. Los Angeles: Natural History Museum of Los Angeles County.

Davis, A. K., and M. S. Garland. 2002. An evaluation of three methods of counting migrating monarch butterflies in varying wind conditions. Southeast. Nat. 1:55–59.

Dhondt, A. A., W. M. Hochachka, S. M. Altizer, and B. K. Hartup. 2001. The house finch hot zone: citizen science on the trail of an epidemic. Living Bird 20:24–30.

Dhondt, A. A., D. L. Tessaglia, and R. L. Slothower. 1998. Epidemic mycoplasmal conjunctivitis in house finches from eastern North America. J. Wildl. Dis. 34:265–80.

Donnelly, E. 1999. Journey North: tracking the migration over the Internet. In J. Hoth, L. Merino, K. Oberhauser, I. Pisantry, S. Price, and T. Wilkinson, eds., The 1997 North American Conference on the Monarch Butterfly, pp. 347–48. Montreal: Commission for Environmental Cooperation.

Garland, M. S., and A. K. Davis. 2002. An examination of monarch butterfly (*Danaus plexippus*) autumn migration in coastal Virginia. Am. Midl. Nat. 147:170–74.

Gauthreaux, S. A., Jr. 1999. Neotropical migrants and the Gulf of Mexico: the view from aloft. In K. P. Able, ed., Gatherings of angels, migrating birds and their ecology, pp. 27–49. Ithaca, N.Y.: Cornell University Press.

Hartup, B. K., A. A. Dhondt, K. V. Sydenstricker, W. M. Hochachka, and G. V. Kollias. 2001. Host range and dynamics of mycoplasmal conjunctivitis among birds in N. Am. J. Wildl. Dis. 37:72–81.

Hartup, B. K., H. O. Mohammed, G. V. Kollias, and A. A. Dhondt. 1998. Risk factors associated with mycoplasmal conjunctivitis in house finches. J. Wildl. Dis. 34:281–88.

Hochachka, W. M., and A. A. Dhondt. 2000. Density-dependent decline of host abundance resulting from a new infectious disease. Proc. Natl. Acad. Sci. USA 97:5303–6.

Journey North. 2002. http://www.learner.org/jnorth/. Accessed 1 August 2002.

Knight, A. L., L. P. Brower, and E. H. Williams. 1999. Spring remigration of the monarch butterfly, *Danaus plexippus* (Lepidoptera: Nymphalidae) in north-central Florida: estimating population parameters using mark-recapture. Biol. J. Linn. Soc. 68:531–56.

Malcolm, S. B., B. J. Cockrell, and L. P. Brower. 1993. Spring recolonization of eastern North America by the monarch butterfly: successive brood or single sweep migration? In S. B. Malcolm and M. P. Zalucki, eds., Biology and conservation of the monarch butterfly, pp. 253–67. Los Angeles: Natural History Museum of Los Angeles County.

Monarch Watch. 2002. Monarch Watch. http://monarchwatch.org. Accessed 1 August 2002.

Prysby, M. D., and K. Oberhauser. 1999. Large-scale monitoring of larval monarch populations and milkweed habitat in North America. In J. Hoth, L. Merino, K. Oberhauser, I. Pisantry, S. Price, and T. Wilkinson, eds., The 1997 North American Conference on the Monarch Butterfly, pp. 379–83. Montreal: Commission for Environmental Cooperation.

Riley, T. J. 1993. Spring migration and oviposition of the monarch butterfly in Louisiana. In S. B. Malcolm and M. P. Zalucki, eds., Biology and conservation of the monarch butterfly, pp. 270–73. Los Angeles: Natural History Museum of Los Angeles County.

Schmidt-Koenig, K. 1985. Migration strategies of monarch butterflies. In M. A. Rankin, ed., Migration: mechanisms and adaptive significance, pp. 786–98. Contributions to Marine Science, Vol. 27 Suppl. Port Aransas, Texas: Marine Science Institute, University of Texas at Austin.

Swengel, A. B. 1995. Population fluctuations of the monarch (*Danaus plexippus*) in the 4th of July Butterfly Count 1977–1994. Am. Midl. Nat. 134:205–14.

Urquhart, F. A. 1976. Found at last: the monarch's winter home. Natl. Geogr. Mag. 150:161–73.

Walton, R. K., and L. P. Brower. 1996. Monitoring the fall migration of the monarch butterfly *Danaus plexippus* L. (Nymphalidae: Danainae) in eastern North America: 1991–1994. J. Lepid. Soc. 50:1–20.

Wells, J. V., K. V. Rosenburg, E. H. Dunn, D. L. Tessaglia-Hymes, and A. A. Dhondt. 1998. Feeder counts as indicators of spatial and temporal variation in winter abundance of resident birds. J. Field Ornithol. 69:577–86.

PART III

Overwintering Biology

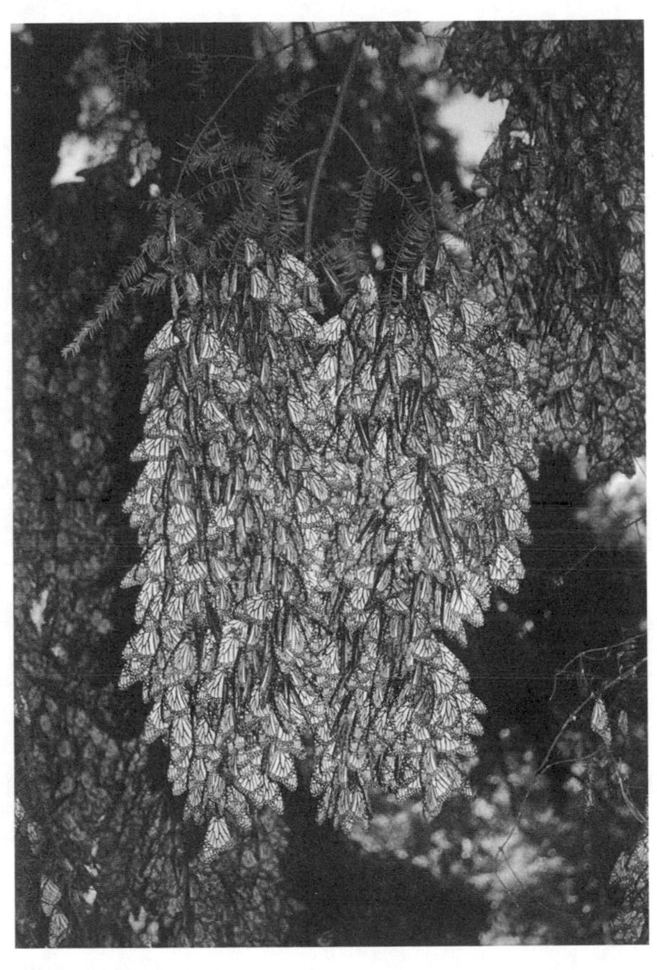

15

Overview of Monarch Overwintering Biology

Michelle J. Solensky

Although monarchs inhabit many areas of the world, the most spectacular overwintering colonies occur in North America. There are two major regions in North America in which monarchs regularly congregate during the winter: central Mexico and coastal California (Brower 1995). Monarchs also reside in southern Florida throughout the year, but the population receives an influx of individuals from the eastern migratory population each fall (Knight 1997; Altizer 2001). The degree to which monarchs from this part of the United States move back into the larger population is not understood.

Monarchs that spend the summer breeding season west of the Rocky Mountains overwinter along the coast of southern California. Here, they roost in wooded areas most often dominated by eucalyptus trees, Monterey pines, and Monterey cypresses located in sheltered bays or farther inland. These areas provide moderated microclimate extremes and protection from strong winds. More than 300 different aggregation sites have been reported (Frey and Schaffner, this volume; Leong et al., this volume).

North American monarchs that spend the summer breeding season east of the Rocky Mountains overwinter in oyamel fir forests in the mountains of central Mexico. The location of these overwintering sites was unknown to the scientific community until 1975 when associates of Fred Urquhart located colonies on Cerro Pelón and Sierra Chincua (Urquhart 1976; Brower 1995). While scientists have learned much about the phenomenon of monarch overwintering in the past few decades, several basic questions remain. Measuring the density of an organism that congregates by the millions, and perhaps billions, presents a formidable challenge. In addition to estimating population size, scientists also seek to understand the characteristics of the overwintering sites that are most important to monarch survival and the factors that influence the patterns of colony formation and dispersal (figure 15.1).

ESTIMATING POPULATION SIZE

Scientists use many methods to estimate abundance, but determining the population size of overwintering monarchs is particularly challenging because of their mobility and numbers. Nearly three decades after the discovery of the Mexican overwintering sites, scientists still search for ways to accurately measure the density of these butterflies. Calvert (chapter 16) used two methods to estimate the number of monarchs in two Mexican overwintering colonies. At one colony, he used mark, release, and recapture techniques to estimate the population density at 7 to 61 million monarchs/ha, with higher densities occurring later in the season when the colony had contracted. At a different colony, he measured the density of monarchs on subsamples of tree branches and trunks to reach an estimate of 12 million monarchs/ha. While some of these densities agree with previous estimates (Brower 1977; Brower et al. 1977), the variation suggests problems with assuming that monarch density remains constant seasonally and between colonies.

García-Serrano and colleagues (chapter 17) have

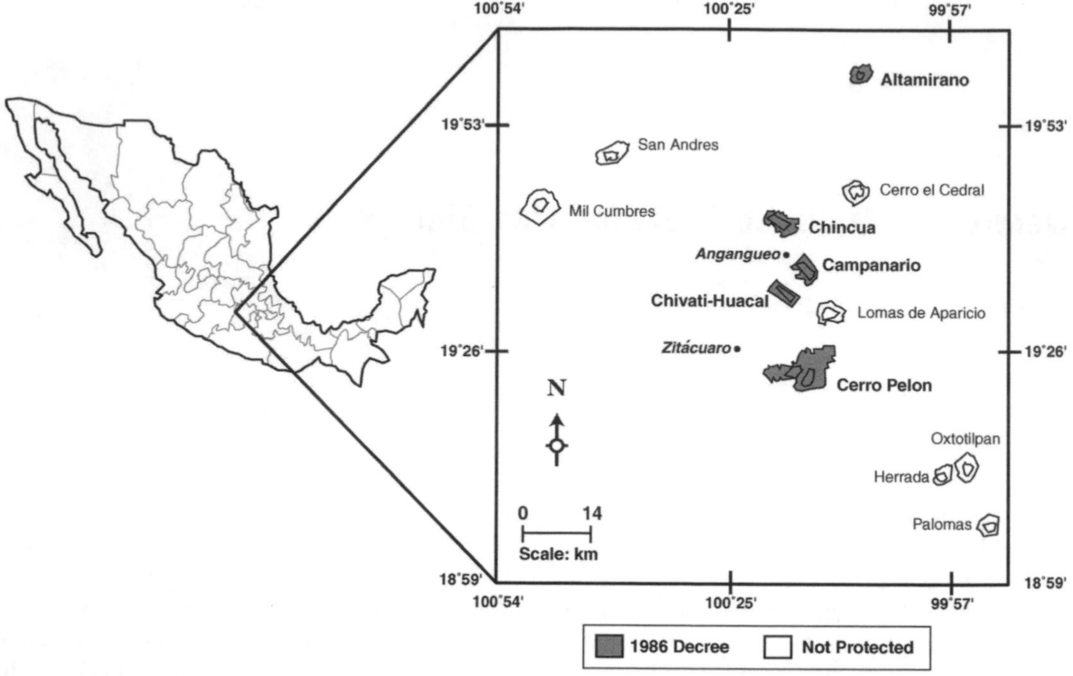

Figure 15.1. Geographic information system (GIS)–generated map of twelve mountain massifs in central Mexico that support monarch overwintering colonies. The total area shown is approximately 11,700 km^2. The five shaded polygons are overwintering areas protected by presidential decree in 1986 (16,100 ha). Lomas de Aparicio was protected in the 2000 decree, but the other six unshaded polygons are sites that currently are not protected. From Brower et al. 2002, reprinted with permission of Blackwell Publishing.

monitored 22 Mexican overwintering sites from 1993 to 2002 and report the location, size, and mortality measured at each site. Using an estimate of 10 million monarchs/ha, they report that the overwintering population ranged from 23 million monarchs in 2000–2001 to 176 million in 1996–1997. They measured the highest mortality (27.7%) during a low-population year (1997–1998, 45.5 million monarchs) and suggest that mortality rate may decrease with increasing population size.

PHYSICAL CHARACTERISTICS AND PROTECTED STATUS OF OVERWINTERING SITES

Monarchs migrate to specific overwintering sites because they require particular environmental characteristics to survive throughout the winter. While researchers have studied the microclimatic conditions that promote monarch survival (e.g., Calvert and Brower 1981; Brower 1999), few address how to promote conservation of the forests in which monarchs overwinter. Keiman and Franco (chapter 18) studied the response of the Mexican oyamel forests to disturbance and describe the processes of regeneration and self-thinning in the absence of human-induced disturbance. They found that trees within forest patches tend to be similar in size, and that homogeneity tends to increase with stand age. They argue that since monarchs typically form colonies in mature forests, we must not only protect the current forests but also ensure replacement as forest patches age.

The Mexican overwintering sites first achieved protected status under a 1986 presidential decree that established the Monarch Butterfly Special Biosphere Reserve. While this was an important first step, this decree did not protect all important overwintering sites (figure 15.1), failed to compensate local landowners for imposed restrictions on land use, and offered no effective economic alternatives to previous means of subsistence (e.g., agriculture, logging). In 1998, an international group of scientists and policy makers joined to redefine the protected area. Missrie (chapter 19) describes the 4-year process that led to a new presidential decree and improved protection of the Mexican overwintering sites. She summarizes the reasoning and models used by scientists to define an optimal protected area, then describes negotiations between government agencies and landowners that resulted in a new reserve more than twice the size of the previous protected area. Perhaps most importantly, the new decree includes provisions for compensation of landowners. However, this new agreement only protects monarchs from human-induced disturbances; they face threats from natural disturbances as well. Brower and coauthors (chapter 20) describe the devastating impact of a severe winter storm in the Mexican overwintering sites in January 2002. They estimate a mortality of 75% to 80% at two overwintering colonies and suggest that similar rates occurred throughout the Mexican sites. Their estimates of the number of monarchs killed per hectare (26 to 72 million) far exceed previous estimates of the number of monarchs occupying these sites, but agree with estimates presented by Calvert (chapter 16) for the same time of year. Calvert suggests that previous estimates of 10 million monarchs/ha may reasonably reflect densities earlier in the overwintering season.

Frey and Schaffner and Leong and coauthors describe patterns of distribution and abundance of monarchs in the western United States. With the same database, each group of authors uses a different model to predict habitat and climatic variables that influence the distribution and numbers of overwintering monarchs. Frey and Schaffner (chapter 21) examined abundance on three temporal scales (spanning 1, 4, and 20 years) and found that sites near the coast that contained eucalyptus, pine, and cypress tended to have more monarchs. Landownership (private or public) and shoreline orientation were not associated with monarch abundance. They also compared the western and eastern North American populations and found similar annual variation in relative abundances. Monarch abundance in Mexico is at least two orders of magnitude greater than that in western North America, but Frey and Schaffner observed that the trends were not in sync, suggesting different sources of variation in the two populations. Leong and coauthors (chapter 22) focused on a regional variation in environmental variables and found that the higher abundance of monarchs in central California was associated with high ambient moisture, substantial morning dew, and moderate winter temperatures. Geographic information system (GIS) analyses showed that most winter groves occurred within 2.4 km from the coastline on slopes with a south to west orientation. Larger winter sites were associated with the lower slopes of valleys, bays, and coastal inlets. Both groups of authors advocate the use of these and similar analyses in evaluating land management practices and structuring conservation goals.

UNDERSTANDING PATTERNS OF COLONY FORMATION AND DISPERSAL

Throughout the winter, North American monarchs cluster together, covering whole tree trunks and branches. Calvert (chapter 16) describes four phases typical of colony development in Mexican sites: recruitment and consolidation, settling and compaction of clusters, expansion and rapid movement, and mating and dispersal. Frey and Schaffner (chapter 21) describe a temporal pattern of abundance in California that is comparable to the first two of Calvert's phases. Initially monarchs occupy many local habitats, but by late November they abandon many of them and join nearby colonies.

The timing of the last phase, mating and dispersal, depends on the timing of completion of reproductive diapause, which varies considerably across individuals within an overwintering colony. Tagging (Urquhart and Urquhart 1978; Monarch Watch 2001) and stable isotope studies (Wassenaar and Hobson 1998) indicate that while the majority of monarchs overwintering in Mexico originate in the Midwest, these overwintering populations are composed of monarchs coming from a wide geographic area subjected to a wide range of environmental conditions. Goehring and Oberhauser (chapter 23) studied postdiapause reproductive development in monarchs overwintering in Mexico. As expected based on the varied histories of the butterflies, they found a great deal of variation in reproductive status. Females that were collected while mating were more likely to have developed oocytes than were females collected from clusters. Furthermore, access to host plants and mating accelerated oocyte development, while increasing daylength had no effect. They suggest that female response to host plants serves to synchronize oogenesis with oviposition opportunities.

The chapters in this section represent exciting developments in our attempts to understand one of the most amazing natural phenomena in the world. They also illustrate the need for continued study and accelerated conservation efforts.

References

Altizer, S. M. 2001. Migratory behaviour and host-parasite co-evolution in natural populations of monarch butterflies infected with a protozoan parasite. Evol. Ecol. Res. 3:611–32.

Brower, L. P. 1977. Monarch migration. Nat. Hist. 84:40–53.

Brower, L. P. 1995. Understanding and misunderstanding the migration of the monarch butterfly (Nymphalidae) in North America: 1857–1995. J. Lepid. Soc. 49:304–85.

Brower, L. P. 1999. Biological necessities for monarch butterfly overwintering in relation to the oyamel forest ecosystem in Mexico. In J. Hoth, L. Merino, K. Oberhauser, I. Pisantry, S. Price, and T. Wilkinson, eds., The 1997 North American Conference on the Monarch Butterfly, pp. 11–28. Montreal: Commission for Environmental Cooperation.

Brower, L. P., W. H. Calvert, L. E. Hendrick, and J. Christian. 1977. Biological observations of an overwintering colony of monarch butterflies (*Danaus plexippus*, Danaidae) in Mexico. J. Lepid. Soc. 31:232–42.

Brower, L. P., G. Castilleja, A. Peralta, J. Lopez-Garcia, L. Bojorquez-Tapia, S. Diaz, D. Melgarejo, and M. Missrie. 2002. Quantitative changes in forest quality in a principal overwintering area of the monarch butterfly in Mexico: 1971 to 1999. Conserv. Biol. 16:346–59.

Calvert, W. H., and L. P. Brower. 1981. The importance of forest cover for the survival of overwintering monarch butterflies (*Danaus plexippus*, Danaidae). J. Lepid. Soc. 35:216–25.

Knight, A. L. 1997. A population study of monarch butterflies in North-central and South Florida. Master's thesis, University of Florida, Gainesville.

Monarch Watch. 2001. Monarch watch migration and tagging. www.monarchwatch.org/tagmig/index.htm. Accessed 21 January 2003.

Urquhart, F. A. 1976. Found at last: the monarch's winter home. Nat. Geogr. Mag. 150:161–73.

Urquhart, F. A., and N. R. Urquhart. 1978. Autumnal migration routes of the eastern population of the monarch butterfly (*Danaus p. plexippus* L.; Danaidae; Lepidoptera) in North America to the overwintering site in the Neovolcanic Plateau of Mexico. Can. J. Zool. 56:1759–64.

Wassenaar, L. I., and K. A. Hobson. 1998. Natal origins of migratory monarch butterflies at wintering colonies in Mexico: new isotopic evidence. Proc. Natl. Acad. Sci. USA 95:15436–39.

16

Two Methods Estimating Overwintering Monarch Population Size in Mexico

William H. Calvert

INTRODUCTION

The fall generation of the eastern North American monarch population migrates to specific areas in Mexico's Transvolcanic Belt, where monarchs cluster in crowns and on trunks of trees. When one first enters the colonies, the number of monarchs seems enormous and uncountable. Mark, release, and recapture (Tuskes and Brower 1978) and subjective estimation techniques have been used at the much smaller California colonies (Sakai and Calvert 1992), but quantitative methods have not been applied in Mexico.

To answer basic questions about monarch choice of and fidelity to particular sites, we must understand survival rates in the overwintering colonies. The major causes of monarch mortality in the Mexican overwintering colonies are well studied (Calvert et al. 1979, 1983; Fink and Brower 1981; Glendinning et al. 1988), but reliable estimates of the population of the colonies are needed to assess the impact of particular mortality agents each year (e.g., severe weather [Brower et al., this volume]).

I describe two methods to estimate the size of the monarch overwintering population. I used the traditional mark, release, and recapture methodology of the Petersen and Jolly-Seber indices in Picacho, a relatively small colony, and an indirect method based on several forest parameters in the larger Sierra Chincua colony.

METHODS: MARK, RELEASE, RECAPTURE

Picacho, now called Lomas de Aparicio (19.6° north latitude and 100.2° west longitude), was selected for a mark, release, and recapture study during the winter of 1985–1986. The biggest challenge of this method was marking a large number of monarchs. Picacho was chosen because of its relatively small size, which allowed us to mark a substantial portion of the monarchs.

The colony periphery was mapped on 12 December 1985 and 12 January 1986 using a Suunto sighting compass and measuring tape. I calculated colony areas using Hewlett-Packard's double meridian distance program (Anonymous 1975).

Monarchs were marked on 12 and 13 December, 27 and 28 December, and 12 and 13 January and captured on 27 and 28 December, 12 and 13 January, and 2 February (table 16.1). On each occasion, approximately 10,000 individuals were marked by six persons. Monarchs were captured from all parts of the colony, including the ground, shrubs, and tree trunks and branches ranging in height from 1 to 6 m. We used an extendible pole with attached net to reach the higher clusters.

After capture, we examined each monarch for marks and then marked each with a colored felt-tipped pen. The colors used were to be changed each marking period. We sought to mark as many monarchs as possible in the limited time available while

Table 16.1. Numbers of monarchs marked and recaptured for the Picacho site

Date	No. captured and marked	No. of marked individuals recaptured	Estimated % marked	Colony area (ha)
12, 13 Dec 1985	10,527 (red)		0.55	0.2728
27 Dec 1985	1,997 (red)	10		
27, 28 Dec 1985	10,781 (red)	59	0.33	
12, 13 Jan 1986	9,707 (green)	53	0.19	0.0839
2 Feb 1986	10,524 (not marked)	42 (red), 19 (green)		

Table 16.2. Population estimates based on mark, release, recapture methods for the Picacho site

Time interval	Estimated no. at beginning of interval	95% confidence limits (millions)	Estimated density (95% confidence interval) (per ha, millions)
11–27 Dec	1,912,266[a]	1.1–3.3	
12–28 Dec	1,891,880[a]	1.5–2.6	6.9 (5.6–9.6)
27 Dec–13 Jan	3,830,833[a]	3.1–5.4	
12 Jan–2 Feb	5,108,834[a]	3.4–8.4	60.9 (40.6–100.0)
12, 13 Jan	2,836,927[b]	1.8–5.8	33.8 (21.1–68.7)

[a] Petersen method.
[b] Jolly-Seber method.

allowing for the possibility of distinguishing marking dates. Due to an error in communication, the marking color was not changed on 27 and 28 December, obviating the use of the Jolly-Seber index for the entire season, though it was still useful for segments of time. I used the Petersen index for most date combinations and the Jolly-Seber index when applicable (Southwood 1966; Krebs 1999; table 16.2).

The formulation of the Petersen index without replacement is:

$$(1)\quad \hat{N} = \frac{(M+1)(C+1)}{(R+1)} - 1,$$

where
$\hat{N}$ = the size of the population at the time of marking,
M = the number of individuals captured and marked during the first sampling period,
C = the total number of individuals captured during the second sampling period, and
R = the number of previously marked individuals observed in the second sample.

The Petersen index assumes no net migration out of the population, an assumption that may have been violated. However, short intervals between marking periods and repeated computation with overlapping periods mitigate problems caused by this violation.

The Jolly-Seber method permits birth, death, immigration, and emigration. This makes it a better choice for the overwintering colonies, but because it requires three sampling periods it can only produce one estimate using the data shown in table 16.1. The formulation of the method (Krebs 1999) is:

$$(2)\quad \hat{\alpha}_t = \frac{m_t+1}{n_t+1} \quad \hat{M}_t = \frac{(s_t+1)Z_t}{R_t+1} + m_t \quad \hat{N}_t = \frac{\hat{M}_t}{\hat{\alpha}_t}$$

where
$\hat{\alpha}_t$ = proportion of the population that is marked,
$\hat{M}_t$ = marked population just before sample time t,
$\hat{N}_t$ = population size at time t,
m_t = number of marked animals caught in sample t,
n_t = number of animals caught in sample t,
s_t = number of animals released after sample t,
R_t = number of animals released at sample t and recaptured in a later sample, and
Z_t = number of animals marked before sample t, not caught in sample t, but caught in a later sample.

RESULTS: MARK, RELEASE, RECAPTURE METHOD

The area covered by the Picacho colony showed a clear decrease between mapping dates (see table 16.1), due to either emigration away from the colony or a seasonal compaction of the clusters.

The population estimates vary with recapture dates, but the estimated number of monarchs generally increased as the season progressed (see table 16.2). All of the Petersen estimates are within the confidence interval of the single applicable Jolly-

Seber estimate. These results suggest that the population did not change substantially before mid-January; if anything, it may have increased.

The Jolly-Seber estimate of 2,836,927 monarchs at the Picacho colony (see table 16.2) yields an estimate of 10,399,293 monarchs/ha when the colony area was 0.2728 ha, but 33,813,194 monarchs/ha when the colony area was 0.0839 ha. The Petersen method produces estimates of 6,935,044 monarchs/ha when the colony area was 0.2728 ha, and 60,891,943 monarchs/ha when the colony area was 0.0839 ha.

METHODS: FOREST PARAMETER

At a 2.69-ha colony in the Sierra Chincua (19.7° north latitude and 100.3° west longitude) during January and February 1979, a number of volunteers and I indirectly estimated the size of the monarch population. We used several forest parameters and sampled monarch densities to estimate the number of monarchs occupying tree crowns and trunks.

Monarchs on tree crowns

I estimated the number of monarchs occupying tree crowns using two empirical relationships established by regression analysis. The first regression estimates average crown dry weight from the easily measured average diameter at breast height (*dbh*) of trees within the colony. This relationship ($R^2 = 0.95$) was established by Brown (1978) for the grand fir, *Abies grandis*, a species similar in crown shape to *A. religiosa* (oyamel fir), the preferred roosting species of monarchs:

$$(3) \quad w_l = e^{[1.3094+1.6076(\ln dbh)]},$$

$$(4) \quad w_{nl} = e^{[3.5638(\ln dbh)-5.3154]},$$

where
w_l = dry live crown weight in kilograms, and
w_{nl} = dry dead crown weight in kilograms.

I determined the average *dbh* for trees selected using the point-centered quarter method (Cottam and Curtis 1956) along two randomly set transects through the colony and a third transect set perpendicular to the slope's strike.

We used a second regression of monarch number against branch weight to estimate the average number of monarchs per tree branch. Twelve branches fully covered with monarchs were removed and lowered onto sheets of polyethylene in the early morning when it was too cold (about 0°C) for the monarchs to move. We chose branches to represent the range of sizes occupied by monarchs. After gently shaking the monarchs from the branch, we weighed 200 or 300 individuals in groups of 100 to determine average monarch weight per branch. The remaining monarchs were weighed, and their number was calculated by dividing their total mass by the average monarch weight. We cut branches into manageable sizes and weighed them with a Pesola spring balance. Monarch number was regressed against branch mass for the twelve branches using a least-squares curve fitting program.

I calculated the number of branches per crown by dividing the crown weight (determined using equations 3 and 4) by average branch weight, and then multiplied that by the estimated number of monarchs per branch to produce an estimate of the number of monarchs per crown. The same trees used to estimate *dbh* were used to estimate tree density, average percentage of cover of crowns by monarchs, average number of trees containing trunk clusters, and average fraction of trunk area occupied by monarchs. The total number of trees in the colony was determined by multiplying tree density by colony area. Finally, the estimate for the number of monarchs per crown was multiplied by the number of trees in the colony, and then adjusted for incomplete crown coverage and the percentage of trees that contained monarchs to give an estimate of the total number of monarchs on the crowns.

Monarchs on tree trunks

I estimated the number of monarchs on trunks based on calculations of the average surface area of a column and the density of monarchs on occupied trunks. The surface area of tree trunks was computed from the formula for the frustum of a cone:

$$(5) \quad SA = \pi(r_b + r_t)\left[h^2 + (r_b - r_t)^2\right]^{1/2},$$

where
SA = surface area,
r_b = average radius at the base of a column,

r_t = average radius at the top, and
h = average height of the column.

Furthermore,

(6) $$r_b = \frac{dbh}{2}\left(\frac{1-b}{n-1.4}\right) \text{ and } r_t = \frac{dbh}{2}\left(\frac{1-t}{n-1.4}\right),$$

where
1.4 = breast height in meters,
b = the average height of the bases of the monarch columns,
n = the average height of a colony tree, and
t = the average height of the tops of the monarch columns.

Parameters were measured with a Spiegel-Relaskop instrument (which can be used to measure stand basal area and tree height and diameter at any point up a tree trunk) from sample trees along the first two transects described above.

The density of monarchs on trunks was measured by counting the number of monarchs within a 20 × 50-cm wire frame superimposed on 17 trees with trunk clusters. Monarchs on the boundary were counted only when at least half of their bodies were within the frame. Densities were determined at different heights within the trunk clusters. We used a ladder or scaffolding where necessary to reach higher clusters. The numbers counted were multiplied by 10 to arrive at a per square meter value.

RESULTS: FOREST PARAMETER METHOD

Monarchs on tree crowns

The average *dbh* of colony trees was 0.31 m. The estimation of dry live crown mass (excluding the bole fraction) for a tree of this *dbh* using equation 3 was 93.2 kg. The mass of nonliving parts (dead weight of the crown) of a tree of this *dbh* using equation 4 was 16.4 kg. Dry live crown mass was converted to wet crown mass using the average percentage of moisture for eleven species of conifers (Brown 1978) and added to the dead mass, giving 189 kg for the average crown mass of a colony tree. I divided this value by the average branch mass (5.252 kg) to estimate the number of branches per tree (approximately 36 branches/tree).

The relationship between branch mass and the estimated number of monarchs on these branches is illustrated in figure 16.1. The least-squares regression of monarch number against branch mass generated the following formula ($R^2 = 0.725$):

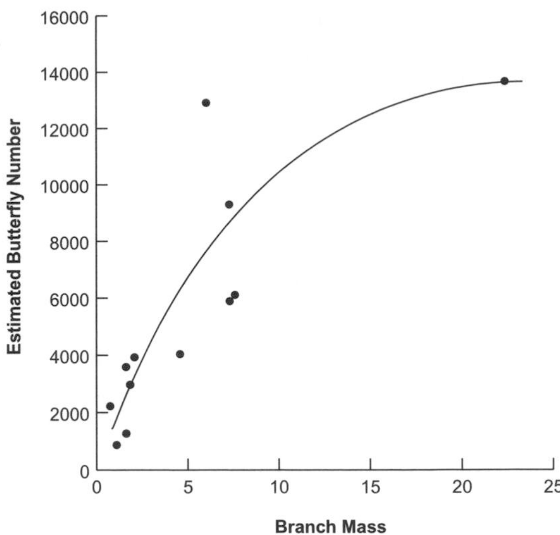

Figure 16.1. Estimated numbers of monarchs on twelve branches of different masses, with trendline from least-squares power function regression.

(7) $$y = 1724m^{0.73},$$

where
y = number of monarchs on a branch, and
m = branch mass.

This regression produced an estimate of 5786 monarchs occupying a branch of average mass (5.252 kg), and an average tree crown weighing 189 kg would have contained 208,296 monarchs if it were fully occupied. But since on average only 16% of the tree crowns were covered with monarchs, the average crown contained only 33,327 monarchs. Therefore, the crowns of the entire colony of 1026 trees were estimated to have contained 24,961,256 monarchs (33,327 monarchs/crown × 1026 trees × 0.73 of trees in the colony with monarchs).

Monarchs on tree trunks

I calculated the number of monarchs on the average tree trunk by computing the surface area of an average column of monarchs on trunks and multiplying by the density of monarchs on trunks. This figure was then multiplied by the number of trees having trunk clusters to give an estimate of the number of monarchs in trunk clusters.

Average surface area, computed from the radius and height at the base and top of a monarch column and the height of the average colony tree, was 2.66 m^2. The number of monarchs in the average column was estimated by multiplying average surface area occupied by monarchs by the average monarch density: 2.66 m^2 × 2992 monarchs/m^2 = 7959 monarchs/tree trunk. However, during the transect surveys, we estimated that 89% of the trunk circumference was covered by monarchs and only 37% of the colony trees contain trunk clusters. The corrected estimate for the number of monarchs on one tree trunk was 2,621, giving a total estimate of 2,688,947 monarchs on the 1026 colony tree trunks.

The estimated total number of monarchs in this colony using this method is the sum of those on the trunks and in the crowns (2,688,947 + 24,961,256 = 27,650,203), or 10,278,886 monarchs/ha (27,650,203/2.69 ha).

DISCUSSION

Mark, release, recapture method

The Petersen and Jolly-Seber mark, release, and recapture indices suggest that there were 6.9 and 10.4 million monarchs/ha in the Picacho colony on 12 December. These numbers increased to 60.9 and 33.8 million for the two methods on 12 and 13 January. While the confidence intervals around these values are large, they represent the first quantitative assessments using this method. Since the Jolly-Seber method allows for emigration, immigration, and death, the assumptions of this method were met in this study. The assumptions of the Petersen method (Southwood 1966; Krebs 1999) are likely met except for a possible net migration out of the colony during the study. If marked monarchs were leaving the colony, the numbers recaptured were lower than expected, and consequently, the population size was estimated to be larger. This inflation of estimated colony size would have been even greater if marked monarchs were more likely to leave the colony. If the monarchs we marked or recaptured were nonrandom samples of the population, our estimates would also be biased. Since the colony location shifted between marking episodes, thorough mixing was likely and sampling biases were unlikely to have been important. Mortality occurred during the period, but marked dead monarchs were as apparent as marked live ones and were counted in the total of recaptured marked monarchs.

The Picacho colony shrank in area between 11 December and 13 January (see table 16.1). The Petersen indices suggest that the total number of monarchs increased during this period, and the Jolly-Seber estimate for mid-January overlaps with the early Petersen estimate. How can the 67% loss in area occupied by the monarchs be reconciled with the lack of change or even an increase in population size?

Our current knowledge on the dynamics of Mexican overwintering colonies is based on a study of the 1978–1979 Chincua colony (Calvert and Brower 1986). This colony went through four phases: (1) recruitment and consolidation from late October to mid-December, (2) settling and compaction of clusters from mid-December to mid-February, (3) expansion and rapid movement beginning about mid-February, and (4) mating and dispersal beginning in early March. The area occupied by the colony grew during November, contracted in December, and then expanded again in February. After December, changes in area were probably due to cluster compaction of and recruitment from other colonies. Large colonies always appear to go through these phases, but the timing varies with the weather. The timing of colony reduction by 67% (0.2728 to 0.0839 ha) at Picacho coincides with the compaction period of the Chincua colony, and thus agrees with our earlier findings.

Similar compaction to more dense configurations has been observed in California colonies. In the fall of 2000, the area occupied by roosting monarchs declined from 0.14 to 0.012 ha (90%) at the Pismo Beach colony between November and the end of December, while monarch abundance actually increased (D. Frey, pers. comm.).

Forest parameter method

Information relating *dbh* to crown weight is not available for *A. religiosa*. Foresters have applied the regression formulae used in this study to congeners with good results, especially when crown shapes are similar, as they are in *A. grandis* and *A. religiosa* (J. Brown pers. comm.). Therefore the regression of *dbh* on crown weight established from *A. grandis*

(Brown, 1978) should also be valid for *A. religiosa*, the oyamel fir used by roosting monarchs in Mexico.

The forest parameter method also assumes that branch masses sampled are an accurate reflection of branches throughout the colony. Anticipating small sample sizes, I chose a range of branch sizes occupied by monarchs (see Valliant et al. 2000). Errors in either direction would tend to cancel each other: if the average branch mass were greater than estimated, there would be more monarchs per branch but fewer branches per crown.

The empirically derived regression from the forest parameter method agrees remarkably well with a model determined from theoretical considerations. The best fitting relationship between branch mass and monarch number using equation 7 ($y = bm^a$) had values of 1724 and 0.73 for b and a, respectively. From a theoretical perspective, monarch number is likely to be proportional to branch surface area. Since surface area is a function of length squared, branch surface area (which is the parameter most likely to be correlated with monarch number) will be proportional to the square of branch length:

(8) $N = cl^2$,

where
N = surface area,
l = branch length, and
c = is a constant.

Similarly, because mass is proportional to volume, which is a function of length cubed, branch mass will be proportional to the cube of branch length:

(9) $m = dl^3$,

where
m = branch mass,
l = branch length, and
d is a constant.

One can simplify these equations to:

(10) $N^3/m^2 = c/d$,

and define c/d as a new constant, "b":

(11) $N = bm^{2/3}$.

This bears remarkable resemblance to the empirically derived equation 7 from the regression analysis: $y = bm^{0.73}$.

Comparison of the two methods and results

I estimated the population size and density for two different colonies in two different years. In January and February 1979, the forest parameter method suggested that there were about 10.3 million monarchs/ha in a colony on Sierra Chincua. The 1985–1986 mark, release, recapture indices suggested population densities of 6.9 (Petersen method) or 10.4 (Jolly-Seber method) million monarchs/ha in December and 33.8 (Jolly-Seber method) or 60.9 (Petersen method) million monarchs/ha in January in the Picacho colony. This variation suggests problems with assuming consistent monarch densities between colonies and years, or within years in a given colony, as has been suggested previously (Calvert and Brower 1986). There are not enough data to assess which method is most accurate, but different methods may be more convenient and less disruptive to the monarchs at different times.

The importance of population estimations

The annual migration of much of the entire eastern North American monarch population to a few small isolated areas provides unparalleled opportunities for demographic analysis. If we can accurately estimate monarch density in the overwintering colonies, simple mapping of all overwintering colonies could provide a good estimate of the entire eastern monarch population after migratory mortality is subtracted. These estimates could be correlated with ecological factors in the breeding area such as parasitic outbreaks, the availability of adult and larval food resources, and abiotic factors such as rainfall and temperature. Perhaps most important is the potential for answering questions about the overwintering strategies of monarchs. A comparative study of the various agents of mortality and their contribution to survivorship among sites differing in ecological characteristics should provide clues as to why monarchs consistently choose specific habitats within the oyamel forest system of Mexico.

Acknowledgments

I thank Lic. Ricardo Enriquez, Roberto Alcantar, and Lorenzo Maldonado of the Mexican Forestry and Wildlife Department and the late Col. Timoteo Mondragon, former owner of the exhacienda Chincua, members of the ejido Cañon del Muerte, Mayor José Martinez, and Secretary Pablo Piña of Angangueo for permission to study monarchs in Mexico. Gary Mathews, Mary Margaret Quadlander, Willow Zuchowski, David Palmer, Melinda Lindquist, Susan Kress, Peter Philips, Richard Lindley, and Margaret Sheppard helped to collect the forest parameter data. Agustin Espinoza Ocampo, Maria Macaria Mejia Mendoza, Maria Concepcion Huerta Zamacona, Maria de la Paz Espitia Cabrera, Juan Cristobal Palatio, Norma Patricia Mendoza Villaseñor, Zion Julio Aguirri T., and Maria Esther Mendez Pugor helped mark the monarchs. Richard Miller provided valuable assistance with the computer analysis of the data. Lincoln Brower, John and Elizabeth Buck, Jim Mallet, Lawrence Cook, and Steve Malcolm at various times made suggestions that helped to augment the study. Dennis Frey, Andrew Schaffner, Michelle Solensky, Karen Oberhauser, and Don Warren made suggestions that greatly improved the manuscript. Daniel Thompson helped edit the manuscript. This study was supported by National Science Foundation grants DEB 75-14265 and 78 10658 (to L. Brower).

References

Anonymous. 1975. Hewlett-Packard HP-25 applications programs. Hewlett-Packard Company, Palo Alto, Calif.

Brown, J. K. 1978. Weight and density of crowns of Rocky Mountain conifers. U.S. Department of Agriculture Forest Service Research Paper INT-197. Ogden, Utah: Forest Service, U.S. Department of Agriculture.

Calvert, W. H., and L. P. Brower. 1986. The location of monarch butterfly (*Danaus plexippus* L.) overwintering colonies in Mexico in relation to topography and microclimate. J. Lepid. Soc. 40:164–87.

Calvert, W. H., L. E. Hedrick, and L. P. Brower. 1979. Mortality of the monarch butterfly (*Danaus plexippus* L.): avian predation at five overwintering sites in Mexico. Science 204:847–51.

Calvert, W. H., W. Zuchowski, and L. P. Brower. 1983. The effect of rain, snow and freezing temperatures on overwintering monarch butterflies in Mexico. Biotropica 15:42–47.

Cottam, G., and J. T. Curtis. 1956. The use of distance measure in phytosociological sampling. Ecology 37:451–60.

Fink, L. S., and L. P. Brower. 1981. Birds can overcome the cardenolide defense of monarch butterflies in Mexico. Nature 291:67–70.

Glendinning, J. I., A. Alonso-Mejía, and L. P. Brower. 1988. Behavioral and ecological interactions of foraging mice (*Peromyscus melanotis*) with overwintering monarch butterflies (*Danaus plexippus*) in Mexico. Oecologia 75:222–27.

Krebs, C. 1999. Ecological methodology. Menlo Park, Calif.: Benjamin and Cummings.

Sakai, W. H., and W. H. Calvert. 1992. Statewide Monarch Butterfly Management Plan for the state of California Department of Parks and Recreation. Sacramento, Calif.: California Department of Parks and Recreation.

Southwood, T. R. E. 1966. Ecological methods. New York: Chapman and Hall.

Tuskes, P., and L. P. Brower. 1978. Overwintering ecology of the monarch butterfly, *Danaus plexippus* L. in California. Ecol. Entomol. 3:141–53.

Valliant, R., A. H. Dorfman, and R. M. Royall. 2000. Finite population sampling and inference: a prediction approach. New York: John Wiley and Sons.

17

Locations and Area Occupied by Monarch Butterflies Overwintering in Mexico from 1993 to 2002

Eligio García-Serrano, Jaime Lobato Reyes, and Blanca Xiomara Mora Alvarez

INTRODUCTION

Monarch migration represents one of the largest movements of conspecific individuals (Rendón Salinas 1997). It is considered an endangered biological phenomenon and the first priority in world butterfly conservation by the International Union for Conservation of Nature and Natural Resources (IUCN), and is now a priority in the conservation agenda of various institutions (Missrie 2000). The high-altitude oyamel forests where monarchs overwinter (2700 and 3600 m in altitude with slopes of 10% to 30% [Gomez-Peralta 1998]) are located on the borders of the states of México and Michoacán and represent one of the most environmentally threatened regions in Mexico. These forests also capture water used by both the monarchs and the communities of the region and feed two large watersheds in México, the Balsas and the Lerma Santiago.

The area decreed by the Mexican government as a biosphere reserve includes enormous biological diversity and hosts five types of vegetation: oyamel forest, pine and oyamel forest, pine forest, cedar forest, and oak forest. It spans the municipalities of Temascalcingo, San Felipe del Progreso, Donato Guerra, and Villa de Allende in the state of México, and the municipalities of Contepec, Senguio, Angangueo, Ocampo, Zitácuaro, and Aporo in Michoacán. The current reserve has a surface area of 56,259 ha divided into three core zones comprising 13,551 ha and a buffer zone comprising 42,707 ha (SEMARNAT 2001; Missrie, this volume).

Monarchs form their colonies at an altitude of 3000 to 3280 m (when the colonies are stable). They generally roost in the oyamel trees, although they also form clusters in other tree species such as *Pinus pseudostrobus*, *Cupressus lindleyi*, and *Quercus* spp. (García-Serrano 1997). On average, the overwintering period of the monarch butterfly is 154 days, with the colonies forming in four characteristic phases (Calvert and Brower 1986; García-Serrano 1997). The first phase begins with the arrival of the butterflies in October and November, though the exact date varies between years. This phase is characterized by intense flights followed by formations of small clusters, though monarchs in this phase do not necessarily congregate in the same location where the final colonies form. During the second phase, the colonies become more stable and activity diminishes. This phase occurs during the coldest months (December to mid-February). On some occasions the colonies move during this phase, depending on forest quality and climatic conditions. At the end of February and March the third phase, characterized by a dramatic increase in butterfly activity, begins. The monarchs move toward places with higher humidity, seeking water in streams within the colonies or agricultural fields outside of the colonies. During this phase a colony may subdivide into two or more smaller colonies and on some occasions may disappear completely, as often happens to the San Andrés colony. The last phase begins when the butterflies initiate their northward migration. They continue to occupy the forest on the edges of the streams, but once they have shifted to the border of the forest and the agricultural areas they move northward to occupy different gullies. The return north occurs when days are clear and winds are favorable. This phase begins in March, and by April all the butterflies have left the overwintering area.

Here, we describe work done through the Monarch Butterfly Biosphere Reserve over nine seasons at the overwintering sites in Mexico.

METHODS

Locating overwintering colonies

Beginning in 1993, we monitored all known colonies within and outside of the protected area during each overwintering season. The number of colonies formed typically depends on the number of monarchs that arrive in Mexico. Permanent reserve colonies are located in Cerro Altamirano ($n = 1$) and Cerros Chivatí-Huacal ($n = 1$), Sierra Chincua ($n \geq 2$), Sierra El Campanario ($n \geq 2$), and Cerro Pelón ($n \geq 2$). Outside of the reserve we typically find colonies in San Andrés, Pizcuaro, Puerto Morillo (Garnica) and Puerto Bermeo Michoacán, and Palomas, Piedra Herrada and San Francisco Oxtotilpan in the state of México.

Monitoring overwintering colonies

Each year, we monitored the occurrence and general characteristics of the four phases of overwintering in Mexico: arrival, colony establishment, colony movement, and dispersal. To allow comparisons between years, we used a standardized data collection protocol during the last 2 weeks of December. For each colony we recorded the date and time of the observation, location, altitude, slope, distance to rivers, number of trees, temperature, cloud cover, wind, exposure, and other general characteristics. In mapping the position of each colony we used topographic maps (1:50,000 scale) for El Oro de Hidalgo, Angangueo, Villa de Allende, Ciudad Hidalgo, and Nevado de Toluca.

To estimate the surface area of each colony, we went to the highest part of the colony and marked a tree located in the periphery. From this point we used a compass and measuring tape to measure the perimeter of the colony, using a series of lines connecting adjacent trees along the perimeter. We used these data to plot colony polygons on paper (1:500 scale) and calculated the surface area using planimetric techniques (H. Silva, pers. comm.).

In January of each year, we estimated the mortality at each site using a method described by Rendón Salinas (pers. comm.). Using the polygon of each colony plotted on the paper, we drew three transects: one through the center of the colony and two in the periphery. We sampled 1-m^2 plots every 5 or 10 m along these three transects. In each plot we collected dead butterflies and recorded the mortality as caused by bird or mouse predation or without apparent cause, separating males and females.

RESULTS AND DISCUSSION

Location of the overwintering colonies

Colony location and permanence both inside and outside of the reserve were different each year. Permanent colonies formed consistently at three sites within the reserve: Sierra Chincua, Sierra El Campanario, and Cerro Pelón. Outside the reserve, permanent colonies formed each year at three sites: San Andrés, Palomas, and Piedra Herrada. Table 17.1 shows the 22 colonies found in the Monarch Butterfly Biosphere Reserve over the 9 years of our study.

The 1986 presidential decree did not protect all important monarch overwintering sites. In contrast, the decree passed on 10 November 2000 (Missrie, this volume) defines a protected area in which 68% of the colonies described in this study are located in the core zone and 32% are outside the protected area (see table 17.1). The new decree also protects other potential sites and provides continuity between the buffer and core zones through corridors. We feel that this is an important change; over the last 25 years the number of known overwintering sites has increased and is likely to continue to increase. During our 9-year study we located and monitored 10 more colonies than had been reported previously (Calvert and Brower 1986; Mejía 1996). This was probably a result of intensified search effort rather than new colony formation, as previous studies had only recorded the main sites in Cerro Altamirano, Sierra Chincua, Sierra El Campanario, and Cerro Pelón. We are still finding new sites, including one (Llano de Koala) during the 2001–2002 season (see Table 17.1).

Table 17.1. Colony characteristics (1993 to 2002)

Sanctuary	Altitude (meters)	Latitude	Longitude	Location in the reserve
Cerro Altamirano				
1. Cañada Oscura[a]	3090	19°58′21″	100°08′07″	Core zone
Corredor Chincua-Campanario-Chivatí-Huacal				
2. El Zacatonal[a]	3260	19°40′10″	100°17′14″	Core zone
3. Mojonera Alta[ab]	3280	19°40′22″	100°17′39″	Core zone
4. Llano del Toro[ab]	3200	19°40′29″	100°18′13″	Core zone
5. Llano de Koala	3000	19°41′12″	100°18′49″	Core zone
6. El Rosario[ab]	3039	19°35′35″	100°15′54″	Core zone
7. Piedra Boluda	3248	19°34′11″	100°14′22″	Core zone
8. Cerro Blanco	3248	19°34′13″	100°14′24″	Core zone
9. El Picacho[a]		19°33′32″	100°12′14″	Core zone
10. Los Trozos	3210	19°31′17″	100°18′02″	Core zone
11. Lomas de Aparicio[b]	3290	19°30′25″	100°12′14″	Core zone
Cerro Pelón				
12. El Cedral[a]	3207	19°23′13″	100°15′27″	Core zone
13. Carditos[ab]	3110	19°23′18″	100°15′40″	Core zone
14. Santa Teresa	3282	19°24′36″	100°13′54″	Core zone
15. Las Lagunitas[a]	3170	19°23′18″	100°16′18″	Core zone
Outside the reserve				
16. Puerto Morillo		19°40′53″	100°49′00″	
17. Pizcuaro		19°47′45″	100°38′57″	
18. San Andrés[ab]	3227	19°42′29″	100°48′39″	
19. Puerto Bermeo		19°44′36″	100°08′50″	
20. Piedra Herrada[ab]	3055	19°06′27″	99°50′48″	
21. San Francisco Oxtotilpan	3199	19°11′51″	99°54′51″	
22. Palomas[b]	3185	19°05′53″	99°52′06″	

Note: These locations are generalized; monarchs often cluster at different sites within each colony in different years.

[a] Studied by Brower and Calvert (1986) and Mejía (1996).

[b] Permanent sites.

Surface area of overwintering colonies

The surface area occupied by each colony is an important indication of the size of the monarch population that arrives in Mexico. Previous researchers have estimated that there are approximately 10 million butterflies/ha (Calvert and Brower 1986; Brower 1995), although this number may be an underestimate (Calvert, this volume; Brower et al., this volume). Based on this estimate, the largest population of monarchs during the years of this study occurred in 1996–1997, when the colonies covered 17.6 ha (figure 17.1) and contained an estimated 176 million monarch butterflies. During the rest of the overwintering seasons, the total colony populations ranged from 23 to 125 million monarchs.

Compiling our results with those of Calvert and Brower (1986) and Mejía (1996) yields estimates of total colony size for the past 25 years (figure 17.1). The peak population size occurred in 1990–1991, when the colonies covered 17.8 ha. The 1996–1997 season was nearly this large. The smallest overwintering population occurred in 1976–1977, when the colonies covered only 1.5 ha. However, as this was the first year for which colony sizes are reported, it is possible that this small size is an artifact of early and still-developing sampling techniques. Problems with the long-term comparisons shown in figure 17.1 include a lack of data and incomplete knowledge of colony locations; new colonies were discovered throughout the 25 years, and in four seasons (1982–1983, 1983–1984, 1991–1992, and 1992–1993) no sampling occurred. Furthermore, previous monitoring focused on permanent sites that are easier to access. To accurately assess the population dynamics of overwintering monarchs, it will be important to continue to monitor all of the 22 recorded colonies to date, search for additional colonies, and more rigorously measure the density of

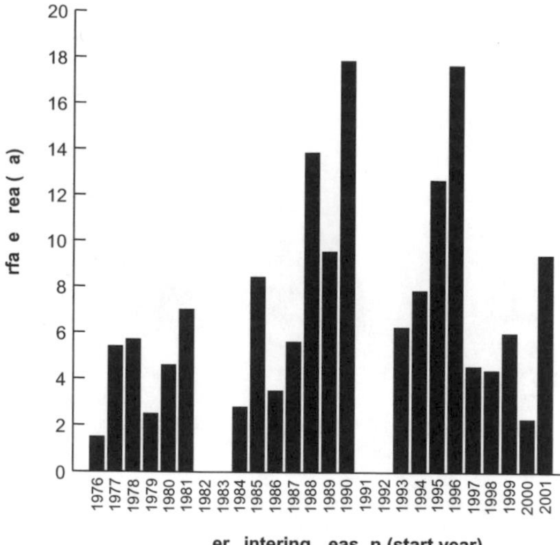

Figure 17.1. Total surface area occupied by the overwintering colonies of the monarch butterfly during 1976 to 2002. Overwintering seasons are labeled by the year in which they started. Data for years 1976 to 1982 are from Brower and Calvert (1986) and for 1984 to 1991 are from Mejia (1996).

monarchs in multiple colonies, rather than extrapolating density estimates from measurements of just one colony (e.g., Brower 1995).

Mortality of overwintering monarchs

We estimated that mortality ranged from 14.7 butterflies/m^2 in the San Francisco Oxtotilpan colony to 335.7 butterflies/m^2 in the San Andrés colony, with differences between sites and years. Arrellano and coworkers (1993) estimated a predation rate of only 3.0 to 3.3 butterflies/m^2 during 1985–1986. Differences in rates and sources of mortality are likely related to the conditions of the forest structure of each site, environmental conditions, and predator assemblages, which are also dynamic and vary with demographic dynamics of the species at local and regional levels (Sáyago 2001).

The main causes of monarch mortality in the overwintering sites are predation from birds and mice, strong winter storms, low temperatures, and depletion of lipid reserves (Alonso and Arellano 1989). We observed the highest level of mortality caused by birds in the San Andrés colony (18.2%) and the lowest in the Herrada colony (1.3%). These results are within the range reported by Brower and Calvert (1985), who estimated that birds eat from 7.2% to 43.6% of the population.

Severe weather can also cause mortality. Snowstorms can be particularly dangerous to overwintering monarchs. During a snowstorm in the winter of 1995–1996 we recorded 36 butterflies/m^2 dead before the snow storm (28 November 1995), 202 butterflies/m^2 lying on the floor because of the snow (31 December 1995), and 83 butterflies/m^2 dead after the storm (5 January 1996). In the end, we estimated 7.7% mortality at Sierra Chincua during this season. A similar effect was observed by Calvert and colleagues (1983), who reported 2.5 million dead butterflies in the Alpha site (El Zapatero) in Sierra Chincua after a winter storm. According to our observations, mortality is highest when storms begin with rain, then winds, followed by snow and freezing temperatures (see also Brower et al., this volume). This causes the butterflies to get wet and then freeze, allowing the formation of crystals in their tissues, ultimately causing their death (Alonso et al., 1992). Anderson and Brower (1993) suggest that these crystals invade the spiracles of the butterfly, acting as a nucleus that promotes freezing of the fluids in the body.

Calvert and coworkers (1979) propose that there is an inversely proportional relationship between the predation intensity and colony size; in the smallest colonies, predation will be relatively higher owing to the area-volume relationship. Our results support this prediction; the total estimated mortality by season was greatest (27.7%) after the arrival of fewer butterflies (1997–1998) and least (0.17%) during one of the seasons with the largest recorded number of butterflies arriving in the last 25 years (figure 17.2).

Acknowledgments

We thank the reserve director, Roberto Solís Calderón, for his suggestions to improve the monitoring program. Our colleagues Alejandro Torres, Hector Silva, Juan Velázquez, José María Suarez, Alberto Morales, Felipe Meza, Guadalupe Rodríguez, and Martín Cruz Piña provided invaluable support in the field. We also thank the ejidatarios and communal landowners who helped us locate the butterfly colonies, and extend heartfelt thanks to the Monarch Butterfly Biosphere Reserve, which has given us a wonderful place to work.

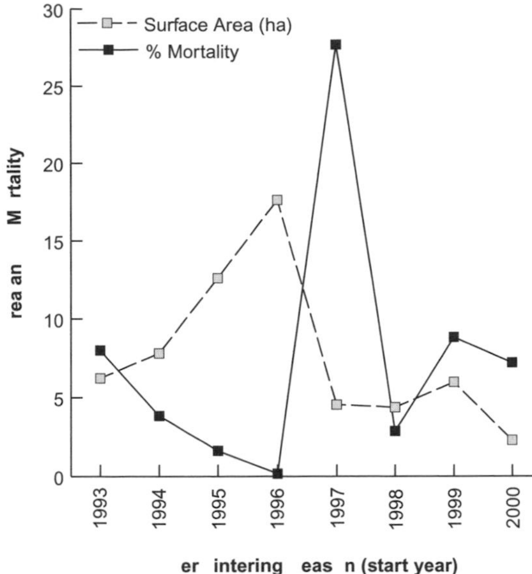

Figure 17.2. Total mortality and surface area in the overwintering colonies during 1993 to 2002.

References

Alonso-Mejía, A., and A. G. Arellano. 1989. Mariposa monarca. Su hábitat de hibernación en México. Ciencias 15:6–11.

Alonso-Mejía, A., A. Arellano, and L. P. Brower. 1992. Influence of temperature, surface body moisture and height above ground on the survival of monarch butterflies overwintering in México. Biotropica 24:415–19.

Anderson, J. B., and L. P. Brower. 1993. Cold-hardiness in the annual cycle of the monarch butterfly. In S. B. Malcolm and M. P. Zalucki, eds., Biology and conservation of the monarch butterfly, pp. 157–64. Los Angeles: Natural History Museum of Los Angeles County.

Arellano, G. A., J. I. Glendinning, J. B. Anderson, and L. P. Brower. 1993. Interspecific comparisons of the foraging dynamics of black-backed orioles and black-headed grosbeaks on overwintering monarch butterflies in Mexico. In S. B. Malcolm and M. P. Zalucki, eds., Biology and conservation of the monarch butterfly, pp. 315–22. Los Angeles: Natural History Museum of Los Angeles County.

Brower, L. P. 1995. Revisión a los mitos de Jurgen Hoth. Ciencias 39:50–51.

Brower, L. P., and W. H. Calvert. 1985. Foraging dynamics of birds predators on overwintering monarch butterflies in Mexico. Evolution 39:852–68.

Calvert, W. H., L. E. Hendrick, and L. P. Brower. 1979. Mortality of the monarch butterfly (*Danaus plexippus* L.): avian predation at five overwintering sites in Mexico. Science 204:847–51.

Calvert, W. H., W. Zuchowski, and L. P. Brower. 1983. The effect of rain, snow and freezing temperatures on overwintering monarch butterflies in Mexico. Biotropica 15:42–47.

Calvert, W. H., and L. P. Brower. 1986. The location of monarch butterfly (*Danaus plexippus* L.) overwintering colonies in Mexico in relation to topography and climate. J. Lepid. Soc. 40:164–87.

García-Serrano, E. 1997. Relación entre la temperatura y humedad con el movimiento de las colonias de mariposa monarca *Danaus plexippus* L. En *sus sitios de hibernación en México.* Tesis licenciatura, Universidad Michoacana de San Nicolás de Hidalgo.

García-Serrano, E. 1999. Manual de métodos de campo para el monitoreo de las colonias de mariposa monarca en México. Reserva de la biosfera mariposa monarca. Documento fotocopiado.

Gómez-Peralta, M. 1998. Evaluación de la extracción comercial de musgo en la reserva especial de la biosfera "mariposa monarca," Sierra Chincua, Michoacán, México. Tesis maestría, Universidad Michoacana de San Nicolás de Hidalgo.

Mejía, M. M. M. 1996. Caracterización de las colonias de la mariposa monarca (*Danaus plexippus* L.) en la reserva especial de la biosfera en el estado de Michoacán, México. Tesis licenciatura, Universidad Michoacana de San Nicolás de Hidalgo.

Missrie, M. 2000. La nueva reserva de la mariposa monarca. Pulso regional. Hacia el desarrollo sustentable de la regiones marginadas 4:19–23.

Rendón Salinas, E. 1997. Diagnóstico de las mariposas monarca hibernantes que intentaron alimentarse y la estructura del rodal del bosque donde se agrupo la colonia del Llano del Toro en la Sierra Chincua, Mich. durante la temporada de hibernación 1993–1994. Tesis licenciatura, Universidad Nacional Autónoma de México, Mexico, DF.

Sáyago, L. R. C. 2001. Efecto de las colonias de mariposa monarca sobre la diversidad de las aves invernantes en la reserva de la biosfera mariposa monarca, México. Tesis profesional, Universidad Michoacana de San Nicolás de Hidalgo.

SEMARNAT. 2001. Programa de manejo reserva de la biosfera mariposa monarca. 1st ed. México, DF.

18

Can't See the Forest for the Butterflies: The Need for Understanding Forest Dynamics at Monarch Overwintering Sites

Andrés F. Keiman and Miguel Franco

INTRODUCTION

The forest for the trees

In order to overcome freezing winters in the United States and southern Canada, monarch butterflies east of the continental divide migrate to overwintering sites in the central region of the Mexican Neovolcanic Axis. The winter ecology of monarchs has been the subject of detailed research (Calvert et al. 1979; Brower and Calvert 1985; Brower 1985, 1995a; Anderson and Brower 1996). These authors agree that successful overwintering depends on a narrow climatic window where temperatures are benign enough for the monarch to avoid death by freezing, but cool enough to maintain a state of metabolic and reproductive diapause until spring arrives (Brower 1999). Despite controversy as to the precise conditions required for successful overwintering (Hoth 1995; Alonso-Mejía et al. 1995; Brower 1995b), there is overwhelming evidence of a positive relationship between the degree of forest disturbance (as measured by canopy opening) and the butterfly's energy expenditure (Calvert et al. 1983; Alonso-Mejía et al. 1997). As a consequence, monarchs favor mature (tree height more than 20 m) closed-canopy forest patches to form overwintering colonies. The middle layer of the forest where monarchs roost is an efficient buffer against daily fluctuations in temperature—it is cooler in the daytime and warmer at nighttime than (1) exposed, treeless areas; (2) the open air above the canopy; and (3) the forest floor (E. Rendón Salinas, pers. comm.).

The forests where monarchs overwinter have long been a source of revenue for their human inhabitants. They provide fuel, building materials, food (e.g., wild rabbits and mushrooms), land where cattle roam and graze freely, and raw materials for industry (Merino 1999). Thus, the forests are subject to a variety of disturbances that are induced or exacerbated by a growing human population. The most important are (see Snook 1993) logging (both legal and illegal [Bojórquez-Tapia et al. 2002; Brower et al. 2002]), insect pests, pathogens, cattle grazing, fire, and perhaps even the double-edged sword of tourism. Additionally, the current low market value of timber encourages the transformation of land use for agricultural and intensive cattle-grazing purposes (Malcolm and Zalucki 1993; Hoth et al. 1999; Merino 1999). These factors vary in their intensity and effects on the forest (Snook 1993), and designing a management strategy to address all of them is a monumental task. However, a great deal can be achieved by increasing our understanding of the optimal forest conditions required for the successful overwintering of monarchs. Regardless of the need for a better understanding of monarch ecology, we believe it is time for attention to focus on preserving the most suitable habitat on which successful overwintering depends. No amount of knowledge on monarch ecology will save the migratory phenomenon if the monarch's overwintering habitat disappears.

The natural dynamics of the forests

The forests where monarchs overwinter are dominated by the oyamel fir *Abies religiosa* H. B. K. Schltdl. et Cham. Although trees of different ages coexist, they tend to be clumped into relatively even-aged patches (E. Rendón Salinas, A. Keiman, and M. Franco unpublished). The tendency to form even-aged stands is due to the high leaf area of *Abies* forests, which results in a deep shadow inhibiting the growth of understory plants. For seedling establishment to occur, high levels of incident light must reach the forest floor. This only occurs after a relatively major disturbance such as the death of several large trees. Although we do not know the precise light requirements of oyamel fir seedlings, they seem to require a minimum daily amount of direct sunlight to survive and grow. Thus, small gaps do not allow sapling recruitment and are soon filled with growth from surviving dominant trees.

Oyamel seeds do not seem to require special light conditions to germinate (Román-Ibarra 2002). They are released in late winter to early spring (February to March) and germinate with the first summer rains. If they do not germinate, they lose viability rapidly within their first year. Even if they survive longer, the weak seedlings produced in subsequent years do not live long. Therefore, under natural conditions they germinate soon after dispersal or die from predation by rodents or from insect and fungal infestation. In years of high seed production the oyamel fir may form a bank of 50 to 100 seedlings/m^2 (pers. observ.). However, unless they fall in a large forest canopy gap, the seedlings will die before the year is over.

When successful establishment occurs in a large gap, the canopy closes after a few years of unimpeded growth. This precludes further recruitment. As in other boreal forests dominated by conifers with a high leaf area, unless disturbance occurs during the development of these forest patches, the temporally short recruitment window constrains variation in the age of individual trees (Oliver and Larson 1996). Nonetheless, the natural variability in growth rate among individual trees, and the heterogeneity in resource acquisition, give rise to a size hierarchy whereby differences between larger and smaller individuals become exaggerated with time (Harper 1977; Weiner and Solbrig 1984; Weiner 1985). Sooner or later, these differences result in the death of smaller individuals. This differential mortality eliminates the lower end of the distribution of tree sizes in a process of growth-driven mortality known as "self-thinning" (White and Harper 1970; Westoby 1984). In forests such as the ones in which monarchs overwinter, this process is most likely determined by competition for light rather than nutrients or water.

METHODS

In order to reconstruct the temporal trajectory of occupancy and self-thinning of oyamel fir, it is necessary to locate reasonably undisturbed forest patches of different ages. Out of the five sanctuaries that the Mexican government has declared as protected (Sierra Chincua, Campanario, Chivatí-Huacal, Cerro Altamirano, and Cerro Pelón), Sierra Chincua is the least disturbed (Brower et al. 2002). In order to reconstruct the natural dynamics of oyamel fir forests, we selected 13 forest patches of different ages in this sanctuary. We subjectively judged their age and stage of development by their relatively homogeneous structure (as observed in tree size) and closed canopy. These also presumably reflect the relatively uniform age of trees within each patch and the lack of disturbance, respectively. Patch areas ranged from 90 to 2500 m^2 (table 18.1), and population density (number of trees per patch) varied from 32 to 385. All sample plots were contained within larger, relatively homogeneous forest stands to avoid possible edge effects. Young plots contained more trees per unit area than did older ones, increasing the sampling effort considerably. In each plot, all trees were numbered and measured (diameter at breast height [DBH] and tree height). We measured DBH with a diameter tape and height with a Spiegel Relaskop instrument (both distributed by Forestry Suppliers, Jackson, Mississippi). Given a fixed, relatively horizontal distance to a tree, the Spiegel Relaskop provides a direct reading of tree height. We then standardized the population density and occupation of space by the trees, using total basal area as a standard metric, on a per hectare basis.

Because we selected patches with closed canopies, we expected the values for leaf area index (LAI) to be close to the maximum attainable by oyamel fir at this locality. The proportion of incident light (light extinction) at the forest floor was measured with a Li-Cor 2000 light meter, which compared the amount of incident light in a minimum of 10 regularly spaced points within each plot and a nearby open site at least 50 m across.

Table 18.1. Oyamel fir plot statistics

Sample plot	Area (m^2)	No. of trees	Mean DBH ± SD (cm)	Mean H ± SD (m)
Mojonera 01	260	32	23.7 ± 11.5	19.6 ± 8.0
Mojonera 02	90	88	25.4 ± 7.4	6.1 ± 4.6
Llano Redondo 01	150	36	13.4 ± 6.2	9.9 ± 4.0
Llano Redondo 02	482	89	13.1 ± 10.2	6.1 ± 5.2
Llano Redondo 03	144	91	11.5 ± 8.7	5.9 ± 4.7
Llano del Toro 01	1250	82	37.3 ± 15.5	23.4 ± 8.3
Llano del Toro 02	625	61	25.1 ± 19.3	14.7 ± 10.2
Llano del Toro 03	100	43	9.3 ± 5.9	8.1 ± 4.6
Llano del Toro 04	2500	109	39.2 ± 14.1	24.3 ± 5.9
Vivero 01	225	385	1.9 ± 1.4	5.2 ± 4.4
Vivero 02	240	125	5.9 ± 4.0	4.7 ± 3.1
Vivero 03	235	210	5.5 ± 0.1	4.5 ± 8.8
Vivero 04	500	116	14.7 ± 10.4	8.8 ± 6.5
Totals	6801	1467		

Note: Trunk diameter at breast height (DBH) and tree height (H) with standard deviation (SD).

RESULTS AND DISCUSSION

Tree height and girth

Trees within each patch tended to be of similar size, with no single patch having the entire range of sizes that we measured in all the patches (table 18.1, figure 18.1). Knowledge of the variation of tree size (hierarchy) within even-aged patches, and of the position that monarchs occupy both within the canopy and among trees in this hierarchy, is essential to guarantee long-term overwintering success. Not only is it necessary for patches of appropriate age (and tree size) to be present on the southwestern slopes where monarchs preferentially overwinter, but it is essential that these patches contain the required (and so far unknown) tree size structure. Monarchs roost in the intermediate layers of the forest canopy. These layers are made up of the lower-middle portion of dominant trees and the upper-middle section of suppressed trees. It would be interesting to know with more precision how the position of butterflies within the heterogeneous canopy affects their probabilities of survival (Anderson and Brower 1996; Alonso-Mejía et al. 1997). It is interesting to note that the coefficient of variation (CV) of both tree diameter and tree height (employed as a measure of hierarchy [Franco and Harper 1988]) decreases with the age of the plot. That is, the variation within a plot decreases during the self-thinning process (figure 18.2). This suggests that older stands, like the ones where monarchs overwinter, are more homogeneous in terms of tree size.

The forest is a mosaic of patches in different stages of development. Because monarchs occupy forest patches in a particular temporal window of their development, not all forest patches are suitable for colony establishment. Preliminary age data suggest a minimum life span of 200 years for this species. This, together with our size data, suggests that this window will last for several decades. Further analysis of the age data of trees at overwintering sites will allow us to determine the useful life span of roosting sites with more precision in the near future. What is important to emphasize is that whatever the span of this window, we must not only guarantee the current existence of the required forest structure, but also its continuing replacement as forest patches age, senesce, and open up. It is a worrisome thought that were this mosaic to lack the required structure for overwintering monarchs in a single year in the future, the whole phenomenon could potentially go extinct in what is essentially an instant in time!

Invasion by secondary shrub species

A poorly understood aspect of the dynamics of the oyamel fir forest is the degree and nature of disturbance required for secondary species to invade. Several species of *Senecio* (e.g., *S. prenanthoides*, *S. angulifolius*, and *S. cardiophyllus*), as well

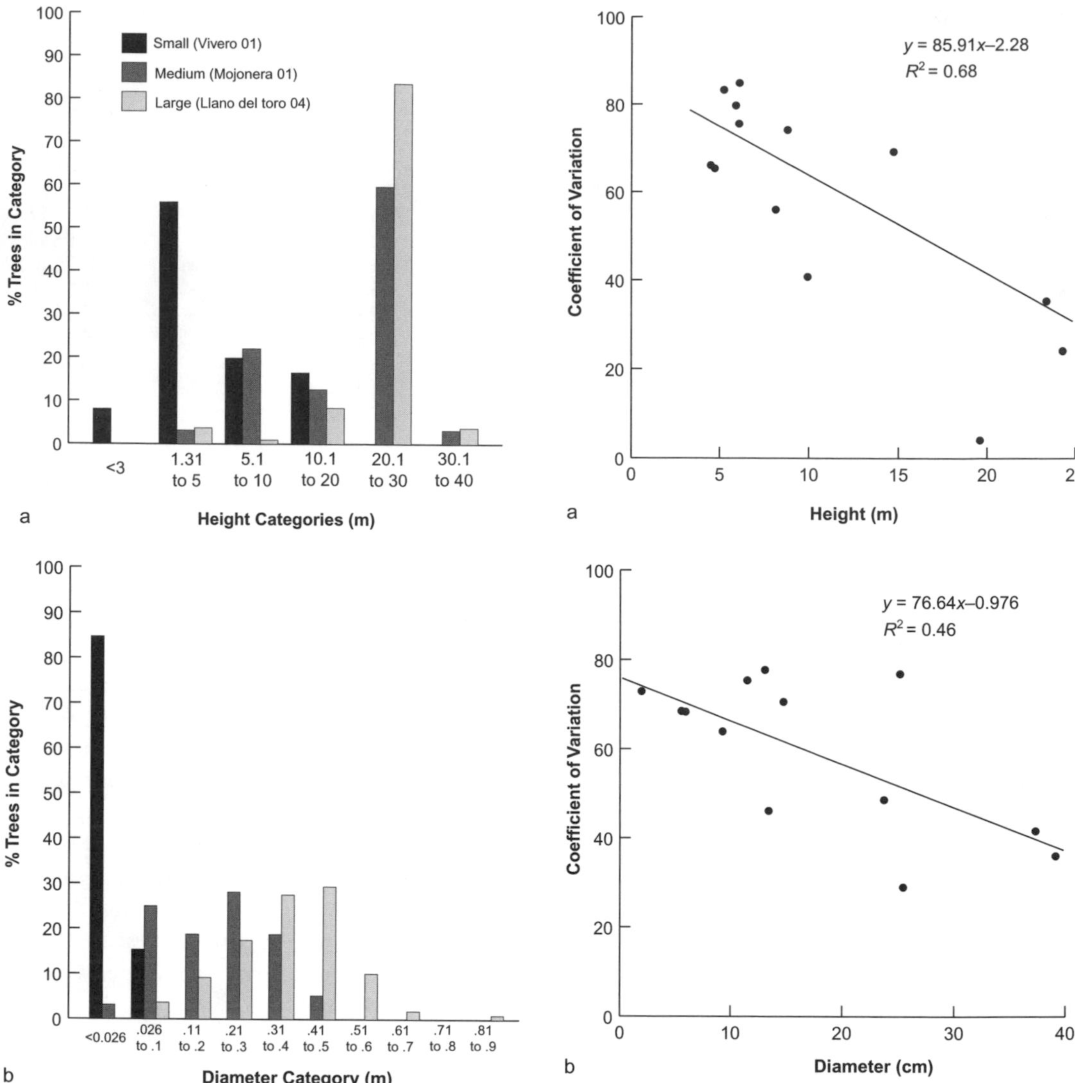

Figure 18.1. Frequency distribution of (a) tree height and (b) tree diameter in three sites of contrasting size structure (indicated in the legend) at Chincua Sanctuary. "Diameter" in (b) refers to the diameter of the tree with the average basal area in each plot.

Figure 18.2. The coefficients of variation of (a) tree height and (b) tree diameter decrease with tree size. "Diameter" in (b) refers to the diameter of the tree with the average basal area in each plot.

as *Baccharis conferta* and *Acaena elongata*, become dominant in the understory, apparently when forest gaps are large enough to permit colonization by these shrubs but not large enough to allow recruitment of fir seedlings. However, there are no data on this hypothesized intermediate disturbance pattern, or on the possible competitive exclusion of fir seedlings or saplings. Once these shrubs become established, it is difficult for oyamel fir seedlings to overcome their dense cover. Fir saplings (e.g., more than 50 cm tall), however, seem vigorous enough to eventually break through this shrub cover. The timing of fir recruitment would therefore seem crucial.

Forest dynamics

Our results suggest that sampled plots can be visualized as a sequence of overcrowded stands from

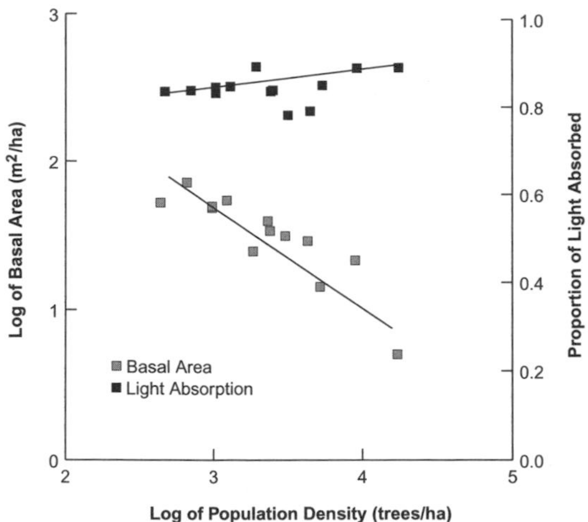

Figure 18.3. The relationships between oyamel basal area per hectare and population density and between the proportion of light absorbed by the canopy and population density. Population density and basal area are graphed on logarithmic scales.

which to reconstruct the temporal dynamics of space occupation and self-thinning. The proportion of incident light reaching the forest floor was below 22% in all plots, with most absorbing between 80% and 90% of incident light (figure 18.3). Despite a large range of ages and tree sizes among plots, there was no correlation between population density (N, in number of trees per hectare) and light extinction (regression $p > 0.1$). If anything, there is a slight positive relationship between density and light absorption, indicating the possibility that older plots actually decrease in LAI (figure 18.3). Several possible explanations exist for this pattern (Ryan et al. 1997; Ryan and Yoder 1997), but their discussion is beyond the scope of this chapter.

Not surprisingly, basal area per plot (BA, in m^2/ha) increased as population density decreased (figure 18.3; BA = 2955 $N^{-0.59}$; $r^2 = 0.79$; $n = 13$, $p < 0.001$).

Next steps

The approach suggested here assumes a homogeneity of physical environmental conditions. It is obvious, however, that heterogeneity occurs at different scales. At the landscape level, variations in productivity determined, for example, by differences in altitude, orientation, and soil characteristics would modify the relationships illustrated in figure 18.3. Finer within-stand variation is assumed, however, to alter the variance of individual tree size, not the position (mean) of populations in this graph. The forest structure of patches where colonies are currently formed, and also of patches that were occupied in the past but have not been used in recent years, is currently being investigated (E. Rendón Salinas and M. Franco, pers. comm.). This information is essential to guarantee that forest patches with the required characteristics are continuously being replaced as older ones die. Detailed dynamics of tree growth and mortality within sample plots, as evidenced by tree rings and dead tree stumps, will allow a finer description of the patterns of occupancy and mortality. Since many areas of the reserve have supported intensive use, the current forest structure likely departs from that expected under self-thinning. It is therefore important to estimate this departure in monarch-occupied areas and its possible consequence on the overwintering of monarchs. Furthermore, the results must be used to predict the time it takes forest structures to return to a state of compatibility with the requirements of monarchs, particularly in areas in which they have been known to overwinter in the past but have recently deserted. Although it is unlikely that our study would suggest monarch-occupied sites may sustain exploitation, it is crucial to learn how far from desertion (both in terms of structure and the time to reach it) currently occupied sites are. The future of the most fascinating insect migration in the world may depend on answering this question accurately.

Acknowledgments

We particularly thank Ruben Pérez-Ishiwara for his skillful support in technical aspects of the project and data collection in the field. We also thank Eduardo Rendón Salinas, Ruth Román-Ibarra, and Celia de Ita-Martinez for data collection and enlightening discussion. The Estación Llano de las Papas of Instituto Nacional de Ecologia provided lodging in Chincua Sanctuary. Karen Oberhauser, Michelle Solensky, and an anonymous reviewer helped us to improve the original manuscript. This work was supported by the Monarch Butterfly Sanctuary Foundation (MBSF), the Universidad Nacional Autónoma de México (UNAM), and more recently, the University of Plymouth.

References

Alonso-Mejía, A., E. Rendón Salinas, and E. Montesinos-Patiño. 1995. Realidades energéticas de la mariposa monarca. Ciencias (Mexico) 38:48–49.

Alonso-Mejía, A., E. Rendón Salinas, E. Montesinos-Patiño, and L. P. Brower. 1997. Use of lipid reserves by monarch butterflies (*Danaus plexippus* L.) overwintering in Mexico: implications for conservation. Ecol. Appl. 7:934–47.

Anderson, J. B., and L. P. Brower. 1996. Freeze-protection of overwintering monarch butterflies in Mexico: critical role of the forest as a blanket and an umbrella. Ecol. Entomol. 21:255–63.

Bojórquez-Tapia, L. A., L. P. Brower, G. Castilleja, S. Sánchez-Colón, M. Hernández, W. Calvert, S. Díaz, P. Gómez-Priego, G. Alcantar, E. D. Melgarejo, M. J. Solares, L. Gutiérrez, and M. L. Juárez. 2003. Mapping expert knowledge: redesigning the Monarch Butterfly Biosphere Reserve. Conserv. Biol. 17:367–79.

Brower, L. P. 1985. New perspectives on the migration biology of the monarch butterfly, *Danaus plexippus* L. In M. A. Rankin, ed., Migration: mechanisms and adaptative significance. Contributions in Marine Science, Vol. 27 Suppl. Port Aransas, Texas: Marine Science Institute, University of Texas at Austin.

Brower, L. P. 1995a. Understanding and misunderstanding the migration of monarch butterfly (Nymphalidae) in North America: 1857–1995. J. Lepid. Soc. 49:304–85.

Brower, L. P. 1995b. Revisión a los mitos de Jurgen Hoth. Ciencias (Mexico) 38:50–51.

Brower, L. P. 1999. Biological necessities for monarch butterfly overwintering in relation to the oyamel forest ecosystem in Mexico. In J. Hoth, L. Merino, K. Oberhauser, I. Pisanty, S. Price, and T. Wilkinson, eds., 1997 North American Conference on the Monarch Butterfly, pp. 11–28. Montreal: Commission for Environmental Cooperation.

Brower, L. P., and W. H. Calvert. 1985. Foraging dynamics of bird predators on overwintering monarch butterflies in Mexico. Evolution 39:17–19.

Brower, L. P., G. Castilleja, A. Peralta, J. Lopez-Garcia, L. Bojórquez-Tapia, S. Diaz, D. Melgarejo, and M. Missrie. 2002. Quantitative changes in forest quality in a principal overwintering area of the monarch butterfly in Mexico: 1971–1999. Conserv. Biol. 16:346–59.

Calvert, W. H., W. H. Hendrick, and L. P. Brower. 1979. Mortality of the monarch butterfly: avian predation at five overwintering sites in Mexico. Science 204:847–51.

Calvert, W. H., W. Zuchowsky, and L. P. Brower. 1983. The effect of rain, snow and freezing temepratures on overwintering monarch butterflies in Mexico. Biotropica 15:42–47.

Franco, M., and J. L. Harper. 1988. Competition and the formation of spatial pattern in spacing gradients: an example using *Kochia scoparia*. J. Ecol. 76:959–74.

Harper, J. L. 1977. Population biology of plants. London: Academic Press.

Hoth, J. 1995. Mariposa monarca, mitos y otras realidades aladas. Ciencias (Mexico) 37:19–28.

Hoth, J., L. Merino, K. Oberhauser, I. Pisanty, S. Price, and T. Wilkinson, eds. 1999. 1997 North American Conference on the Monarch Butterfly. Montreal: Commission for Environmental Cooperation.

Malcolm, S. B., and M. P. Zalucki, eds. 1993. Biology and conservation of the monarch butterfly. Los Angeles: Natural History Museum of Los Angeles County.

Merino, L. 1999. Reserva Especial de la Biósfera Mariposa Monarca: problemática general de la región. In J. Hoth, L. Merino, K. Oberhauser, I. Pisanty, S. Price, and T. Wilkinson, eds., 1997 North American Conference on the Monarch Butterfly, pp. 239–48. Montreal: Commission for Environmental Cooperation.

Oliver, C. D., and B. C. Larson. 1996. Forest stand dynamics. New York: John Wiley and Sons.

Román-Ibarra, R. E. 2002. Ecología de semillas y plántulas de *Abies religiosa* en el Pargue Nacional Cumbres del Ajusco. Tesis licenciatura, Facultad de Estudios Superiores Zaragoza, Universidad Nacional Autónoma de México, Mexico, D.F.

Ryan, M. G., D. Binkley, and J. H. Fownes. 1997. Age-related decline in forest productivity: pattern and process. Adv. Ecol. Res. 27:213–62.

Ryan, M. G., and B. J. Yoder. 1997. Hydraulic limits to tree height and tree growth. Bioscience 47:235–42.

Snook, L. C. 1993. Conservation of the monarch butterfly reserves in Mexico: focus on the forest. In S. B. Malcolm and M. P. Zalucki, eds., Biology and conservation of the monarch butterfly. pp. 363–75. Los Angeles: Natural History Museum of Los Angeles County.

Weiner, J. 1985. Size hierarchies in experimental populations of annual plants. Ecology 66:743–52.

Weiner, J., and Solbrig, O. T. 1984. The meaning and measurement of size hierarchies in plant populations. Oecologia 61:334–36.

Westoby, M. 1984. The self-thinning rule. Adv. Ecol. Res. 14:167–225.

White, J., and Harper, J. L. 1970. Correlated changes in plant size and number in plant populations. J. Ecol. 58:467–85.

19

Design and Implementation of a New Protected Area for Overwintering Monarch Butterflies in Mexico

Mónica Missrie

INTRODUCTION

Located in the states of México and Michoacán, the Monarch Butterfly Biosphere Reserve legally protects the oyamel-pine-oak forest ecosystem that serves as a winter habitat for hundreds of millions of monarch butterflies that migrate southward in the fall from eastern Canada and the midwestern United States. The survival of these overwintering monarchs in Mexico from November through March depends on a delicate balance of macro- and microclimatic factors that characterize the oyamel forests located within the reserve (Calvert and Brower 1986; Alonso-Mejía et al. 1993, 1997). These forests, however, have been degraded by excessive and illegal commercial logging, wood harvesting for domestic use, forest conversion to agriculture, and damage from periodic fires. A study by the Geography Institute of Universidad Nacional Autónoma de México (UNAM) showed that between 1984 and 1999, 44% of high-quality forest inside the reserve had been degraded (Brower et al. 2002). In fact, habitat loss and forest degradation in this region were most likely caused by inadequate protection of a system of reserves whose boundaries were delineated prior to extensive ecological research and established without a mechanism of economic or social compensation.

Ecologists rely on a variety of approaches to designate land areas as nature reserves, with the overarching goal of preserving species, groups of species, or ecosystems of special interest. Recently, geographic information system (GIS) methods, geographic approaches to planning using the Gap Analysis Program created by the U.S. Geological Survey of the Department of the Interior, and iterative, optimizing algorithms have been used to establish reserve boundaries that minimize land area while protecting the maximum number of species, unique sites, or combinations of essential site characteristics (Kiester et al. 1996; Pressey et al. 1996; Possingham et al. 2000). Despite these efforts, multiple issues determine the boundaries for reserve systems, and governments have historically set aside land for nature reserves based more on political issues or lobbying efforts by special interest groups than on ecological guidelines (Dobson 1996).

THE FIRST MONARCH BUTTERFLY RESERVE

The first attempt to legally protect the overwintering habitats of the monarchs culminated in 1986 with a presidential decree that created the Monarch Butterfly Special Biosphere Reserve, encompassing an area of 16,110 ha (Diario Oficial 1986). The decree included five conservation areas, one for each of the known principal overwintering sites (Calvert and Brower 1986). Each area, or sanctuary, had a core zone in which no logging was allowed and a buffer zone in which controlled logging could occur. Only 28% of the total area was delimited as core. Owing to incomplete biological knowledge available when the 1986 decree was established, the polygons defining the five protected areas did not protect a large proportion of colonies, and the shapes of the sanctuaries (polygons) did not conform to the natural distribution pattern of the colonies (Hoth 1994). In the 1993–1994 season, only 11 of the 20 known colony sites were within the reserve areas (Hoth 1994; García-Serrano et al., this volume). In addition, the butterflies' movements to lower altitudes throughout the season were poorly understood, resulting in inadequate protection of the lower watershed areas. Furthermore, forest practices (e.g., timber removal) were permitted within watersheds of the decreed buffer zones, which were subsequently determined to be essential for monarch survival at the end of the overwintering season (Brower 1999). Forest exploitation patterns and land use changes in surrounding areas further endangered the survival and health of the remaining forest massifs (Brower 1999). Thus, the design did not protect or adequately manage the forests within the larger matrix in which the reserve was immersed.

Perhaps most problematic was the fact that the 1986 decree imposed a limit on forest use without offering effective economic alternatives to the legal owners, the campesinos and indigenous communities (Chapela et al. 1995; Hoth 1995; Merino and Gerez 1996; Merino 1997). As a result, most of the subsequently proposed conservation schemes have tried simultaneously to preserve the sanctuaries, protect the butterflies, and offer economic alternatives to logging and habitat destruction that were lacking in the 1986 original decree (Diario Oficial 1986). The concept of sustainable development, however, often stumbles in attempting to simultaneously accommodate economic, social and biological needs.

In a meeting between the World Wildlife Fund (WWF) Mexico and the National Ecology Institute (INE) in February 1998, both institutions agreed to collaborate in redefining the natural protected area for the monarch butterfly sanctuaries. The need to redefine this area emerged from commitments adopted by Canada, the United States, and Mexico during the North American Conference on the Monarch Butterfly held in Morelia, Michoacán, Mexico, in November 1997 (Hoth et al. 1999). In particular, the WWF committed to developing a technical proposal that considered the minimum ecological requirements for successful overwintering of the monarch butterflies in Mexico. During this process, the WWF had two specific goals: (1) to determine the habitat required for the long-term protection of the monarch butterfly's migratory phenomenon based on a comprehensive analysis of current biological data and a GIS model; and (2) based on these analyses, to propose and cartographically delineate new reserve boundaries congruent with the conservation needs of the overwintering colonies.

MODIFYING THE RESERVE DESIGN: METHODS AND ECOLOGICAL RECOMMENDATIONS

To identify potential habitats to protect, the WWF sponsored a participatory planning workshop in October 1998. A team of 15 academic and government scientists (table 19.1) who have engaged in field research and monitoring of the overwintering sites in Mexico over the past 21 years gathered for a 3-day workshop. Habitat Suitability Evaluation (HSE) and Multi-Criteria Group Decision-Making (MCGDM) techniques (Pereira and Duckstein 1993; Malczewski et al. 1997; Bojórquez et al. 2002) were used to attain consensus among the experts on a conservation agenda, with the goal of redesigning the Monarch Butterfly Special Biosphere Reserve. Multivariate statistical modeling and a 0–1 mathematical programming model were implemented to analyze data. A detailed explanation on the use of these techniques is provided by Bojórquez-Tapia and coauthors (2002). Participants considered biological criteria only, without addressing socioeconomic and political issues. Workshop participants addressed three specific objectives: (1) to outline the physical and biological conditions of known overwintering habitats used by the monarch butterfly, (2) to locate potential overwintering areas to be included in a new reserve, and (3) to delimit the minimum indispensable area necessary to guarantee the long-term conservation of the monarch butterfly's migratory phenomenon.

Prior to this workshop, participants compiled a digital database with all known available data on the locations of the overwintering colonies, including 315 records of colonies in 149 separate geographic locations compiled over a 21-year period (1977 to 1998). Overwintering occurs on at least 12 general mountain massifs that include the five polygons defined by the 1986 presidential decree and seven additional ones proposed by the PROFEPA (Environmental Federal Attorney) (table 19.2; see figure 15.1). A GIS model was used to superimpose

Table 19.1. World Wildlife Fund workshop participants

Participant	Institution
Dr. Alfonso Alonso-Mejía	Smithsonian Institution, Washington, D.C.
Dr. Gerardo Bocco	Instituto de Ecología, UNAM, Mexico City, Mexico
Dr. Luis Bojórquez-Tapia	Instituto de Ecología, UNAM, Mexico City, Mexico
Dr. Lincoln P. Brower	University of Florida, Gainesville, and Sweet Briar College, Sweet Briar, Virginia
Dr. William H. Calvert	University of Texas, Austin
Ing. Rodolfo Campos	Universidad de Chapingo, Chapingo, Mexico
Dr. Guillermo Castilleja	World Wildlife Fund, Mexico Program, Mexico City, Mexico
Dr. Miguel Franco	Instituto de Ecología, UNAM, Mexico City, Mexico
Biól. Eligio García-Serrano	Insitituto Nacional de Ecología, Michoacán, Mexico
M. S. Jurgen Hoth	Mexican embassy, Ontario, Canada
Biól. María Macaria Mejía	Procuraduría Federal de Protección al Ambiente, Michoacán, Mexico
Lic. Mónica Missrie	World Wildlife Fund, Mexico Program, Mexico City, Mexico
Biól. Eduardo Rendón Salinas	Instituto de Ecología, UNAM, Mexico City, Mexico
Geog. Roberto Solis	Reserva Especial de la Biosfera Mariposa Monarca, Michoacán, Mexico
Biól. Alejandro Torres	Reserva Especial de la Biosfera Mariposa Monarca, Michoacán, Mexico

Note: Meeting took place on 26–28 October to outline ecological requirements of overwintering monarchs in Mexico.

several digitized layers: topography, colony site coordinates, 1986 polygons, vegetation types, and watershed boundaries.

Analyses of the spatial data determined that the preferred habitats of overwintering monarchs shared four features: (1) high elevations (91% of the colony sites were located at altitudes greater than or equal to 2890 m), (2) proximity to streams (the majority of the sites occurred less than 400 m from permanent [57%] or ephemeral streams [83%], (3) moderately steep slopes (41% of the sites occurred on land sloping between 23° and 26°), and (4) south-southwest orientation (58% of the sites were located on mountains facing south to southwest). Although the experts initially assumed that fir forests are the prime habitat for the overwintering monarchs, colony sites also existed below these forests, primarily because the butterflies move to lower altitudes (where mixed forest stands occur) as spring advances.

A comparison of vegetation layers between 1973 and 1993 showed that 23% of the colonies occurred in areas converted from primary butterfly habitat to other land uses, and 41% were located within areas with a high deforestation risk (Bojórquez-Tapia et al. 2003). Another disturbing fact revealed by the analyses was that 20% of the colonies were located in the buffer zones and 30% were completely outside of the buffer and core zones of the 1986 polygons (Bojórquez-Tapia et al. 2003). Thus at best, the 1986 decree resulted in fully protecting only half of the currently known overwintering sites.

During the workshop, 45 reserve configurations were generated and the one that protected the maximum number of butterfly colonies in the minimum area was selected using an iterative algorithm. A second probabilistic model identified areas with a high probability of being critical monarch habitat based on vegetation, altitude, and hydrologic features. The experts concluded that the optimal dimensions of the monarch butterfly reserve should combine features of both models, and generated proposed protected areas totaling 226,000 ha (873 sq mi) of potential habitat. Because such a large area would be challenging if not impossible to protect, the group selected more conservative altitudinal limits, leading to the reduction of potential habitat from 226,000 to 70,000 ha (270 sq mi). A second major conclusion of the group was that watershed protection was essential to overwintering habitats. Thus, the 70,000 ha (270 sq mi) was distributed across 158 watersheds.

In January 1999, WWF Mexico sponsored a second participatory planning workshop to refine and reduce the reserve design based on both biological and socioeconomic factors. Following the recommendations of the participating experts (L. Brower, W. Calvert, A. Alonso, J. Hoth, and G. Castilleja) all of the watersheds containing butterfly colonies were defined as conservation units. Based

Table 19.2. Colony site descriptions (1977 to 1998)

The 12 massifs and 64 sites	Source	Longitude	Latitude	Main stream and watershed	Map
Altamirano					
Camino de las Cruces	PROFEPA	381375	2207334	Cañada El Aile	E14A16
Cañada de las Cruces	Mejía	380936	2208597	Unnamed between Cañada El Pastor and Cañada El Aile	E14A16
Unnamed	García-Mora	381216	2208709	Unnamed between Cañada El Pastor and Cañada El Aile	E14A16
Puerto Borrego	PROFEPA	381307	2208733	Unnamed between Cañada El Pastor and Cañada El Aile	E14A16
Chincua					
Mojonera Alta	Hoth	364209	2175622	La Plancha	E14A26
Sengio Ridge	Alonso-Mejía				
Arroyo Barranca Honda	PROFEPA	363713	2174995	La Plancha	E14A26
Peña Cargada	Calvert/Brower	364053	2175383	La Plancha	E14A26
Llano del Toro	Calvert/Brower	363208	2176088	Zapatero	E14A26
Zapatero	Calvert/Brower	362357	2176392	Zapatero	E14A26
Sendero el Japonés	Rendón Salinas	363464	2176094	La Plancha	E14A26
El Zacatonal	PROFEPA	364549	2175806	Garatachea	E14A26
Rincón de Villalobos	Rendón Salinas	365500[a]	2174800[a]	Limpio	E14A26
Cañada del Muerto	Rendón Salinas	NA	NA	Limpio	E14A26
Acuña	Calvert/Brower	368696	2173104	El Charco	E14A26
Campanario (northern part)					
El Sendero	Mejía	367296	2166486	Los Conejos	E14A26
Los Horcones	Mejía	367651	2167237	Los Conejos	E14A26
Los Letreros	Mejía	367355	2167737	Carrillos	E14A26
Las Palmas	Mejía	366797	2167243	El Gracera	E14A26
Llano Cruzado	Mejía	367302	2167387	El Gracera	E14A26
Balsitas	Mejía	367100	2167189	El Gracera	E14A26
Llano de los Conejos	Mejía	367373	2167113	Los Conejos	E14A26
El Sautrillo	PROFEPA				E14A26
Campanario (southern part)					
Llano El Picacho	PROFEPA	371635	2162898	La Hacienda	E14A26
Cerro Blanco	García-Serrano/Mora	369931	2164210	La Hacienda	E14A26
Piedra Boluda	García-Serrano/Mora	369989	2164210	La Hacienda	E14A26
El Picacho	Calvert/Brower	369897	2162793	La Hacienda	E14A26
Los Enjonches					
Cerro Las Palomas	PROFEPA	370081	2164215	La Hacienda	E14A26
Lomas de Aparicio	PROFEPA	373895	2156185	Grande	E14A36
Chivatí/Huacal					
San Cristóbal	Mejía	362988	2160653	El Establo	E14A26
Mesa Alta	PROFEPA	364253	2159701	El Sauz	E14A26
Los Trozos	García-Serrano/Mora	363537	2158908	El Borbollón	E14A26
Pelón					
El Cedral	García-Serrano/Mora	367947	2143996	El Pedregal	E14A36
El Cardito	PROFEPA	367095	2144104	El Pedregal	E14A36
La Ciénega	PROFEPA	371745	2146360	Guadalupe	E14A36
Santa Teresa	García-Serrano/Mora	370678	2146528	Gudalupe	E14A36
La Gotita	PROFEPA	367454	2143507	El Pedregal	E14A36
El Jara	PROFEPA	366120	2142229	Jaral	E14A36
Las Latas	PROFEPA	366487	2142909	El Pedregal	E14A36
Loma Larga	Mejía	366598	2145002	Seco	E14A36
El Terrero	Mejía	368257	2146933	Seco	E14A36
Llano Tres Gobernadores	Mejía	367936	2143695	Barranca Honda[b]	E14A36

Table 19.2. Continued

The 12 massifs and 64 sites	Source	Longitude	Latitude	Main stream and watershed	Map
Cerro de las Nieves	García-Serrano/Mora	370090	2145794	Seco	E14A36
Los Chiqueros	PROFEPA	371755	2145905	Guadalupe	E14A36
San Andrés					
La Paloma Muerta	PROFEPA	331620	2190416	Colorado	E14A15
Hoyo de la Nieve	PROFEPA	332036	2190108	Colorado	E14A15
El Zorrillo	PROFEPA	331729	2188985	Colorado	E14A15
San Andrés 1	Calvert/Brower	332076	2187875	Agua Azul	E14A15
San Andrés 2	Calvert/Brower	332375	2187795	Unnamed west Branch Barranca Honda[b]	E14A15
San Andrés 3	Rendón Salinas	331818	2189863	Unnamed	E14A15
Mil Cumbres					
Cerro de Garnica	PROFEPA	310461	2178055	El Carrizo	E14A24
Puerto de Las Papas	PROFEPA	310461	2178055	El Carrizo	E14A24
Puerto Murillo	PROFEPA	309853	2179282	El Real	E14A24
Cerro el Cedral					
Puerto Bermeo	PROFEPA	380274	2183672	El Cedral	E14A26
Herrada					
Piedra Herrada	PROFEPA	399120	2122064	Los Hoyos	E14A47
Herrada 1	Calvert/Brower	399515	2121062	Palomas	E14A47
Herrada 2	Calvert/Brower	399453	2120939	Palomas	E14A47
Herrada 3	Rendón Salinas	399011	2121971	La Alameda	E14A47
Oxtotilpan					
Los Hoyos	Rendón Salinas	404066	2122642	Unnamed	E14A47
Palomas					
Cerro Las Palomas 1	PROFEPA	408517	2111923	Palo Amarillo	E14A47
Cerro Las Palomas 2	SEMARNAP	407277	2110339	Palo Amarillo	E14A47
Cerro Las Palomas 3	Rendón Salinas	408626	2111316	Palo Amarillo	E14A47
Cerro Las Palomas 4	Rendón Salinas	408657	2111777	Palo Amarillo	E14A47
Cerro Las Palomas 5	Rendón Salinas	410941	2112811	Agua Blanca	E14A47

Note: The sources listed are the last names of scientists or the names of organizations who identified each site; full names of sources are listed in the acknowledgments. For each site, Universal Transverse Mercator longitude and latitude and map references are listed, along with the names of the major drainage stream along which the colonies form. "Map" refers to the 1 : 50,000 Instituto Nacional de Estadística, Geografía e Informática topographic maps. Sengio Ridge is the same as Mojonera Alta; Arroyo Barranca Honda, same as Arroyo La Plancha; Sendero el Japonés, same as El Mirador; Los Enjonches, same as Lomas de Aparicio; Mesa Alta, same as Mesa Chica; El Cardito, same as Ranchitos de los Carditos; La Gotita, same as Gota de Agua.

[a] Estimated from topographic map.

[b] Chincua, Pelón, and San Andrés all have arroyos (streams) called Barranca Honda.

on the selection criteria described in table 19.3, the minimum optimal habitat was reduced to 22,250 ha (86 sq mi) in 38 watersheds.

Using an optimization procedure (Bojórquez-Tapia et al. 2003), participants reduced the minimum optimal habitat to 19,929 ha and defined this as a core zone. They proposed an additional 25,580 ha as a buffer zone to create a reserve with a total area of 45,000 ha that encompassed a total of 93 watersheds. This proposal established five priorities for site protection: (1) protect all known overwintering colonies on a watershed-by-watershed basis, (2) protect potential overwintering sites with suitable habitat but no known records of large colony formation, (3) provide protection on westerly and southwesterly slopes of watersheds adjacent to those in which the colonies regularly occur, (4) provide interconnectivity of the protected areas by means of corridors, and (5) avoid protecting areas within which extensive deforestation has occurred in the past.

NEGOTIATIONS BETWEEN AGENCIES AND LANDOWNERS

In June 1999, the WWF presented the reserve design proposed at the January meeting to the Ministry of the Environment, Natural Resources

Table 19.3. Interative optimization model results

Rule description	Lower altitudinal limit (meters above sea level)	No. of watersheds	No. of adjacent watersheds	Total area (ha)
1. Watersheds with colonies, with no evident deforestation	3000	2	0	560
	2900	15	0	5370
	2800	16	0	6330
	2700	16	0	6810
	2600	16	0	7360
2. Watersheds with colonies with evident deforestation (<20% of the area between altitudinal limits within the watershed)	3000	24	0	16,030
	2900	24	0	17,220
	2800	24	0	18,210
	2700	24	0	18,210
	2600	24	0	18,210
3. Same as 2 but including adjacent watersheds	3000	34	10	20,400
	2900	36	2	21,420
	2800	37	1	22,220
	2700	38	1	22,250
	2600	38	1	22,250

Note: Results used to set final ecological recommendations for size and location of monarch butterfly reserves, following a January 1999 meeting sponsored by the World Wildlife Fund.

and Fisheries (SEMARNAP) in Mexico with positive results. SEMARNAP (the key environmental agency of the Mexican federal government) agreed to promote the proposal among the local landowners and to provide the WWF with digital information on land tenure to include in the GIS maps. Concerned about the reactions from the campesinos, in November 1999 SEMARNAP presented a new proposal with a core zone around the butterfly colonies where absolutely no activities (including logging) would be permitted, a buffer zone where some activities (i.e., mushroom collecting, reforestation, watershed management) would be allowed but logging would be prohibited, and an influence zone with controlled logging.

In January 2000, a compromise agreement was reached melding SEMARNAP's design with the WWF's original proposal. The idea of the influence zone was discarded, and the area was designed to include two core areas where logging would be banned and a buffer zone where controlled amounts of all other activities, including logging, would be allowed. The continuous core and buffer areas of this design protected both the current and potential habitat of the monarchs as well as the watersheds. Because of a delay in receiving the data layer from SEMARNAP, land tenure information had not been included up to this point. In May 2000, however, the land tenure layer was added to the GIS maps. Adjustments were made according to the number of hectares each landowner had within the core zone. If the majority of a given property was within the core, the remainder was incorporated. When only a small portion of a property was in the core, it was removed to become part of the buffer. This was done to facilitate negotiations with the campesinos and indigenous communities who own the land. The adjustment resulted in a bigger reserve with a smaller core zone than the one originally proposed by the WWF in June 1999. The core was now reduced to 15,306 ha (59 sq mi) and the buffer increased to 40,953 ha (158 sq mi) for a total of 56,259 ha (217 sq mi).

THE MONARCH BUTTERFLY CONSERVATION FUND

During the negotiation process with SEMARNAP, the WWF worked independently to develop a mechanism to compensate the local landowners for the loss of their logging rights that would result from the expansion of the core area. With a $5 million donation from the David and Lucile Packard Foundation, and in collaboration with the Fondo Mexicano para la Conservación de la Naturaleza (FMCN), the WWF established the Monarch Butterfly Conservation Fund (MBCF) to finance the purchase of logging permits inside the new core area of the proposed Monarch Butterfly Biosphere Reserve.

The fund was designed to accomplish three specific goals: (1) to purchase all logging permits operating inside the new core area of the proposed Monarch Butterfly Biosphere Reserve, (2) to sponsor forest conservation activities by local communities included in the management program of the reserve, and (3) to promote economic activities by local communities that are compatible with the conservation objectives of the reserve.

Negotiations between SEMARNAP and the local landowners followed from June to October 2000, during which both the boundaries of the reserve and the terms of compensation payments were discussed. An additional $1 million contribution by the Mexican government was added to the fund during the process. By the end of October 2000, negotiations ended and the final boundaries were established. The total area recommended in the May 2000 proposal (56,259 ha) remained, but the hectares designated as core zone were reduced. The final boundaries of the reserve were set at 13,552 ha in the core and 42,707 ha in the buffer (figure 19.1). Legal agreements accepting the new boundaries and the compensation mechanism were signed with the local landowners on 24 October 2000.

The negotiation process culminated with the promulgation of a new decree by President Ernesto Zedillo on 10 November 2000, expanding the reserve from 16,100 to 56,259 ha, and changing its official designation from the Monarch Butterfly *Special* Biosphere Reserve to the Monarch Butterfly Biosphere Reserve (Diario Oficial 2000). Table 19.4 describes the changes in the proposed sizes of the reserve throughout the negotiation process. The new reserve is more than triple the size of the original 1986 reserve, but the proportion of core areas remains low with respect to the total size of the reserve. In 1986, 28% of the total reserve consisted of core areas; currently the core areas are 24% of the total. The key difference between the two reserves lies in the fact that the new reserve protects a contiguous area instead of separate "islands." This reduced fragmentation should result in better long-term protection of the ecosystem.

Table 19.4. Negotiated changes in the reserve

	Core	Buffer	Total
Reserve 1986 decree	4491	11,619	16,110
Defined optimal habitat (October 1998)	20,300	21,400	41,700
WWF and SEMARNAP proposal (May 2000)	15,306	40,953	56,259
Final reserve decree (November 2000)	13,552	42,707	56,259

As part of the laws regarding protected area management, no forest exploitation activities are allowed in the core area, although illegal logging still poses a challenge. The majority of local campesinos want to see an end to illegal cutting, which benefits only a few. Local women, in particular, are concerned about the diminishing water supply (pers. observ.).

In theory, the payments from the Monarch Butterfly Conservation Fund will effectively halt logging in the core area, but enforcement of the no-logging rule needs to be addressed. This has been a problematic issue since the local economy has traditionally focused on logging. Through the payments for conservation activities, the fund hopes to gradually phase out logging and transform the economy into one based on sustainable activities.

DISCUSSION

It is evident that long-term conservation of ecosystems can only be achieved if the needs of the communities in and close to them are addressed. When establishing protected areas, social, economic, and political factors must be considered along with biological criteria. Traditionally, most reserves are designed with the needs of the species or ecosystem in mind, disregarding the human dimension. An important lesson learned through the process of designing and negotiating the Monarch Butterfly Biosphere Reserve was that there is a strong need to form multidisciplinary teams to tackle conservation issues. The complexities involved in conservation, and the socioeconomic and political factors that affect it, can only be addressed if representatives of all disciplines collaborate.

The Monarch Butterfly Conservation Fund represents an attempt to incorporate the human dimension into conservation. It has set a precedent for conservation efforts in Mexico since it is the first time incentives were offered to local communities affected by the establishment of a protected area. Trust funds as conservation tools are now being promoted in several areas of biological importance throughout the world, and the case of the Monarch Butterfly Biosphere Reserve will serve as an example.

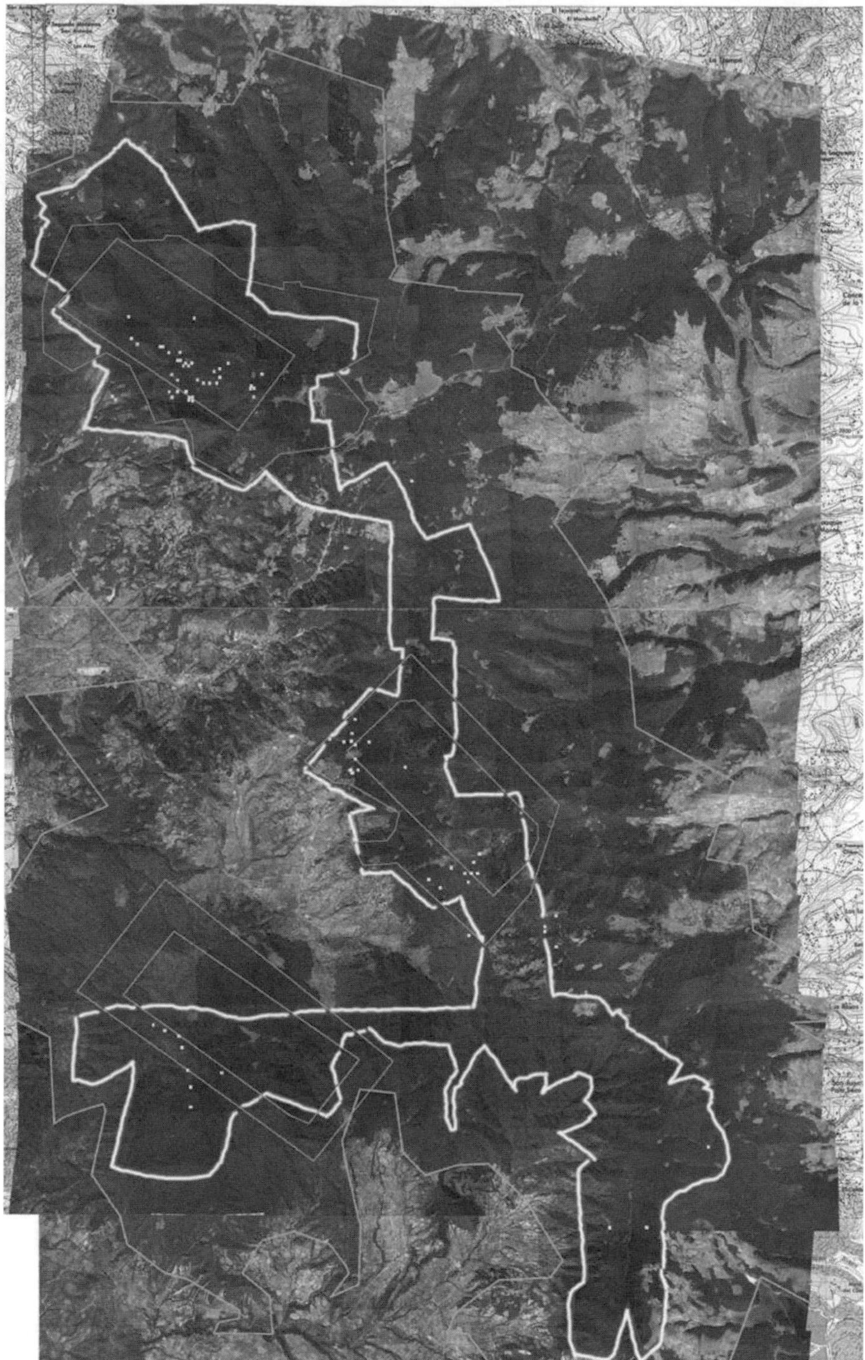

Figure 19.1. Monarch Butterfly Biosphere Reserve boundaries established in October 2000. Bold white lines show the core area of the new reserve and the gray line outside of the core encloses the new buffer. The three central polygons are core zones established by the 1986 decree (surrounding, from top to bottom, the Chincua, Campanario, and Chivatí-Huacal sites), and the polygons that surround them enclose the 1986 buffers. White dots represent known monarch overwintering sites. Prepared for World Wildlife Fund Mexico with the collaboration of A. Peralta, G. Castilleja, L. Bojórquez-Tapia, S. Diaz, D. Melgarejo, M. Missrie, W. Calvert, A. Alonso, J. Hoth, and L. Brower.

However, time will tell if indeed the trust fund–compensation mechanism proves to be a sustainable option.

Acknowledgments

Thanks to Dr. Armando Peralta, Dr. José Lopez, and Salomón Diaz for their help in developing maps and to many colleagues for assembling colony location data over 21 years: Alfonso Alonso-Mejía, Lincoln Brower, William Calvert, Jurgen Hoth, María Macaria Mejía, Xiomara Mora, Eligio García-Serrano, Eduardo Rendón Salinas, and Alejandro Angulo from PROFEPA; to Lincoln Brower for reviewing the manuscript; to Michelle Solensky for her encouragement and her revisions; and to Sonia Altizer whose suggestions greatly improved this manuscript.

The new Monarch Butterfly Biosphere Reserve would not have become a reality without the financial support of the Rufford Foundation (United Kingdom), World Wildlife Fund (Canada), the Monarch Butterfly Sanctuary Foundation (United States) and the David and Lucile Packard Foundation (United States). I am grateful to the Monarch Butterfly Sanctuary Foundation for their support during the reserve design process, and for inviting me to participate in the Monarch Population Dynamics meeting in Lawrence, Kansas, in May 2001.

Dr. Lincoln Brower, my colleagues at the WWF, the Fondo Mexicano para la Conservación de la Naturaleza, SEMARNAP, and INE all contributed significantly. Dr. Guillermo Castilleja led the project brilliantly. Dr. Alberto Szekely was instrumental in designing the structure for the creation of the Monarch Butterfly Conservation Fund and the legal agreements with the campesinos. Eligio García-Serrano provided us with additional data for our GIS analysis. I appreciate their commitment to the monarchs and am grateful for having had the opportunity to collaborate with them.

References

Alonso-Mejía., A., J. I. Glendinning, and L. P. Brower. 1993. The influence of temperature on crawling, shivering, and flying in overwintering monarch butterflies in Mexico. In S. B. Malcolm and M. P. Zalucki, eds., Biology and conservation of the monarch butterfly, pp. 309–14. Los Angeles: Natural History Museum of Los Angeles County.

Alonso-Mejía, A., Rendón Salinas, E. Montesinos-Patino, and L. P. Brower. 1997. Use of lipid reserves by monarch butterflies (*Danaus plexippus* L.) for overwintering in Mexico: implications for conservation. Ecol. Appl. 7:934–47.

Bojórquez-Tapia, L. A., L. P. Brower, G. Castilleja, S. Sanchez-Colón, M. Hernández, W. H. Calvert, S. Diaz, P. Gomez-Priego, G. Alcantar, E. D. Melgarejo, M. J. Solares, L. Gutiérrez, and M. D. L. Juárez. 2003. Mapping expert knowledge: redesigning the monarch butterfly biosphere reserve. Conserv. Biol. 17:367–79.

Brower, L. P. 1999. Oyamel forest ecosystem conservation in Mexico is necessary to prevent the extinction of the migratory phenomenon of the monarch butterfly in North America. In P. Canevari, ed., Proceedings of the CMS Symposium on Animal Migration (Gland, Switzerland, 13 April 1997), pp. 41–50. Bonn: United Nations Environment Programme/Convention on the Conservation of Migratory Species of Wild Animals (UNEP/CMS).

Brower, L. P., G. Castilleja, A. Peralta, J. Lopez-Garcia, L., Bojórquez-Tapia, S. Diaz, D. Melgarejo, and M. Missrie. 2002. Quantitative changes in forest quality in a principal overwintering area of the monarch butterfly in Mexico, 1971–1999. Conserv. Biol. 16:346–59.

Calvert, W. H., and L. P. Brower. 1986. The location of monarch butterfly (*Danaus plexippus* L.) overwintering colonies in Mexico in relation to topography and climate. J. Lepid. Soc. 40:164–87.

Chapela, G., Y. Mendoza, and D. Barkin. 1995. Mariposas y campesinos: estrategia de desarrollo sustentable en el oriente de Michoacán. México, DF: Centro de Ecología y Desarrollo, A.C.

Diario Oficial. 1986. Órgano del Gobierno Constitucional de los Estados Unidos Mexicanos, pp. 33–41. México, DF. 10 de septiembre.

Diario Oficial. 2000. Órgano del Gobierno Constitucional de los Estados Unidos Mexicanos, pp. 6–29. México, DF. 10 de noviembre.

Dobson, A. P. 1996. Conservation and biodiversity. New York: Scientific American Library.

Hoth, J. 1994. Posicionamiento de los santuarios de la mariposa monarca y observaciones ecológicas cualitativas. 15 pp. Reporte de campo presentado al Instituto Nacional de Ecología, México.

Hoth, J. 1995. Mariposa monarca, mitos y otras realidades aladas. Ciencias 37:19–28.

Hoth, J., L. Merino, K. Oberhauser, I. Pisanty, S. Price, and T. Wilkinson, eds. 1999. The 1997 North American Conference on the Monarch Butterfly. Montreal: Commission for Environmental Cooperation.

Kiester, R., J. M. Scott, B. Csuti, R. F. Noss, B. Butterfield, K. Shar, and D. White. 1996. Conservation prioritization using GAP data. Conserv. Biol. 10:1332–42.

Malczewski, J., R. Moreno-Sanchez, L. A. Bojórquez-Tapia, and E. Ongay-Delhumeau. 1997. Multicriteria group decision-making model for environmental conflict analysis in the Cape Region, Mexico. J. Environ. Plan. Manag. 40:339–74.

Merino, L. 1997. El manejo forestal comunitario en México y sus perspectivas de sustentabilidad. Mexico City: Universidad Nacional Autónoma de México.

Merino-Perez, L., and P. Gerez-Fernandez. 1996. Status of the conservation of the monarch butterfly in Mexico, pp. 1–32. Report for the Commission for Environmental Cooperation (CEC) of North America. Jalapa: Consejo Civil Mexicano para la Silyicultura Sostenible.

Pereira, J. M. C., and L. Duckstein. 1993. A multiple criteria decision-making approach to GIS-based land suitability evaluations. Int. J. Geogr. Inf. Syst. 7:407–24.

Possingham, H. I. B., and S. Andelman. 2000. Mathematical methods for identifying representative reserve networks. In S. Ferson and M. Burgman, eds., Quantitative methods for conservation biology, pp. 291–305. New York: Springer-Verlag.

Pressey, R. L., H. P. Possingham, and J. R. Day. 1997. Effectiveness of alternative heuristic algorithms for identifying indicative minimum requirements for conservation reserves. Biol. Conserv. 80:207–19.

20

Catastrophic Winter Storm Mortality of Monarch Butterflies in Mexico during January 2002

Lincoln P. Brower, David R. Kust, Eduardo Rendón Salinas, Eligio García-Serrano, Katherine R. Kust, Jacob Miller, Concha Fernandez del Rey, and Karen Pape

INTRODUCTION

Monarchs form their overwintering colonies at high-altitude sites in the oyamel fir (*Abies religiosa*) forests in central Mexico. The butterflies are subject to freezing when northern cold fronts generate winter storms that impinge on high areas in the region. Since 1977 many storms have occurred, but their frequency, severity, and effects on the monarchs have not been systematically documented.

Calvert and coauthors (1983) reported on the effects of a prolonged frontal incursion that severely affected the Zapatero overwintering colony in the Sierra Chincua during January 1981. The storm system was accompanied by snow and sleet alternating with rain over 10 days. With subsequent clearing, the temperature in the butterfly colony dropped to −5°C. They estimated that 418 monarchs were killed per square meter in the 0.65-ha colony, totaling 2.7 million dead monarchs.

Heavy mortality occurred again at the Sierra Herrada overwintering colony, located at 3164 m, in 1992 (Culotta 1992; L. Brower, pers. observ.). Prolonged cloudy, cold, and wet weather had occurred in the central overwintering region during January. A major cold front moved through during the early morning of 4 February, and by noon the whole of central Mexico was spectacularly clear. At 12:30 AM, the temperature was 2.5°C and the area was still very wet. Dead monarchs littered the ground and the colony area had been reduced by 90% (W. H. Calvert, pers. comm.). Brower and Calvert (unpub.) estimated that more than 80% of the monarchs had been killed. Heavy mortality had also occurred in the Sierra Chincua and Sierra Campanario colonies (C. Gottfried and Rosario guides, pers. comm.). We hypothesized that the butterflies had been killed by the combination of wetting and the subsequent clearing that results in extreme radiant heat loss to the cloudless sky. Anderson and Brower (1993, 1996) tested this hypothesis at a field laboratory in the Sierra Chincua. They measured the cumulative mortality that occurred as the body temperatures of individual monarchs were experimentally lowered to 15°C below freezing. The study determined that dry butterflies have a modicum of cryoprotection and can super-cool, but by −8.1°C, 50% had frozen to death and by −15°C, all were killed. When misted, they lost much of their natural cryoprotection: 50% died as their body temperatures dropped to only −4.4°C, and by −7.8°C, all were dead. Larsen and Lee (1994) showed that wetting also accelerates the freezing process: monarchs held at −4°C froze within 3 hours when wet, whereas dry individuals survived the same treatment for the 24-h duration of the experiment. These studies are definitive: wetting of butterflies prior to the short-term temperature plunges that follow winter storms in the overwintering region greatly increases the percentage of monarchs that will freeze to death.

Continuing microclimatic research at the overwintering sites in Mexico demonstrated that forest thinning exacerbates the monarchs' risk of freezing (Calvert and Brower 1981; Calvert and Cohen 1983;

Calvert et al. 1982, 1983, 1984, 1986; Alonso-Mejía et al. 1992; Anderson and Brower 1993). Removal of trees within and adjacent to the overwintering colonies subjects monarch clusters to increased wetting and their individual body temperatures drop below the ambient temperature when it is clear. This happens because body heat is lost by radiation through gaps in the forest canopy to the colder sky (Anderson and Brower 1996).

Recognition during the 1980s that forest thinning in and near the overwintering sites posed a severe threat to monarchs resulted in the designation of their migration and overwintering biology as an endangered biological phenomenon (Wells et al. 1983; Brower and Malcolm 1991). Brower (1996b, 1999a, 1999b) synthesized the evidence that forest thinning and the overwintering of monarchs are incompatible and called for more effective protection of the oyamel-pine ecosystem. A geographic information system (GIS) analysis of deforestation between 1971 and 1999 revealed that 44% of the high-quality forest has been degraded and fragmented in the past 28 years, and that the rate of cutting is accelerating (Brower et al. 2002).

Misunderstandings about monarch biology, combined with insufficient data, have resulted in erroneous reports in the press and a general public confusion over rates and causes of winter mortality. In December 1995, for example, an early winter storm dropped 31 cm of snow on the Sierra Chincua. Clearing was accompanied by heavy winds that dislodged millions of butterflies from their clusters. It was reported in the press that up to 35% of the colony had been killed (e.g., Preston 1996). In fact, because little rain accompanied the storm, its impact was minimal. Most of the butterflies recovered and the mortality estimate was changed to 5% to 7% (Brower 1996a). This and a spate of other press reports resulted in accusations of exaggeration of the effects of logging (e.g., Huriash 1996).

Once again in January 2001, lack of understanding of the biology of monarch overwintering generated severe controversy about what had killed tens of thousands of monarchs at the San Andrés overwintering colony. Iniquitous pesticide spraying was implicated as the cause by concerned visitors to the area and then widely reported in the press and popular monarch literature (Aridjis 2001; Fullerton 2001; Marriott 2001). The pesticide hypothesis received no support from independent chemical analyses done for the Mexican federal environmental enforcement agency (PROFEPA 2001). Brower (2001) concluded that the most likely explanation was a winter storm that soaked and then froze thousands of monarchs, followed by the colony's partial recovery and subsequent movement to a nearby location.

On 12 to 14 January 2002, a heavy winter storm occurred in the monarch overwintering region in central Mexico. We describe the storm and the impact it had on four different overwintering colonies (Conejos and Rosario [Sierra Campanario], Zapatero [Sierra Chincua] and Capulin [Cerro Pelón]) and discuss conservation implications.

METHODS

Locations, altitudes, and sizes of the colonies

Figure 15.1 illustrates the locations of the mountains on which monarch colonies are known to form. During January and March 2002 we used an Eagle Explorer global positioning device to determine the coordinates of overwintering sites, and a Thommen altimeter to determine altitudes, referenced against 1:50,000 topographic maps (Anonymous 1974, 1987). One of us (E. García-Serrano) measured colony areas on 13 to 20 December 2001 (table 20.1). The Zapatero and Rosario colonies have formed nearly every year since 1976 and 1980, respectively, when they were first reported (Urquhart 1976; Calvert and Brower 1986; Bojórquez-Tapia et al. 2003).

Weather observations

To reconstruct the storm climatology and the likely minimum temperatures reached in the Zapatero colony, we pieced together three sources of information. First, during and after the storm, one of us (D. R. Kust) recorded temperatures, rainfall, and qualitative weather descriptions in an open courtyard in the town of Angangueo, in a grove of low-growing juniper trees next to Chincua Station, and along the 4-km dirt road leading from the station into the Zapatero colony. Temperature was measured with a Springfield Precise Digital thermometer.

Second, hourly satellite weather images (GOES-EAST 2002) posted on the Internet by David Dempsey showed the genesis and movements of an

Table 20.1. Approximate center locations and altitudes of the overwintering colonies and weather stations

Location	Area (ha)	Massif	Latitude (N)	Longitude (W)	Altitude (m)
Rosario colony	0.10[a]	Campanario	19°35′56″	100°15′55″	3200
Conejos colony	2.59[a]	Campanario	19°35′45.2″	100°15′50.0″	3277
Zapatero colony	2.96	Chincua	19°40′41.3″	100°18′25.6″	3206
Capulin colony	0.98	Pelón	19°23′33.7″	100°16′44.2″	2896
Campamento colony		Pelón	19°23′48″	100°16′52″	2752
Chincua station		Chincua	19°39′42.8″	100°16′4.0″	3182
Town of Angangueo		Chincua	19°37′30.0″	100°16′46.0″	2630

[a] Areas of the closely adjacent Rosario and Conejos colonies are combined in the analyses as 2.69 ha. Also shown are pre-storm areas of the four monarch overwintering colonies measured in December 2001. Zapatero was measured on 13 December; Rosario and Conejos, on 14 December; and Capulin, on 20 December.

extensive storm system that passed across the overwintering region from 11 to 14 January. We examined 72 hourly visible and infrared images and selected six of the latter to construct figure 20.1.

Third, we compared the daily minimum temperature measurements made by D. Kust during and immediately after the storm with temperatures measured in March, and estimated the likely minimum temperatures in the Zapatero colony on the three clear mornings following the storm. We recorded the air temperature for 15 days (5 to 19 March 2002) at 15-min intervals using four precalibrated Hobo XLT electronic thermometers. One Hobo was set in the courtyard in Angangueo, two were suspended in the center of a standard weather box at the Chincua Station (both recordings were virtually identical), and one was set in what had been the center of the Zapatero colony at the time of the storm. To avoid vandalism, we placed the latter sensor inconspicuously in contact with the surface bark of an oyamel fir. Previous research in the Sierra Chincua indicated that the daily minimum ambient temperature is at least 1°C lower than the minimum temperature recorded on the bark surface (Brown, Lear, García-Serrano, pers. observ.). A difference in 1° can have a substantial impact on the probability of wet monarchs freezing (Anderson and Brower 1996).

Measuring monarch mortality

Initial qualitative observations: 1 to 4 days after the storm

D. Kust visited the Zapatero colony immediately after the storm on 14 and 16 January and the Rosario and Conejos colonies on 18 January. During these visits, he qualitatively assessed the level of mortality caused by the storm.

Quantitative mortality estimates: 7 to 8 days after the storm

We (except for E. García-Serrano and E. Rendón-Salinas) visited the Rosario and Conejos colonies on 21 January and the Zapatero colony on 22 January. At Rosario, we collected three samples of butterflies in gallon-size plastic bags from the ground beneath the roost trees, about 5 m off the path and a few meters apart from each other. To ascertain their status, we emptied the samples onto the ground in a nearby open field and spread the butterflies out to warm for several minutes in the bright sun. The ambient shade temperature was 22°C, well above flight threshold. Any individuals showing movement of their appendages were grasped and tossed into the air. As in the study by Calvert and colleagues (1983), those that flew normally were categorized as alive; those that flew abnormally or plummeted to the ground were categorized as moribund (effectively dead); and those that showed no signs of movement of their legs, wings, antennae, or proboscis were categorized as dead. We tallied and sexed the butterflies in each category between 2:55 and 3:40 PM, during which the weather was clear with occasional light clouds. Immediately after this, we moved to the Conejos site and followed the same procedure to categorize butterfly condition. We completed data collection before 5:45 PM, while it was still sunny.

The following day, we sampled six 25 × 25-cm (625-cm^2) plots in the southwestern quadrant of the Zapatero colony. We finished collecting our samples too late to warm them in the sun, so we punched holes in the plastic bags and took them to

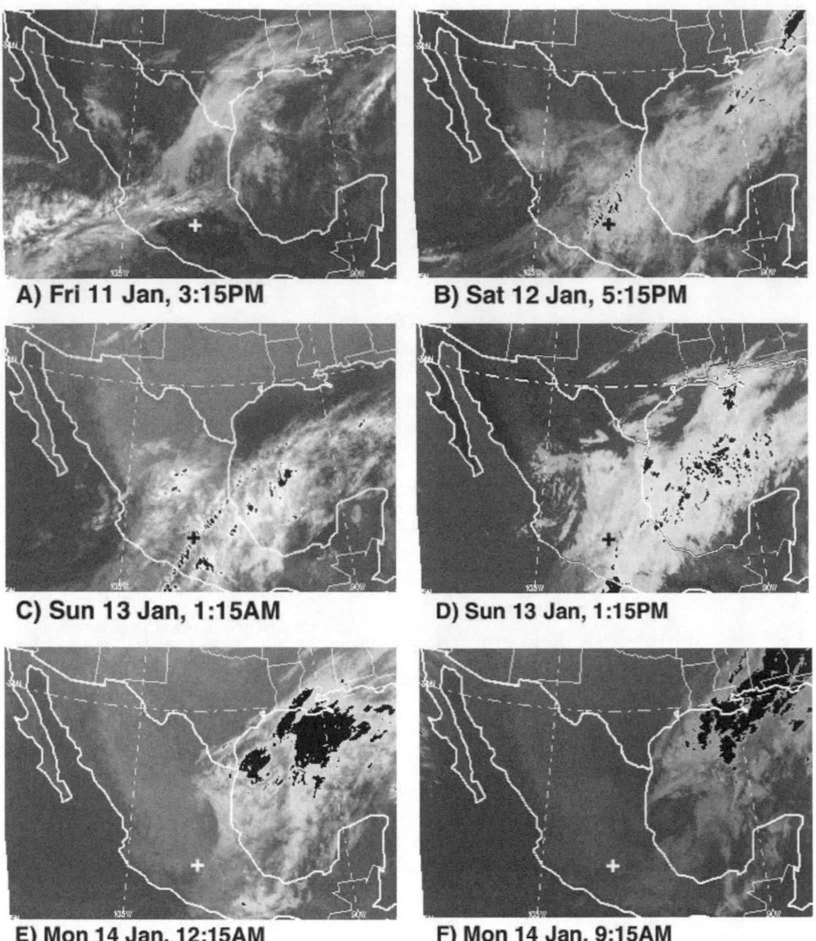

Figure 20.1. Six infrared satellite images generated for 11 to 14 January 2002 document a major North American winter storm system that penetrated Mexico. The white or black plus signs denote the center of the Sierra Chincua sanctuary. The GOES infrared image numbers from (a) to (f) are 02011-121, -223, -307, -319, -406, and -415, respectively, and have been converted to central standard time (GOES EAST 2002). The storm system moved from the Pacific Ocean northeastwardly across Mexico while the precipitation line (blackened areas) swept across the overwintering region with a southeasterly trajectory. In agreement with these satellite data, our ground observations indicated that heavy rain occurred on Saturday and Sunday, followed by extreme clearing beginning late on Sunday night.

Angangueo. We transferred each sample into a pillowcase, spread the monarchs out as thinly as possible, and left them overnight on an open, cold patio floor, next to a thick wall to prevent freezing by radiational cooling during the night. The next day the weather was again clear and we tallied the monarchs from 10:10 AM to 4:30 PM. We split each sample into several separate pillowcases and hung the cases on a clothesline in the sun for about 15 min. This enabled us to separate the dead from the living because the latter crawled up and could be seen in silhouette. We then tossed the survivors individually into the sunlit patio and recorded their condition as just described. We emptied the remaining monarchs onto a table and discarded those that had long been dead or killed by birds, categorized according to Fink and Brower (1981). The total of long-dead and bird-killed monarchs provides an estimate of the cumulative mortality caused by factors other than the storm.

Quantitative mortality estimates: 16 days after the storm

D. Kust and Rendón Salinas returned to Zapatero on 30 January, 16 days after the initial freeze. They established a reference line through the center of what, in December, had been an elliptical colony that embraced the dry streambed. They then marked two 140-m sampling lines parallel to and 20 m to the left and right of the reference line. At 10-m intervals they alternately walked perpendicularly for 5 m to the left and then 5 m to the right off of the main line, establishing 14 sampling positions on one line and 15 on the other. The position of the samples was at the end of each 5-m arm. They followed this procedure to obtain 29 additional samples along two 150-m transects through the Conejos colony on 31 January.

At each sampling position monarchs were gathered from 20 × 20-cm squares (0.04 m^2) and put into labeled plastic bags. After removing the butterflies from each sample square, D. Kust and Rendón-Salinas measured the depth (cm) of the stacked butterflies on one edge of the cleared sample area. In assessing butterfly condition, they discarded long-dead individuals and categorized the rest as alive, moribund, dead with evidence of bird predation, or dead from other cause (attributed to the storm).

RESULTS

Weather observations

Local observations

From 2 to 11 January 2002, the region was clear with few clouds and no precipitation (table 20.2). On 12 January a storm front moved in from the southwest and, as observed in Angangueo, was accompanied by alternating periods of light and heavy rain. Rain continued intermittently through the night and the next day until 10:00 PM, accumulating to a total of 5.8 cm. No snow accumulated in Angangueo, but by midday on 13 January at Chincua Station the rain had turned to snow. Clearing occurred by 11:00 PM on 13 January and it remained clear through 17 January (table 20.2).

Table 20.2. Weather observations

Date	Time	Location	Temperature (°C)	Remarks
3–10 Jan		Entire region		Generally clear with few clouds, no precipitation
11 Jan	7:00 AM	Angangueo	5.4	Clear all day
12 Jan		Angangueo		Storm front arrives, continuous light rain during day, intermittently harder all evening
13 Jan	7:00 AM	Angangueo	5.6	Rain continues all day, intermittently heavy
		Chincua Station		Rain turns to snow in afternoon, accumulating at high elevations throughout the area
	6:30 PM	Angangueo	7.5	Rain continues; cold front arrives with increasing wind
	10:00	Angangueo		Rain ends
	11:00	Angangueo	3.5	Clear, total rain accumulation = 5.8 cm
14 Jan	7:00 AM	Angangueo	–0.2	Clear, thin ice layer in bucket
	7:00	Zapatero colony	–4.4	(Temperature estimated)
	10:30	Angangueo	7.5	Clear
	12:00 PM	Chincua Station		Clear; 5 cm of snow on ground in shaded areas, people making snowmen
	12:00 PM	Road to Zapatero		Ground extremely wet, with snow and ice, refrozen crunchy snow in shaded areas
15 Jan	7:30 AM	Angangueo	1.4	Clear
	7:30	Zapatero colony	–2.8	(Temperature estimated)
	12:00 PM	Chincua Station		Snow remains and puddles frozen in shaded areas, water and mud in road where sun hit
16 Jan	7:30 AM	Angangueo	5.7	Clear
	7:30	Zapatero colony	1.5	(Temperature estimated)
	8:00	Chincua Station	–4.2	Clear; ambient shade temperature measured in juniper grove
	8:30	Road into colony		Heavy rime ice and frost on vegetation, many puddles frozen sufficiently to walk on
	1:00 PM	Zapatero colony	13.8	Ambient shade temperature in colony; snow melt running down road adjacent to colony
17 Jan	7:00 AM	Angangueo	7.1	Clear
	7:00	Zapatero colony	2.9	(Temperature estimated)

On 14 January, about 5 cm of snow covered the ground at Chincua Station and along the road to the Zapatero colony (table 20.2). Based on a snow-to-rain conversion factor of 4:1 for wet snow (Anonymous 2002), 5 cm of snow would be equivalent to about 1.25 cm of rain. Assuming that the Zapatero colony area received the same amount of precipitation as Angangueo (5.8 cm), the butterfly colony would have received 4.55 cm of rain in addition to the 5.0 cm of snow. Angangueo and Zapatero are located only 6 km apart on the Chincua-Campanario massifs, and the colony is 580 m higher in altitude. Because of the adiabatic effects of the wet air mass being forced up over the Sierra Chincua, more precipitation than this probably fell on the butterfly colony area.

At 8:00 AM on 16 January the temperature at Chincua Station was −4.2°C with large puddles frozen sufficiently to walk on. The ground and surrounding vegetation (grass, herbs, bushes, and trees) were frosted with rime ice. Since rime forms by deposition of super-cooled water drops floating in a driving fog that crystallizes on surfaces (Geiger 1950), its presence was another indication of how wet the area had become.

Satellite images support D. Kust's local weather observations and indicate that this storm system affected all the known monarch overwintering massifs (see figure 20.1).

Temperature estimates for the Zapatero colony

The difference between the minimum temperatures recorded on 16 January at Angangueo and the Chincua Station was 9.9°C (table 20.2). The average difference of the daily minimum temperatures in Angangueo and Chincua Station measured for 15 days in March was 9.2°C (Angangueo mean = 10.08°C, Chincua mean = 0.90°C). The closeness of these two values suggests that we can use the measured temperature differences in March to estimate the Zapatero colony temperatures after the storm from measurements taken in Angangueo. The average minimum temperatures in March were 10.1°C in Angangueo and 5.9°C in the Zapatero colony, a difference of 4.2°C. Subtracting 4.2°C from the minimum temperatures measured in Angangueo on 14 to 17 January, we estimated the minimum temperatures attained on these four clear mornings following the storm in the Zapatero colony (table 20.2). If the ambient temperature in Zapatero was on average 1° colder than the oyamel bark temperature as described earlier, then these minima would be reduced accordingly.

Even though the Zapatero colony and Chincua Station are at nearly the same altitude, the average minimum temperature inside the colony in March was 5.0°C warmer than at the station (Zapatero = 5.86°C, Chincua Station = 0.90°C). This is likely because the station weather box was located within a large clearing, whereas the intact forest above the butterfly colony acted as a microclimatic blanket.

Monarch mortality

Initial qualitative observations (1 to 4 days after the storm)

D. Kust and one of the Chincua Station guides were the first to arrive at the Zapatero colony after the storm, at 1:30 PM on 14 January. They walked only a meter into the colony to avoid damaging the many downed and very wet monarchs. Binocular viewing indicated little movement of live butterflies in the colony, and the clusters on the oyamel branches seemed still intact. There were no large accumulations of monarchs on the ground, but D. Kust observed individual monarchs plummeting to the forest floor with regularity.

He returned to the Zapatero colony on 16 January and reported that many monarchs were now on the tops of the understory shrub layer. The scene seemed less severe than on Monday, though many monarchs continued to fall from the trees. He noted that the shade temperature by 1:00 PM had risen to 13.8°C, less than 2° below flight threshold (Masters et al. 1988). Thousands of monarchs were basking in the sun on tree boughs and understory vegetation and drinking water in sun-lit puddle areas. Later in the afternoon many were airborne, and both the trees and the ground were festooned with butterflies. A temperature mosaic in the colony was indicated by the presence of snow and ice patches. It appeared that fewer monarchs were falling from the trees than 2 days previously. At this time, D. Kust was not certain whether the accumulated monarchs on the ground were dead.

On 18 January, D. Kust arrived at the Rosario colony at 10:00 AM. The guards had swept dead monarchs from the main tourist path into piles and had blocked several other paths through the colony. The logging road through the Conejos colony was covered with thick layers of immobile monarchs. In both colonies there was little butterfly movement, and it appeared that many of the intact clusters that D. Kust had seen on 11 January prior to the storm were no longer present on the tree branches. At this time, he estimated mortality to be highest in Conejos, intermediate in Rosario, and least in Zapatero, and reported his findings on Journey North (2002).

Quantitative mortality estimates: 7 to 8 days after the storm

Rosario colony. When we arrived at Rosario on 21 January, the weather, except for a general haze, was clear and the ambient shade temperature in the oyamel forest at 2:30 PM was 15°C, very close to flight threshold. The scene was unlike anything one of us (L. Brower) had witnessed over 25 seasons; had any monarchs on the ground been alive, they would have been fluttering and crawling onto the understory vegetation and tree trunks. Instead, deep layers of motionless butterflies littered the forest floor. D. Kust observed that many more had accumulated on the ground since 16 January. Of the 745 butterflies we counted in three separate samples, 1% were alive, 1% were moribund, and 98% were dead. There was a significant excess of males (64%).

Conejos colony. On reaching Conejos, we observed masses of dead monarchs on the logging road through the center of the colony. A few meters into the north central side, accumulations on the ground beneath the formerly monarch-laden oyamels ranged from 0 to over 20 cm deep. Numerous butterflies lay motionless on the tree boughs while many of the oyamels had intact, seemingly normal clusters. We shook several smaller trees and determined that both the motionless butterflies and those in the clusters had frozen in situ. The understory vegetation showed considerable frost damage, especially the *Senecio angulifolius* D.C. bushes, the leaves of which were blackened and shriveled. A 3-m-high *Cupressus benthamii* var. *lindleyi* Kotsch tree in the understory had many quiescent monarchs hanging on its boughs. We picked off 100 and gently blew on them in our cupped hands. If they had still been healthy, this would have warmed them sufficiently to fly. All were dead. We collected three (nonrandom) separate ground samples from measured areas. Of 965 monarchs sampled, 5 were moribund, and the rest were dead. The calculated numbers of dead monarchs/m^2 were 4297, 4502, and 2290. The sex ratio was approximately even.

Zapatero colony. As we approached Zapatero colony via a road from the Llanos de los Villalobos along the north face of the Sierra Chincua, we noticed severe frost damage on the understory *S. angulifolius* bushes in thinned areas beneath the oyamels. Most were browned except for their lowermost leaves. They still had snow on them and the ground was very wet. The colony was located at the head of El Zapatero watershed in virtually the same location as in several previous years (Calvert and Brower 1986).

We saw similar mortality patterns as in Conejos, with layers of monarchs covering both the forest floor and the adjacent logging road. Heterogeneity in the depth of the accumulations was evident: where tree branches extended from the oyamels, many more monarchs were on the ground than beneath the many forest gaps.

The leaves of the 1.5-m *S. angulifolius* bushes in the colony beneath the oyamels on the southwestern side of the creek bed were still mostly green, compared to the severe frosting on the ridge about 160 m above the colony. Many monarchs clung to the upper leaves of these bushes. We cupped several in our hands, gently blew ten breaths on them, and then tossed them into the air. Twelve (8%) of 146 monarchs flew normally while the rest were moribund. We collected six ground samples from measured areas, totaling 4288 monarchs. In five of the six samples, only 1.2% to 2% of the butterflies were alive, but in the deepest (20-cm) sample, many monarchs (38%) were buried alive. The butterflies that covered them probably kept these individuals alive, but the weight of the tightly packed dead butterflies on top of them would likely have caused their eventual death. From these six samples we estimated an average of 9854 dead monarchs/m^2 (standard deviation [SD] = 7540, range = 1456 to 18,112). These estimates of mortality were 3 to 43 times larger than the 418 estimated killed per square meter during the 1981 storm (Calvert et al. 1983).

Quantitative mortality estimates: 16 days after the storm

Preliminary data from the Rosario, Conejos, and Zapatero colonies indicated high sample variability

Table 20.3. Monarch conditions in 29 random samples made in the Zapatero and Conejos colonies

	Sample means (SD) and ranges for 0.04-m² plots					
Colony	No. dead	No. moribund	No. live	No. killed by birds	Depth (cm)	Estimated no. dead / m²
Zapatero ($n = 3136$)	99.4 (89.1) 0–337	5.8 (7.6) 0–35	1.5 (3.7) 0–16	1.5 (1.4) 0–5	3.8 (2.9) 0–9	2628
Conejos ($n = 8489$)	289.8 (504.5) 1–2347	0.4 (1.3) 0–7	0.03 (0.19) 0–1	2.6 (6.4) 0–32	6.5 (8.5) 0–33	7253

Note: The estimated number of dead monarchs per square meter includes dead and moribund monarchs [(99.4 + 5.8) × 25], [(289.8 + 0.4) × 25]. SD, standard deviation.

Table 20.4. Mortality estimates in the Zapatero and Conejos colonies

Colony	Colony size before storm (ha)	Colony size after storm (ha)	% of colony eliminated	No. of monarchs killed / m²	No. of monarchs killed / ha (millions)	Total no. of monarchs killed (millions)
Zapatero	2.96	0.76	74.3%	2628	26.3	77.8
Conejos	2.69	0.54	80.1%	7253	72.5	195.1

and heterogeneity in the depth of accumulations of dead monarchs. We therefore deemed it critical to obtain a larger number of samples collected systematically from within the pre-storm colony boundaries. This was facilitated by García-Serrano having marked the colony borders in December.

Zapatero colony. By 24 January, the surviving monarchs had deserted the area in which the mortality had occurred. Dropping about 35 m in altitude, they moved slightly down the dry streambed and re-formed a smaller (0.76-ha) colony on the trees on both sides of the arroyo.

Table 20.3 summarizes the conditions of the butterflies in the 29 0.05 m² samples. Of 3136 butterflies collected, 44 (1.4%) were alive, 167 (5.3%) were moribund, 43 (1.4%) were preyed on, and 2882 (91.9%) were dead from other causes, assumed to be storm-related mortality (mean numbers in each category are illustrated in table 20.3). There was a small deficiency of females in all categories. The average depth of accumulated dead butterflies was 3.8 cm. Using the mean number of dead and moribund monarchs per sampling plot, we calculated the mean number of dead and moribund monarchs per square meter (number/0.04-m² plot × 25 = number/m²). The average of 2628 dead or dying monarchs per square meter is more than six times the mortality estimated during the 1981 storm (Calvert et al. 1983). By multiplying the mean number of dead or dying monarchs per square meter by the pre-storm colony size, we estimated the total mortality at the Zapatero colony to be 77.8 million monarchs (table 20.4). Because the post-storm cluster densities were substantially less than they had been prior to the storm, we feel confident that this is a conservative estimate of the mortality caused by this storm.

Conejos colony. As in Zapatero, the surviving butterflies deserted the original colony area. They moved slightly up the slope where they formed a distinct new colony. D. Kust and Rendón-Salinas revisited the area on 31 January and concluded that the colony architecture was so disturbed and fragmented that its post-storm area could not be accurately measured. However, García-Serrano had estimated that 942 trees were occupied by butterfly clusters on 14 December, and D. Kust and Rendón-Salinas now counted 187 trees in the recovery colony, an 80.1% reduction. We used this percentage to estimate the reduction in colony size from the pre-storm value of 2.69 ha to a post-storm size of 0.535 ha (table 20.4).

Of the 8489 monarchs collected in 29 samples at Conejos, 1 was alive, 11 were moribund, 74 were preyed on, and 8412 (99%) were dead (see table

20.3). Sex ratios were nearly even. The average depth of accumulated dead butterflies was 6.5 cm (figure 20.2). We estimated an average of 7253 dead or dying monarchs per square meter at the Conejos colony, yielding an overall estimate of 195.1 million monarchs killed. As was true for the Zapatero colony after the storm, visual inspection indicated that the post-storm clusters were substantially less dense. We therefore are again confident that our data provide a conservative estimate of the mortality caused by this storm.

Additional transect samples

García-Serrano had also sampled the Zapatero and Conejos colonies to estimate mortality, and his methods yielded substantially different estimates than the sampling by D. Kust and Rendón Salinas just described. He had collected 57 samples along three transects through Zapatero on 23 January and 59 samples along three transects through Conejos on 24 January. His collecting and sampling methods differed in three important ways: (1) they were collected 9 and 10 days after the 14 January freeze, whereas D. Kust and Rendón-Salinas collected samples 16 and 17 days after the freeze; (2) García-Serrano collected monarchs from 1.0-m^2 areas, while D. Kust and Rendón-Salinas's were from 0.04-m^2 areas; and (3) García-Serrano stored his samples in numbered plastic bags at the Sierra Chincua research station and did not himself tally or supervise the tallying of his samples. It was not possible to obtain counts of all of his 116 samples, but in early February, D. Kust and Rendón Salinas tallied 15 from each colony.

They estimated 749 and 245 dead monarchs/m^2 at the Conejos and Zapatero colonies, respectively. These two estimates were 9.7 and 10.7 times less than those from the samples collected later (7253/749 and 2628/245). The similar ratios suggest a biological basis for the discrepancy. Monarchs continued to fall from the trees and accumulate on the ground for several weeks after a similar previous freezing event (Calvert et al. 1983), and D. Kust observed the same phenomenon occurring in both colonies, with dead monarchs still falling out of the Zapatero trees on 30 January. Four of us (García-Serrano, Rendón Salinas, D. Kust, and L. Brower) discussed the apparent discrepancy and agreed that the differences between our estimates had likely resulted from continued accumulation of dead monarchs on the ground during the time between the two sampling periods.

Comparison of mortality in the Conejos and Zapatero colonies. Although the 2.76-fold difference in mean densities of dead and moribund monarchs between Conejos and Zapatero was not statistically significant (Mann-Whitney $Z = 0.91$, $p = 0.363$), several lines of evidence led us to conclude that Conejos was harder hit. First, the largest number of dead monarchs per sample in Zapatero was 337. In contrast, six samples in Conejos had more than 450 dead monarchs, including one with 2347, more than six times the maximum in Zapatero (see table 20.3). Second, the mean depth of accumulations in Conejos was 1.72 times that of Zapatero, and the maximum depth recorded in Conejos was 33 cm compared to 9 cm in Zapatero (see table 20.3). However, the high variance again precluded showing a significant difference in the depth of the samples ($t = 1.64$, $df = 56$, $p = 0.11$). Third, in all samples from Zapatero combined (from the 21 and 30 to 31 January collection dates), 643 of 7424 butterflies were alive. In contrast, in the Conejos samples, only 1 of the 9454 monarchs was alive. The numbers of moribund butterflies showed the same pattern. Fourth, the leaves on the *Senecio* understory in Zapatero showed only minor damage, whereas in Conejos the apical stems and leaves were bent over, shriveled, and blackened and had entombed many monarchs. Finally, the separate set of samples gathered in the two colonies by García-Serrano indicated a similar magnitude of difference (3.06 times as many dead and moribund monarchs in Conejos as in Zapatero).

Qualitative observations: 7 weeks after the storm

Rosario, Conejos, and Zapatero colonies. We revisited the Rosario and Conejos colonies on 5 March and the Zapatero colony on 4 and 6 March and confirmed that the surviving butterflies had deserted their original sites and re-formed colonies in locations within approximately 0.2 to 1.0 km of the positions they occupied during the January storm. As we describe later, the Pelón colony responded similarly. It therefore appears that after suffering a major mortality event, monarchs move and reestablish their overwintering colony some distance from the accumulated dead butterflies.

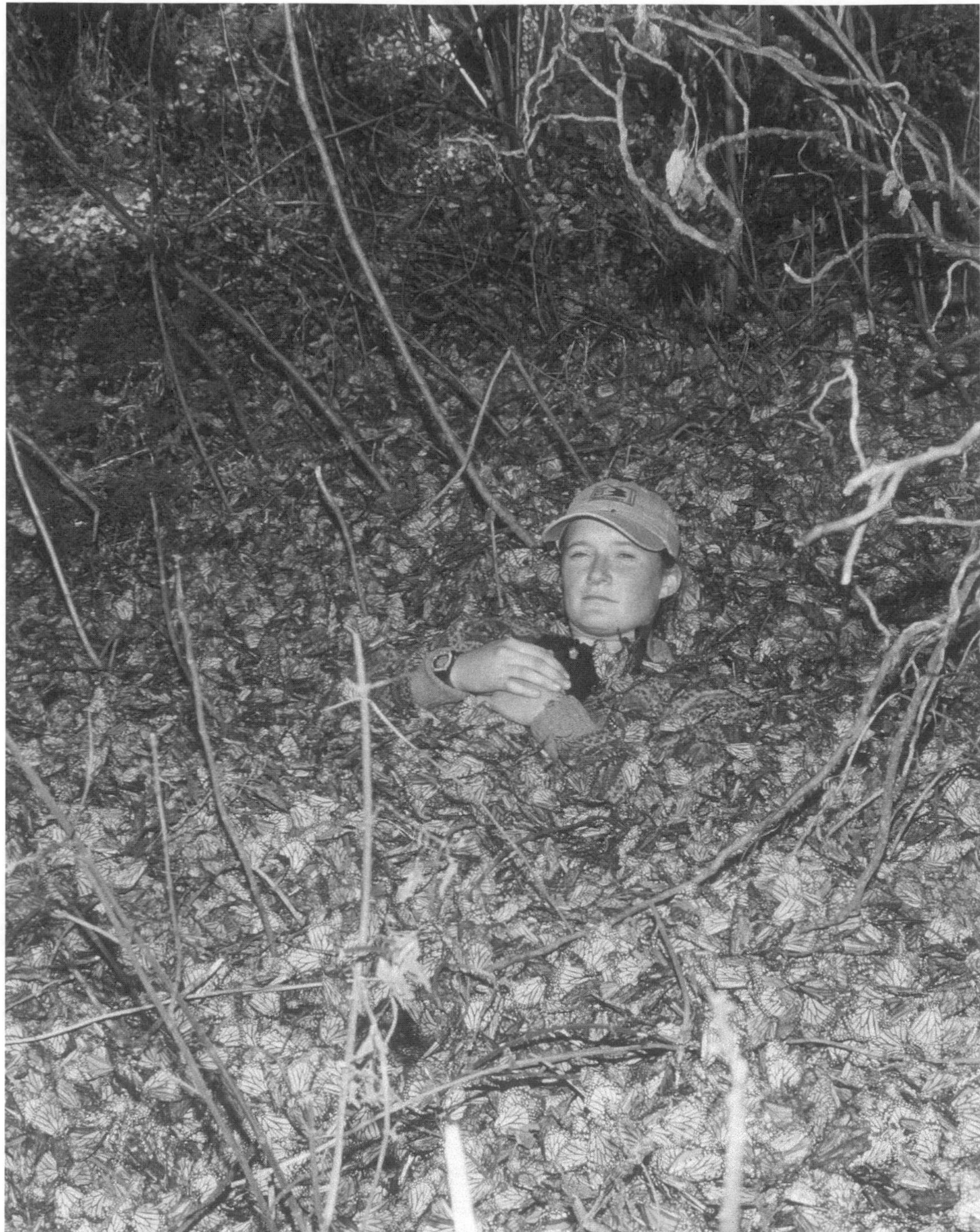

Figure 20.2. Chris Kisiel is shown covered in dead monarchs in the Conejos overwintering colony on Sierra Campanario. This exemplifies the severe mortality caused by the January 2002 storm. We estimated that 195 million monarchs were killed in this colony (see table 20.4). Photo by L. P. Brower, 5 March 2002.

The general appearances of the surviving remnant colonies were very different from what they had been before the storm. In addition to occupying smaller areas and fewer trees, bough clusters on individual trees were fewer, smaller, and more dispersed. In all sites except Zapatero, the new locations of the colonies were in more thinned areas of the forest and therefore more exposed to the sky.

Colonies typically move down their arroyo as the season progresses (Calvert and Brower 1986). In contrast, the monarchs in Conejos moved upward into a section of the oyamel forest that had been heavily thinned in the late 1980s (L. Brower, pers. observ.). In Rosario, they moved laterally and slightly up into the oyamel forest that has been progressively thinned. Finally, as we describe later, in the heavily damaged forest on Pelón, the El Capulin colony that had formed at a perilously low altitude moved even farther down the arroyo into a largely deciduous forest.

These observations suggest that normal colony movements to lower altitudes in the watershed were disrupted. Ending up in more, rather than less, exposed areas of the forests further jeopardizes the monarchs because of the potential for sequential winter storms.

Our return in March to the pre-storm colony areas confirmed our observations on the vastness of the mortality. Many monarchs that had accumulated on the oyamel boughs still had not fallen to the ground. The heavy and compressed butterfly packs were now molding and decomposing. The large stores of lipids in the butterfly abdomens were leaking out and penetrating the wings, turning them shiny and black. The air was scented with a disturbing mixture of ammonia and sweetness.

Cerro Pelón. Manos-Jones and Taylor (2002) reported that an overwintering colony on Cerro Pelón had not been impacted by the January storm. This position was also strongly espoused by a prominent ecotourism leader, Astrid Fritsch Jordan, who also maintained that the storm had missed the Herrada colony (pers. comm.). The Pelón and Herrada massifs are about 20 to 60 km southeast of the Chincua and Campanario massifs (see figure 15.1). Brower was skeptical because of a report that the storm had damaged the original Herrada colony, and that the surviving butterflies had moved and reformed a colony at lower altitude (J. Honey-Rosés, pers. comm.).

To resolve the issue, we visited the El Capulin colony at the Cerro Pelón overwintering area on 3 March via the small village of Macheros, located at 2490 m on the southwest side of Cerro Pelón. The weather was brilliantly clear and the ambient temperature well above the monarch flight threshold. At 2740 m we encountered several thousand monarchs roosting in moderate-sized pine trees and flying against the azure sky. On reaching the 0.98-ha monarch colony that García-Serrano had measured in December (see table 20.1), we observed that the devastation caused by the storm seemed at least as severe as in Conejos. We saw no live monarchs within the bounds of the now deserted colony area, dead butterflies littered the ground, thousands were buried in layers of dry pine needles, huge piles had accumulated beneath oyamel and pine boughs, and many of these boughs cradled monarchs that had frozen in situ.

The center of the deserted Capulin colony was at 2896 m, nearly 300 m lower in altitude than the current and past Rosario, Conejos, and Campanario colonies (see table 20.1). We attribute this anomalous altitude (see also Calvert and Brower 1996) to the severe habitat deterioration. We did not quantify the mortality, but it was clear that reports of no storm impact on the Cerro Pelón monarchs were incorrect. Leaving the colony, we walked 0.5 km northwest into the arroyo that drains the entire watershed (Las Canoas). Here we encountered several people viewing another colony of live monarchs called the Campamento colony (see table 20.1). We learned that Campamento can be accessed via two routes: the one we had taken on the southwest side of Cerro Pelón, or an alternative route on the northwest side of Cerro Pelón.

We concluded that the Campamento colony was actually a small surviving remnant of the Capulin colony that had moved several hundred meters down the arroyo after the January storm. As in the case of the Conejos and Zapatero colonies, the monarchs that survived the January storm deserted the Capulin colony area and formed another colony in the same arroyo at 2752 m, dropping about 0.5 km and 145 m in altitude below the original colony. Because of the near absence of oyamels and pines in the new site, the monarchs had reestablished most of their clusters on the moderate-sized oak trees growing along the sides of the arroyo. These clusters were less structured and much less dense than usual, probably owing to both the deciduous tree architecture and the diminished numbers of monarchs now more scattered within the colony area.

We are confident that Campamento was not a distinct colony that had formed the previous fall because García-Serrano had passed through the Campamento site in December and had observed no monarchs. Local residents confirmed that this was a newly formed site, and we observed very few dead butterflies on the ground beneath the new colony, further evidence that it had formed after the storm.

We were impressed by the severe dryness of the Pelón area compared to the colony locations on the Sierra Campanario and Sierra Chincua. Although one small dammed water pool was present slightly above the Campamento colony, we found no springs, seeps, or running water as we descended the arroyo until we encountered plastic pipes capturing spring water at 2646 m, about the same altitude as Angangueo (see table 20.1). The extensive deforestation appears to have disrupted the hydrology of the entire Canoas watershed on this part of Cerro Pelón. Thus monarchs, heavily impacted by the January storm in the exposed remnant oyamel pine forest, had moved down into an area where they normally would have had access to water, but which was now severely desiccated.

DISCUSSION

Widespread effects of January 2002 storm

Satellite weather images indicate that contrary to early rumors, the January storm occurred throughout central Mexico and broadly impacted the entire overwintering region of the monarchs (see figure 20.1). Heavy rain and snow caused extreme wetting of the clustering butterflies, which reduced their natural cryoprotection. When the weather cleared early in the morning on the 14th, the temperature dropped to about −4°C, killing a historically unprecedented number of butterflies. The geographic extent and pattern of the storm strongly suggest that all known overwintering colonies in Mexico were severely affected.

Quantitative estimates of the mortality

Systematic sampling of monarch mortality led to an estimate of 4940 dead monarchs/m^2, averaged across the two colonies sampled (see tables 20.3 and 20.4). Our March visit suggested that mortality in the El Capulin colony was at least as severe as it had been in these two colonies. It therefore seems reasonable to use this average mortality estimate, rounded to 5000 killed/m^2, as a conservative estimate for the entire overwintering region.

In December 2001, García-Serrano (2002) estimated that most of the known overwintering colonies comprised a total area of 9.35 ha. Multiplying this by the average mortality per square meter gives an estimated 467.5 million monarchs killed by the storm. Since García-Serrano did not visit all the known overwintering areas (Bojórquez-Tapia et al. 2002), we revise this estimate upward to 500 million monarchs killed across the overwintering region. Averaging the percentage of colony loss across the two colonies sampled (see table 20.4), we estimate an average 75% colony mortality.

The average percentage of monarchs killed in the two colonies was remarkably consistent with the predictions based on the cryobiological experiments of Anderson and Brower (1996). According to their data, 5% of monarchs with water on their bodies freeze to death as the temperature falls to −3.0°C, 50% die at −4.0°C, and 80% die at −5°C. We show that the monarchs were wetted by the storm prior to freezing and that the post-storm (14 January) temperatures in the Zapatero colony dropped to between −4° and −5°. Thus the 50% to 80% mortality predicted by the experimental data was realized by the 75% mortality that we estimated to have occurred in the two colonies.

Variation in estimates of dead monarchs per square meter

Both natural and anthropogenic factors contribute to the extreme variability in the numbers of monarchs killed per square meter. The main factor was likely heterogeneity of the oyamel tree cover that ranges from large forest gaps to complete canopy closure. Most of our low sample counts were collected from the floor beneath large forest gaps where no butterflies could have been roosting during the storm. The densest samples were from beneath and adjacent to the large healthy oyamels, on which the majority of butterflies roosted. Natural variation occurs in the numbers, size, and quality of available lower branches on the oyamels. There is also variation in the densities of the monarch clusters on the tree branches and trunks. Other factors might include the position of the colony with respect to the direction from which the storm approached, slope inclination, the degree to which the colony had nestled into an arroyo, the presence of diseased and lightning-struck trees, and the age distribution of the forest.

Historical underestimate of the density of monarchs in the overwintering colonies

On first visiting the Zapatero colony in January 1977, Brower conservatively estimated 1000 live monarchs/m^2 or 10 million/ha (Brower 1977; Brower et al. 1977). This value has been used to estimate the size of the fall migratory populations (e.g., García-Serrano et al., this volume). However, the data presented in this chapter indicate that the actual number far exceeds the early estimate (see also Calvert, this volume). We now suggest revision of the numbers of living monarchs in a typical colony based on our estimate of the mean number dead per square meter (5000) and our estimate of average colony mortality (75%). Thus we now suggest that there were 6667 monarchs/m^2 in the pre-storm colony. Rounding to 6500, we estimate 65 million monarchs/ha at Mexican overwintering sites. This revision will require a reevaluation of the published estimates of the sizes of migratory fall populations of eastern North American monarchs (e.g., Taylor 1999; Taylor et al. 2000).

The mortality estimation controversy

Lack of understanding of the continued accumulation of dead butterflies over several weeks after the storm and the incomplete data analyses of García-Serrano's collections led to the release of conflicting statements to the Mexican press shortly after the storm. Based on information provided by Roberto Solis, then director of the Monarch Butterfly Biosphere Reserve, Elorriaga (2002a) reported on 25 January that 2 to 5 million, or only 2% to 5% of the monarchs, had been killed in the Rosario and San Andrés colonies. On 8 February, World Wildlife Fund Mexico (in Bezaury and Rojas 2002), having first provided the information to the highest-level officials in SEMARNAP and COANANP (Comisión Nacional de Areas Naturales Protegidas [National Commission of Natural Protected Areas]), made a formal press release based on our 58 samples summarizing the much higher mortality. Brower released these data to the *New York Times* for a 12 February report (Yoon 2002). Aware of our findings, Solis revised his estimate upward on 12 February to 35 million, stating that all five of the sanctuaries in Michoacán had been hit, and that about 30% of the known overwintering monarchs had been killed (Elorriaga 2002b). Solis apparently based his revision on the incompletely analyzed data from García-Serrano. Not realizing the difference in the dates on which the samples were collected and the continuing accumulation of dead butterflies on the forest floor, he ascribed our higher estimates to "an error, or bad faith" (Stevenson 2002).

Given the history of confrontation and confusion in the Mexican and international press over the pesticide issue in 2001, we were extremely cautious about the possibility of exaggeration based on our initial mortality estimates. It was exactly for this reason that we performed the systematic transect counts (see table 20.3). We have extensively reviewed our methods and analyses and are confident that these data, although highly variable, do not overestimate the mortality.

Post-storm colony movement and effects of human disturbance

Earlier studies in the Sierra Chincua determined that overwintering colonies of monarchs drop in altitude as the headwater streams shrink with the advancing dry season. This colony movement is slow at first but accelerates prior to the butterflies' spring remigration northward (Calvert and Brower 1986) and is almost certainly a desiccation avoidance behavior (Calvert and Lawton 1993).

The present study established a second category of colony response: the storm survivors in the Zapatero, Rosario, Conejos, and Capulin colonies all deserted the area of severe mortality and formed new colonies. Because northern cold fronts regularly cause winter storms in central Mexico and have probably done so back to the Pleistocene, it is likely that monarchs at these high-altitude sites have been under strong selective pressure favoring various adaptive responses. Thus we propose that the post-storm movement is an evolved behavioral response different from the seasonal desiccation movement. One possible adaptive benefit would be to avoid pathogens from the mass decomposition of the millions of carcasses on the forest floor. Another would be to move to an area of the forest that provides increased canopy shelter. Herein lies a serious conflict because of human encroachment on the forests: if adjacent areas have been thinned, then moving can result in the colony re-forming in a site providing even less protection if another storm impacts the area.

Extensive human disturbance of the forests in and adjacent to the butterfly colonies has been documented elsewhere (Brower et al. 2002) and undoubtedly affects monarch survival in all the known overwintering massifs. For example, during the dry El Niño spring of 1998, agricultural carelessness caused a forest fire that spread up the Sierra Chincua ridge into the southwestern rim of Arroyo Zapatero (Brower and Missrie 1998). This, plus a wide boundary cut and prior forest thinning on the colony's border area, increased the exposure of the Zapatero colony to the January 2002 storm. The aforementioned degradation of the forest and hydrology on Cerro Pelón and our observation that the surviving remnant of the Rosario colony moved about 200 m laterally into a sparsely forested area further illustrate effects of human-induced disturbance. The important forest on the edge of this principal ecotourism colony has been subjected to incremental illegal tree removal over the past several years (L. Brower, pers. observ.). Finally, the survivors in the Conejos colony moved upslope into an area that had been heavily thinned by selective cutting in March 1989 (L. Brower, pers. observ.).

More generally, the effects of this severe weather event in January 2002 support predictions of the relationship between weather events, forest conditions, and overwintering monarch mortality. The larger picture is that a vegetation analysis documented that the forest in the area surrounding both colonies was seriously degraded between 1986 and 1999 (Brower et al. 2002). These facts are a resounding wake-up call for more effective protection of the Monarch Butterfly Biosphere Reserve.

Call for a stronger Mexico research program

Our study demonstrates the need to establish a more effective ongoing research program that monitors the overwintering colonies and collects basic data needed to responsibly manage the Monarch Butterfly Biosphere Reserve. As a start, electronic weather-monitoring stations should be installed in the overwintering colonies, and the methodology for monitoring and estimating mortality within the colonies needs to be standardized. Employment of trained local research biologists, in strong collaboration with the international scientific community, would also help, as would renovation of the Sierra Chincua research station.

Acknowledgments

We thank Jordi Honey-Rosés of World Wildlife Fund Mexico for assistance and insights in the fieldwork, Jose Luis Alvarez and Ed Rashin of the Michoacán Reforestation Fund in Santa Clara del Cobre for logistical and diplomatic assistance, the Erasto Romero family of Angangueo for gracious hospitality, and Valentine Rendón of Mexico City for help in tallying the quantitative samples. We are also grateful to Serena Basten and Christine Kisiel for help in the field. We are especially grateful to Elizabeth Howard, director of Journey North, whose foresight and communication skills resulted both in the fortuitous assembling of our research team in Mexico and in obtaining the satellite weather data, so ably synthesized by Dr. David Dempsey of San Francisco State University. Dr. Giselle Mora kindly helped with translations. We thank Linda Fink of Sweet Briar College, Karen Oberhauser, and Michelle Solensky for critical reviews of the manuscript. The research was supported by Scion Natural Science Association, the Monarch Butterfly Sanctuary Foundation, K. Reinhold, P. Reinhold, World Wildlife Fund-Mexico, and an anonymous donor.

References

Alonso-Mejía, A., A. Arellano-Guillermo, and L. P. Brower. 1992. Influence of temperature, surface body moisture and height aboveground on survival of monarch butterflies overwintering in Mexico. Biotropica 24:415–19.

Anderson, J. A., and L. P. Brower. 1993. Cold-hardiness in the annual cycle of the monarch butterfly. In S. B. Malcolm and M. P. Zalucki, eds., Biology and conservation of the monarch butterfly, pp. 157–64. Los Angeles: Natural History Museum of Los Angeles County.

Anderson, J. B., and L. P. Brower. 1996. Freeze-protection of overwintering monarch butterflies in Mexico: critical role of the forest as a blanket and an umbrella. Ecol. Entomol. 21:107–16.

Anonymous. 1974. Carta Topographica, Villa de Allende. E14A36. Michoacán y Mexico. Escala 1:50,000. Mexico City, Mexico 8, DF: Cetenal, San Antonio de Abad No.124.

Anonymous. 1987. Carta Topographica, Angangueo. E14A26. Mexico y Michoacán. Escala 1:50,000. Mexico City, Mexico 8, DF: Cetenal, San Antonio de Abad No.124.

Anonymous. 2002. Rain: a water resource. United States Geological Survey website. http://wa/water/usgs.gov/rain.html. Accessed 22 August 2002.

Aridjis, H. 2001. Monarchs in the time of democracy. Reforma, 13 May 2001.

Bezaury, J., and S. Rojas. 2002. Severe monarch butterfly mortality due to cold storm. World Wildlife Fund Mexico home page, Mexico City. http://www.wwf.org.mx/news_monarch_mortality.php. Accessed 8 February 2002.

Bojórquez-Tapia, L. A., L. P. Brower, G. Castilleja, S. Sánchez-Colón, M. Hernández, W. Calvert, S. Díaz, P. Gómez-Priego, G. Alcantar, E. D. Melgarejo, M. J. Solares, L. Guttiérrez, and M. L. Juárez. 2003. Mapping expert knowledge: redesigning the Monarch Butterfly Reserve. Conserv. Biol. 17:367–79.

Brower, L. P. 1977. Monarch migration. Nat. Hist. 86:40–53.

Brower, L. P. 1996a. Monarch mortality estimate from winter storm in Mexico. Monarch Newsletter 6:1.

Brower, L. P. 1996b. Forest thinning increases monarch butterfly mortality by altering the microclimate of the overwintering sites in Mexico. In S. A. Ae, T. Hirowatari, M. Ishii, and L. P. Brower, eds., Decline and conservation of butterflies in Japan III, pp. 33–44. Proceedings of the international symposium on butterfly conservation, Osaka, Japan, 1994. Osaka: Lepidopterological Society of Osaka.

Brower, L. P. 1999a. Oyamel forest ecosystem conservation in Mexico is necessary to prevent the extinction of the migratory phenomenon of the monarch butterfly in North America. In P. Canevari, ed., Proceedings of the CMS Symposium on Animal Migration (Gland, Switzerland, 13 April 1997), pp. 41–50. Bonn: United Nations Environment Programme/Convention on the Conservation of Migratory Species of Wild Animals (UNEP/CMS).

Brower, L. P. 1999b. Biological necessities for monarch butterfly overwintering in relation to the oyamel forest ecosystem in Mexico. In J. Hoth, L. Merino, K. Oberhauser, I. Pisantry, S. Price, and T. Wilkinson, eds., The 1997 North American Conference on the Monarch Butterfly, pp. 11–28. Montreal: Commission for Environmental Cooperation.

Brower, L. P. 2001. Report to World Wildlife Fund Mexico regarding recent news reports that monarch butterflies had been purposely killed by loggers spraying pesticides in their overwintering sites, pp. 1–3. 24 April. World Wildlife Fund, Mexico City, http://www.wwf.org.mx.

Brower, L. P., W. H. Calvert, L. E. Hedrick, and J. Christian. 1977. Biological observations on an overwintering colony of monarch butterflies (*Danaus plexippus* L., Danaidae) in Mexico. J. Lepid. Soc. 31:232–42.

Brower, L. P., G. Castilleja, A. Peralta, J. Lopez-Garcia, L. Bojorquez-Tapia, S. Diaz, D. Melgarejo, and M. Missrie. 2002. Quantitative changes in forest quality in a principal overwintering area of the monarch butterfly in Mexico: 1971 to 1999. Conserv. Biol. 16:346–59.

Brower, L. P., and S. B. Malcolm. 1991. Animal migrations: endangered phenomena. Am. Zool. 31:265–76.

Brower, L. P., and M. Missrie. 1998. Fires in the monarch butterfly sanctuaries in Mexico, spring 1998. Que Pasa 3:9–11.

Calvert, W. H., and L. P. Brower. 1981. The importance of forest cover for the survival of overwintering monarch butterflies (*Danaus plexippus*, Danaidae). J. Lepid. Soc. 35:216–25.

Calvert, W. H., and L. P. Brower. 1986. The location of monarch butterfly (*Danaus plexippus* L.) overwintering colonies in Mexico in relation to topography and climate. J. Lepid. Soc. 40:164–87.

Calvert, W. H., and J. A. Cohen. 1983. The adaptive significance of crawling up onto foliage for the survival of grounded overwintering monarch butterflies (*Danaus plexippus*) in Mexico. Ecol. Entomol. 8:471–74.

Calvert, W. H., M. B. Hyatt, and N. P. Mendoza-Villasenor. 1986. The effects of understory vegetation on the survival of overwintering monarch butterflies (*Danaus plexippus* L.) in Mexico. Acta Zool. Mex. 18:1–17.

Calvert, W. H., and R. O. Lawton. 1993. Comparative phenology of variation in size, weight, and water content of eastern North American monarch butterflies at five overwintering sites in Mexico. In S. B. Malcolm and M. P. Zalucki, eds., Biology and conservation of the monarch butterfly, pp. 299–307. Los Angeles: Natural History Museum of Los Angeles County.

Calvert, W. H., W. Zuchowski, and L. P. Brower. 1982. The impact of forest thinning on microclimate in monarch butterfly (*Danaus plexippus* L.) overwintering areas of Mexico. Bol. Soc. Bot. Mex. 42:11–18.

Calvert, W. H., W. Zuchowski, and L. P. Brower. 1983. The effect of rain, snow, and freezing temperatures on overwintering monarch butterflies in Mexico. Biotropica 15:42–47.

Calvert, W. H., W. Zuchowski, and L. P. Brower. 1984. Monarch butterfly conservation: interactions of cold weather, forest thinning and storms on the survival of overwintering monarch butterflies (*Danaus plexippus* L.) in Mexico. Atala 9:2–6.

Culotta, E. 1992. The case of the missing monarchs. Science 256:1275.

Elorriaga, E. M. 2002a. Mueran mas de 2 milliones de mariposa monarca. La Cronica (Mexico City). 26 January 2002.

Elorriaga, E. M. 2002b. La muerte de mariposas en Michoacan, parte del equilibrio natural: funcionario. Han fallecido 35 milliones, acepta; antes dijo que cinco. La Jornada (Mexico City). 13 February 2002.

Fink, L. S., and L. P. Brower. 1981. Birds can overcome the cardenolide defense of monarch butterflies in Mexico. Nature 291:67–70.

Fullerton, E. 2001 March 6. Mexico loggers said to decimate butterflies. Reuters News Service Limited.

García-Serrano, E. 2002 January. Informe preliminar del monitoreo de rutas migratorias y sitios de hibernacon temporada 2001–2002. Preliminary report to Secretaria del Medio Ambiente Recursos Naturales y Pesca, Instituto Nacional de Ecologia, Reserva de la Biosphera Mariposa Monarca, pp. 1–2.

Geiger, R. 1950. The climate near the ground. Cambridge: Harvard University Press.

GOES-EAST. 2002. GOES-EAST satellite IR and visible weather images. http://virga.sfsu.edu/crws/specials/gif/mex_cold_frt. Accessed 12–14 January 2002.

Huriash, L. J. 1996 December 9. Flight of monarchs may end in Mexico. Sun-Sentinel, Broward Metro Edition (Fort Lauderdale, Fl.).

Journey North. 2002. Monarch butterfly migration update, 7 February 2002. http://www.learner.org/jnorth/. Accessed 30 August 2002.

Larsen, K. L., and R. E. Lee Jr. 1994. Cold tolerance including rapid cold-hardening and inoculative freezing of fall migrant monarch butterflies in Ohio. J. Insect Physiol. 40:859–64.

Manos-Jones, M., and C. Taylor. 2002. Fatal storm in Mexico. Monarch Quarterly 12:10–13, 18.

Marriott, D. F. 2001. Butterfly deaths alarm monarch ecologists. Monarch Quarterly 11:16–18.

Masters, A. R., S. B. Malcolm, and L. P. Brower. 1988. Monarch butterfly (*Danaus plexippus*) thermoregulatory behavior and adaptations for overwintering in Mexico. Ecology 69:458–67.

Preston, J. 1996 January 3. Snow in Mexico winter home lethal to monarch butterflies. New York Times.

PROFEPA. 2001. Mortalidad de mariposa monarca registrada en el "Cerro de San Andres" Municipio de Maravatio, Michoacan. Procuraduria Federal de Proteccion al Ambiente, Subprocuraduria de Recursos Naturales, Mexico City.

Stevenson, M. 2002. Monarch butterflies dying in Mexico. Page News Release. The Associated Press, Mexico City. http://forests.org/articles/reader.asp?linkid = 7664. Accessed 13 February 2002.

Taylor, O. R. 1999. Monarch population size. Monarch Watch 7:18–20.

Taylor, O. R., D. Wilfong, and C. Walters. 2000. Monarch population size. Monarch Watch 8:11–13.

Urquhart, F. A. 1976. Found at last: the monarch's winter home. Natl. Geogr. Mag. 150:160–73.

Wells, S. M., R. M. Pyle, and N. M. Collins. 1983. The IUCN invertebrate red data book. Gland, Switzerland: International Union for Conservation of Nature and Natural Resources.

Yoon, C. K. 2002 February 12. Storm in Mexico devastates monarch butterfly colonies. New York Times.

21

Spatial and Temporal Pattern of Monarch Overwintering Abundance in Western North America

Dennis Frey and Andrew Schaffner

INTRODUCTION

Monarchs winter across an extensive landscape in western North America. These habitats occur in a variety of topographic and biotic settings that are generally more diverse than the ones used by eastern monarchs wintering in Mexico (Calvert and Brower 1986; Sakai and Calvert 1991; Lane 1993). Variation in macroclimates, in combination with local topography and plant community structure, results in similar microclimates in the two overwintering domains (Calvert and Brower 1981; Calvert et al. 1982; Leong et al. 1991; Leong and Frey 1992).

The overwintering phenomena and population abundance of monarchs have both temporal and spatial dimensions. Compelling arguments exist for the necessity of studying natural processes, such as these, at several scales simultaneously (Allen and Hoekstra 1992). Zalucki and Rochester (1999) used a climate modeling approach to predict the pattern of relative monarch abundance at a continent-wide spatial scale. Likewise, Brower and colleagues (2002) employed a large-scale landscape ecology approach to reveal a dramatic decline in closed-canopy habitat over a 30-year period at the monarch's wintering grounds in Mexico. Studies of wintering habitat and population dynamics have focused almost exclusively on small-scale issues rather than more inclusive approaches. Microclimate analyses and descriptions of abiotic conditions at the monarch's wintering sites are typical of this small-scale approach (e.g., Leong 1990; Leong et al. 1991; Calvert and Lawton 1993; Calvert and Brower 1981). Studies of wintering dynamics in western North America are likewise limited in scope (Harvey et al. 1982; Frey 1995), and little large-scale synthesis of population dynamics has been carried out.

We examined databases and historical archives on several scales for both temporal and spatial patterns of the abundance of monarchs overwintering in western North America. Our approach is primarily descriptive, but information derived from these databases allowed us to test a number of hypotheses associated with the spatial aspects of the monarch's wintering habitats and both spatial and temporal patterns of winter-generation abundance. The specific objectives of our study were to (1) describe the short-term system-wide abundance pattern of monarchs (1997 to 2000), (2) describe longer-term system-wide abundance (1976 to 1997) using a different database, (3) describe the spatial abundance pattern at a county-wide scale within a single season, (4) describe variation of site attributes among western overwintering habitats, and (5) explore relationships between abundance patterns and variation in site attributes.

METHODS

Short-term system-wide abundance

We used data primarily from reports of the Monarch Program Thanksgiving Count (Marriott 2001) from 1997 to 2000 to describe short-term temporal and spatial patterns of monarch abundance. This Monarch Program has organized and coordinated annual monarch counts at western

North American habitats since 1997. These counts are modeled after the July 4th Lepidoptera surveys by the North America Butterfly Association, but are conducted during a 2-week period around Thanksgiving.

Long-term system-wide abundance

We drew information for the longer-term analyses from the California Department of Fish and Game Natural Diversity Data Base (NDDB), a computerized geographic information system that classifies and inventories location and habitat data on sensitive taxa and natural communities throughout California. The wintering habitat of monarchs is considered a sensitive natural community in California because of its limited distribution and the unique pattern of migration and overwintering behavior (Wells et al. 1983). The earliest entry in the NDDB regarding the habitats and population estimates of monarchs is from 1976 (D. McGriff, pers. comm.).

The NDDB contains information for 332 monarch winter habitats located in 17 California counties: Alameda, Contra Costa, Inyo, Kern, Los Angeles, Mendocino, Monterey, Marin, Orange, Santa Barbara, Santa Cruz, San Diego, San Francisco, San Luis Obispo, San Mateo, Solano, and Ventura (figure 21.1). The database provides habitat descriptions for most sites and estimates of population abundance. We analyzed site elevation, latitude, longitude, abundance, habitat ownership (i.e., private or public), and species of trees used for roosting. For sites located within 5 km of the Pacific Ocean, we measured the orientation of the nearest shoreline along the ocean or its inlets. We located these coastal habitats using ArcView 3.2 software with coordinates from the NDDB and measured the orientation of a line tangent to the "smoothed" shoreline at a point nearest to a specific habitat. Orientation was recorded as clockwise deviations from due north (0°).

We wanted to know the position of each habitat in relation to the coast so that it was independent of latitude and longitude, that is, whether it was located "up" the coast or "down" the coast and whether it occurred "near shore" or "away from the coast." This was important because western North American coastal habitats that are farther north are also farther west (figure 21.1). We derived an independent measure of location by subjecting the latitude and longitude coordinates of each site to principal components analysis (S-Plus 2000, Insightful Corporation). Individual component scores of the first and second principal components described these two aspects of geographic location.

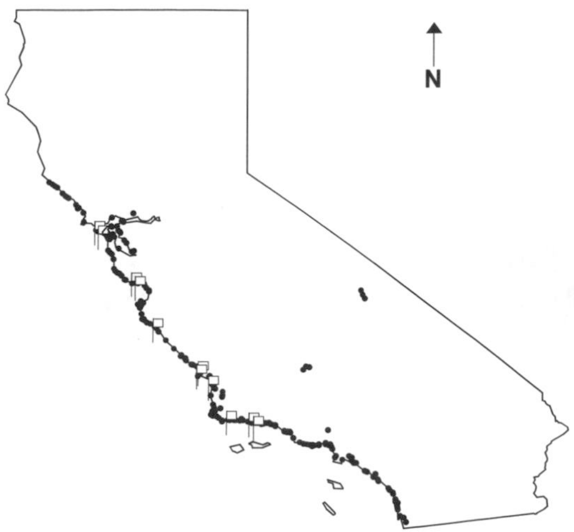

Figure 21.1. Location of winter habitats in western North America. The position of the California habitats were plotted from Natural Diversity Data Base (NDDB) coordinates. Flags indicate the location of 11 monarch winter habitats in western North America with long-term maximum abundance greater than 50,000.

Of primary interest to us was information on long-term historical abundance at wintering habitats. Some abundance entries in the NDDB include only general qualitative information (e.g., Site 22788: "Monarchs have used this site for at least 4 years. During winter 1985–86, thousands arrived in mid-September and left by mid-November. In October 1990, none were observed."). Others include specific counts or visual estimates made on several dates within a season (e.g., Site 2795: "Fifty observed in 1988–89. Low 100's observed in 1989–90. Five flyers observed in 1990–91. Hundreds observed in December 1991 [ten by January 1992]. A single flyer observed in 1993–94. None observed in 1994–95. Two-three hundred observed in November 1995; 20 by January 1996."). When we conducted statistical tests of hypotheses regarding abundance, we used only habitats with quantitative data (counts or estimates) for a population on a specific date. For standardization, we used the maximum count listed for each habitat that had multiple-year information or more than one abundance record within a single season. We recorded the year associated with these "maximum" estimates.

County-wide seasonal abundance pattern, rate of habitat loss, and underestimation of population abundance

The rate at which monarch winter habitat is lost or extirpated was derived from a study of the winter habitats of Santa Barbara County, California (Meade 1999). This study identified 93 winter habitats in the 1998–1999 wintering season and tracked monthly abundance at each one. We plotted the geographic coordinates of these habitats and analyzed their small-scale county-wide population dynamics for the 1998–1999 overwintering season (i.e., their seasonal and spatial abundance pattern).

Weather data

We downloaded historical weather information from the website of the California Irrigation Management Information System (CIMIS) for 1997 to 2000. CIMIS weather stations are located throughout California and provide data on regional weather conditions. We used weather data from two randomly chosen stations within each county included in the Monarch Program Thanksgiving Counts. Several weather variables were used as predictors of late-spring and summer milkweed productivity within each county, including precipitation (January through August), evapotranspiration (Et_o) (May through August), and soil temperature (May through August). Variation in early-season precipitation has been associated with late-season primary production in plant species occupying areas with little or no summer rainfall (Boyer 1982). Much of western North America is subject to this seasonal precipitation pattern. Bell (1998) showed that increased soil water availability resulted in increased late-season longevity of *Asclepias eriocarpa* Benth., one of the host plants of monarchs in western North America. Similarly, evapotranspiration correlates with primary production in a variety of plant communities (Rosenzweig 1968).

RESULTS

Short-term patterns

Monarch Program Thanksgiving Counts are archived on a "county-wide" basis. Sixteen counties or regions were surveyed during the period from 1997 to 2000: Mendocino, Sonoma, Marin, San Francisco, Solano, Contra Costa, Alameda, Santa Cruz, Monterey, San Luis Obispo, Santa Barbara, Ventura, Los Angeles, Orange, and San Diego Counties, and the coastal region between the U.S. border and Ensenada, Baja California, Mexico (table 21.1). Solano County was not surveyed during 1997, 1998, and 2000, and Mendocino County was not surveyed during 2000. Sampling effort, as measured by the number of sites visited, varied from 101 habitats in 1997 to 141 habitats in 2000. San Diego and Santa Barbara were the most extensively sampled counties in 1997 and 1998, and 1999 and 2000, respectively. Santa Barbara County had the highest estimated population size during the 1997, 1999, and 2000 counts, while San Luis Obispo County had the largest reported abundance in 1998.

Abundance at habitats ranged from 0 to 120,000 monarchs, and the majority of western habitats had very small populations; 60% of sites during the last

Table 21.1. Monarch Program Thanksgiving Count: short-term abundance summary

	Year			
	1997	1998	1999	2000
No. of counties or regions surveyed	15	16	15	14
No. of sites surveyed	101	112	118	141
Total population estimate	1,266,490	564,352	267,574	391,057
Range of population estimate	0–120,000	0–115,100	0–60,000	0–58,000
Median of population estimate	2000	250	100	25
% sites with estimate <500	32	56	60	65
% sites with estimate 501–10,000	40	35	35	27
% sites with estimate >10,000	28	9	5	8

3 years of the survey had counts of less than 500. At the other extreme, less than 10% of the habitats between 1998 and 2000 had counts greater than 10,000 monarchs. Santa Cruz, Monterey, San Luis Obispo, and Santa Barbara Counties each had at least one site reporting more than 10,000 monarchs during each of the 4 years. These counties are located in the middle of the coastal overwintering range, suggesting that this region tends to have larger populations than those farther up or down the coast.

The year-to-year abundance patterns were tested by pair-wise sign tests using counts only from sites that were surveyed in both seasons of successive year-year paired comparisons. Short-term system-wide abundance significantly declined between 1997 and 1998 and 1998 and 1999, but significantly increased between 1999 and 2000 (Table 21.1; 1997 vs. 1998: $p = 0.0005$, $n = 86$; 1998 vs. 1999: $p = 0.0005$, $n = 88$; 1999 vs. 2000: $p = 0.0024$, $n = 99$ where n refers to the number of habitats compared).

We used Spearman's rank correlation analyses to describe the relative abundance pattern or ranking among the habitats between years (table 21.2). All year-year pair comparisons were highly correlated, suggesting that the relative short-term rankings of habitats were consistent throughout the four years. Habitats with a relatively low (or high) population count in one year tended to have low (or high) counts in other years. Furthermore, the relative abundance ranking of habitats in 1997 was highly predictive of the system-wide abundance pattern for as many as 3 years into the future.

Table 21.2. Monarch Program Thanksgiving Count: year-year abundance correlation (Spearman rank)

Year	1998	1999	2000
1997	$z = 5.82$ $p < 0.0005$ $n = 40$	$z = 6.40$ $p < 0.0005$ $n = 46$	$z = 5.62$ $p < 0.0005$ $n = 69$
1998	-	$z = 6.85$ $p < 0.0005$ $n = 57$	$z = 6.14$ $p < 0.0005$ $n = 80$
1999	-	-	$z = 8.56$ $p < 0.0005$ $n = 86$

Influence of regional weather on local short-term abundance

We used an analysis of covariance to model the log-abundance over a 4-year period (1997 to 2000) as a function of evapotranspiration, precipitation, and soil temperature. The model included terms to account for year-to-year and county-to-county variation and was weighted to reflect the number of sites sampled in each county. The model was carried out using S-Plus software. There was no significant relationship between the weather variables and log-abundance (table 21.3; F statistic $= 1.987$, $df = 3, 31$, $p = 0.136$).

Long-term and large-scale patterns

The majority of the 332 NDDB winter habitats occurred near the Pacific coastline. Only 7 habitats (2%) occur in inland counties (Inyo and Kern Counties). Abundance data for these 7 habitats are limited and qualitative in nature. Furthermore, they do not specify the month during which abundance was estimated. We used ArcView 3.2 software to delineate a 5-km region inland from the Pacific Ocean and computed the number of habitats within this area. Two hundred thirty-two (over 70%) of the 332 habitats occurred within this coastal zone. In

Table 21.3. Regional weather influence on local short-term overwintering abundance

Variable	*df*	SS	MS	*F* value	*p* value
Evapotranspiration	1	23.66	23.66	1.04	0.314
Precipitation	1	74.38	74.38	3.28	0.079
Soil temperature	1	0.13	0.13	0.01	0.939
Year	3	1544.30	514.76	22.70	<0.001
County	13	2137.11	164.39	7.25	<0.001
Residuals	31	702.94	22.67		

Note: Weighted analysis of covariance. Type III sum of squares presented.
SS, Sum of squares; MS, mean square.

addition, all 14 of the habitats with the greatest long-term historical abundance (i.e., those with over 50,000 monarchs) fell within this region (see figure 21.1).

Ownership was given for 287 of the 332 NDDB listed winter habitats. Of these, 199 (60%) occurred on private property and 133 (40%) on public land. Of the latter category, the greatest number of habitats occurred on California Department of State Parks property. Half of the 14 large-abundance habitats (i.e., those with over 50,000 monarchs) occurred on private lands.

Three types of trees were used most frequently by roosting monarchs: eucalyptus (75% of the habitats; primarily *Eucalyptus globulus* Labill.), pine (20% of the habitats; primarily *Pinus radiata* Don.), and cypress (16% of the habitats; *Cupressus macrocarpa* Hartw.). Twelve other tree species were identified in the NDDB with a combined prevalence of only 10%. These included alder, coast live oak, cottonwood, Douglas fir, redwood, sycamore, and willow.

Of the NDDB habitat listings, 205 met our "quantitative" criteria regarding long-term maximum abundance estimates. The year for which the greatest abundance had been reported at specific habitats was extracted from the database in an effort to reveal the temporal pattern of abundance in western North America. This was problematic because "sampling effort" was not consistent between years (W. Sakai and D. McGriff, pers. comm.). Over half of the 205 habitats had their maximum abundance reported for one of three wintering seasons (1990–1991, 1995–1996, and 1997–1998). Of the 14 largest listings (more than 50,000; see figure 21.1), 10 were reported in the 1997–1998 season, 3 for 1995–1996, and 1 for 1990–1991.

Maximum counts for the 205 sites ranged from 4 to 200,000 monarchs (median = 3000). We used multiple regression (S-Plus software) to investigate the relation between maximum wintering abundance (Y) over the 20-year history of the NDDB record and 15 attributes (x_i) associated with the wintering habitats across their relative large-spatial scale. The model took the form:

$$\text{Log}(Y) = B_0 + B_1x_1 + B_2x_2 + \ldots + B_px_p + e$$

We found a significant predictive relationship (table 21.4; F statistic = 1.879, df = 15, 174, p = 0.028, R^2 = 0.139).

Table 21.4. Habitat attributes in relation to long-term habitat abundance

Term	Description	Type of variable
Ownership1	Public ownership of habitat	Indicator (0 or 1)
Ownership2	Private ownership of habitat	Indicator (0 or 1)
Ownership3	Ownership unknown	Indicator (0 or 1)
Orientation1	Sine of nearest shore-line angle–East vs. West	Continuous
Orientation2	Cosine of nearest shore-line angle–North vs. South	Continuous
Elevation1	Habitat elevation–linear term	Continuous
Elevation2	Habitat elevation–quadratic term	Continuous
Location1	PC1 score[a]–up vs. down the coast–linear term	Continuous
Location2	PC1 score–up vs. down the coast–quadratic term	Continuous
Location3	PC2 score[b]–near shore vs. inland–linear term	Continuous
Location4	PC2 score–near shore vs. inland–quadratic term	Continuous
Species1	Pine used–roosting tree	Indicator (0 or 1)
Species2	Eucalyptus–roosting tree	Indicator (0 or 1)
Species3	Cypress–roosting tree	Indicator (0 or 1)
Species4	Other species–roosting tree	Indicator (0 or 1)

[a] PC1 refers to the first principal component of the coastal location variable.
[b] PC2 refers to the second principal component of the coastal location variable.
Note: Predictor variables included in multiple regression model. See text for more detail of variables.

We next used a stepwise procedure to identify potential key predictor variables. The program sequentially added or dropped terms based on their reduction of Mallow's C_p statistic (Weisberg 1985). The reduced model included six terms that had a low C_p and a good set of diagnostics, such as normality of residuals, homoscedastic error, and so on (table 21.5). The model had significant predictive power and identified two terms that were significantly associated with variation in the abundance pattern. The strongest predictor was the quadratic term for the "up/down coast location" variable (table 21.5). Its negative sign indicates that historical abundance has been greatest in the middle of the wintering range and lesser at the extremes. The remaining significant predictor variable from the reduced model was the roosting tree species category "others" (table 21.5). The negative sign for this indicator variable means that habitats had smaller populations when the roosting tree type was a species other than eucalyptus, pine, or cypress.

Table 21.5. Multiple regression analyses summary

Variable	Coefficient	*p* value
Up/down coast location (linear)	0.429	0.8993
Up/down coast location (quadratic)	−12.045	0.0002
Tree type–eucalyptus	0.170	0.7382
Tree type–pine	0.594	0.2396
Tree type–cypress	0.333	0.5607
Tree type–others	−1.236	0.0314

Note: F statistic = 3.246, df = 6, 194, p = 0.0046, R^2 = 0.0912.

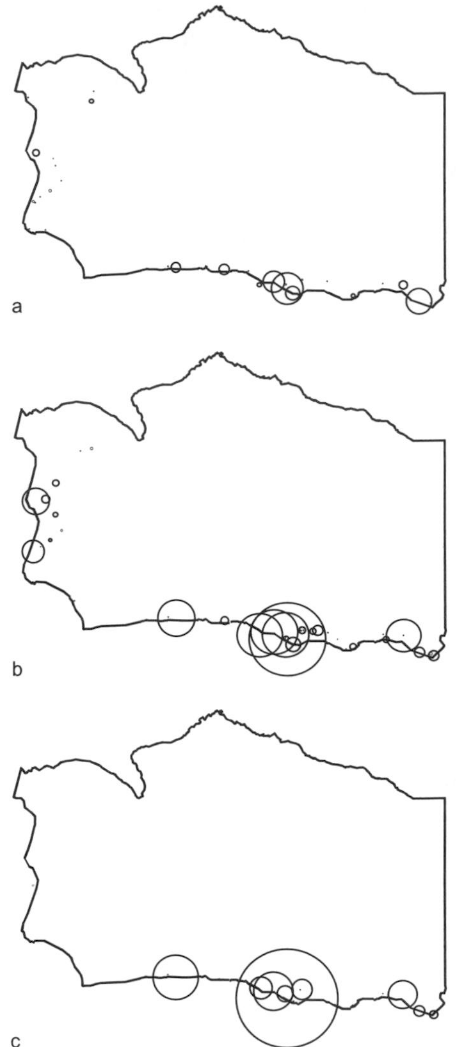

Figure 21.2. Seasonal pattern of abundance along the Santa Barbara County coastal zone during (a) October, (b) November, and (c) December 1998. Data derived from Meade 1999. Points or circles are scaled to indicate relative monthly abundance.

County-wide seasonal abundance pattern, rate of habitat loss, and underestimation of population abundance

Meade (1999) compared monarch wintering habitat abundance in Santa Barbara County, California, during the 1998–1999 season to that of an extensive study done 8 years earlier (Calvert 1991). Eleven of the 88 monarch habitats documented by Calvert (1991) had disappeared during the intervening period. This was a decline in the number of habitats by 12.5%, or approximately 1.5% annually. Habitat loss was attributed to agricultural, commercial, and municipal development.

Data for 16 previously unknown habitats were included in the report (Meade 1999). This increased the number of identified habitats by 20% over the earlier study. The abundance at these new sites ranged from a few individuals, to nearly 13,000 monarchs present at some time during the overwintering season. The Ellwood Main site had the greatest abundance overall, with approximately 40,000 monarchs in January and February. The median abundance estimate during November for these new sites was 41 individuals, and they collectively accounted for 14% and 13% of the Santa Barbara county-wide abundance during November and December, respectively. Only 4 (i.e., 25%) of these 16 habitats still had monarchs present by December, suggesting that the majority of them were autumnal-type habitats.

Small-scale temporal and spatial patterns associated with Meade's (1999) study of monarchs wintering in Santa Barbara County, California, are summarized in figure 21.2. The number of sites used by monarchs in October, November, and December were 74, 71, and 39, respectively. By December, the 4 sites with the greatest abundance accounted for over 63% of the Santa Barbara county-wide total monarch population.

DISCUSSION

Small-scale movements and accompanying changes in local abundance early in the wintering season are salient features of the population dynamics of monarchs in western North America. This is clearly demonstrated by our analysis of Meade's study of Santa Barbara County (Meade 1999). As fall migrants reach the coastal zone in October, more habitats become occupied (see figure 21.2a). In November the number of occupied habitats levels off, but by December more than half of these habitats are abandoned (see figure 21.2b, 2c), and populations at some of the remaining habitats increase (e.g., Meade 1999). A similar pattern occurred during the 2000–2001 overwintering season at 12 focal habitats in San Luis Obispo County (pers. observ.). These patterns are consistent with the autumnal habitat concept (Sakai and Calvert 1991; Lane 1993; Bell et al. 1993), whereby weather-induced dispersal is followed by nonrandom settlement at nearby habitats. Fall dispersal from these autumn habitats is frequently abrupt, with 90% to 100% of the population departing within a few days (pers. observ.). In contrast, while spring dispersal can occur over a short period of time, it is usually more gradual in nature (Tuskes and Brower 1978; Frey 1995; Meade 1999; Frey et al. 2002).

Localized movement to alternative habitats may minimize any cumulative negative consequences of physiological stressors such as desiccation or thermal excess. These stressors may have cascading effects of higher metabolic rate and increased use of energy reserves (Chaplin and Wells 1982; Alonso-Mejia et al. 1997; Brower 1999; Frey et al. 2002). During fall 2000, some San Luis Obispo County habitats were abandoned following several days of unseasonably hot dry conditions (pers. observ.). In other years, butterflies disappeared from habitats with relatively open canopy following autumn storms that included extremely high winds (pers. observ.).

Variation in system-wide long-term abundance in the West was not dependent on habitat ownership category; habitats on privately held land had abundances similar to those on public lands. Abundance patterns were also unrelated to the elevation of habitats. It has been suggested that most habitats and the largest populations of monarchs in western North America occur on coastlines that are oriented east-west rather than north-south because they are more protected (Lane 1993). However, our analysis indicated that variation in abundance was independent of shoreline orientation.

Our short-term (Monarch Program data) and long-term (NDDB data) analyses revealed similar geospatial patterns of monarch abundance. While habitats spanned a distance of approximately 1000 km along the Pacific Ocean, the majority of monarchs, and the largest populations, occupied habitats located over a more restricted range. While the Monarch Program Thanksgiving Count data could be biased by differences in the size of counties and sampling effort, our similar finding based on the NDDB information was independent of geopolitical spatial units. This prominent spatial pattern (see table 21.5, figure 21.1), in addition to year-to-year correlation of the relative abundance ranking of habitats, suggests that much of the variation in monarch abundance in the West may be associated with a variation in system-wide or large-scale factors such as weather patterns.

In contrast, a smaller-scale or "regional conditions" hypothesis is sometimes invoked to explain the nonrandom spatial pattern of abundance in the West. It implies that monarchs migrate in rather uniform densities across the western breeding range toward the coastal region. On reaching the Pacific Ocean many butterflies in the north supposedly move down the coast in search of optimal local habitat, while those arriving in the south search up the coast, leaving habitats at the extremes less heavily populated. Few data exist in support of this model. A study of monarch transfer patterns at twelve focal habitats in San Luis Obispo County during fall 2000 revealed that intersite transfer beyond the nearest neighboring habitats was extremely rare. For example, only 7 of 186 transfers of monarchs that occurred during October and November (i.e., less than 4%) involved movements greater than 7 km (J. Walth, pers. comm.).

A model to account for the annual variation in the spatial pattern of overwintering monarchs has been proposed (Harris 1986; Wenner and Harris 1993). This "local recruitment" hypothesis discounts the role of monarch migration from an extensive recruitment range in the West and views the overwintering phenomenon as a range contraction from late-summer coastal breeding habitats. A prediction of this model is that variation in coastal milkweed productivity, on a regional basis, ought to be correlated with a variation in regional abundance of overwintering monarchs. Since we were unable to obtain data on milkweed productivity directly, we examined the relationship between predictors of milkweed productivity (evapotranspiration, precipitation, and soil temperature) and overwintering abundance. We found no significant relationship between abundance and the three surrogate productivity variables, even after accounting for annual and regional variation. This result suggests that variation in local milkweed abundance and productivity does not play a large role in the pattern of local overwintering abundance, refuting the local recruitment hypothesis. Our failure to find a significant relationship between these variables does not preclude the possibility that such a relationship exists; it merely suggests a lack of strong evidence for the local recruitment hypothesis.

One way to identify the recruitment range for western wintering monarchs is to "overlay" the general eastern North American migratory pattern for monarchs onto the region adjacent to western winter habitats. We define the eastern migratory pattern as an average flight trajectory of 195° (Rogg et al. 1999). Putative late-summer recruitment grounds should theoretically occur within this macroregion (figure 21.3). While over 100 species of milkweed occur in North America, only *Asclepias fasicularis* Dene. and *A. speciosa* Torr. occur widely over this range and *A. eriocarpa* Benth. to a lesser extent (Woodson 1954). Western North America comprises large tracts with extremely dry conditions, which undoubtedly limit the abundance, diversity, and productivity of milkweed compared to eastern North America (Woodson 1954; Zalucki and Rochester 1999). The majority of late-summer recruitment for the migratory generation probably originates from six bioregions within California: Bay Area-Delta, South-Central Coast, Sacramento Valley, San Joaquin Valley, Northern Sierra, and Southern Sierra. Limited tracts of irrigated agricultural land and widely spaced watercourses across other areas of this large-scale corridor may also contribute to the winter abundance pattern to a lesser extent.

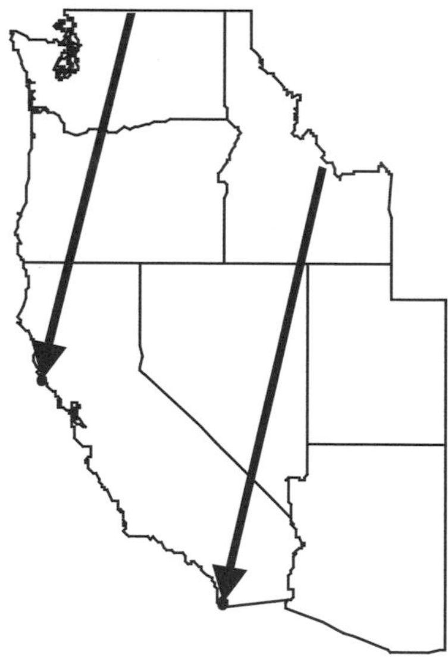

Figure 21.3. Putative recruitment range for the wintering generation of monarchs in western North America. Range boundaries, shown by the arrows, are based on the mean orientation (195°) for monarch migration given by Rogg and colleagues (1999) and extensions of these vectors inland from the overwintering range limits along the Pacific Ocean.

We do not wish to minimize the importance of microlevel factors or conditions that are well documented for their influence on the geography of monarch overwintering (e.g., Calvert and Brower 1981, Calvert et al. 1982; Leong et al. 1991; Leong and Frey 1992). In fact, our long-term analysis showed that abundance has historically been greater at habitats dominated by eucalyptus, pines, or cypress than at those with "other" species. Stands of these three signature taxa may be more likely to produce a community structure and associated microclimate that increases the residence time of monarchs. Furthermore, these taxa may produce a more attractive landscape architecture in terms of sensory cues to migratory monarchs arriving in a certain region.

Finally, to place patterns of monarch population dynamics into a continent-wide context, we compared the recent population trends in the western and eastern North American populations. While the eastern population may exceed abundance in the West by at least two orders of magnitude (Brower 1985), their relative annual variation is comparable, approximately one half order of magnitude (pers. observ.; Journey North 2001). The direction of year-to-year trends in abundance for the western population, however, is opposite that of the eastern population (figure 21.4). The abundance patterns, though opposite, are probably caused by unrelated phenomena that are not addressed here (e.g., Urquhart 1974; Bell 1998).

Acknowledgments

We thank Amy Prokenpek and Jim Walth for helping transcribe data. We are grateful to Rosemary

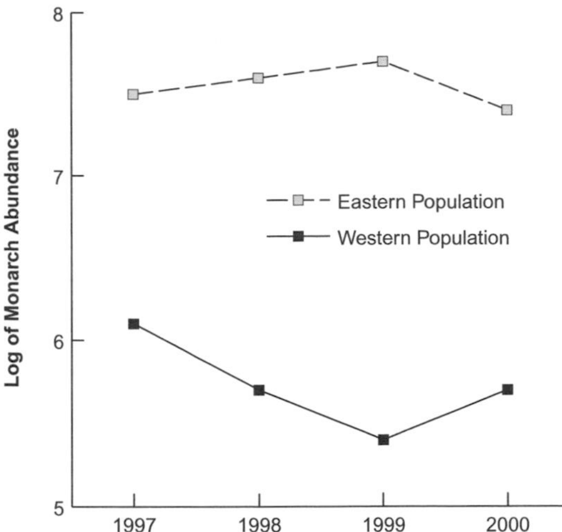

Figure 21.4. Pattern of relative abundance at overwintering habitats for western and eastern monarch populations. Data for western populations were based on the Monarch Program Thanksgiving Count. Data for eastern populations are from Journey North (2001).

Bowker for assistance with geographic information system (GIS) applications and to Darlene McGriff for providing information regarding the California Department of Fish and Game Natural Diversity Data Base. We acknowledge Lincoln Brower, Walt Sakai, and Jim Walth for sharing valuable information and unpublished data. Finally, we extend our appreciation to California Polytechnic State University for their support in the preparation of this manuscript.

References

Allen, T., and T. Hoekstra. 1992. Toward a unified ecology. New York: Columbia University Press.

Alonso-Mejía, A., E. Réndon Salinas, E. Montesinos-Patino, and L. Brower. 1997. Use of lipid reserves by monarch butterflies overwintering in Mexico: implications for conservation. Ecol. Appl. 7:934–47.

Bell, E. 1998. Multitrophic level influences on the population ecology of the monarch butterfly (*Danaus plexippus* L.). Ph.D. thesis, University of California at Santa Cruz.

Bell, E., L. Brower, W. Calvert, J. Dayton, D. Frey, K. Leong, D. Murphy, R. Pyle, K. Snow, and S. Weiss. 1993. The monarch project's conservation and management guidelines for preserving the monarch butterfly migration and monarch overwintering habitat in California. Portland, Ore.: Xerces Society.

Boyer, J. S. 1982. Plant productivity and environment. Science 218:443–48.

Brower, L. P. 1985. New perspectives on the migration biology of the monarch butterfly, *Danaus plexippus* L. In M. A. Rankin, ed., Migration: mechanisms and adaptive significance, pp. 748–85. Contributions to Marine Science, Vol. 27 Suppl. Port Aransas, Texas: Marine Science Institute, University of Texas at Austin.

Brower, L. 1999. Biological necessities for monarch butterfly overwintering in relation to the oyamel forest ecosystem in Mexico. In J. Hoth, L. Merino, K. Oberhauser, I. Pisantry, S. Price, and T. Wilkinson, eds., The 1997 North American Conference on the Monarch Butterfly, pp. 11–28. Montreal: Commission for Environmental Cooperation.

Brower, L. P., G. Castilleja, A. Peralta, J. Lopez-Garcia, L. Bojorquez, S. Diaz, D. Melgarejo, and M. Missrie. 2002. Quantitative changes in forest quality in a principal overwintering area of the monarch butterfly in the states of Michoacan and Mexico: 1971 to 1999. Conserv. Biol. 16:346–59.

California Irrigation Management Information System. http://www.cimis.water.ca.gov/, Accessed 9 August 2001.

Calvert, W. 1991. Monarch butterfly overwintering site location in Santa Barbara County, California. Report to the Planning and Development Department of Santa Barbara County, Santa Barbara, California.

Calvert, W., and L. Brower. 1981. The importance of forest cover for the survival of overwintering monarch butterflies (*Danaus plexippus*, Danaidae). J. Lepid. Soc. 35:216–25.

Calvert, W., and L. Brower. 1986. The location of monarch butterfly (*Danaus plexippus* L.) overwintering colonies in Mexico in relation to topography and climate. J. Lepid. Soc. 40:164–87.

Calvert, W., and R. Lawton. 1993. Comparative phenology of variation in size, weight, and water content of eastern North American monarch butterflies at five overwintering sites in Mexico. In S. B. Malcolm and M. P. Zalucki, eds., Biology and conservation of the monarch butterfly, pp. 299–307. Los Angeles: Natural History Museum of Los Angeles County.

Calvert W., W. Zuchowski, and L. Brower. 1982. The impact of forest thinning on microclimate in monarch butterfly (*Danaus plexippus* L.) overwintering sites in Mexico. Bol. Soc. Bot. Mex. 42:11–18.

Chaplin, S., and P. Wells. 1982. Energy reserves and metabolic expenditures of monarch butterflies overwintering in southern California. Ecol. Entomol. 7:249–56.

Frey, D. 1995. Monarch population trend-California overwintering sites. Monarch Newsletter 5:6–7.

Frey, D., R. Roman, and L. Messett. 2002. Dew-drinking by male monarch butterflies (*Danaus plexippus* L.). J. Lepid. Soc. 56:96–103.

Harris, E. 1986. Natural history of the monarch butterfly (*Danaus plexippus*) in the Santa Barbara region. Master's thesis, University of California at Santa Barbara.

Harvey, H., R. Stecker, J. Dayton, W. Peeler, and M. Schmelzer. 1982. Monarch butterfly monitoring study—natural bridges and moran lake. Project No. 104–02. Harvey and Stanley Associates, Alviso, California.

Journey North. 2001. http://www.learner.org/jnorth/tm/monarch/PopulationMexico.html#Size. Accessed 5 July 2001.

Lane, J. 1993. Overwintering monarch butterflies in California: past and present. In S. B. Malcolm and M. P. Zalucki, eds., Biology and conservation of the monarch butterfly, pp. 335–44. Los Angeles: Natural History Museum of Los Angeles County.

Leong, K. L. H. 1990. Microenvironmental factors associated with the winter habitat of the monarch butterfly (Lepidoptera: Danaidae) in central California. Ann. Entomol. Soc. Am. 83:906–10.

Leong, K., and D. Frey. 1992. Monarch butterfly winter habitat study. Final report. Sacramento: California Department of Parks and Recreation.

Leong, K., D. Frey, G. Brenner, S. Baker, and D. Fox. 1991. Use of multivariate analyses to characterize the monarch butterfly (Lepidoptera: Danaidae) winter habitat. Ann. Entomol. Soc. Am. 84:263–67.

Marriott, D. 2001. Results from the fourth annual Thanksgiving count. Monarch Quarterly 11:14–17.

Meade, D. 1999. Monarch butterfly overwintering sites in Santa Barbara County, California. Report to Planning and Development Department of Santa Barbara County, California. Prepared by Althouse and Meade, Biological and Environmental Services, Paso Robles, California.

Rogg, K., O. Taylor, and D. Gibo. 1999. Mark and recapture during the monarch migration: a preliminary analysis. In J. Hoth, L. Merino, K. Oberhauser, I. Pisantry, S. Price, and T. Wilkinson, eds., The 1997 North American Conference on the Monarch Butterfly, pp. 133–38. Montreal: Commission for Environmental Cooperation.

Rosenzweig, M. 1968. Net primary productivity of terrestrial communities: predictions from climatological data. Am. Nat. 102:67–74.

Sakai, W., and W. Calvert. 1991. Statewide monarch butterfly management plan for the state of California Department of Parks and Recreation. Final report. Sacramento: California Department of Parks and Recreation.

Tuskes, P., and L. Brower. 1978. Overwintering ecology of the monarch butterfly, *Danaus plexippus* L., in California. Ecol. Entomol. 3:141–53.

Urquhart, F. 1974. Fluctuations in monarch butterfly populations. News Lepid. Soc. 3:1–2.

Weisberg, S. 1985. Applied linear regression. 2nd ed. New York: Wiley and Sons.

Wells, S., R. Pyle, and N. Collins. 1983. The IUCN invertebrate red data book. Gland, Switzerland: International Union for Conservation of Nature and Natural Resources (IUCN).

Wenner, A., and A. Harris. 1993. Do California monarchs undergo long-distance directed migrations?. In S. B. Malcolm and M. P. Zalucki, eds., Biology and conservation of the monarch butterfly, pp. 209–18. Los Angeles: Natural History Museum of Los Angeles County.

Woodson, R. E., Jr. 1954. The North American species of *Asclepias* L. Ann. Mo. Bot. Gard. 41:1–211.

Zalucki, M., and W. Rochester. 1999. Estimating the effect of climate on the distribution and abundance of *Danaus plexippus*: a tale of two continents. In J. Hoth, L. Merino, K. Oberhauser, I. Pisantry, S. Price, and T. Wilkinson, eds., The 1997 North American Conference on the Monarch Butterfly, pp. 151–63. Montreal: Commission for Environmental Cooperation.

22

Analysis of the Pattern of Distribution and Abundance of Monarch Overwintering Sites along the California Coastline

Kingston L. H. Leong, Walter H. Sakai, Walter Bremer, Dan Feuerstein, and Gwen Yoshimura

INTRODUCTION

Mass winter aggregations of monarchs in North America are mainly Mexican and Californian phenomena. Current theory defines two populations separated by the Rocky Mountains. In the fall, monarchs east of the Rocky Mountains migrate to Mexico, while those west of this natural divide migrate to forested areas on the California coastline (Tuskes and Brower 1978; Nagano and Lane 1985; Nagano and Sakai 1990; Brower and Malcolm 1991).

In California, monarchs begin to arrive at coastal overwintering sites in mid-October (Hill et al. 1976; Leong et al. 1995) and only occupy sites that possess specific combinations of microclimatic conditions (Leong 1990; Leong et al. 1991). These conditions include the absence of freezing temperatures, shelter from strong winds, sources of moisture for hydration, cool grove temperatures to conserve energy reserves, and exposure to filtered sunlight for radiant energy, permitting daily activities (Leong 1990, 1999; Leong et al. 1991). Depending on the stability of these conditions, monarchs may remain at a site for part or all of the winter season. Sites where clustering occurs throughout the winter season provide protection against prevailing winds from the north and northwest and winter storm winds from the south (Leong 1999). Barriers to winter storm winds, however, must also permit exposure to filtered sunlight (Leong 1990). Monarchs leave the coast in February and March.

Winter sites are found along the California coastline from northern Mendocino County to as far south as Baja California, Mexico, and the number of active wintering sites varies seasonally from 150 to over 250 (Nagano and Sakai 1990; Sakai et al. 1989; Sakai and Calvert 1991). Wintering sites may support from a few dozen to several hundred thousand monarchs (Sakai and Calvert 1991). Notably, the groves supporting the most monarchs occur in the central coast, which includes coastal areas between Santa Cruz and Santa Barbara Counties. The causes of this pattern are poorly understood.

Geographic information system (GIS) analyses examine this distribution and abundance pattern on a larger geographic scale. Regional comparisons can be made of the topographic and environmental variables associated with the central coast and areas north and south of this region.

The objectives of this study were to (1) determine the environmental variables that may account for high numbers of monarchs wintering along the central coast, (2) determine the factors limiting their northern and southern distribution and abundance, and (3) describe the geographic features associated with winter aggregation sites using GIS technology.

METHODS

We obtained data on winter sites from the California Department of Fish and Game Natural Diversity Data Base (NDDB). Over 390 winter aggregation sites are recorded for California; some of these sites were recently discovered and reported by Meade (1999) for Santa Barbara County. We used only the 331 sites monitored from 1990 to 2000 for which geographic location and population size were described.

To determine the attributes, distribution, and frequency of habitats supporting larger winter aggregations along the California coastline, winter habitats were divided into six population categories: less than 12,500, 12,500 to 24,999, 25,000 to 49,999, 50,000 to 99,999, 100,000 to 199,999, and more than 200,000 overwintering monarchs. We used the maximum population size of roosting monarchs recorded for any single winter season during the ten seasons to categorize each site. Maximum seasonal numbers were summed to estimate the maximum overwintering population for the California coastline during each season from 1990 to 2000. We define a winter season as the period from October to February.

Data on rainfall, wind, temperatures (maximum, minimum, and average), relative humidity (average), and dew point (average) during the months of October to February, from 1989 to 2000, were obtained from 121 weather stations in coastal counties through four Internet sources (University of California 2002; National Weather Service 2002; California Department of Water Resources 2002; California Irrigation Management Information System 2002). We calculated the 10-year average values of each environmental variable for each month of the winter season.

We obtained digital topographic maps of California from the U.S. Geological Survey (2002) and digital rainfall maps from the Parameter-elevation Regression Independent Slope Model (PRISM) (Oregon State University 2002). The data were formatted to ArcInfo 8 grids using Solaris Unix. The distance of sites from the coastline, elevation, and slope were analyzed using ArcView 3.2 software.

The data were analyzed using BioStat 1 for simple linear regression, analysis of variance (ANOVA), and chi-square tests of significance.

RESULTS AND DISCUSSION

Location and winter populations of sites along California

Winter aggregations of monarchs were found mainly in forested areas along the California coastline from northern Mendocino County to southern San Diego County, with six small inland sites reported by Cherubini (1993) (table 22.1). Based on the NDDB records during 1990 to 2000, the estimated maximum number of overwintering monarchs for a single season was 2,347,865. More than 70% of overwintering monarchs occurred in groves along the central coast, with an equal percentage of butterflies occurring in groves north of Santa Cruz County (northern region) and south of Santa Barbara County (southern region). Their abundance along the coastline fits a bell-shaped curve, with most in the center of their distribution and lower but equal numbers occurring north and south of this region (figure 22.1). A similar relationship exists for the number of wintering sites.

Table 22.1. Wintering site population

Population size	No. of sites		
	Northern region	Central region	Southern region
<12,000	33	76	35
12,000 but <25,000	3	18	3
25,000 but <50,000	2	8	4
50,000 but <100,000	2	6	1
100,000	0	4	0
Total	40	112	43

Note: Regions are shown in figure 22.2.

Dynamics of three types of overwintering habitats

Nagano and Sakai (1990) initially classified California wintering sites as "permanent" and "autumnal." The former indicated the presence of monarchs throughout the entire winter and the latter indicated sites where monarchs were not present for the entire winter. However, neither term describes the dynamic nature of a habitat that may account for the duration of residency of the overwintering monarchs during the season. Furthermore, "permanent" implies an enduring, unchanging, or lasting state while "autumnal" implies the use of winter sites only during autumn or fall, but permanent sites can become unsuitable while autumnal sites can support roosting monarchs the entire season during mild winters (pers. observ.).

We use the terms "climax" and "transitional" to describe overwintering habitats, rather than "permanent" and "autumnal," because they better depict overwintering sites as living and ever-changing dynamic plant communities. We define climax

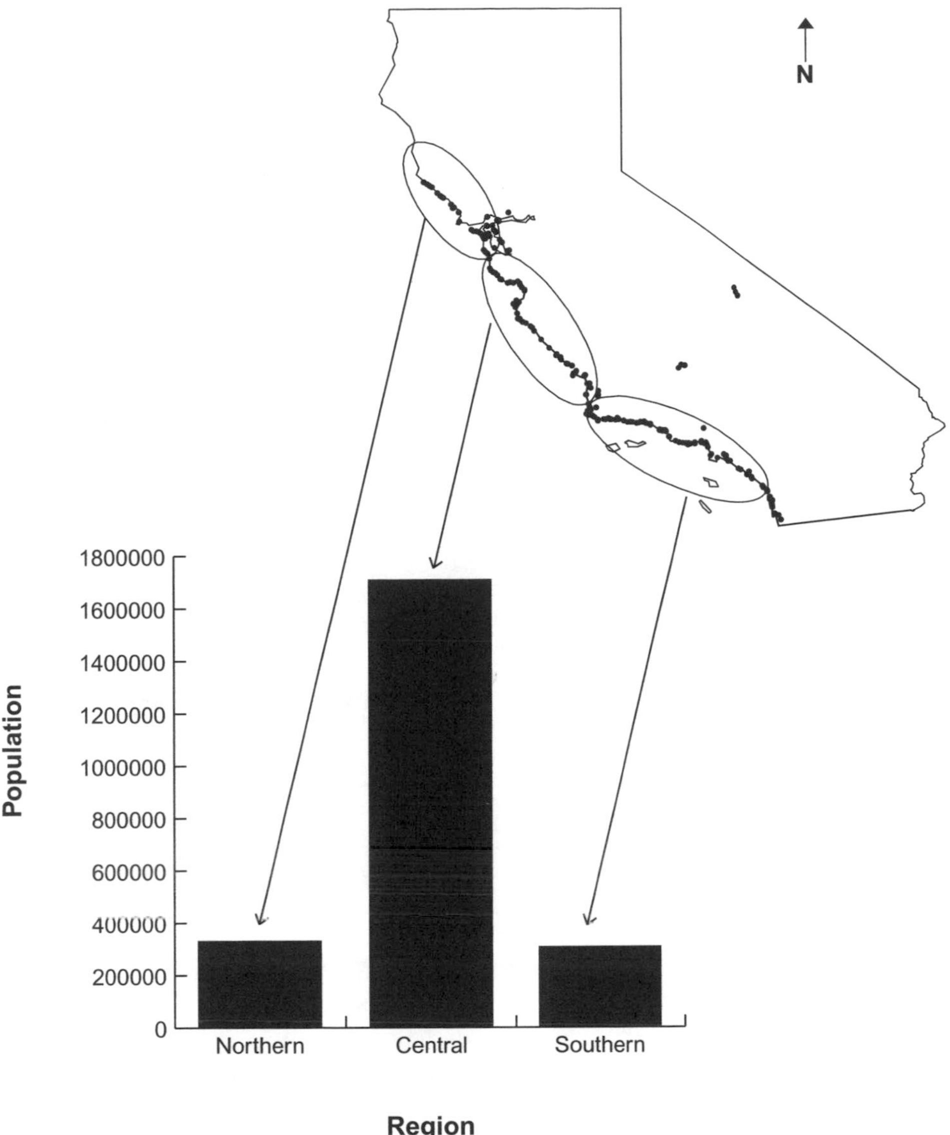

Figure 22.1. Distribution of 331 wintering sites (small circles) along the California coastline, including six inland sites. Ovals distinguish three regions: the northern region encompasses sites north of Santa Cruz County, the central region encompasses sites from Santa Cruz County (lat 122°20′30″W, long 37°8′26″N) to Santa Barbara County (lat 119°24′18″W, long 34°20′4″N), and the southern region encompasses sites south of Santa Barbara County. The population level for each region represents the sum of the maximum numbers of overwintering butterflies recorded for a site during a 10-year period.

habitats as those that maintain conditions suitable for winter aggregations throughout the winter season. Transitional habitats are evolving overwintering habitats with ephemeral conditions for roosting. These often support roosting monarchs early in the season but are generally abandoned when weather conditions, such as strong winds, disrupt the roosting area (Leong 1999). Climax habitats may provide optimal conditions for several decades, but eventually grove conditions change owing to various factors. These include tree growth that results in increased shading, as found at Sweet Spring Marsh and Monarch Lane, Los Osos, in San Luis Obispo County, California, and tree senescence and losses due to insect infestation, diseases, natural catastrophes, and urban development such that the site becomes unsuitable for monarch aggregation. Depending on the degree of deterioration, these groves may revert to transitional sites. Likewise, transitional sites may develop into climax habitats or fail to do so because they lack one or more essential features, such as optimal tree density. Changes may occur at overwintering sites both in forested areas and in surrounding areas including ravines, sand dunes, and man-made structures that comprise the habitat (Tuskes and Brower 1978; pers. comm.).

Transitional and climax sites

Of the 331 sites monitored during the 10-winter seasons (1990 to 2000), 136 had no winter aggregations during this time period. These unoccupied sites had supported from a few dozen to several thousand monarchs at some time prior to 1990 (Sakai and Calvert 1991; NDDB). Whether these sites served as transitional or climax habitats a decade earlier cannot be determined. The loss of these habitats has been attributed to a loss of trees due to urban or agriculture development, diseases, insects, tree trimming and selective cutting, natural storms, fires and flooding, and grove senescence (Sakai and Calvert 1991; Leong et al. 1991; pers. observ.). The remaining 195 active sites (those recording butterflies at least once during the decade) were classified as a climax site if they had winter aggregations during each of the last four annual site visitations and as a transitional site if winter aggregations were absent at least once during the last four annual site visitations. Climax sites not only were occupied every year but also supported more monarchs (figure 22.2).

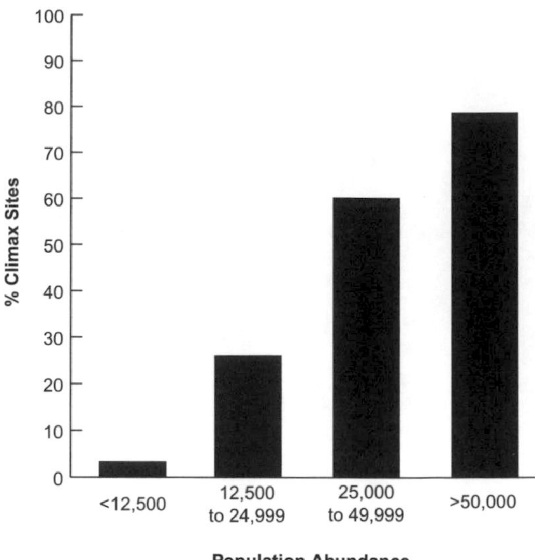

Figure 22.2. The percentage of climax sites in the four population categories.

Table 22.2. Distance of wintering sites from the California coastline

Region	No. of sites	Distance (km ± SE)
Northern	66	1.8 ± 0.7
Central	187	2.4 ± 0.3
Southern	78	2.9 ± 0.3

Distance of sites from the coastline

The distances of wintering sites from the coastline were similar throughout their range ($F = 1.34$, $df = 2, 329$, $p = 0.262$) and averaged 2.37 km ± 0.39 standard error (SE) from the Pacific Ocean (table 22.2). Thus, sites were within the influence of the maritime climate. Inland sites described by Cherubini (1993) were considered statistical outliers and were not included in the analysis.

Site elevation and wind velocities

The elevations at wintering sites ranged from 8 to 800 m, with an average of 19.3 m ± 2.8 SE. We found no statistically significant relationship between winter population size and site elevation ($R^2 = 0.0001$, $df = 1, 193$, $p = 0.8962$). Wind velocities did not vary significantly among the regions (table 22.3).

Slope orientation

Site location was correlated with geographic orientation of the slope on which the habitat occurred. Of 195 winter habitats supporting roosting monarchs, 136 of 195 (70%) occurred on slopes with south to west orientations (figure 22.3a). We believe that these grove orientations provide protection from prevailing north to northwest winds and optimal exposure to solar radiant energy. These conditions resembled conditions previously described as favoring winter aggregations (Leong 1990; Leong et al. 1991; Frey et al. 1992). Sites with large aggregations (more than 25,000 monarchs) showed similar

Table 22.3. Environmental variable comparisons

Variable	Region	October	November	December	January	February
Wind (ft/s)	N	3.4 ± 0.4	3.1 ± 0.3	3.8 ± 0.5	3.7 ± 0.5	3.6 ± 0.4
	C	4.7 ± 0.4	4.4 ± 0.4	4.2 ± 0.1	4.2 ± 0.3	4.7 ± 0.3
	S	3.6 ± 0.3	3.8 ± 0.3	3.8 ± 0.4	3.9 ± 0.3	4.0 ± 0.4
Precipitation (in.)	N	0.05 ± 0.11	0.06 ± 0.01	$0.13^{a} \pm 0.03$	$0.21^{a} \pm 0.05$	0.21 ± 0.02
	C	0.02 ± 0.00	0.08 ± 0.02	$0.07^{b} \pm 0.01$	$0.11^{ab} \pm 0.02$	0.16 ± 0.01
	S	0.01 ± 0.00	0.03 ± 0.00	$0.06^{b} \pm 0.01$	$0.12^{ab} \pm 0.02$	0.11 ± 0.05
Relative humidity (%)	N	62.0 ± 3.2	$68.6^{a} \pm 2.4$	$69.0^{a} \pm 2.0$	$73.0^{a} \pm 2.0$	73.6 ± 1.8
	C	69.0 ± 2.3	$69.6^{a} \pm 1.32$	$71.5^{a} \pm 1.1$	$72.1^{a} \pm 1.6$	71.4 ± 2.3
	S	65.1 ± 2.2	$59.9^{b} \pm 1.8$	$57.7^{b} \pm 2.5$	$63.0^{b} \pm 2.9$	66.6 ± 1.9
Average temperature (°C)	N	$16.2^{a} \pm 0.8$	$12.4^{a} \pm 0.4$	$8.9^{a} \pm 0.8$	$9.8^{a} \pm 0.7$	$10.7^{a} \pm 0.6$
	C	$16.1^{a} \pm 0.2$	$12.1^{a} \pm 0.2$	$9.9^{a} \pm 0.4$	$10.4^{a} \pm 0.3$	$11.4^{a} \pm 0.2$
	S	$18.2^{b} \pm 0.6$	$14.6^{b} \pm 0.6$	$11.8^{b} \pm 0.6$	$12.1^{b} \pm 0.6$	$12.4^{b} \pm 0.6$
Maximum temperature (°C)	N	23.8 ± 1.01	$18.9^{a} \pm 0.27$	$14.8^{a} \pm 0.77$	$15.3^{a} \pm 0.66$	$16.3^{a} \pm 0.6$
	C	23.6 ± 0.67	$19.3^{a} \pm 0.38$	$16.6^{b} \pm 0.24$	$17.1^{b} \pm 0.49$	$18.0^{b} \pm 0.3$
	S	25.6 ± 0.93	$22.4^{b} \pm 0.05$	$19.4^{c} \pm 0.33$	$19.4^{c} \pm 1.04$	$18.0^{b} \pm 0.5$
Minimum temperature (°C)	N	$8.6^{a} \pm 0.4$	5.8 ± 0.8	3.0 ± 0.8	4.2 ± 0.8	5.1 ± 0.7
	C	$8.5^{a} \pm 0.3$	4.9 ± 0.5	3.3 ± 0.6	3.8 ± 0.4	4.9 ± 0.4
	S	$10.7^{b} \pm 0.5$	6.7 ± 0.9	4.1 ± 1.0	4.7 ± 1.0	5.7 ± 1.0
Dew point (°C)	N	$8.8^{a} \pm 0.7$	6.7 ± 0.8	3.5 ± 1.0	5.1 ± 0.8	6.1 ± 0.7
	C	$10.3^{ab} \pm 0.2$	6.7 ± 0.4	5.0 ± 0.3	5.6 ± 0.2	6.3 ± 0.5
	S	$11.5^{b} \pm 0.7$	6.8 ± 0.6	3.7 ± 0.7	5.1 ± 0.9	6.3 ± 0.7

Note: Comparisons made throughout the winter season and across three aggregation regions along the California coastline: North (N), Central (C), and South (S). Means $\pm$ 1 standard error are shown. Values within each group of variables and month (column) with different superscript letters are significantly different at $p \leq 0.05$ based on analyses of variance.

slope orientations, with the highest frequency occurring on slopes with a southwest orientation (figure 22.3b).

The slope orientation of winter sites does not always reflect the habitat's wind protection and exposure to sunlight. Two sites in Monterey occurred on slopes with a north and northwest orientation (figure 22.4), but both were on a coastal peninsula with access to winter sunlight. Another site in Bolinas (northern region) was on flat terrain but on a south-facing coastal inlet, again allowing ample exposure to sunlight.

Twenty of 27 large sites (more than 25,000 monarchs) were associated with a coastal inlet, bay, or valley mouth, while the remaining 7 were found in more wind-exposed locations. Wintering sites occurred in wind-sheltered regions significantly more often than in wind-exposed areas ($\chi^2 = 7.79$, $df = 1, p = 0.005$). Winter sites on the lower terrain of coastal inlets, bays, or valleys, especially those associated with the northern barriers, would be shielded from the direct effects of northwesterly winds, and many were on slopes that had the best exposure to sunlight. This kind of shelter is not a necessary feature of a suitable habitat, since one fourth (7/27) of the large winter aggregation sites were not in major valleys, bays, or inlets. Sufficient tree densities, grove configurations, and local terrain such as ravines and deep streambeds could also provide protection from strong winds. These characteristics were not analyzed in this study but may play a major role in the suitability of cluster sites.

Relationship of colony occurrence to climate

Since a disproportionate number of roosting monarchs was found in the central coast, the environment of this region likely features the conditions most favorable for winter aggregations. The average monthly temperatures during the colder months of

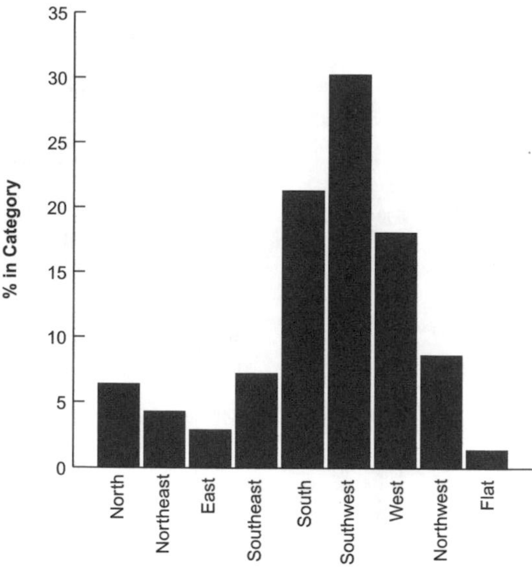

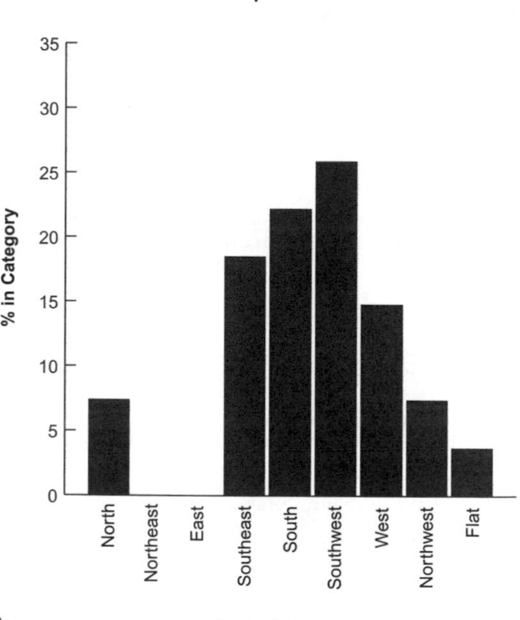

Figure 22.3. The slope orientation of (a) 195 wintering sites with monarchs and (b) 27 of these sites with more than 25,000 monarchs along the California coastline.

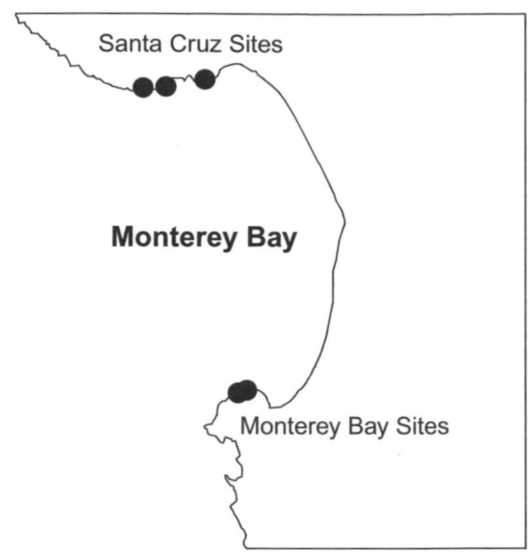

Figure 22.4. Circles show large winter sites associated with Monterey Bay, California. Santa Cruz sites are on the northern border of the bay and Monterey sites are on a peninsula, but within the influence of the bay.

December and January were below the flight threshold of monarchs (12.7°C, figure 22.5b, see table 22.3). This allows for energy conservation (Chaplin and Wells 1982; James 1984; Masters et al. 1988). The average maximum temperatures for these months were frequently high enough to allow for thermoregulation and foraging for water and nectar (Tuskes and Brower 1978; Brower 1988; Masters 1993).

The central coast region has abundant morning dew as indicated by average monthly dew points, which averaged 1.7°C above the monthly minimum temperatures (figure 22.5b). The monthly relative humidity averages for the central coast were very similar to those recorded for the northern region. Moreover, for the months of November to January, they were significantly higher than in the southern region (see table 22.3). A high relative humidity reduces the monarchs' risk of excessive water loss due to evaporation (Church 1960; May 1979).

Low winter temperatures and high rainfall may limit monarch abundance in the northern region. The average monthly maximum temperatures recorded for December and January for regions north of Santa Cruz County were 14.8°C and 15.3°C (see figure 22.5a, table 22.3), just a few degrees above the flight threshold of monarchs. The narrow range between flight threshold and maximum temperatures in the northern locations may limit foraging and metabolic time (Masters 1993). December and January were significantly colder in the northern region than in the central region (see table 22.3). In addition, the northern region had significantly more

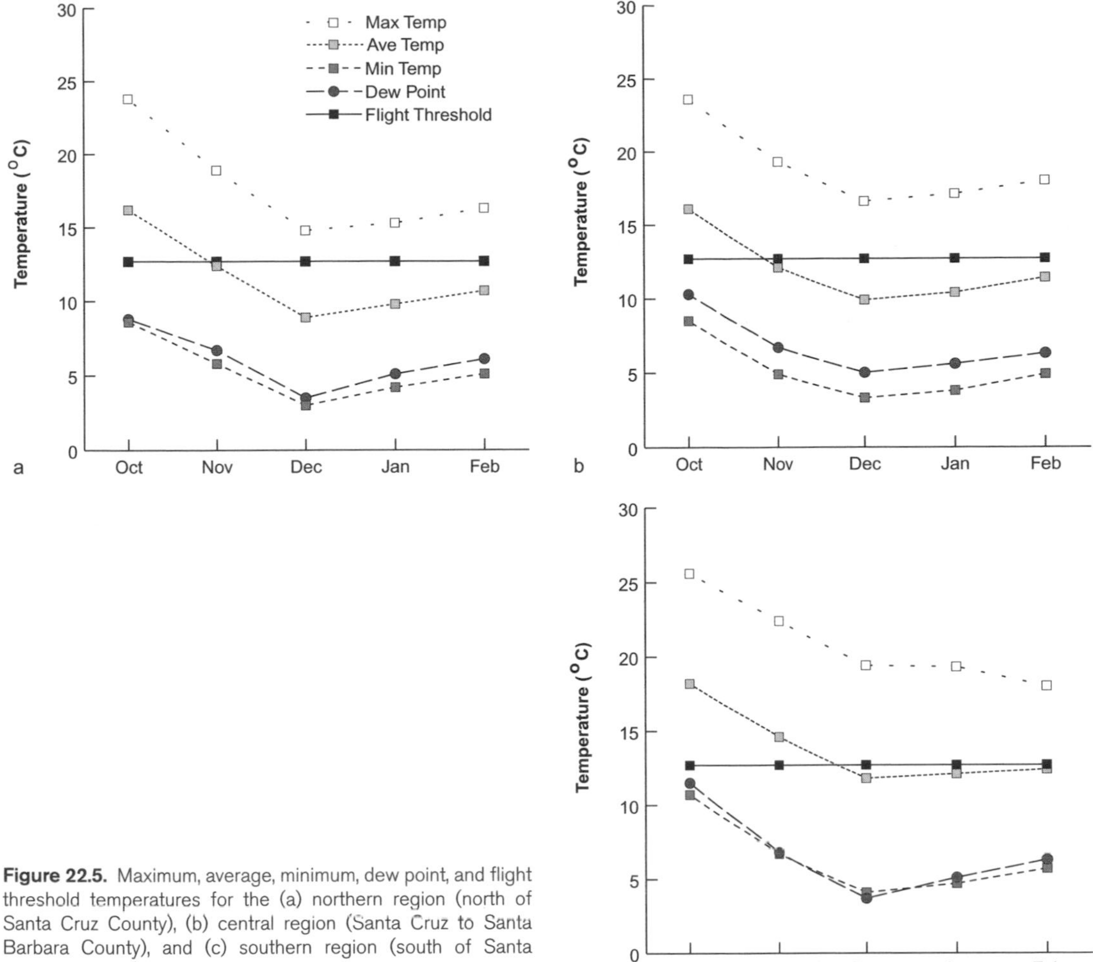

Figure 22.5. Maximum, average, minimum, dew point, and flight threshold temperatures for the (a) northern region (north of Santa Cruz County), (b) central region (Santa Cruz to Santa Barbara County), and (c) southern region (south of Santa Barbara County).

precipitation and rainy days during December and January than either the central or southern region (figure 22.6, see table 22.3). Monarchs are seldom active on rainy days, even when temperatures are above the flight threshold.

Factors affecting the metabolic and dehydration rates in monarchs, including high temperatures (maximum and average), low relative humidity, and the little morning dew, may limit the abundance of cluster sites in the southern region. The average temperatures of December and January were only 0.9°C and 0.6°C below flight threshold (see table 22.3), and average maximum temperatures suggest that this region had more warm winter days than did the central or northern region. Roosting monarchs would easily have reached flight threshold temperatures (Masters 1993) and higher body temperatures would have increased metabolism and reduced energy reserves. To keep thoracic temperatures low, monarchs would have to spend more time gliding or soaring (Brower 1988; Masters et al. 1988). In addition, average relative humidity values of this region were significantly lower from November to January than those recorded for the other two regions (see table 22.3). Such conditions would increase water loss (Church 1960; May 1979), requiring more frequent flights to search for water and reduce their body temperatures. Morning dew in the south may also limit abundance, as dew points were close to the minimum temperatures (see figure 22.5c, table 22.3). When morning dew was present, it was available only briefly because of greater evaporation rates due to high winter temperatures and low relative humidity. Consequently, overwintering monarchs

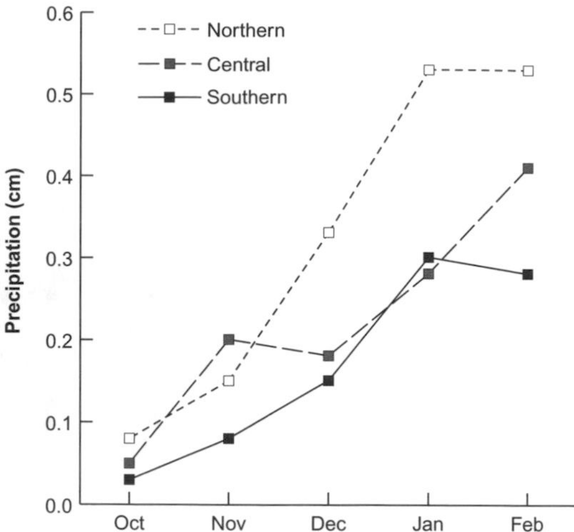

Figure 22.6. The northern region had significantly more precipitation during the months of December and January than the central and southern regions.

may have to seek other sources of water from ponds, streams, winter flowering plants, or irrigated gardens and lawns to hydrate (Chaplin and Wells 1982; Brower 1995).

CONCLUSION

Based on information from the NDDB from 1990 to 2000, roosting monarchs and wintering sites were concentrated along the central coast of California. Regions north and south of the central coast had fewer winter aggregations. Sites supporting more than 25,000 overwintering butterflies tended to be climax sites, while those having less than 12,000 butterflies were more often transitional.

Most sites were within 2.4 km from the ocean shores and were consequently under the influence of the maritime climate. The majority of the sites were on slopes that provided optimal exposure to winter sunlight. Cluster sites experienced similar wind conditions, and the elevation of the habitat had little influence on monarch abundance.

Environmental conditions in the central coast region favor aggregations for several reasons. This region has copious amounts of morning dew and high relative humidity, which protect roosting monarchs from desiccation. Average winter temperatures below the flight threshold help conserve stored lipids. Furthermore, moderate maximum temperatures allow monarchs to hydrate, thermoregulate during clear winter days, and metabolize stored energy for body maintenance. The environmental data strongly support the hypothesis that high rainfall and low temperatures limit the northern distribution of monarchs, while low relative humidity, high winter temperatures, and minimum availability of morning dew limit their southern abundance.

The GIS analysis revealed three topographic features associated with winter aggregations of monarchs. First, the greatest numbers of wintering sites were on south- to west-facing slopes, which offer the best exposure to sunlight and possibly protection from wind. Second, the population density of a winter site was not related to its elevation. Lastly, large winter aggregations occurred in groves associated with slopes of valleys, bays, and inlets significantly more often than exposed areas.

The preservation of the winter aggregations of monarchs in California depends on long-term management of the habitat at climax and certain transitional sites. Management practices should focus on grove enhancement activities to favor winter aggregations. Leong (1999) demonstrated that monarchs will return to a former climax grove if conditions for winter aggregations are reestablished. Management plans should target climax sites in all three regions. Transitional sites with the highest likelihood of becoming climax sites are in the central coast region and are associated with terrain that has protection from strong winds and ample exposure to winter sunlight. These sites may require grove enhancement activities, such as tree plantings to increase wind protection and selective tree trimming and removal for better exposure to sunlight, to establish stable conditions for the entire winter season.

Acknowledgments

We thank Michael Yoshimura and Lincoln Brower for their critical editorial comments. We also would like to thank Chris Nagano and John Lane for their contributions to the California Department of Fish and Game's Natural Diversity Data Base of monarch overwintering sites used in this study.

References

Brower, L. P. 1988. A place in the sun. Anim. Kingdom 91:42–51.

Brower, L. P. 1995. Understanding and misunderstanding the migration of the monarch butterfly (Nymphalidae) in North America: 1857–1995. J. Lepid. Soc. 49:304–85.

Brower, L. P., and S. B. Malcolm. 1991. Animal migrations: endangered phenomena. Am. Zool. 31:265–76.

California Department of Water Resources. 2002. http://wwwdpla.water.ca.gov/cgi-bin/cimis/main.pl. Accessed 10 July–15 August 2000.

California Irrigation Management Information System. 2002. http://www.ceresgroup.com/weather/cimis/index.html. Accessed 10 July–6 August 2000.

Chaplin, S. B., and P. H. Wells. 1982. Energy reserves and metabolic expenditure of monarch butterflies overwintering in southern California. Ecol. Entomol. 7:249–56.

Cherubini, P. 1993. Inland overwintering sites in California. Monarch Newsletter 3:6–7.

Church, H. K. 1960. Heat loss and the body temperature of flying insects. II. Heat conduction within the body and its loss by radiation and convection. J. Exp. Biol. 37:187–212.

Frey, D., K. L. H. Leong, D. Fredericks, and S. Raskowitz. 1992. Clustering patterns of monarch butterfly (Lepidoptera: Danaidae) at two California central coast overwintering sites. Ann. Entomol. Soc. Am. 83:907–10.

Hill, H. F., A. M. Wenner, and P. H. Wells. 1976. Reproductive behavior in an overwintering aggregation of monarch butterflies. Am. Midl. Nat. 95:10–19.

James, D. G. 1984. Phenology of weight, moisture and energy reserves of Australian monarch butterflies, *Danaus plexippus*. Ecol. Entomol. 9:421–28.

Leong, K. L. H. 1990. Microenvironmental factors associated with the winter habitat of the monarch butterfly (Lepidoptera: Danaidae) in central California. Ann. Entomol. Soc. Am. 83:906–10.

Leong, K. L. H. 1999. Restoration of an overwintering grove in Los Osos, San Luis County, California. In J. Hoth, L. Merino, K. Oberhauser, I. Pisantry, S. Price, and T. Wilkinson, eds., The 1997 North American Conference on the Monarch Butterfly, pp. 211–17. Montreal: Commission for Environmental Cooperation.

Leong, K. L. H., D. Frey, G. Brenner, D. Fox, and S. Baker. 1991. Use of multivariate analyses to characterize the monarch butterfly (Lepidoptera: Danaidae) winter habitat. Ann. Entomol. Soc. Am. 84:263–67.

Leong, K. L. H., E. O'Brien, K. Lowerisen, and M. Colleran. 1995. Mating activity and status of overwintering monarch butterflies in central California. Ann. Entomol. Soc. Am. 88:45–50.

Masters, A. R. 1993. Temperature and thermoregulation in the monarch butterfly. In S. B. Malcolm and M. P. Zalucki, eds., Biology and conservation of the monarch butterfly, pp. 145–55. Los Angeles: Natural History Museum of Los Angeles County.

Masters, A. R., S. B. Malcolm, and L. P. Brower. 1988. Monarch butterfly (*Danaus plexippus*) thermoregulation behavior and adaptations for overwintering in Mexico. Ecology 69:458–67.

May, M. L. 1979. Insect thermoregulation. Annu. Rev. Entomol. 24:313–49.

Meade, D. E. 1999. Monarch butterfly overwintering sites in Santa Barbara County, California. Paso Robles, Calif.: Althouse and Meade Biological and Environmental Services.

Nagano, C. D., and J. Lane. 1985. A survey of the location of monarch butterfly (*Danaus plexippus* L.) overwintering roosts in the state of California, U.S.A.: first year 1984/85. Report of the World Wildlife Fund United States. Portland, Ore.: Monarch Project.

Nagano, C. D., and W. H. Sakai. 1990. The monarch butterfly. In W. J. Chandler and L. Labate, eds., Audubon wildlife report 1989/1990, pp. 367–85. San Diego: Academic Press.

National Weather Service. 2002. National weather station for Los Angeles/Oxnard. http://www.nwsla.noaa.gov/climate/. Accessed 17 July–6 August 2000.

Oregon State University. 2002. Climate mapping with PRISM. http://www.ocs.orst.edu/prism/prism_new.html. Accessed 20 July–30 July 2000.

Sakai, W. H., and W. C. Calvert. 1991. Statewide monarch butterfly management plan for the state of California Department of Parks and Recreation. Report no. 88-11-050. Sacramento: California Department of Parks and Recreation.

Sakai, W. H., J. Lane, A. V. Evans, J. Schrumpt, and M. Monroe. 1989. The wintering colonies of monarch butterfly (*Danaus plexippus* L.: Nymphalidae: Lepidoptera) in state of California, U.S.A. Contract report no. FG7551. Sacramento: California Department of Fish and Game.

Tuskes, P. M., and L. P. Brower. 1978. Overwintering ecology of monarchy butterfly, *Danaus plexippus* L. (Lepidoptera: Danaidae). J. Aust. Entomol. Soc. 25:31–35.

University of California. 2002. Statewide Integrated Pest Management project. http://www.ipm.ucdavis.edu/WEATHER/weather1.html. Accessed 17 July–15 August 2000.

U.S. Geological Survey. 2002. http://www.usgs.gov/. Accessed 5 July–6 July 2000.

23

Environmental Factors Influencing Postdiapause Reproductive Development in Monarch Butterflies

Liz Goehring and Karen S. Oberhauser

INTRODUCTION

Organisms living in temperate regions face seasonal challenges, such as absence of food, harsh winter conditions, and the need to synchronize reproduction with suitable conditions for breeding. Insect adaptations to these challenges include migration, dormancy, and seasonal phenotypic variation; various combinations of these traits constitute a diapause syndrome (Andrewartha 1952; Tauber et al. 1986; Danks 1987; Leather et al. 1993). Diapause is a state of arrested development, characterized by low metabolic activity, reduced motor activity, and increased resistance to environmental extremes, and is usually hormonally controlled in insects (Nijhout 1994). Diapause can occur during any insect life stage; "reproductive diapause" refers to delayed reproductive development in the adult stage.

The course of development during diapause includes changes in the insect's physiology and sensitivity to environmental stimuli against a backdrop of seasonal changes. After the onset of diapause, there are three steps: intensification, maintenance, and termination. These steps are referred to as "diapause development" (Tauber et al. 1986). Diapause development either follows a predetermined course not influenced by external cues, or terminates in response to external stimuli. Hodek (1983) refers to these pathways as "horotelic" (Greek *hora* = right time, *telos* = fulfillment) and "tachytelic" (Greek *tachys* = quick), respectively. The pathways may operate singly or together. The rate of diapause development is often driven by temperature, but other stimuli include photoperiod, food, moisture, parasitoid-host interactions, and mating (reviewed in Tauber et al. 1986; Danks 1987).

In reproductive diapause, once diapause development is complete, characteristics such as reduced metabolism and cold-hardiness disappear, and the insect is capable of reproducing. If prevailing environmental conditions are not suitable for reproduction, the insect may remain dormant, in a postdiapause "quiescence" (Tauber et al. 1986).

Many researchers have noted a lack of reproductive activity and undeveloped reproductive organs in overwintering monarchs, and referred to this as "reproductive diapause" (Urquhart and Urquhart 1976; Brower et al. 1977). Herman (1981) reported a period of minimal reproductive tract development in monarchs collected in Californian overwintering sites from September to December even after they were incubated under conditions that are normally favorable to reproductive development (16-h:8-h light-dark cycle; 25°C), clearly demonstrating the refractory period necessarily associated with diapause. Subsequent work comparing California and Mexico overwintering butterflies revealed qualitatively similar diapause patterns, with longer diapause in the eastern population (Herman et al. 1989). More recent work in Mexican overwintering sites followed male reproductive development and mating strategies (Van Hook 1993, 1996). Van Hook identified significant variation in the degree of male diapause and suggested that this leads to multiple mating strategies in the overwintering colonies. In Australia, monarch ovarian dormancy is more accurately classified as "oligopause," an intermediate condition that lacks the refractory period associated with diapause (James 1982).

Goehring and Oberhauser (2002) reported on environmental factors influencing the induction of monarch diapause. Here, we report studies on the effects of photoperiod, access to milkweed, and mating on diapause completion and postdiapause ovarian development in eastern-population females.

METHODS

Collection from the overwintering colony

We collected adult monarchs from the Arroyo Barranca Honda colony in the Sierra Chincua, located in the transvolcanic mountains of Central Mexico, during the 1996 and 1997 overwintering seasons. In both years, we collected during a time of increased activity (e.g., flying, drinking, nectaring, and mating), but before mass dispersal for spring migration. We collected 324 females and 72 males on 28 February 1996, and 300 females and 100 males on 5 March 1997. These dates roughly correspond to the average start of the mass mating period (Van Hook 1996).

We sampled butterflies from three hypothesized subpopulations—roosting, mating, and active—following Van Hook (1996). Roosting butterflies were collected from trees in the center of the colony. These butterflies were hanging immobile on tree trunks or branches 3.5 to 6 m from the ground. Mating butterflies were collected *in copula*, also in the colony center. Active butterflies were collected in flight in a clearing or near a stream downhill from the colony. Collections from the three populations were made at the same time. In 1996, equal numbers of adults were collected from each subpopulation. In 1997, to ensure male mating readiness, all males were collected *in copula*. In 1997, the nucleus of the colony moved downhill on the day prior to collection, possibly mixing subpopulations.

We marked butterflies at the time of collection and then placed them in glassine envelopes. Mating pairs were stored together in the same envelope and allowed to separate on their own. Butterflies were kept on ice in a cooler and transported to St. Paul, Minnesota, within 3 days of collection.

Dissections and general measurements

We measured butterfly mass, wing length, and wing condition (scale loss and tatter along the edges) immediately on arrival in Minnesota. We assessed scale loss on an ordinal scale from 1 to 5 (no loss to severe loss) and wing edge tatter on an ordinal scale from 0 to 4 (no wing tatter to all 4 wings tattered). Scale loss may approximate age, and wing tatter may indicate distance traveled, damage from mating struggles, or encounters with predators (Frey and Leong 1995; Van Hook 1996; Borland et al., this volume).

Females in reproductive diapause have small ovarioles with no ovarian development (Herman 1973). We examined ovaries for the presence of unyolked, yolked, and mature (chorionated) oocytes, and counted mature oocytes, if present (for details on dissection methods, see Oberhauser and Hampton 1995). Although we measured and report all of the stages in diapause development, we used the presence of mature oocytes as the indication that diapause was completed.

We determined mating status by examining the contents of the bursa copulatrix for spermatophores and spermatophore remains (Van Hook 1996). Thus we had two indicators of mating: mating activity at the time of collection (i.e., "mating" if collected *in copula*) and mating status found at dissection (i.e., "mated" if female had one or more spermatophores).

Experimental design

To establish a baseline on degree of ovarian development and mating status at the time of collection, we dissected a random sample of females from each activity category (active, mating, and roosting) (1996 $n = 20$ each category; 1997 $n = 16$ each). These butterflies were dissected on day 0 of the experiments. Remaining butterflies were used in environmental chamber experiments designed to test the hypothesis that exposure to certain environmental cues (host plant access, increasing daylength, and mating) will stimulate postdiapause ovarian development.

1996 Experiment: Host plant and daylength

In 1996, we tested the effects of photoperiod and access to milkweed on postdiapause reproductive development. Butterflies in the overwintering colony experience a daylength of 11 h and 45 min at the end of February; this increases with time and northward movement. By early April, monarchs in the southern United States (approximately 30° north latitude) experience 12 h and 30 min of daylight, an increase of 45 min or a gain of over 1 min/day. To simulate these changes, we used programmable timers on standard shop fluorescent fixtures with 40-watt fluorescent tubes to control daily light-dark cycles, increasing the amount of daylength 2 min/day. To test the effect of access to milkweed on ovarian development, we used potted *Asclepias curassavica* in host plant treatments and potted *Cassia fasciculata* (partridge pea) in nonhost plant treatments.

We used a 2 × 2 factorial design, testing increasing daylength (12-h : 12-h light-dark +2 min/day) versus constant daylength (12-h : 12-h light-dark), and access to milkweed versus no access. We used two controlled-environment growth chambers (4 × 3 × 2 m), each subdivided with black opaque (157 μm) plastic sheeting to allow two light treatments in the same chamber (2 × 3 × 2 m each). Milkweed and nonmilkweed treatments were in separate chambers.

Sixty females (20 randomly selected from each activity category) and 12 males were put in each treatment, divided evenly into two net cages (0.75 m^3). We kept temperatures at 24 ± 1°C, which is suitable for ovarian development (Barker and Herman 1976; Malcolm et al. 1987). Adults were fed ad libitum from sponges soaking in honey-water (20% honey). Relative humidity was 59 ± 3.3% in the milkweed chamber and 60 ± 2.7% in the nonmilkweed chamber.

To assess ovarian development, we randomly selected one fourth of the females from each activity category on days 1, 3, 7, and 12 for dissection.

1997 Experiment: Host plant and mating

After observing an ad hoc effect of mating on ovarian development in 1996, we explicitly tested the effects of mating in 1997. We omitted the photoperiod treatment after observing no effect of this independent variable but included a host plant access variable. We conducted a 2 × 2 factorial experiment, with access to males versus no access to males, and potted *Asclepias physocarpa* for host plant treatments versus potted *Leucanthemum x superbum* (chrysanthemum) in nonhost plant treatments. Temperature and humidity were the same as in 1996, and the photoperiod was 12-h : 12-h light-dark.

We used 63 females in each treatment (21 randomly selected from each activity category) and 40 males in mating treatments. To keep cage densities relatively even, we divided mating treatments into two cages. We recorded mating daily. Butterflies were fed as before, and temperature and humidity were similar to those in the previous experiment. On days 2, 4, 6, and 8, we dissected one fourth of the females from each activity category. We dissected these as before with the exception of more precise examination of the bursa copulatrix to count the number of spermatophores present.

Statistical analyses

We assessed postdiapause development by the presence or absence of mature oocytes (a yes/no, or binary, variable) and used stepwise analysis of deviance and logistic regression models to examine the relationship between oocyte presence and the independent variables of subpopulation, butterfly size and wing condition, mating status, and experimental treatment (Hardy and Field 1998; K. Chaloner, pers. comm.). Probabilities of 0.05 or less indicate statistical significance.

RESULTS

Baseline condition

Figure 23.1 shows the degree of ovarian development in females before the experimental treatments. In both years, most females had undeveloped ovaries at the time of collection: 70% in 1996 and 92% in 1997. Ovarian development differed between activity category as well as between years. Females collected *in copula* were more likely to contain oocytes than roosting or active females, and fewer females showed any degree of ovarian development in 1997 even though we collected them 5 days later that year.

In both years, many females were mated at the time of collection (figure 23.2): 54% in 1996 and 25% in 1997 (spermatophores received during the mating in progress for females collected *in copula* were not included in the data illustrated in figure 23.2). The proportion of females that had mated previously differed between activity categories, as did mating frequency. Butterflies collected *in copula* were more likely to have mated previously and more frequently in both years.

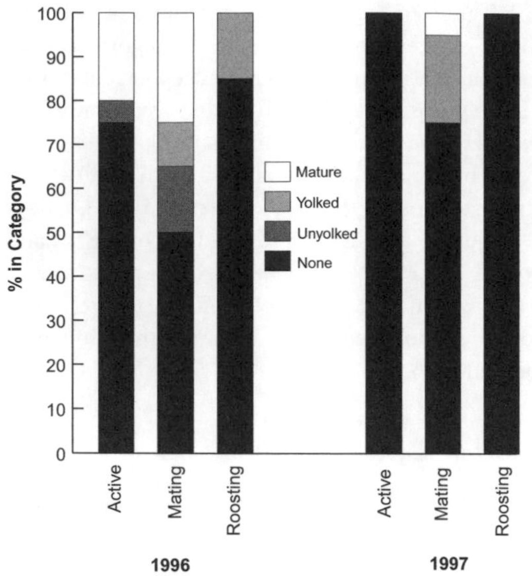

Figure 23.1. Oocyte presence in "baseline" active, mating, and roosting females. Females collected while mating were more likely to contain oocytes than were other females (1996: Kruskall-Wallis [KW] statistic H = 9.013, df = 2, p = 0.011; 1997: H = 8.53, df = 2, p = 0.014). Females collected in 1996 were more likely to contain oocytes than were those collected in 1997 (χ^2 corrected for continuity = 6.44, p = 0.011).

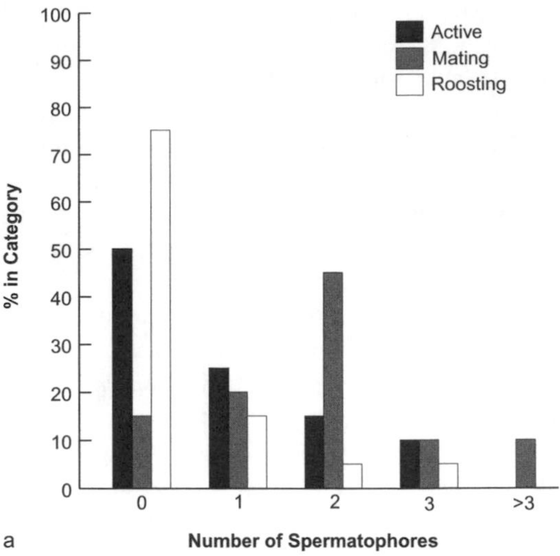

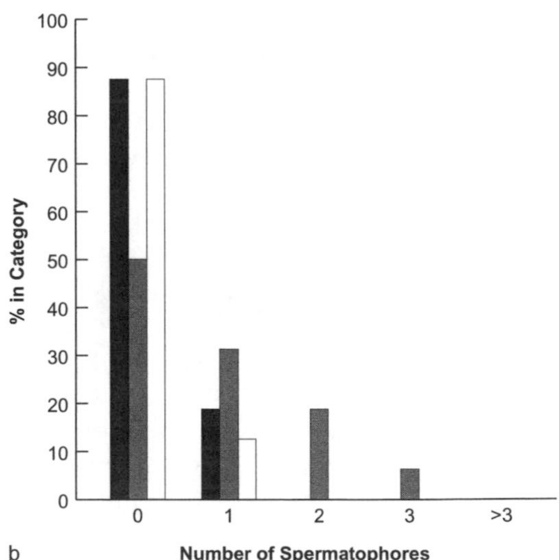

Figure 23.2. Mating history by activity at the time of collection in "baseline" females in (a) 1996 and (b) 1997. Females collected while mating were more likely to have mated previously (1996: H = 13.5, df = 2, p = 0.001; 1997: H = 7.83, df = 2, p = 0.020) and more frequently (1996: χ^2 = 20.62, df = 2, p < 0.001; 1997: χ^2 = 13.57, df = 2, p = 0.001) than were other females.

Figure 23.3 shows the degree of ovarian development for baseline females by mating status at the time of collection, with all activity categories combined. Given the small degree of ovarian development, there is not sufficient power to test for a relationship between mating status and ovarian development. However, there is an association between mating status and the presence of any oocytes. In 1997, mated females were significantly more likely to show some degree of ovarian development than nonmated females. This relationship was almost statistically significant in 1996 (figure 23.3).

We tested for relationships between wing condition and the degree of ovarian development; given the minimal ovarian development in 1997, we analyzed only 1996 baseline data. There is a suggestion that females with more scale loss had more developed ovaries, although this relationship was not statistically significant (correlation coefficient r_s = 0.1612, t = 1.24, df = 58, p = 0.11). There is a significant correlation between wing tatter and ovarian development (correlation coefficient r_s = 0.3829, t = 3.16, df = 58, p = 0.001). Wing tatter was not greater than expected in mated females (Kruskall-Wallis [KW] statistic H = 1.99, df = 1, p = 0.158) or greater with increased mating frequency (KW statistic H = 4.85, df = 4, p = 0.435).

Postdiapause reproductive development

In the following description, it is important to distinguish different mating categories. In 1996, all experimental females were kept in cages with males. However, they did not all mate during the experiment. In 1997, half of the experimental females had access to males (the mating *treatments*), but not all females in these treatments actually mated. In addition, since females were randomly assigned to treatments, some females in all treatments had mated before they were collected (their mating *status*).

Photoperiod and host plant access

Figure 23.4 illustrates the progression of ovarian development for 1996 females. Across all treatments, 59% (36/61) of the females had some degree of ovarian development after 1 day, compared with 30% (see figure 23.1) of the females from the baseline group. By days 7 and 12, over 77% and 100% had mature oocytes, respectively. Although our experimental design did not explicitly test for an effect of mating, we determined whether females had mated when we dissected them and included their mating status as a predictor in our model. Table 23.1 summarizes the analysis of postdiapause ovarian development, as measured by the presence of mature oocytes. In addition to the experimental variables of photoperiod and host plant access, we tested the effects of activity at the time of collection, mating status, mass, and wing length. The most parsimonious model for predicting mature oocyte presence includes days in treatment, mating status, and access to milkweed. The odds of full reproductive development in mated females, given access to milkweed, are 11 times the odds for unmated females. The odds of reproductive development in females with access to milkweed, given having mated, are 5 times the odds for females without access to milkweed. There were no significant effects of photoperiod, activity at collection, mass, or wing length.

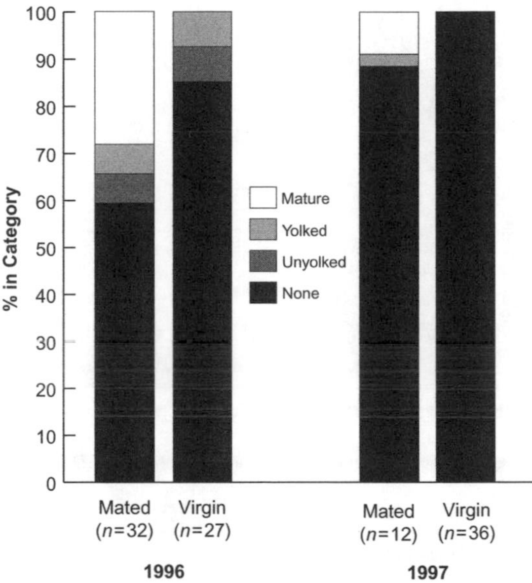

Figure 23.3. Degree of ovarian development in "baseline" mated and virgin females. Mated females were more likely to contain oocytes than were virgin females (1996: χ^2 corrected for continuity = 3.58, p = 0.06; 1997: Fisher exact test p = 0.0025).

Host plant access and mating

Figure 23.5 shows the progression of ovarian development in 1997. A greater proportion of females with access to milkweed and males developed mature oocytes than did those without access to milkweed or males. A large proportion of those in treatments without milkweed or males were still undeveloped 6 days into the experiment, and the majority contained only yolked oocytes by the end of the experiment. Other treatments reveal intermediate patterns of ovarian development.

Table 23.2 summarizes the analysis of postdiapause ovarian development in the 1997 experiment.

Table 23.1. Effect of milkweed access and photoperiod on mature oocyte development

Predictor		Coefficient	SE	*p* value	Log-odds	95% CI
Constant		−4.681	0.666	<0.0001		
Days in treatment		0.530	0.081	<0.0001	1.70	1.45–1.99
Mated		2.357	0.499	<0.0001	10.56	3.97–28.07
Access to host plant		1.557	0.423	0.0002	4.74	2.07–10.87
Deviance	159.57					
df	218					

Note: Summary of binomial regression model for 1996 experiment. SE, standard error; CI, confidence interval.

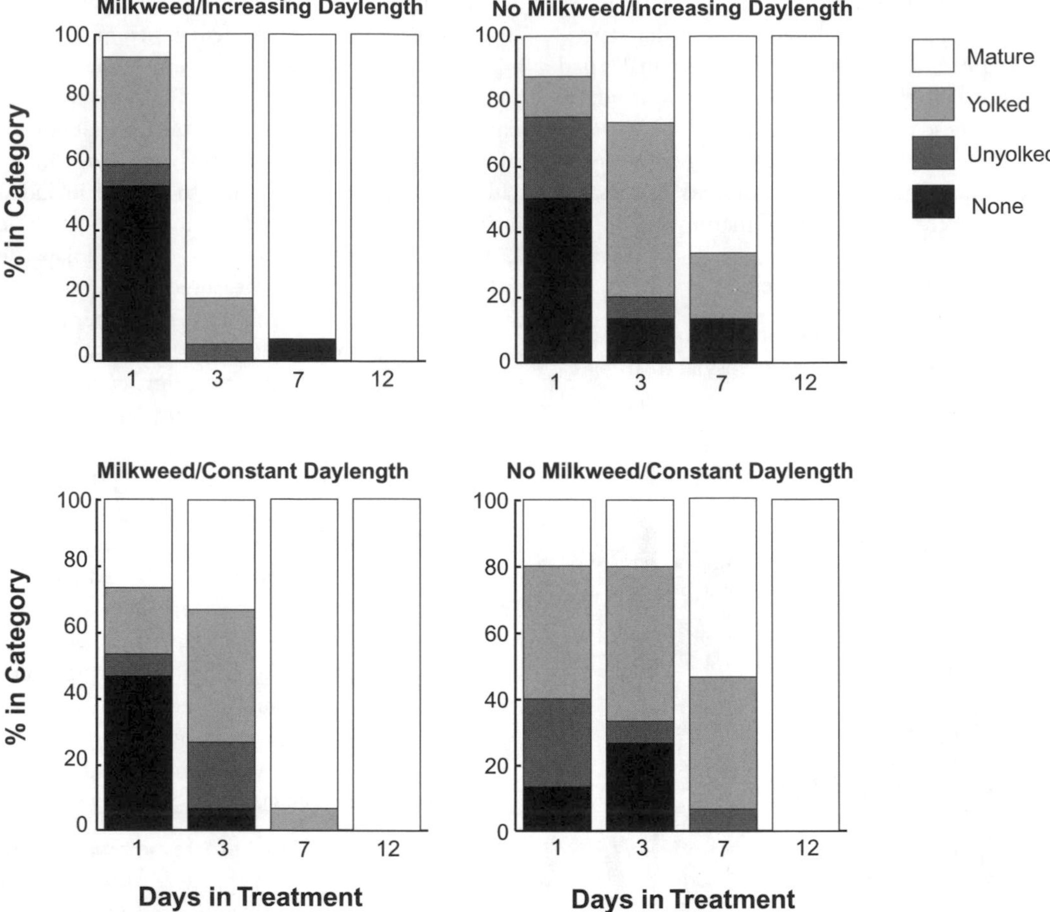

Figure 23.4. Degree of ovarian development over time in each treatment of photoperiod and host plant experiment (1996).

Table 23.2. Effect of milkweed and mating access on mature oocyte development

Predictor		Coefficient	SE	*p* value	Log-odds	95% CI
Constant		−26,213.0	3,895.9	<0.001		
Days in treatment		0.7383	0.110	<0.001	2.18	1.74–2.73
Access to host plant		2.919	0.459	<0.001	19.60	7.79–49.35
Mated		1.826	0.399	<0.001	6.42	2.88–14.3
Activity at time of collection		1.155	0.418	0.006	3.17	1.40–7.21
Deviance	178.29					
df	237					

Note: Summary of binomial regression model for 1997 experiment. SE, standard error; CI, confidence interval.

We tested the effects of access to milkweed and males, activity at the time of collection, mating status, mass, and wing length. The resulting model includes days in treatment, access to milkweed, mating status, and activity at the time of collection. Access to milkweed had the greatest effect on postdiapause ovarian development, followed by mating status and activity at the time of collection. Figure 23.6 shows the proportion of females with mature oocytes over time by milkweed treatment and

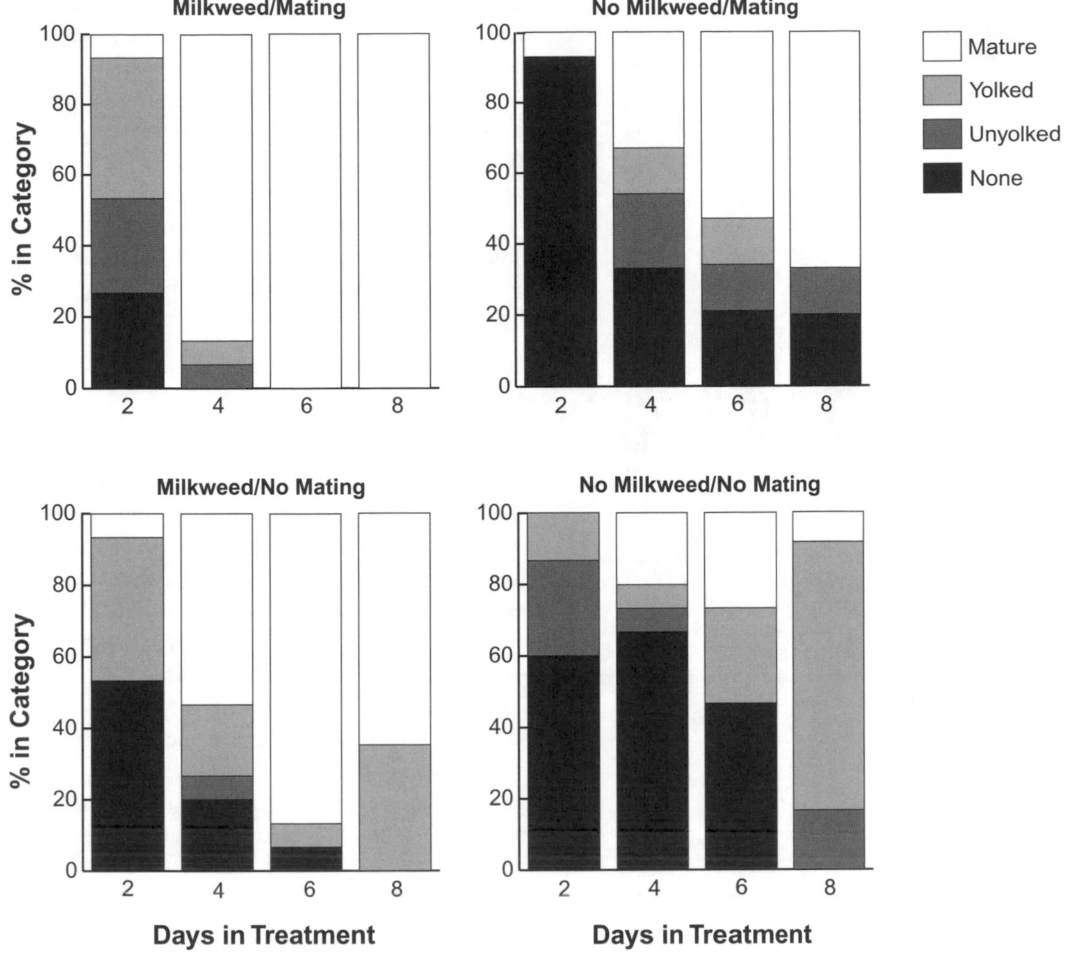

Figure 23.5. Degree of ovarian development over time in each treatment of mating and milkweed experiment (1997).

mating status. Most unmated females without access to milkweed remained undeveloped.

These variables are not independent. Access to milkweed has an effect on the probability of mating within the experiment. In treatments with males, more females mated when milkweed was present than when it was not present: 55 (89%) of 62 and 43 (72%) of 60, respectively, $\chi^2 = 5.6$, $p = 0.018$. They also mated more frequently (table 23.3, KW statistic $H = 20.66$, $p < 0.001$). Although some matings occurred prior to collection, the frequency of mating prior to collection was not different between milkweed and nonmilkweed treatments (25% and 23%, respectively, $\chi^2 = 0.11$, $p = 0.741$).

Table 23.3. Mating frequency in milkweed versus nonmilkweed treatments

No. of spermatophores	Milkweed treatments	Nonmilkweed treatments
0	7	17
1	11	22
2	19	16
3	10	4
>3	15	1

Note: Only females in treatments with males are included.

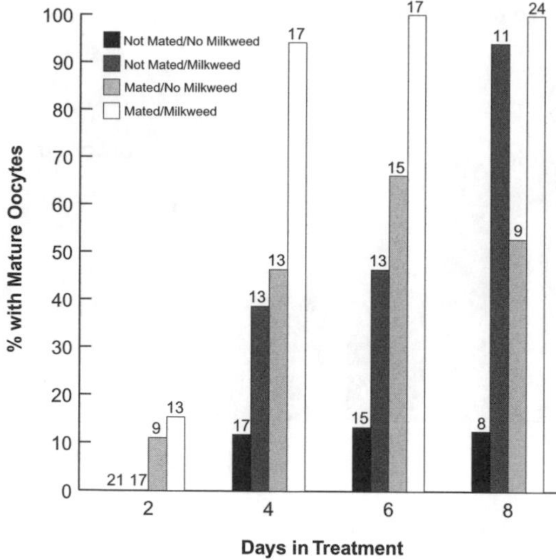

Figure 23.6. Effect of mating and milkweed on mature oocyte production over time in the mating and milkweed experiment. The numbers over the columns represent the number of females in each sample. Females were put into a category depending on their actual mating status, since some females held without males had already mated in the colonies, which does not always match their mating treatment.

DISCUSSION

Diapause development is a progressive physiological process. While diapause induction is initiated in response to particular cues (e.g., Goehring and Oberhauser 2002), diapause development typically follows a predetermined course not necessarily terminated by specific cues (Tauber et al. 1986). The progression may be influenced by external factors that speed the completion of diapause, and response to these factors often varies as a function of diapause intensity. Given the wide geographic range and environmental conditions experienced by North American monarchs, diapause intensity is likely to be variable, making characterization of diapause development complex.

Monarchs used in this study were collected during the last third of the overwintering period, a time of increasing mating activity. Mating dynamics change dramatically during the overwintering period, from very little mating in early November to mass mating during the last 6 weeks in the Mexican colonies (Brower et al. 1977; Brower 1985; Calvert and Brower 1986; Van Hook 1996). The onset of mating is quite consistent from year to year; mass mating begins in mid-February and increases until monarchs disperse from the overwintering sites (Van Hook 1996). Although mating marks the end of diapause in males, it does not necessarily signify the same in females because they can be forced to mate. Females with undeveloped ovaries during this period either may be nearing completion of diapause or are in a postdiapause quiescence awaiting suitable conditions for reproduction.

Status of diapause development and mating at the time of collection

In both years, most females showed no ovarian development at the time of collection. Herman and coauthors (1989) reported similar findings for monarchs obtained in March 1983 and 1984 from two Mexican sites. However, we found that oogenesis had commenced in some females in late February and early March. Females with ovarian development were most likely to be collected while mating (see figure 23.1) or to have mated prior to collection (see figure 23.3), suggesting an association between ovarian development and mating. However, 15% of unmated females in 1996 showed ovarian development, indicating that mating is not required for postdiapause development.

The fact that more females in our samples had produced oocytes in 1996 than in 1997 suggests that females were further along in postdiapause development in 1996, even though they were collected earlier. Previous work has shown that the course of diapause is primarily influenced by temperature (Hodek 1983; Tauber et al. 1986; Danks 1987); unfortunately temperature data were not available for comparison.

Postdiapause ovarian development in experimental treatments

Ovarian development progressed rapidly under experimental conditions. While a significant proportion of females without access to milkweed or males remained undeveloped, most of those exposed to milkweed and allowed to mate developed mature oocytes within 3 days (see figures 23.4 to 23.6). This rapid development suggests that females were in a state of postdiapause quiescence (Tauber et al. 1986) awaiting stimuli to activate and accelerate postdiapause morphogenesis. Mating and access to milkweed appear to serve as such stimuli.

Given the importance of synchronizing reproduction with host plant availability, it is not surprising that milkweed is an external stimulus for postdiapause development in monarchs. Similarly, the presence of host plant *Vigna unguiculata* pods stimulate diapause termination in the seed beetle *Bruchidius atrolineatus* (Lenga et al. 1993; Tran et al. 1993; Glitho et al. 1996), as does host plant presence for the leek moth, *Acrolepiopsis assectella* (Abo-Ghalia and Thibout 1983).

Although mating has been shown to stimulate the rate of nondiapause oocyte production in monarchs, it is not required for oogenesis (Herman and Barker 1977; Oberhauser and Hampton 1995; for other insects, see review in Barth and Lester 1973). Few studies have assessed the effect of mating on postdiapause ovarian development (review in Danks 1987). In *A. assectella,* Abo-Ghalia and Thibout (1983) found that along with host plant presence, mating significantly increases the postdiapause mean number of oocytes, and that these factors have a synergistic effect. In our study, mating was associated with postdiapause oogenesis, both in the baseline analysis and in the experimental treatments. However, our results do not allow us to distinguish whether mating stimulates diapause completion or if it just results in faster postdiapause development.

Photoperiod

Although photoperiod has been shown to affect diapause completion, it does not usually affect postdiapause development (e.g., McNeil and Fields 1985; Tanaka and Sadoyama 1997). An increasing daylength, simulating that experienced by northward migrants, did not affect monarch postdiapause ovarian development in our 1996 experiment. Photoperiod may affect diapause termination, but our study did not address that question.

Variation in diapause development

Given the effect of mating on postdiapause ovarian development, it is instructive to consider male diapause development. While the course of insect diapause is influenced by environmental conditions experienced by both sexes, it does not always proceed identically in males and females. In general, it has been postulated that given the greater energy requirement to maintain eggs versus sperm and the smaller metabolic change required to enter diapause in males, male diapause is usually less intense and of shorter duration (Danks 1987). In monarchs, diapause appears to last longer in females than males (Herman 1981; Lessman and Herman 1983; Herman et al. 1989). Wiklund and colleagues (1992) proposed that the difference in the timing of diapause between sexes is an example of protandry, where males are expected to benefit by emerging or being ready to mate before females; Nylin and coworkers (1995) suggested this is the case in overwintering monarchs. Males may complete diapause earlier and begin mating at the overwintering sites to maximize their number of matings.

Diapause termination typically occurs over a considerable time span subject to individual and environmental variation, even in species with synchronous cohorts. Overwintering populations of monarchs are composed of individuals coming from a wide geographic area, subjected to a wide range of environmental conditions. The range of physiological ages and diapause intensities could lead to an even greater span of time for diapause termination. In addition, there are probably complicated relationships among postdiapause development and mating. The fact that females with access to milkweed mated more suggests that females may be more amenable to male mating attempts when they contain mature oocytes.

While the factors that trigger the development of diapause in monarchs remain to be determined, our results suggest that postdiapause reproductive development is strongly influenced by external factors such as host plant availability and mating, serving to synchronize reproduction with the seasonal availability of breeding habitat.

Acknowledgments

We thank Alfonso Alonso-Mejía, Eduardo Rendón Salinas, and Eneida Montesinos-Patiño for the many ways they helped with this work; Tonya Van Hook for important insights on sampling; Michelle Prysby, Kari Geurtz, and Sonia Altizer for help in collection; Amy Alstad and Leah Alstad for help measuring and recording data; and Imants Pone for laboratory assistance. This work was supported in part by a National Science Foundation grant to K. Oberhauser (DEB-9220829), Monarchs in the Classroom, and a James W. Wilkie Award to L. Goehring.

References

Abo-Ghalia, A., and E. Thibout. 1983. The influence of the host plant (*Allium porrum*) on the reproductive activity of the female leek moth, *Acrolepiopsis assectella*, after the termination of its reproductive diapause. Entomol. Exp. Appl. 33:188–94.

Andrewartha, H. C. 1952. Diapause in relation to the ecology of insects. Biol. Rev. 27:50–107.

Barker, J. F., and W. S. Herman. 1976. Effect of photoperiod and temperature on reproduction of the monarch butterfly, *Danaus plexippus*. J. Insect Physiol. 22:1565–68.

Barth, R. H., and L. J. Lester. 1973. Neuro-hormonal control of sexual behavior in insects. Annu. Rev. Entomol. 18:445–72.

Brower, L. P. 1985. New perspectives on the migration biology of the monarch butterfly, *Danaus plexippus* L. In M. A. Rankin, ed., Migration: mechanisms and adaptive significance, pp. 748–85. Contributions in Marine Science, Vol. 27 Suppl. Port Aransas, Texas: Marine Science Institute, University of Texas at Austin.

Brower, L. P., W. H. Calvert, L. E. Hendrick, and J. Christian. 1977. Biological observations of an overwintering colony of monarch butterflies (*Danaus plexippus*, Danaidae) in Mexico. J. Lepid. Soc. 31:232–42.

Calvert, W. H., and L. P. Brower. 1986. The location of monarch butterfly (*Danaus plexippus* L.) overwintering colonies in Mexico in relation to topography and climate. J. Lepid. Soc. 40:164–87.

Danks, H. V. 1987. Insect dormancy: an ecological perspective. Ottawa: Entomological Society of Canada.

Frey, D. F., and K. L. H. Leong. 1995. Reply to Nylin, Wickman and Wiklund regarding sex ratios of California overwintering monarch butterflies. Anim. Behav. 49:515–18.

Glitho, I. A., A. Lenga, D. Pierre, and J. Huignard. 1996. Changes in the responsiveness during two phases of diapause termination in *Bruchidius atrolineatus* Pic (Coleoptera: Bruchidae). J. Insect Physiol. 42:953–60.

Goehring, L., and K. S. Oberhauser. 2002. Effects of photoperiod, temperature and host plant age on induction of reproductive diapause and development time in *Danaus plexippus*. Ecol. Entomol. 27:674–85.

Hardy, I. C., and S. A. Field. 1998. Logistic analysis of animal contests. Anim. Behav. 56:787–92.

Herman, W. S. 1973. The endocrine basis of reproductive inactivity in monarch butterflies overwintering in central California. J. Insect Physiol. 19:1883–87.

Herman, W. S. 1981. Studies on the adult reproductive diapause of the monarch butterfly, *Danaus plexippus*. Biol. Bull. 160:89–106.

Herman, W. S., and J. F. Barker. 1977. Effect of mating on monarch butterfly oogenesis. Experientia 33:688–89.

Herman, W. S., L. P. Brower, and W. H. Calvert. 1989. Reproductive tract development in monarch butterflies overwintering in California and Mexico. J. Lepid. Soc. 43:50–58.

Hodek, I. 1983. Role of environmental factors and endogenous mechanisms in the seasonality of reproduction in insects diapausing as adults. In K. V. Brown and I. Hodek, eds., Diapause and life cycle strategies in insects, pp. 9–33. The Hague: Junk.

James, D. G. 1982. Ovarian dormancy in *Danaus plexippus* (L.) (Lepidoptera Nymphalidae)—oligopause not diapause. J. Aust. Entomol. Soc. 21:31–35.

Leather, S. R., K. F. A. Walters, and J. S. Bale. 1993. The ecology of insect overwintering. Cambridge: Cambridge University Press.

Lenga, A., I. Glitho, and J. Huignard. 1993. Interactions between photoperiod, relative humidity and host-plant cues on the reproductive diapause termination in *Bruchidius atrolineatus* Pic (Coleoptera Bruchidae). Invertebr. Reprod. Dev. 24:87–96.

Lessman, C. A., and W. S. Herman. 1983. Seasonal variation in hemolymph juvenile hormone of adult monarchs *Danaus p. plexippus* (Lepidoptera). Can. J. Zool. 61:88–94.

Malcolm, S. B., B. J. Cockrell, and L. P. Brower. 1987. Monarch butterfly voltinism: effects of temperature constraints at different latitudes. Oikos 49:77–82.

McNeil, J. N., and P. G. Fields. 1985. Seasonal diapause development and diapause termination in the European skipper, *Thymelicus lineola* Ochs. J. Insect Physiol. 31:467–70.

Nijhout, H. F. 1994. Insect hormones. Princeton: Princeton University Press.

Nylin, S., P. Wickman, and C. Wiklund. 1995. An adaptive explanation for male-biased sex ratios in overwintering monarch butterflies. Anim. Behav. 49:511–14.

Oberhauser, K. S., and R. Hampton. 1995. The relationship between mating and oogenesis in monarch butterflies (Lepidoptera: Danainae). J. Insect Behav. 8:701–13.

Tanaka, S., and Y. Sadoyama. 1997. Photoperiodic termination of diapause in field-collected adults of the Bombay locust, *Nomadacris succincta* (Orthoptera: Acrididae) in southern Japan. Bull. Entomol. Res. 87:533–39.

Tauber, M. J., C. A. Tauber, and S. Masaki. 1986. Seasonal adaptations of insects. New York: Oxford University Press.

Tran, B., J. Darquenne, and J. Huignard. 1993. Changes in responsiveness to factors inducing diapause termination in *Bruchus rufimanus* Boh. (Coleoptera: Bruchidae). J. Insect Physiol. 38:769–74.

Urquhart, F. A., and N. R. Urquhart. 1976. The overwintering site of the eastern population of the monarch butterfly (*Danaus p. plexippus*; Danaidae) in southern Mexico. J. Lepid. Soc. 30:153–58.

Van Hook, T. 1993. Non-random mating in monarch butterflies overwintering in Mexico. In S. B. Malcolm and M. P. Zalucki, eds., Biology and conservation of the monarch butterfly, pp. 49–60. Los Angeles: Natural History Museum of Los Angeles County.

Van Hook, T. 1996. Monarch butterfly mating ecology at a Mexican overwintering site: proximate causes of non-random mating. Ph.D. thesis, University of Florida, Gainesville.

Wiklund, C., P. Wickman, and S. Nylin. 1992. A sex difference in the propensity to enter direct/diapause development: a result of selection for protandry. Evolution 46:519–28.

PART IV

Integrated Biology

24

Modeling the Distribution and Abundance of Monarch Butterflies

Karen S. Oberhauser

THE COMPLEXITY OF THE MONARCHS' ANNUAL CYCLE

Monarch butterflies utilize diverse habitats spanning most of temperate North America during their annual migratory cycle, and populations fluctuate dramatically within and between years. In the course of an annual cycle—which includes breeding in the United States and southern Canada, migrating over a broad latitudinal range, and overwintering in central Mexico and coastal California—monarchs exhibit micro-scale movement as foraging larvae; meso-scale movement as foraging, breeding, and overwintering adults; and macro-scale movement as adult migrants (Ackery and Vane-Wright 1984; Vane-Wright 1993). During each of these stages, the distribution and abundance of monarchs are affected by both current environmental conditions and events that occurred during preceding stages. For example, the numbers of monarchs in Minnesota in June may be affected by weather conditions in Texas during April and May, since these monarchs probably spent their egg, larva, pupa, and early adult stages far south of Minnesota. A late freeze in Minnesota (not unheard of in June!) will also affect monarch populations, as will monarch or milkweed diseases, other milkweed-consuming herbivores, and monarch predators. In addition to these natural factors, monarch populations are vulnerable to land use change (Malcolm and Zalucki 1993; Hoth et al. 1999) and, owing to their susceptibility to temperature extremes, human-induced climatic change (Rawlins and Lederhouse 1981; Zalucki 1982; Malcolm et al. 1987; Zalucki and Rochester 1999; York and Oberhauser 2002).

These factors require that the study of monarch populations involve a large range of temporal and spatial scales, and a variety of research approaches including laboratory, field, and mathematical studies. The first three sections of this book presented results of empirical studies conducted in the laboratory and the field. These studies were designed to document, and in some cases explain, how monarchs interact with their environment throughout their annual cycle of breeding, migrating, and overwintering. In this section, we present chapters that have combined empirical data with mathematical models to further our understanding of the population dynamics of monarchs.

ECOLOGICAL MODELS

The study of ecology involves trying to understand the interactions of many systems and environments, and these interactions are often too complex to understand simply by documenting patterns and following our intuition about the causes of these patterns. When this is the case, a clear analysis requires a simple and explicit mathematical presentation. Ecologists use mathematical models to help understand the complex patterns and processes that link all of the parts of ecological systems. While models almost always involve intentional simplifications of ecological patterns, they force us to state clearly our assumptions about these patterns and their causes and consequences. They can be used to tell us what could happen in a system given changes in the living or nonliving environment, what factors are likely to be most important in causing observed patterns, and in some cases, what else we need to know to better understand the patterns we observe.

Scientists have used mathematical models to explain ecological patterns since the eighteenth century, although early modeling focused on human populations. In his essay on population, Malthus (1798) used simple mathematics to show that although numbers of organisms can increase exponentially (e.g., 1, 2, 4, 8, 16, . . .), their food supply is unlikely to do the same. Thus, he reasoned that reproduction must eventually be checked by food supply. This kind of mathematical reasoning spawned an interest in the study of population growth rates. Other early models looked at relationships between organisms; pioneering work by Ross (1908, 1911) used mathematical models to explain the propagation of malaria in mosquitoes and humans. Malthus, Ross, and others made explicit assumptions about how important features of the environment interacted, and then constructed mathematical equations to model these interactions.

The science of ecology is advanced by a better understanding of the ways in which organisms interact with their environment. Mathematical modeling is one methodology for precisely defining such interactions and for defining relationships that can be tested against observed data. Thus the relationships defined by ecological models have both basic and applied importance. From an applied perspective, models allow us to test hypotheses related to the impact of various factors on population dynamics. For example, we could use models to assess the potential effect of anthropogenic changes in land use and agricultural practices on monarch populations, or to predict potential impacts of future changes in climate. Models can help identify factors that affect monarchs during each period of their annual cycle, and additional research required for a more complete understanding of the population dynamics of these butterflies. Understanding these factors will benefit policy makers concerned with conservation, members of the public with an interest in monarch biology and conservation, and industries whose activities may affect monarch populations.

POPULATION MODELS

Chapter 25 by Altizer and colleagues follows the work of Malthus and other ecologists who model how populations change over time. Altizer and coworkers studied a protozoan parasite called *Ophryocystis elektroscirrha* that has negative effects on the fitness of monarchs (Altizer and Oberhauser 1999) and is usually transmitted from mothers to their offspring. Theory predicts that parasites that are only transmitted from mothers to offspring should not harm their hosts, since their success depends on the reproductive success of these hosts. The researchers combined empirical work (measuring the rates of transmission of *O. elektroscirrha* from male and female monarchs to their offspring) and mathematical modeling to understand the factors that might allow this parasite to persist in monarch populations. The chapter represents an exciting combination of lab, field, and mathematical work to understand basic questions about monarch populations, and is an important contribution to our understanding of disease dynamics in general. The model is clearly a simplification; in a natural environment, a multitude of factors will play an important role in determining abundance. However, this study helps us to understand how *O. elektroscirrha* can have negative consequences on fitness and still persist in monarch populations, and how the parasite might affect the abundance of monarchs.

Whereas Chapter 24 helps us to understand abundance, the other two chapters in this section focus on the distribution of monarchs. Zalucki and Rochester, and Feddema and coauthors use knowledge of monarch growth and development, flight speeds, and weather patterns over large scales to indicate where and when monarchs are expected to occur. Zalucki and Rochester's model (Chapter 26) predicts the effects of weather and arrival times of monarchs from Mexico on the timing and synchrony of spring and summer generations. The model incorporates data collected by many researchers on monarch development under different climatic conditions, arrival times at different locations, and temperature conditions that are lethal to monarchs. By simulating monarch development throughout the North American range using data from hundreds of weather stations, the model predicts the proportion of the monarch population that is in each life stage at each location throughout the season. Not surprisingly, the model suggests that climate should have an important influence on the distribution of monarchs, with large differences in the timing of the relative abundance of different monarch stages across years and space. Zalucki and Rochester used actual data to test the model and found that it correctly predicted the timing of monarch generations across several years. While factors such as the abundance and density of milkweed and the presence of predators will also affect monarch numbers, by narrowing the scope of the model to weather alone, Zalucki and Rochester are able to make simple predictions about the likely exposure of monarchs to potential risks such as those imposed by changes in agricultural practices.

Whereas Rochester and Zalucki model when and where monarchs are expected to occur based on local conditions, Feddema and coworkers (Chapter 27) model monarch movement explicitly. They simulated spring and fall migration, using information on when and whether monarchs leave and arrive at given locations as a function of meteorological and seasonal conditions. In addition to simulating movement, the model predicts the number of generations that are produced each year, based on temperature. Users can input many parameters, such as the daily distance traveled by monarchs as they migrate, the number of degree-days required for each stage of development, and the number of days that female monarchs lay eggs. By varying the value of each parameter and observing the sensitivity of the model's output to this variation, we can learn which features might be most important in determining the distribution and abundance of these butterflies. The inclusion of so many parameters in the model helps us to understand how several environmental factors affect population dynamics, and provides more realism than simpler models that include only a few features of the environment. A potential drawback of this complexity is that the effects of one parameter may depend on the values of other parameters.

Real data are important to ecological models. Data collected in both field and laboratory studies allow us to use realistic values in our models, and also to test model output. Of particular note in models of monarch distribution is the use of data collected by volunteer citizen scientists. Monarch Watch (Taylor 1999; Monarch Watch 2002), Texas Monarch Watch (Calvert and Wagner 1999), Journey North (Journey North 2002; Howard and Davis, this volume), and the Monarch Larva Monitoring Project (Monarch Larva Monitoring Project 2002; Prysby and Oberhauser, this volume) all involve members of the public in long-term, large-scale data collection efforts, and result in data that will continue to allow us to develop realistic models and provide a means to test their validity.

Modeling monarch populations is an important exercise, and the models presented here represent an exciting beginning. More comprehensive models of the population dynamics of monarchs over large spatial and temporal scales are possible, and we hope that future models incorporate their biology and ecology; the phenology, abundance, and distribution of milkweed; the dynamics of vegetation; and climate. These models will be interesting for their own sake, but will be of paramount importance in gauging the impact of biotic and abiotic influences, including patterns of land use and anthropogenic climate change, on the stability of monarch populations.

References

Ackery, P. R., and R. I. Vane-Wright. 1984. Milkweed butterflies: their cladistics and biology. Ithaca, N.Y.: Cornell University Press.

Altizer, S. M., and K. S. Oberhauser. 1999. Effects of the protozoan parasite *Ophryocystis elektroscirrha* on the fitness of monarch butterflies (*Danaus plexippus*). J. Invertebr. Pathol. 74:76–88.

Calvert, W. H., and M. Wagner. 1999. Patterns in the monarch butterfly migration through Texas—1993–1995. In J. Hoth, L. Merino, K. Oberhauser, I. Pisanty, S. Price, and T. Wilkinson, eds., 1997 North American Conference on the Monarch Butterfly, pp. 119–25. Montreal: Commission for Environmental Cooperation.

Hoth, J., L. Merino, K. Oberhauser, I. Pisanty, S. Price, and T. Wilkinson, eds. 1999. 1997 North American Conference on the Monarch Butterfly. Montreal: Commission for Environmental Cooperation.

Journey North. 2002. Engaging students in a global study of wildlife migration and seasonal change. http://www.learner.org/jnorth/orientation/About.html. Accessed 10 December 2002.

Malcolm, S. B., and M. P. Zalucki. 1993. Biology and conservation of the monarch butterfly. Los Angeles: Natural History Museum of Los Angeles County.

Malcolm, S. B., B. J. Cockrell, and L. P. Brower. 1987. Monarch butterfly voltinism: effects of temperature constraints at different latitudes. Oikos 49:77–82.

Malthus, T. R. 1798. An essay on the principle of population as it affects the future improvement of society. London: Johnson.

Monarch Larva Monitoring Project. 2002. http://www.mlmp.org. Accessed 10 December 2002.

Monarch Watch. 2002. http://www.monarchwatch.org. Accessed 10 December 2002.

Rawlins, J. E., and R. C. Lederhouse. 1981. Developmental influences of thermal behavior on monarch caterpillars (*Danaus plexippus*): an adaptation for migration. J. Kans. Entomol. Soc. 54:387–407.

Ross, R. 1908. Reports on the prevention of malaria in Mauritius. London: Waterloo.

Ross, R. 1911. The prevention of malaria. 2nd ed. London: Waterloo.

Taylor, O. R. 1999. Monarch Watch: education, conservation and research. In J. Hoth, L. Merino, K. Oberhauser, I. Pisanty, S. Price, and T. Wilkinson, eds., 1997 North American Conference on the Monarch Butterfly, pp. 355–60. Montreal: Commission for Environmental Cooperation.

Vane-Wright, R. I. 1993. The Columbus hypothesis: an explanation for the dramatic 19th century range expansion of the monarch butterfly. In S. B. Malcolm and M. P. Zalucki, eds., Biology and conservation of the monarch butterfly, pp. 179–88. Los Angeles: Natural History Museum of Los Angeles County.

York, H., and K. S. Oberhauser. 2002. Effects of temperature stress on monarch (*Danaus plexippus* L.) development. J. Kans. Entomol. Soc. 75:290–98.

Zalucki, M. P. 1982. Temperature and rate of development in *Danaus plexippus* L. and *D. chrysippus*. L. J. Aust. Entomol. Soc. 21:241–46.

Zalucki, M. P., and W. A. Rochester. 1999. Estimating the effect of climate on the distribution and abundance of *Danaus plexippus*: a tale of two continents. In J. Hoth, L. Merino, K. Oberhauser, I. Pisanty, S. Price, and T. Wilkinson, eds., 1997 North American Conference on the Monarch Butterfly, pp. 151–63. Montreal: Commission for Environmental Cooperation.

25

Transmission of the Protozoan Parasite *Ophryocystis elektroscirrha* in Monarch Butterfly Populations: Implications for Prevalence and Population-Level Impacts

Sonia M. Altizer, Karen S. Oberhauser, and Kari A. Geurts

INTRODUCTION

Insect parasites are transmitted in a variety of ways, but few studies have quantified the relative importance of different transmission modes to parasite maintenance in natural populations (Fine 1975; Lipsitch et al. 1995; Kover et al. 1997). Mathematical models and empirical studies predict that different transmission modes have major implications for both disease spread and the evolution of parasite virulence (e.g., Ewald 1994; Herre 1995; Lockhart et al. 1996; Thrall et al. 1998). For example, parasites transmitted by direct or indirect social contact (horizontal transmission) require a threshold density of susceptible hosts to invade and persist, but parasites spread by other types of horizontal transmission, such as sexual contact or biting vectors, may persist at low host densities (Getz and Pickering 1983; Anderson and May 1991; Thrall et al. 1993; Thrall and Antonovics 1997). Parasites with vertical (parent to offspring) transmission are predicted to lack a host-density threshold for invasion, but will fail to spread if they have even minor negative effects on host fitness (Fine 1975; Lipsitch et al. 1995; Altizer and Augustine 1997). This is because maternally infected lineages decline to extinction if infected females experience decreased survival or reproductive success.

In general, negative effects of parasites on host survival (i.e., virulence) will remove diseased hosts from the population and decrease transmission opportunities that are necessary for disease spread. Therefore, parasites with high virulence should spread only when host density and transmission opportunities are high (Ewald 1983; Lenski and May 1994; Levin 1996). Parasites that are transmitted vertically depend on the reproductive success of infected hosts and are predicted to evolve toward lower virulence (Herre 1993; Lipsitch et al. 1995; see Kover and Clay 1998; Kover et al. 1997). However, virulent parasites that utilize both vertical and horizontal transmission can be maintained at high prevalence in host populations even when most new infections are derived from vertical transmission (Lipsitch et al. 1995; Altizer and Augustine 1997).

We investigated transmission of the neogregarine protozoan parasite *Ophryocystis elektroscirrha* in monarch butterflies. Vertical transmission from infected females to their offspring has been suggested as the primary mode of transfer (McLaughlin and Myers 1970; Leong et al. 1997b). Laboratory studies have demonstrated measurable virulence (Altizer and Oberhauser 1999), and some populations show nearly 100% prevalence (Altizer et al. 2000), suggesting that additional transmission routes exist. To examine modes of parasite transmission, we measured the effects of maternal, paternal, and horizontal transmission on the survival and parasite loads of captive monarch butterflies. We then explored the consequences of varying the relative importance of different transmission modes for parasite prevalence and virulence using a deterministic model of disease spread.

Ophryocystis elektroscirrha was first recovered from monarch and queen butterflies in Florida in 1966 (McLaughlin and Myers 1970). New infections occur when parasite spores are ingested by larvae that feed on contaminated eggs or milkweed (McLaughlin and Myers 1970). Following ingestion, spores lyse in the larval gut, and emerging sporozoites penetrate the gut wall, enter the hypoderm, and undergo two phases of asexual replication. After host pupation, the parasite undergoes sexual reproduction and forms dormant spores around the scales of the developing adult butterfly (McLaughlin and Myers 1970). Most spores form on the adult abdomen, although spores also develop on the wings, head, and thorax (Leong et al. 1992). Heavily infected adults have difficulty emerging from their pupal cases and expanding their wings, although adults with low parasite loads appear normal (McLaughlin and Myers 1970; Altizer and Oberhauser 1999). High parasite doses decrease larval survival, butterfly mass, and adult life spans (Altizer and Oberhauser 1999; Altizer 2001).

The prevalence of *O. elektroscirrha* is highly variable among host populations (Leong et al. 1997a; Altizer et al. 2000). Monarchs in southern Florida and Hawaii (nonmigratory populations) bear the highest parasite loads (over 70% heavily infected). Approximately 30% of monarchs from a migratory population in western North America are heavily infected (Leong et al. 1992; Altizer et al. 2000). Similar prevalence (ranging from 10% to 40%) has been reported among monarchs from Australia, Cuba, and northern South America (Altizer et al. 2000). Less than 8% of monarchs from the eastern migratory population (the longest-distance migrants) are heavily infected. Some of these differences among populations have persisted for over 30 years and suggest an association between host ecology, parasite transmission, and prevalence (Altizer et al. 2000).

Differences in parasite prevalence among populations may result from a negative association between migration distance and the survival of infected hosts (Altizer et al. 2000). Alternatively, the relative importance of maternal, paternal, and horizontal transmission might vary among different monarch populations. Maternal transmission occurs when females infect their own offspring by scattering spores on eggs or host plants during oviposition (McLaughlin and Myers 1970). Paternal transmission occurs when spores from infected males are transferred to females during mating. In this case, the females do not become infected themselves but may transmit parasites to their offspring. Horizontal transmission may occur if spores from adults are scattered onto milkweed plants and consumed by unrelated larvae (Vickerman et al. 1999). Populations that breed continuously and reside in one area could experience higher rates of horizontal transmission via spore accumulation on milkweed plants. Other factors that might vary among populations and affect parasite transmission include milkweed phenology, leaf morphology, mating frequency, and interoviposition intervals.

Variation in the relative importance of transmission modes among monarch populations should have important consequences for disease spread and the evolution of parasite virulence. In fact, recent work has shown that parasites from the eastern migratory population are less virulent than those from both the western migratory population and a resident population in southern Florida (Altizer 2001). Higher parasite virulence in populations with little or no migration is expected for at least two reasons: (1) continuously breeding populations should experience greater horizontal and paternal parasite transmission, and (2) infected hosts may experience higher relative mortality in migratory populations.

In this study, we explored the effectiveness of different modes of parasite transmission in generating new infections among captive monarchs. Using a deterministic mathematical model, we then simulated host-parasite dynamics to investigate the relative importance of different transmission modes for parasite prevalence and impacts on host population size.

METHODS

Eggs for all experiments were obtained by enclosing mated females in 0.6-m^3 mosquito-net cages. Caged females were fed ad libitum from sponges soaked in 20% honey-water. Greenhouse-reared, potted milkweed (*Asclepias curassavica*) plants were placed into cages and checked for eggs twice daily, and then were removed or replaced after 20 to 50 eggs had been deposited. Unless otherwise indicated, larvae remained on natal host plants until the late second instar. Plants were then clipped at the base, and larvae were transferred to 11 × 17 × 30-cm plastic, containers with metal window-screen lids, at densities of 10 to 15 larvae/container. Larvae were reared to pupation as described in Altizer and Oberhauser 1999. When all monarchs in a container had pupated, they were moved to another laboratory to prevent contamination of the larval rearing area. After adults emerged and their wings hardened (roughly 6 h after emergence), they were placed in individual glassine envelopes. To minimize accidental infection of larvae, all laboratory surfaces and tools that contacted larvae or adults were sterilized with 95% ethanol, with 20% Clorox bleach, or by autoclaving materials at 122°C for 20 min.

To obtain healthy and infected adults for experimental matings, offspring from wild-captured, uninfected monarchs (examined for parasite presence using the methods we describe later) from east central Minnesota were inoculated with a calibrated dose of 0, 10, or 100 *O. elektroscirrha* spores. Inoculum was prepared and parasite spores were fed to larvae as described in Altizer and Oberhauser 1999. Following inoculation, larvae were transferred to plastic containers and reared to adulthood as already described.

Parasite loads of all adults were evaluated within 48 h after emergence by pressing transparent Scotch tape cut into 1-cm^2 units against the ventral surface of each butterfly's abdomen, and putting the tape onto a microscope slide. All spores on the tape were counted, and butterflies were scored for parasite loads according to the following scale: 0 = no spores, 1 = 1 spore, 2 = 2 to 20 spores, 3 = 21 to 100 spores, 4 = 101 to 1000 spores, and 5 = more than 1000 spores. Parasite loads estimated in this manner are highly correlated ($R^2 = 0.81$) with estimates based on hemacytometer counts of spores from monarch abdomens (Leong et al. 1992; Altizer et al. 2000).

Experiment 1: Measuring maternal and paternal transmission

In June 1995, we examined the effects of transmission mode (maternal or paternal) on the survival and parasite loads of offspring. To obtain healthy and infected parents, each offspring of three wild-caught uninfected females was inoculated with either 0 (control) or 100 spores. We inoculated 40 larvae/treatment and assessed parasite loads on all emerging adults. To measure maternal transmission, we randomly selected 4 heavily infected females to mate with uninfected males (parasite load classes 4 and 5; table 25.1). To measure paternal transmission, 8 uninfected females were selected to mate with infected males (parasite load classes 4 and 5; table 25.1). No experimental monarchs had visible abnormalities due to the parasite infections. It is important to note that by removing parasites to classify infection status in this experiment, we may have biased transmission rates downward.

Matings were accomplished by enclosing pairs of adults in 0.6-m^3 field cages for a maximum of 48 h. We maintained a continuous culture of butterflies from uninfected parents in the laboratory to serve as a control population for measuring "background" laboratory infection rates. Following mating, all females were transferred to separate field cages (sterilized in 20% Clorox bleach) kept outdoors on a concrete surface. Each female was assigned a cage with a single *A. curassavica* plant. To measure maternal transmission, approximately 50 eggs from each infected female were obtained 1 day after mating. Heavily infected females bear 2 to 3 orders of magnitude more spores on their abdomens relative to females that acquire spores from infected males (see

Table 25.1. Matings and parental parasite load class summary for experiment 1

Transmission mode	Parasite load of infected parent	No. of matings	No. of females ovipositing on		
			Day 1	Day 5	Day 10
Maternal	4	2	2		
	5	2	2		
Paternal	4	4	4	3	2
	5	4	4	2	2

Note: Parasite load categories represent approximate $\log_{10}$-transformed counts of abdominal spore density and are described in Methods.

table 25.1). Therefore, to minimize contamination of the study area, we assumed that maternal transmission rates would remain relatively constant over time, and removed heavily infected females from cages after 24 h.

To measure paternal transmission, 25 to 50 eggs from each uninfected female mated to an infected male were obtained on each of days 1, 5, and 10 after mating. Plants were checked twice daily and removed after 20 to 50 eggs had been deposited. New plants were used for each oviposition date, and these were later transferred to the laboratory where larvae were reared as described earlier. Females were kept individually in cages without plants between egg-laying dates. For each female and oviposition date, we measured the proportion of offspring that survived to adulthood and the parasite loads of emerging adults. We also measured adult mass and forewing length (from point of attachment to distal tip) for offspring 1 day after emergence.

Experiment 2: Effects of parasite load and time after mating on paternal transmission

In June 1997, we measured the effects of male parasite load and time since mating on paternal transmission and the transfer of spores to females. To obtain healthy and infected parents, the offspring of 5 wild-captured, uninfected females were divided among the following treatments: control inoculum (uninfected group), low dose (10 spores/larva), and high dose (100 spores/larva). We reared monarchs to adulthood and measured parasite loads in all control treatment adults. For the high- and low-dose parasite treatments, we assessed the mean parasite loads of adults that were not used in mating tests to avoid removing spores from the abdomens of infected males prior to assessing paternal transmission. Thus, unlike experiment 1, we did not artificially reduce parasite loads prior to transmission experiments. We assessed parasite loads on all remaining adults following completion of the experiment.

Three types of matings were divided equally among oviposition cages: a control, low-dose, or high-dose male was placed inside a cage with an uninfected female. Cages were erected outdoors on a concrete surface and checked twice daily. If adults mated within 48 h, the male was removed and assessed for infection status following separation, and the female was transferred to a sterile cage with a potted *A. curassavica* plant. Because we noted a marked decline in paternal transmission between days 1 and 5 after mating in experiment 1, we collected 15 to 30 eggs/female/day for each of 5 days after mating in experiment 2. Females were transferred to sterile cages with fresh plants each day to limit transmission via cage materials. Following oviposition, plants were transferred to the laboratory and larvae were reared as described earlier. We measured the parasite loads of all emerging offspring.

For a different set of 40 mating pairs, we sampled the number of spores transferred to females (rather than paternal transmission to offspring). We used the same protocol described earlier, except that female parasite loads were assessed immediately following mating (table 25.2).

Experiment 3: Horizontal transmission via contaminated plants

In July 1996, we measured horizontal transmission of *O. elektroscirrha* via parasite accumulation on milkweed plants in natural populations. To determine whether horizontal transmission varied among populations, we compared parasite loads of

Table 25.2. Attempted and successful matings for experiment 2

Male parasite treatment	Horizontal transfer		Paternal transmission		No. of females ovipositing on day				
	Attempted matings	Successful matings	Attempted matings	Successful matings	1	2	3	4	5
Control	13	7	26	16	14	13	12	9	5
Low dose	13	6	26	21	15	12	11	7	4
High dose	15	9	27	19	11	11	10	6	5

larvae reared in the laboratory on wild *A. curassavica* from near Miami, Florida; wild *A. syriaca* from Minnesota; and greenhouse-raised *A. curassavica*. Plants from Florida were collected from two fields where wild monarchs were observed ovipositing. Several hundred *A. syriaca* plants were collected from two sites in Minnesota and western Wisconsin where females were observed. Field-collected plants were stored in large plastic bags at 4°C until use.

Two uninfected wild-caught females laid eggs on potted *A. curassavica* plants that were reared in a greenhouse and kept separated from field-collected plants. When larvae reached the second instar, they were transferred to the assigned milkweed treatment and reared as described earlier. We reared four replicate containers (at densities of 15 larvae/container) on each of the three milkweed types, for a total of 60 larvae/treatment. Milkweed stalks were placed in florist tubes and replaced daily. We recorded the proportion of larvae that survived to adulthood and the parasite loads of emerging adults.

Statistical analysis

Chi-square analysis (SPSS 1999) was used to investigate the effects of transmission mode (maternal vs. paternal) and time after mating on offspring mortality and the proportion of offspring that emerged deformed or heavily infected in experiment 1. Analysis of variance (ANOVA; GLM procedure, SAS/STAT 2001) was used to examine the effects of transmission mode, female nested within transmission mode, and time after mating on the parasite loads, mass, and wingspan of offspring in experiments 1 and 2. We used ANOVA to evaluate the effect of milkweed type on parasite loads in experiment 3. Here, we constructed *F* tests using the mean square for the container (nested within milkweed source) term as the denominator, to limit the contribution of the larval rearing environment to differences among treatments. To assess parasite transfer from males to females during mating, we analyzed counts of spore numbers from female abdomens in a two-way ANOVA, using male inoculation treatment (high dose, low dose, or control) and female mating status (whether or not the female mated during her 48 h in the cage with a male) as independent variables. We used Tukey's test (significance level = 0.05) for multiple comparisons among means for significant effects in ANOVA.

RESULTS

Experiment 1: Maternal and paternal parasite transmission

Rates of both maternal and paternal transmission in captive monarchs exceeded 75% for offspring laid 1 day after mating (figure 25.1). Maternally infected offspring were more likely to emerge heavily infected than were paternally infected offspring (figure 25.1a, $\chi^2 = 21.96$, $df = 1$, $p < 0.001$) and also had significantly higher parasite loads (figure 25.1b, table 25.3). Less than 8% of the control monarchs in experiment 1 were infected, with approximately half of the infected subset in spore class 4 or 5. This "background infection rate" is difficult to avoid when heavily infected adults are present in the laboratory.

A higher proportion of maternally infected than paternally infected offspring died before reaching adulthood (see figure 25.1c, $\chi^2 = 9.8$, $df = 1$, $p < 0.002$), and among surviving adults, the progeny of infected females were more likely to emerge with deformed wings than were the offspring of infected males (see figure 25.1d, $\chi^2 = 29.0$, $df = 1$, $p < 0.0001$). Although the wingspan of nondeformed adults was not affected by transmission mode (see table 25.3), offspring from infected females weighed less than those from infected males (0.500 g ± 0.028 standard deviation [SD] vs. 0.531 g ± 0.016 SD, see table 25.3).

For monarchs infected paternally, mortality and infection rates declined significantly with increasing time between mating and oviposition, but the decline in the proportion with crumpled wings was statistically insignificant (proportion heavily infected $\chi^2 = 157.92$, $df = 2$, $p < 0.0001$, figure 25.2a; survival from egg to adulthood $\chi^2 = 7.67$, $df = 2$, $p = 0.022$, figure 25.2c; proportion with deformed wings $\chi^2 = 4.68$, $df = 2$, $p = 0.09$, figure 25.2d). Average parasite loads of monarchs laid immediately following mating were also higher than those laid on days 5 and 10 after mating (figure 25.2b, table 25.4), and monarchs laid immediately after mating weighed significantly less (0.531 g ± 0.053 SD) than those laid on days 5 and 10 after mating (0.575 g ± 0.084 SD and 0.554 g ± 0.079 SD, respectively, see table 25.4).

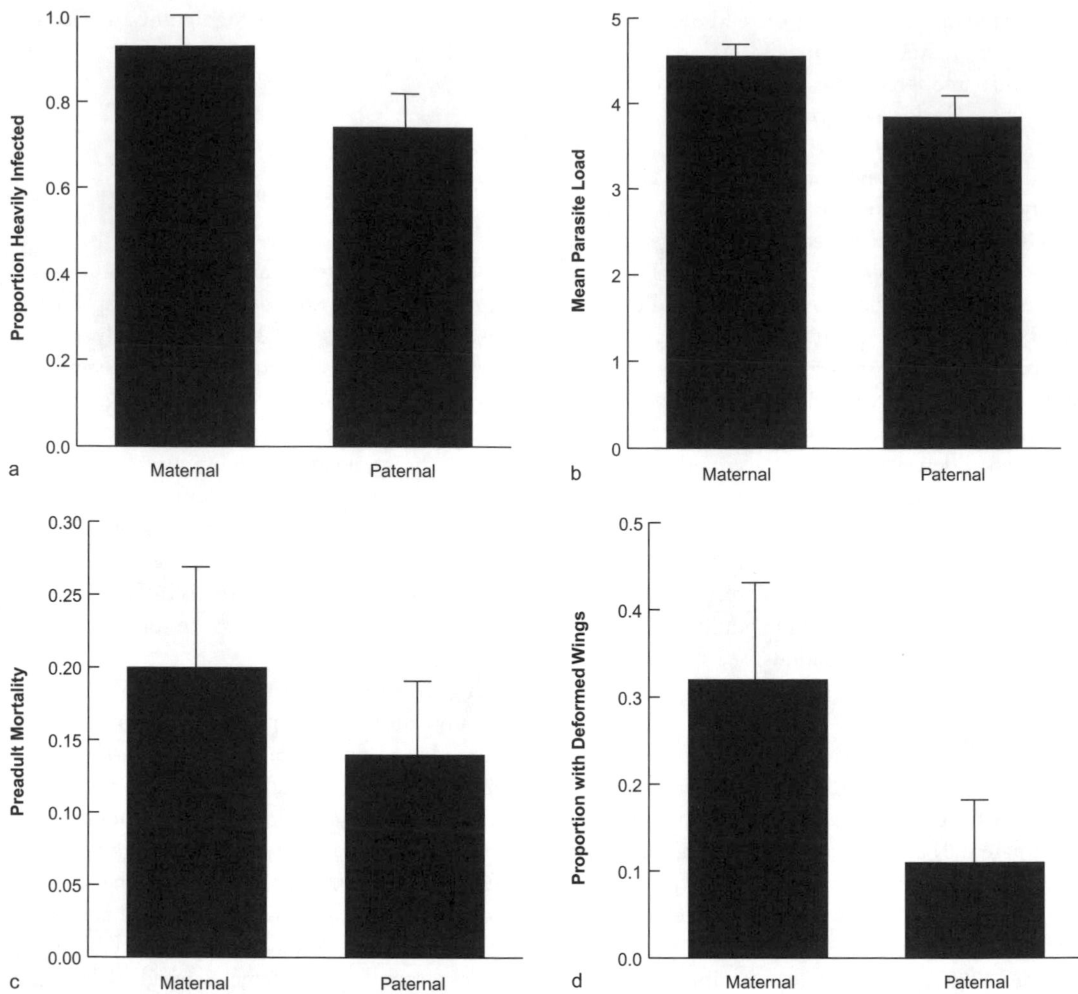

Figure 25.1. Effects of maternal and paternal transmission 1 day after mating on (a) the proportion of heavily infected offspring (in spore classes 4 and 5), (b) the average parasite loads of emerging offspring, (c) the proportion of offspring that died before reaching adulthood, and (d) the proportion of emerging adults with crumpled or deformed wings. Error bars represent 95% confidence intervals based on the variance among females for each transmission mode. *Note*: Parasite loads of emerging offspring in (b) are based on the categorical assessment (0 to 5 scale) described in the methods section and represent approximate $\log_{10}$-transformed counts of abdominal spore density.

Table 25.3. Effect of transmission type (paternal vs. maternal) on parasite loads, mass, and wingspan of offspring in experiment 1

Dependent variable	Independent variable	*df*	MS	*F* value	*p* value
Parasite load	Transmission mode	1	59.15	15.94	0.003
	Female (transmission mode)	10	3.71	2.27	0.013
Mass	Transmission mode	1	0.09	6.22	0.032
	Female (transmission mode)	10	0.02	2.69	0.003
Forewing length	Transmission mode	1	0.39	0.04	0.840
	Female (transmission mode)	10	9.10	2.02	0.031

Note: Analysis of variance (ANOVA) model: dependent variable = transmission mode + female (nested within transmission mode). Only offspring from eggs laid 1 day after mating were included in the analysis. MS, mean square.

Table 25.4. Effect of time since mating on average parasite loads of offspring from infected males in experiment 1

Dependent variable	Independent variable	*df*	MS	*F* value	*p* value
Parasite load	Time	2	212.25	16.30	0.002
	Female*time	7	13.022	5.98	0.001
Mass	Time	2	0.073	4.80	0.049
	Female*time	7	0.015	3.20	0.003

Note: Analysis of variance (ANOVA) model: parasite load = time + female + time*female. Because eggs laid by each female for each oviposition date were reared as cohorts until they reached third instar, we used the mean square (MS) for the time*female interaction term as the error term in constructing tests of significance for time. (Main effects of females were not significant and are therefore not reported here.)

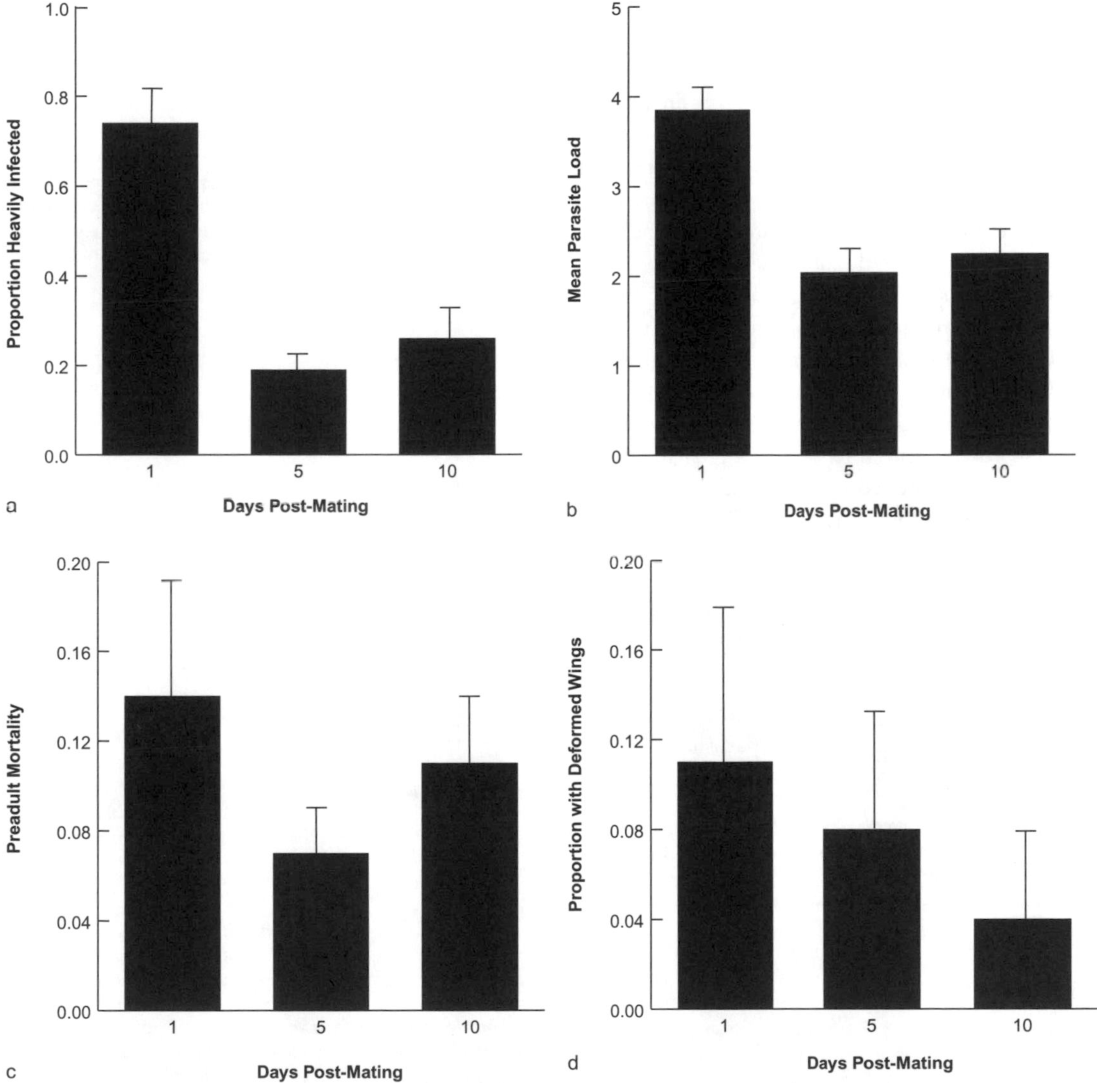

Figure 25.2. Effect of time (number of days after mating) on paternally infected offspring: (a) the proportion of heavily infected offspring (in spore classes 4 and 5), (b) the average parasite loads of offspring, (c) the proportion of offspring that died before reaching adulthood, and (d) the proportion of emerging adults with crumpled or deformed wings. Error bars represent 95% confidence intervals based on the variance among females for each day. *Note*: Parasite loads of emerging offspring in (b) are based on the categorical assessment (0 to 5 scale) described in the methods section and represent approximate $\log_{10}$-transformed counts of abdominal spore density.

Experiment 2: Paternal transmission to females and offspring

In experiment 2, monarchs used as parents that were inoculated with higher parasite doses emerged with higher parasite loads (ANOVA model: parasite load = dose treatment; $df = 2$, $F = 46.27$, $p < 0.001$). The average parasite load of control males (based on the scale described earlier) was 0.15, whereas average parasite loads for males in the low- and high-dose treatments were 2.36 and 4.47, respectively.

Tape samples from uninfected females placed in cages with infected males subsequently contained between 1 and 258 spores/cm^2. Males infected with high parasite loads transferred more spores to females than did males with few or no parasites (figure 25.3, table 25.5). Females that did not mate had few spores, irrespective of male dose treatment (figure 25.3, table 25.5), indicating that spore transfer resulted primarily from mating rather than confinement with infected males.

Male parasite load and the number of days between mating and oviposition affected the proportion of paternally infected offspring and their average parasite loads (figure 25.4, table 25.6). Offspring of high-dose males emerged with the highest parasite loads, and infection rates declined with increased time between mating and oviposition. Over 95% of the high-dose male offspring laid 1 day after mating emerged heavily infected, but no offspring laid on day 5 after mating were heavily infected (figure 25.4). Offspring of low-dose males emerged with lower parasite loads, and most offspring of the control males were uninfected (figure 25.4). Post-hoc comparison of means (Tukey's test) showed that the mean offspring parasite loads from

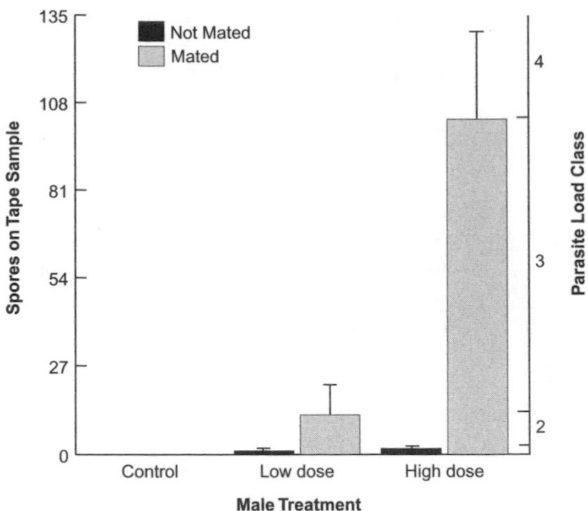

Figure 25.3. Spore transmission from infected males to females: effects of male parasite treatment and whether or not mating occurred on the parasite loads of uninfected females. Error bars represent 95% confidence intervals. Female parasite loads are shown as both the actual number of spores on tape samples (left y-axis) and the parasite load class (right y-axis).

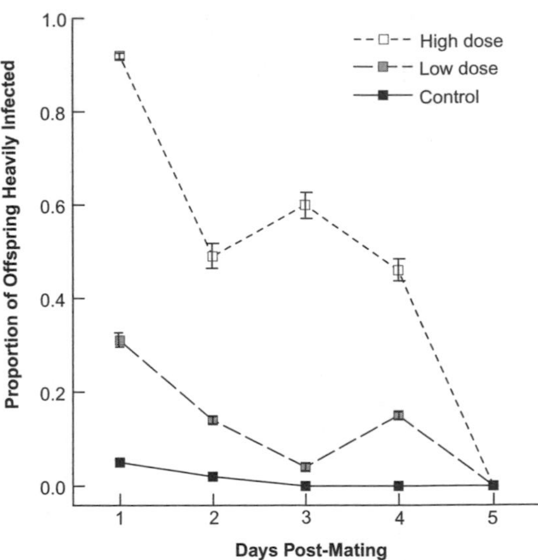

Figure 25.4. Paternal transmission to offspring: effects of male parasite treatment and the number of days after mating on the proportion of heavily infected offspring. Error bars represent 95% confidence intervals based on the variance among females within each treatment-by-day combination. *Note:* Parasite loads of emerging monarchs were based on the categorical assessment (0 to 5 scale) described in the methods section and represent approximate $\log_{10}$-transformed counts of abdominal spore density.

Table 25.5. Effects of male dose treatment and whether or not mating occurred (= mating status) on the number of spores transferred to females in experiment 2

Independent variable	*df*	MS	*F* value	*p* value
Male load	2	4.81	34.77	<0.001
Mating status	1	3.56	25.72	<0.001
Male load*mating	2	2.18	15.73	<0.001
Error	36	0.14		

Note: Analysis of variance (ANOVA) model: spore transfer = male load + mating status + male load*mating status. Actual counts of spore numbers were log-transformed before analysis to normalize the error variance, and one was added to each count to avoid taking the log of zero. MS, mean square.

Table 25.6. Effects of male dose treatment (= male load) and number of days after mating on paternal transmission to offspring in experiment 2

Independent variable	*df*	MS	*F* value	*p* value
Male load	2	195.5	14.7	<0.001
Days	4	25.3	4.44	0.003
Male load*days	8	13.45	2.36	0.025
Female (male load)	41	13.3	2.33	<0.001
Days*female (male load)	80	5.7	5.1	<0.001
Error	1273	1.117		

Note: Analysis of variance (ANOVA) model: offspring parasite load = male load + days + male load*days + female (male load) + days*female (male load). Because eggs laid by each female for each oviposition date were reared as cohorts until they reached third instar, days*female (male load) was used as the error term in constructing most tests of significance. MS, mean square.

all three male dose treatments were significantly different (means for uninfected, low-dose, and high-dose males were 0.519, 1.245, and 3.595, respectively). Moreover, average parasite loads associated with days 1 through 5 after mating were also significantly different (load on day 1 more than those on days 2, 3, 4, which are more than that on day 5; means were 2.250, 1.773, 1.445, 1.185, and 0.379, respectively).

Experiment 3: Horizontal transmission via contaminated milkweed

Monarchs reared in the laboratory on three different types of milkweed emerged with significantly different parasite loads (figure 25.5). Over 98% of monarchs reared on *A. curassavica* from southern Florida were heavily infected. In contrast, 3.6% of monarchs reared on *A. syriaca* collected in Minnesota and Wisconsin were heavily infected, and less than 1.7% of monarchs reared in greenhouse-raised *A. curassavica* were heavily infected. Monarchs reared on both wild *A. syriaca* and greenhouse *A. curassavica* emerged with parasite loads within the range of background laboratory contamination.

Statistical analysis (ANOVA model: parasite load = plant origin + container [plant origin]) showed that effects of both host plant origin (mean square [MS] = 309.52, $F_{2,160} = 87.38$, $p = 0.0001$) and container nested within host plant origin (MS = 3.54, $F_{9,160} = 5.81$, $p = 0.0001$) were highly significant. Comparison of means (Tukey's test) shows that the average parasite loads for all three host plant treatments were significantly different at the 0.05 level (means for wild *A. curassavica*, wild *A. syriaca*, and greenhouse *A. curassavica* were 4.607, 0.696, and 0.167, respectively).

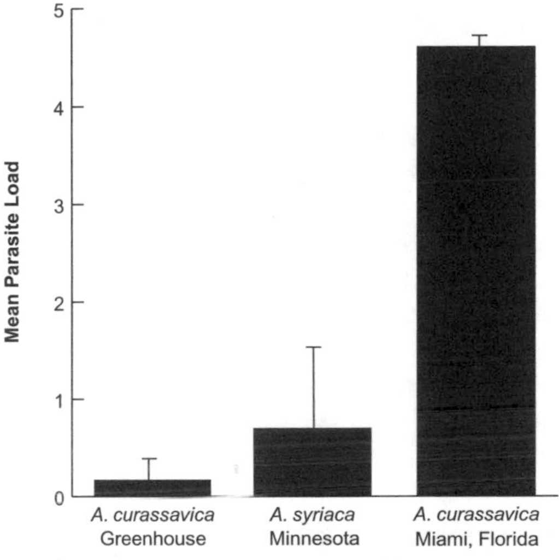

Figure 25.5. Effects of host plant origin on the parasite loads of monarchs in experiment 3. Error bars represent 95% confidence intervals based on the variance among containers within each host plant treatment.

A mathematical model of parasite transmission

To understand the potential implications of variation in paternal transmission to parasite prevalence and virulence, we simulated host-parasite dynamics using a deterministic model modified from Altizer and Augustine (1997). This model assumes that the probability of offspring infection depends on the number and sex of infected parents, and that

Table 25.7. Mating frequency and probability of offspring infection used to derive equations (1)-(3)

Mating class	Mating probability	Birth rate: infected offspring	Birth rate: healthy offspring
Healthy female × healthy male	$H\left(\frac{H}{N}\right)$	0	a
Healthy female × infected male	$H\left(\frac{I}{N}\right)$	$a\beta v$	$a(1-\beta v)$
Infected female × healthy male	$I\left(\frac{H}{N}\right)$	av	$a(1-v)$
Infected female × infected male	$I\left(\frac{I}{N}\right)$	$a[v+(1-v)\beta v]$	$a(1-v)(1-\beta v)$

Note: Equation 1 illustrates the change in the number of healthy individuals over time (dH/dt) and was obtained by summing the products of each mating probability and the birth rate of healthy offspring, and then subtracting mortality. The change in the numbers of infected individuals (dI/dt, equation 2) was calculated similarly, and the change in the total population size (dN/dt, equation 3) is the sum of the other two equations. All parameters are described in the text.

matings between healthy and infected parents occur in proportion to their population-level frequency (table 25.7). Uninfected offspring arise when healthy females mate with healthy males, or when the offspring of infected parents avoid parasite transmission. Similarly, a proportion of the offspring of infected males and females will become infected through maternal or paternal transmission and experience the negative effects of disease. We examined transmission given a single mating episode per generation, although this assumption underestimates actual mating frequencies in wild and captive monarchs (the mean number of matings for captive males and females is 3 to 6/lifetime, with some monarchs mating 10 or more times [Oberhauser 1989; Altizer and Oberhauser 1999]). Assuming a 50:50 sex ratio at birth, this system is described by the following equations (for an explanation of equation derivation, see table 25.7):

$$(1)\quad \frac{dH}{dt}=\frac{a}{N}[H+I(1-\nu)][H+I(1-\beta\nu)] -H(b_0+b_1N),$$

$$(2)\quad \frac{dI}{dt}=\frac{aI\nu}{N}(H\beta+\{H+I[1+\beta(1-\nu)]\}(1-\alpha_+)) -I(b_0+b_1N+\alpha_a),$$

$$(3)\quad \frac{dN}{dt}=N(a-b_0-b_1N)-I\{[1+a(\nu\alpha_1-1)]+\alpha_a\},$$

where H is the number of uninfected hosts,
I is the number of infected hosts,
N is the total population size,
a is the host birth rate, and
b_0 and b_1 are density-independent and -dependent host mortality, respectively.

Maternal transmission is described by v, the proportion of offspring from infected females that emerge heavily infected. Paternal transmission from infected males to females is described by β; hence, βv describes the fraction of offspring that are infected paternally. We assume that $\beta \leq 1$ (paternal transmission does not exceed maternal transmission). Parasite virulence is determined by two variables: α_1 describes parasite-induced mortality during larval and pupal stages, and α_a accounts for reductions in adult life expectance due to infection (as described in Altizer and Oberhauser 1999). In the absence of infected hosts, the population approaches an equilibrium density (N^*) denoted by $K=(a-b_0)/b_1$. The conditions for parasite invasion and coexistence are nearly identical to those described by Altizer and Augustine (1997).

We simulated the dynamics of this host-parasite interaction using a range of parameter values derived from empirical observations of monarch butterflies during breeding periods. Birth and death rates in our model are defined for a single generation; depending on climatic conditions, this period averages 30 days from egg to adult eclosion (Zalucki 1982). Birth rate, the number of new adults per female per generation, is the product of fecundity and preadult survival. Average female fecundity ranges from 220 to 715 eggs/female under captive conditions (Oberhauser 1997; Altizer and Oberhauser 1999), but depends on environmental characteristics in the field (Zalucki 1981). Records from natural populations suggest that 2% to 10% of monarch eggs survive to the pupal stage, and that most mortality occurs during the earliest larval instars (Zalucki and Kitching 1982; Prysby and Oberhauser, this volume; Zalucki and Rochester, this volume). Assuming that 10% of eggs survive to adulthood and that an average female lays 500 eggs during her lifetime, we selected a baseline birth rate of $a = 50$ offspring/female (but varied birth rates from 1, 2, 10, 20, 50, and 100).

We assumed that monthly host death rate, b_0, was approximately 0.8 based on measures of adult life span in outdoor enclosures (Oberhauser 1997; Altizer and Oberhauser 1999), although mortality rates may increase in natural conditions (Zalucki 1981). Because larvae that ingest high parasite doses have a lower probability of surviving to adulthood (see figure 25.1), we estimated preadult virulence (α_1) to be 0.2. Effects of parasites on adult survival are less severe (Altizer and Oberhauser 1999), and we therefore assumed that $\alpha_a = 0.1$. Monarchs breeding in eastern North America during the summer are unlikely to experience strong density-dependent mortality, but negative feedback from increasing density may be stronger in the southeastern United States and in nonmigratory populations such as Hawaii and southern Florida. In the absence of strong empirical justification, b_1 was conservatively set to 0.1.

Our study of parasite transmission indicates that the proportion of heavily infected offspring from infected females is high ($v \approx 0.9$; see figure 25.1). Because paternal transmission varies between 0.1 and 0.75 depending on male parasite load and time after mating, we simulated host-parasite dynamics for a range of paternal transmission rates. It is important to note that because we assume that each female mates only once whereas mating frequency in the wild is actually higher, our model will likely underestimate the contribution of paternal transmission to new infections.

Model results

For the above-described parameter values, parasite invasion and persistence hinge on rates of paternal transmission. As paternal transmission rate increases, the prevalence of infected hosts increases, with most of the population becoming infected for high values of βv. Specifically, parasite invasion requires that $\beta > \{[(\alpha_a/a) + 1]/v(1 - \alpha_1)\} - 1$, assuming that equilibrium host population size in the absence of disease (N^*) is greater than 100. Thus, β, or the ratio of paternal relative to maternal transmission, must exceed this threshold for the parasite to initially spread. These results suggest that for the range of host population parameters described, a slight increase in paternal transmission could lead to a large increase in the proportion of heavily infected hosts. Figure 25.6 illustrates the importance of paternal transmission: when paternal transmission is low, the parasite does not become established (figure 25.6a); as it increases to medium (figure 25.6b) and high levels (figure 25.6c), the proportion of hosts that are infected increases over time.

To further explore the effects of paternal transmission on prevalence and parasite virulence, we simulated host-parasite dynamics for 100 generations across a wide range of host and parasite life history parameters. We varied baseline host mortality ($0 < b_0 < 1$) and parasite-induced larval mortality ($0 < \alpha_1 < 1$) at intervals of 0.2. For each combination of death rates, we also varied host birth rates (from $1 < a < 100$). Maternal and paternal transmission rates were increased by intervals of 0.1 ($0.5 < v < 1$; $0 < \beta v < 1$). We kept density-dependent host mortality and adult virulence constant ($b_1 = 0.1$, $\alpha_a = 0.1$).

For a majority of host life history parameters, large changes in parasite prevalence occurred over a narrow window of paternal transmission rates (figure 25.7), but the explicit relationship between prevalence and paternal transmission depended on maternal transmission and virulence. For example, parasite invasion was highly unlikely for any degree of paternal transmission if maternal transmission was less than 0.5. Parasite invasion was more likely when birth rates exceeded 2 (and otherwise required extremely high transmission and low virulence), but the relationship between prevalence and paternal transmission remained consistent across a wide range of birth rates. Invasion and high

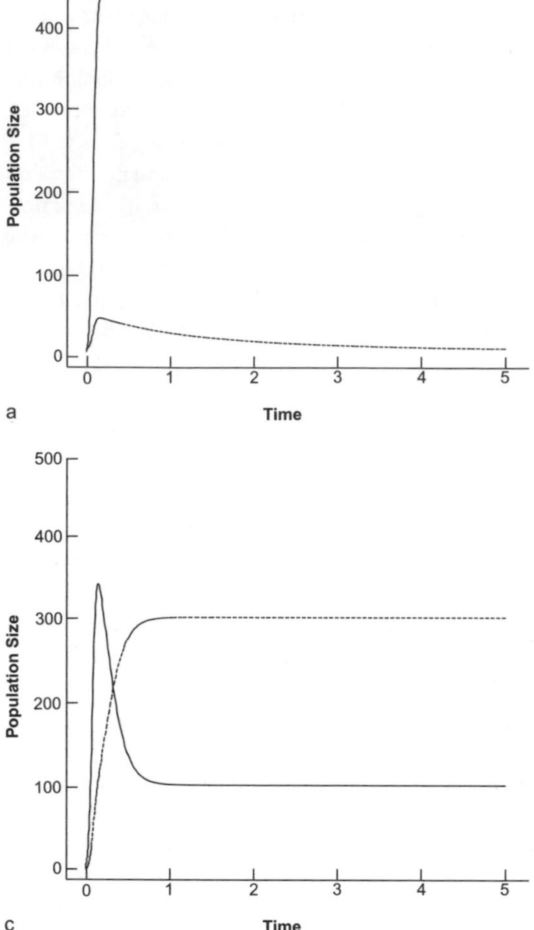

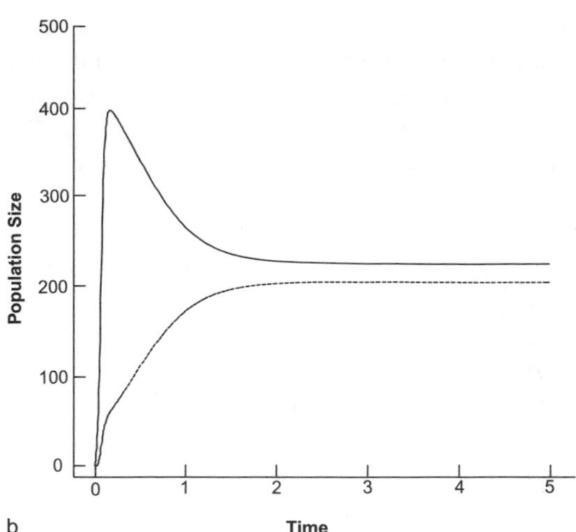

Figure 25.6. Simulation results of equations 1 and 2, illustrating different dynamical outcomes for increasing rates of paternal transmission. Solid lines represent uninfected hosts, and dashed lines represent heavily infected hosts. For all results, the following parameters were used: $a = 50$, $b_0 = 0.8$, $b_1 = 0.1$, $\alpha_1 = 0.2$, $\alpha_a = 0.1$, and $v = 0.9$. (a) When paternal transmission is low ($\beta v = 0.27$), the parasite fails to establish. (b) When paternal transmission is increased ($\beta v = 0.34$), the prevalence of heavily infected hosts approaches 50%. (c) For a high rate of paternal transmission ($\beta v = 0.45$), a majority of hosts in the population become heavily infected (prevalence higher than 75%).

prevalence were favored by low parasite virulence (figure 25.7).

Parasite transmission and larval virulence had large effects on equilibrium prevalence and host population size. Parasite extinction occurred for combinations of low transmission rates and high virulence, and high transmission rates and low virulence favored high prevalence. The range of parameters that led to intermediate prevalence (between 0 and 0.5) was very narrow (figure 25.7). Virulent parasites ($\alpha_1 > 0.5$) reached high prevalence only when paternal transmission was sufficiently high.

Substantial reductions of host population density occurred when high or moderate larval mortality was combined with high prevalence. When parasite-induced preadult mortality was low ($\alpha_1 \leq 0.2$), high infection rates had little impact on host population density, but when parasite-induced larval mortality was high ($\alpha_1 = 0.8$), equilibrium host density was less than half of that of an uninfected host population. However, parasite invasion for this scenario required high rates of maternal and paternal transmission. In general, the degree of host population suppression was most extreme when transmission rates were high and virulence was intermediate, which also resulted in a majority of the host population being infected at equilibrium.

DISCUSSION

In monarch butterflies, the protozoan parasite *O. elektroscirrha* is transmitted to larvae that consume spores deposited on host plants and eggs. We have

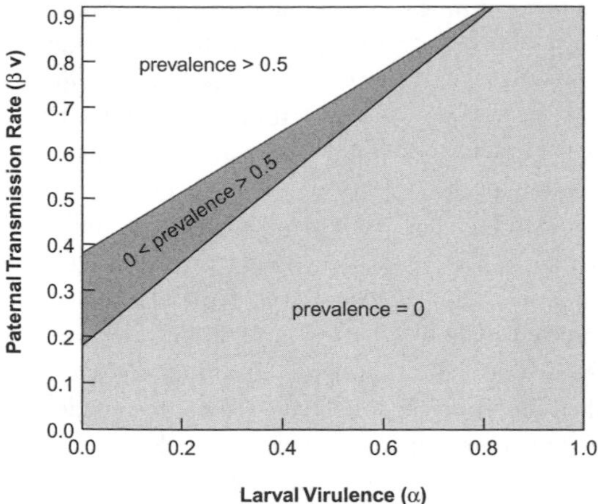

Figure 25.7. Phase diagram showing the regions of parasite extinction, persistence, and high prevalence for different values of parasite-induced larval mortality (α_1) and paternal transmission (βv). Values for other parameters are: $a = 50$, $b_0 = 0.8$, $b_1 = 0.1$, $\alpha_a = 0.1$, and $0.8 < v < 0.9$.

demonstrated that these spores can be transferred vertically from infected males or females to their offspring, or horizontally to larvae via unrelated adults. Maternal transmission in captive monarchs was very high; nearly 95% of the offspring of infected females were heavily infected. In comparison, 75% to 90% of the offspring laid immediately following matings to heavily infected males were heavily infected. These infection rates are probably higher than the transmission rate in natural populations, where monarchs are less likely to oviposit repeatedly on the same plants (as they did in our cages). However, because oviposition cages were exposed to natural weather conditions, our results captured potential environmental effects on spore transfer and parasite viability.

Differences in infection rates resulting from paternal versus maternal transmission are probably caused by the dose of spores deposited during oviposition. Monarchs infected as larvae typically have between 10^3 and 10^5 spores/1-cm^2 tape sample from their abdomens (Altizer and Oberhauser 1999), whereas females that mated with infected males had a maximum of 258 spores/tape sample. Thus, females infected as larvae transferred more parasites to their offspring than did females that acquired spores from males. Past studies of the fitness consequences of *O. elektroscirrha* (Altizer and Oberhauser 1999) indicated that differences in parasite exposure are responsible for lower offspring survival rates, smaller size, and more frequent wing deformities. In fact, because the offspring of infected females are less likely to survive or transmit the disease themselves, the contribution of maternal transmission to new infections may be reduced.

Our study of spore transfer from infected males to females demonstrated that most spore transmission resulted from mating rather than joint confinement in cages (see figure 25.3). Mating in monarchs often involves struggles during which males can force females to copulate, and successful males remain paired with females for up to 16 h (Oberhauser and Frey 1999). If one partner is infected, many spores may be transferred between male and female abdomens during this time. Although infected females may pass spores to uninfected males, the contribution of this transmission mode to future infections will likely be small, because males must then transfer these parasites to uninfected females to generate new infections. Paternal transmission and spore transfer to females increased with male parasite loads, and heavily infected males caused the highest rates of paternal transmission. Males with low parasite doses are unlikely to contribute significantly to new infections in natural populations.

The proportion of paternally infected offspring declined with time since mating, with a large drop in offspring parasite loads between days 1 and 5 after mating (see figures 25.2 and 25.4), probably due to a loss of spores in flight or during oviposition. Although declining parasite doses over time should occur for both maternal and paternal transmission, declines in the fraction of infected offspring are less likely to occur when females are heavily infected themselves. In fact, parasite doses as low as 10 spores/larva can cause heavy offspring infections (Altizer and Oberhauser 1999), and spore densities on heavily infected females are not likely to drop below this transmission threshold.

Parasite loads of paternally infected offspring declined more quickly with time after mating in experiment 2 than in experiment 1 (see figures 25.2 and 25.4). This was probably because we sterilized cages between each day of egg collection in experiment 2, eliminating the likelihood that parasite spores accumulated on cage surfaces. Maximum paternal transmission on day 1 after mating was higher in experiment 2 than experiment 1, possibly due to the removal of male abdominal spores before mating in experiment 1.

For paternal transmission, the total fraction of infected offspring will depend on both age-specific female fecundity and time-specific paternal transmission rate. Assuming that females mate only once, only offspring laid during the first week after mating should emerge heavily infected. Results from experiment 2 suggest that 90% of the offspring laid on day 1 after mating become heavily infected, and 50% of the offspring laid on days 2 to 4 become heavily infected. For newly mated females, the average proportion of total fecundity on day 1 is approximately 0.05, and eggs laid on days 2 to 4 represent 0.2 of lifetime fecundity (Oberhauser 1997). Therefore, the overall fraction of paternally infected offspring would be slightly less than 20%/female, assuming only one mating. However, because monarchs mate multiply, the actual contribution of paternal transmission in natural populations should be higher than indicated by our model.

Our model demonstrated the importance of paternal transmission to variation in parasite prevalence; an increase in paternal transmission on the order of 15% translated to the difference between parasite extinction and a majority of the population being infected (see figures 25.6 and 25.7). This phenomenon holds across a wide range of host demographic parameters and suggests that variation in paternal transmission may underlie the large variation in prevalence among natural monarch populations. Higher rates of maternal transmission also favored high prevalence, and our model suggested that maternal transmission rates lower than 50% are unlikely to sustain the disease. However, paternal transmission is more likely to vary between host populations than maternal transmission. For example, paternal transmission is likely to be higher in nonmigratory populations owing to the timing of mating and oviposition behavior. In the eastern migratory population, many females mate at the end of overwintering and fly long distances to reach new host plants (Brower and Malcolm 1991). Heavily infected males are likely to be in poor condition, and thus more likely to mate in the overwintering colonies rather than remigrate north with ovipositing females (Van Hook 1993, 1996; Oberhauser and Frey 1999). Because paternal transmission depends on the time between mating and oviposition, the overall fraction of paternally infected offspring will be lower in migratory populations than in populations that breed year-round in the same location. This effect could contribute to the divergence in parasite prevalence among natural populations. Other ecological factors could also play a role in causing differences in infection patterns between these populations. For example, variation in milkweed density and distribution could generate variation in temporal oviposition patterns; females mated to an infected male in an environment with dense milkweed populations might lay more eggs before shedding spores transferred to them from males.

Our model indicates that paternal transmission has important consequences for the maintenance of virulent parasites and the depression of host population density. Higher rates of paternal transmission can maintain virulent parasites at a high prevalence, thus depressing host population density below the disease-free carrying capacity. Historically, it has been assumed that vertically transmitted parasites should be avirulent because new infections depend on the reproductive success of infected hosts (Fine 1975; Ewald 1983). However, our model shows that high rates of both maternal and paternal transmission can propel a virulent parasite to a high prevalence (similar work has shown that horizontal transmission has the same effect [Lipsitch et al. 1995; Kover et al. 1997]). Such parasites can have large impacts on host population density, because a majority of hosts will experience the negative effects of disease. Therefore, in monarch populations where parasites are not strictly maternally transmitted, prevalence may be extremely high and parasites may be more virulent. Interestingly, recent work has shown that among parasites isolated from different monarch populations, more virulent strains persist in populations that breed continuously or migrate shorter distances (Altizer 2001).

Horizontal parasite transmission via contaminated milkweed was much higher for milkweed collected from a Florida population than for milkweed collected in an upper midwestern state (see figure 25.5). Spore deposition leading to horizontal transmission may occur when infected adults fly, land, or oviposit on milkweed plants. In areas with high densities of infected adults and milkweed plants that persist year-round, spores will likely accumulate on plant surfaces, leading to horizontal transmission between adults and unrelated offspring. In contrast, milkweed plants in more seasonal climates die back each winter, eliminating opportunities for parasites to persist on vegetation beyond a single season.

Our host-parasite model did not incorporate horizontal transmission via parasite accumulation on milkweed plants. However, past models that addressed the combined effects of horizontal and vertical transmission showed that horizontal transmission will further increase parasite prevalence and allow more virulent parasites to persist (Lipsitch et al. 1995). Therefore, differences in opportunities for horizontal transmission between resident and migratory populations should further contribute to population differences in prevalence and parasite virulence.

The mode of parasite transfer to new hosts is a critical component of host-parasite interactions (Anderson and May 1981; Getz and Pickering 1983; Thrall et al. 1993; Antonovics et al. 1995; Lipsitch et al. 1995). Knowledge of specific transmission routes and rates is essential to predict the probability of parasite invasion, persistence, and equilibrium abundance. We have shown that *O. elektroscirrha* has multiple transmission modes that are associated with different infection probabilities and are likely to vary among populations. Our model indicates that parasite prevalence is highly sensitive to fluctuations in transmission rates, with prevalence switching from near 0% to greater than 50% for minor changes in paternal transmission. Since monarch populations that vary in breeding ecology and migratory behavior are likely to experience different rates of horizontal and paternal parasite transmission, differences in transmission opportunities may underlie the observed differences in prevalence and should thus influence the population-level impacts of this parasite.

Acknowledgments

We thank Don Alstad, Peter Thrall, Scott Pletcher, Clarence Lehman, Dennis Frey, and Myron Zalucki for discussion and comments on earlier drafts of this manuscript. We thank Imants Pone and Lorelle Berkeley for laboratory assistance. This work was supported by National Science Foundation (NSF) grants (DEB-9220829 and ESI-9554476) to K. Oberhauser, an Undergraduate Research Opportunities Program award from the University of Minnesota to K. Geurts, and an NSF grant (DEB-9700916) and two Minnesota Center for Community Genetics Graduate Research Awards to S. Altizer.

References

Altizer, S. M. 2001. Migratory behaviour and host-parasite co-evolution in natural populations of monarch butterflies infected with a protozoan parasite. Evol. Ecol. Res. 3:611–32.

Altizer, S. M., and D. J. Augustine. 1997. Interactions between frequency-dependent and vertical transmission in host-parasite systems. Proc. R. Soc. Lond. B 264:807–14.

Altizer, S. M., and K. S. Oberhauser. 1999. Effects of the protozoan parasite, *Ophryocystis elektroscirrha*, on the fitness of monarch butterflies (*Danaus plexippus*). J. Invertebr. Pathol. 74:76–88.

Altizer, S. M., K. S. Oberhauser, and L. P. Brower. 2000. Associations between host migration and the prevalence of a protozoan parasite in natural populations of monarch butterflies. Ecol. Entomol. 25:125–39.

Anderson, R. M., and R. M. May. 1981. The population dynamics of microparasites and their invertebrate hosts. Proc. R. Soc. Lond. B 291:451–524.

Anderson, R. M., and R. M. May. 1991. Infectious disease of humans: dynamics and control. Oxford: Oxford University Press.

Antonovics, J., Y. Iwasa, and M. P. Hassel. 1995. A generalised model of parasitoid, venereal, and vector-based transmission processes. Am. Nat. 145:661–75.

Brower, L. P., and S. B. Malcolm. 1991. Animal migrations: endangered phenomena. Am. Zool. 31:265–76.

Ewald, P. W. 1983. Host-parasite relations, vectors, and the evolution of disease severity. Annu. Rev. Ecol. Syst. 14:465–85.

Ewald, P. W. 1994. Evolution of infectious disease. New York: Oxford University Press.

Fine, P. E. 1975. Vectors and vertical transmission: an epidemiologic perspective. Ann. N.Y. Acad. Sci. 266:173–94.

Getz, W. M., and J. Pickering. 1983. Epidemic models: thresholds and population regulation. Am. Nat. 121:892–98.

Herre, E. A. 1993. Population structure and the evolution of virulence in nematode parasites of fig wasps. Science 259:1442–45.

Herre, E. A. 1995. Factors affecting the evolution of virulence: nematode parasites of fig wasps as a case study. Parasitology Suppl. 111:179–91.

Kover, P. X., and K. Clay. 1998. Trade-off between virulence and vertical transmission and the maintenance of a virulent plant pathogen. Am. Nat. 152:165–75.

Kover, P. X., T. E. Dolan, and K. Clay. 1997. Potential versus actual contribution of vertical transmission to pathogen fitness. Proc. R. Soc. Lond. B 264:903–9.

Lenski, R. E., and R. M. May. 1994. The evolution of virulence in parasites and pathogens: reconciliation between two competing hypotheses. J. Theor. Biol. 169:253–65.

Leong, K. L. H., H. K. Kaya, M. A. Yoshimura, and D. F. Frey. 1992. The occurrence and effect of a protozoan parasite, *Ophryocystis elektroscirrha* (Neogregarinida: Ophryocystidae) on overwintering monarch butterflies, *Danaus plexippus* (Lepidoptera: Danaidae) from two California winter sites. Ecol. Entomol. 17:338–42.

Leong, K. L. H., M. A. Yoshimura, and H. K. Kaya. 1997a. Occurrence of a neogregarine protozoan, *Ophryocystis elektroscirrha* in populations of monarch and queen butterflies. Pan-Pac. Entomol. 73:49–51.

Leong, K. L. H., M. A. Yoshimura, H. K. Kaya, and H. Williams. 1997b. Instar susceptibility of the monarch butterfly (*Danaus plexippus*) to the neogregarine parasite, *Ophryocystis elektroscirrha*. J. Invertebr. Pathol. 69:79–83.

Levin, B. R. 1996. The evolution and maintenance of virulence in microparasites. Emerg. Infect. Dis. 2:93–102.

Lipsitch, M., M. Nowak, D. Ebert, and R. M. May. 1995. The population dynamics of vertically and horizontally transmitted parasites. Proc. R. Soc. Lond. B 260:321–27.

Lockhart, A. B., P. H. Thrall, and J. Antonovics. 1996. Sexually transmitted diseases in animals: ecological and evolutionary implications. Biol. Rev. Camb. Philos. Soc. 71:415–71.

McLaughlin, R. E., and J. Myers. 1970. *Ophryocystis elektroscirrha sp* N. a neogregarine pathogen of the monarch butterfly *Danaus plexippus* L. and the Florida queen butterfly *Danaus gilippus berenice* Cramer. J. Protozool. 17:300–5.

Oberhauser, K. S. 1989. Effects of spermatophores on male and female monarch butterfly reproductive success. Behav. Ecol. Sociobiol. 25:237–46.

Oberhauser, K. S. 1997. Fecundity, lifespan and egg mass in butterflies: effects of male-derived nutrients and female size. Funct. Ecol. 11:166–75.

Oberhauser, K., and D. Frey. 1999. Coercive mating by overwintering male monarch butterflies. In J. Hoth, L. Merino, K. Oberhauser, I. Pisantry, S. Price, and T. Wilkinson, eds., The 1997 North American Conference on the Monarch Butterfly, pp. 67–78. Montreal: Commission for Environmental Cooperation.

SAS/STAT. 2001. SAS/STAT software. Ver. 8.0.2, Carey, N.C.

SPSS, Inc. 1999. SPSS software. Ver. 8.0. Chicago. Ill.

Thrall, P. H., and J. Antonovics. 1997. Polymorphism in sexual versus non-sexual disease transmission. Proc. R. Soc. Lond. B 264:581–87.

Thrall, P., J. Antonovics, and D. Hall. 1993. Host and pathogen coexistence in sexually transmitted and vector-borne diseases characterized by frequency dependent disease transmission. Am. Nat. 142:543–52.

Thrall, P. H., J. Antonovics, and W. G. Wilson. 1998. Allocation to sexual versus nonsexual disease transmission. Am. Nat. 151:29–45.

Van Hook, T. 1993. Non-random mating behavior in monarch butterflies overwintering in Mexico. In S. B. Malcolm and M. P. Zalucki, eds., Biology and conservation of the monarch butterfly, pp. 49–60. Los Angeles: Natural History Museum of Los Angeles County.

Van Hook, T. 1996. Monarch butterfly mating ecology at a Mexican overwintering site: proximate causes of non-random mating. Ph.D. thesis, University of Florida, Gainesville.

Vickerman, D., A. Michels, and P. Burrowes. 1999. Levels of infection of migrating monarch butterflies, *Danaus plexippus* (Lepidoptera: Nymphalidae) by the parasite *Ophryocystis elektroscirrha* (Neogregarinidia: Ophryocystidae), and evidence of a new mode of spore transmission between adults. J. Kans. Entomol. Soc. 72:124–28.

Zalucki, M. P. 1981. The effects of age and weather on egg laying in *Danaus plexippus* L. (Lepidoptera: Danaidae). Res. Popul. Ecol. 23:318–27.

Zalucki, M. P. 1982. Temperature and rate of development in *Danaus plexippus* and *D. chrysippus*. J. Aust. Entomol. Soc. 21:241–46.

Zalucki, M. P., and R. L. Kitching. 1982. Temporal and spatial variation of mortality in field population of *Danaus plexippus* and *D. chrysippus* L. larvae (Lepidoptera: Nymphalidae). Oecologia 53:201–7.

26

Spatial and Temporal Population Dynamics of Monarchs Down-Under: Lessons for North America

Myron P. Zalucki and Wayne A. Rochester

INTRODUCTION

Predicting the population dynamics of any insect is problematic. Many factors influence the local and regional abundance of insects by influencing the vital processes of development, survival, reproduction, and movement. Our understanding of such processes is usually summarized in some kind of model, and inferences are drawn as to the likely changes in abundance that may result from changes in model parameters. Such models and the predictions of change are important as we assess risks to a species' local or regional existence from anthropogenic changes to the environment. In conservation biology we often need to distinguish between declines in abundance due to anthropogenic changes to a species' habitat and changes in abundance due to natural variation in conditions. These issues are particularly relevant for monarchs in North America.

In North America the monarch population is confronted with a number of potential threatening processes. These include changes to the area of, and land use within, oyamel fir forests in central Mexico where the eastern monarch population overwinters (Malcolm and Zalucki 1993; Brower et al., this volume) and changes in the abundance, distribution, and quality of milkweeds within the summer breeding areas, such as those caused by the use of herbicides and potential exposure of monarchs to transgenic corn pollen (Losey et al. 1999; Jesse and Obrycki 2000, this volume). Whether these processes will significantly impact the abundance of monarchs in eastern North America is a matter of some conjecture, but will require a fundamental understanding of the population dynamics of monarchs on a continental scale. Here we describe our understanding of some development, reproduction, and survival parameters based on ecological research in Australia. We use this understanding and modeling tools to make predictions on the seasonal spatial distribution and abundance of monarchs in North America.

Monarchs in Australia

The first confirmed report of monarchs in Australia is generally considered to be late 1870 or early 1871. It is a matter of some contention as to how monarchs arrived (Brower 1995), but allozyme studies indicate a classic founder effect and independent introductions to Hawaii and Australia (Shephard et al. 2002). Since the early 1870s the species has spread to most parts of eastern Australia and a small portion of Western Australia (Zalucki 1986). Its seasonal distribution is controlled by suitable climate and the presence of milkweed, which in turn is restricted in its distribution and abundance by intolerance to dry conditions and frost (Woodson 1954; Zalucki and Rochester 1999).

The majority of the Queensland population breeds year-round. A range contraction occurs from southern Queensland and northern New South Wales with the onset of autumn, leading to the development of three eastern population centers: the southern Queensland/northern New South

Wales coastal strip extending up in to the tropics, the Sydney Basin/Hunter Valley region, and the Adelaide area (Zalucki and Rochester 1999).

The Sydney Basin population divides into reproductive and nonreproductive overwintering aggregations, but nothing on a scale comparable with the North American monarchs (Kitching and Scheermeyer 1993). Populations south of 34° south latitude are usually nonreproductive from autumn onward (James 1979), with the ratio of nonreproductive to reproductive individuals being determined by temperature.

Mark and recapture studies by James (1993) have confirmed long-distance autumn migrations in the New South Wales region of up to 380 km. However, there is little evidence for a regular long-distance movement (Dingle et al. 1999). Our research in Australia ("down-under") on monarch development (Zalucki 1982), reproduction (Zalucki 1981a), survival (Zalucki and Kitching 1982a), and spatial abundance (Zalucki and Rochester 1999; Rochester and Zalucki 2000) has been based on the southern Queensland population. Here we summarize published and unpublished results from these areas and make "predictions" for North America.

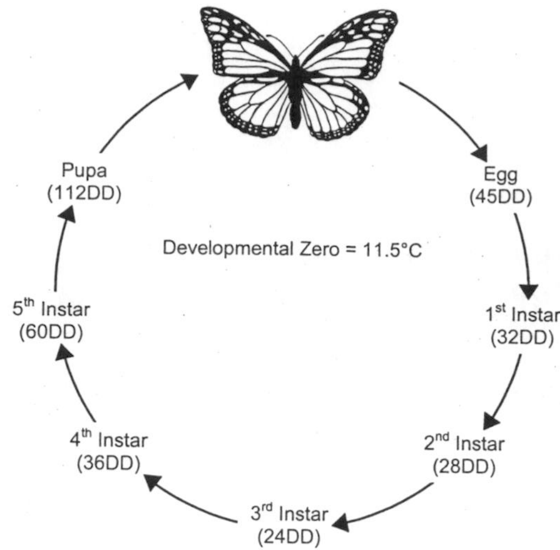

Figure 26.1. Monarch life cycle showing day-degree requirements of each stage above a development threshold (D.Z.) of 11.5°C (after Zalucki 1982).

METHODS

Monarch physiological time scales and predicting phenology in North America

Using detailed observations of stadia durations over a range of constant temperature conditions, Zalucki (1982) derived physiological time scales for the immature stages of monarchs, including developmental thresholds and development times in day-degrees (figure 26.1). These observations have been used to interpret the phenology of the monarch population and execute population curve analysis for life table work (see, e.g., Malcolm et al. 1987; Cockrell et al. 1993; Oberhauser et al. 2001).

Cockrell and colleagues (1993) present a conceptual model of the seasonal colonization of eastern North America that predicts the timing and likely sources of colonization of different parts of the monarch's range. Here we extend this model to predict the effects of weather variation and arrival times of butterflies migrating from Mexico on variation among years in the timing and synchrony of monarch generations. Such a model can be used to predict the degree of synchrony between susceptible immature stages and *Bacillus thuringiensis* (Bt) corn pollen anthesis.

We estimated spatial and temporal demographics of the population in different years and under different scenarios by Monte Carlo simulation. A Monte Carlo model estimates the probability that a system will be in each of all of the possible states in which it can exist. In our case the system was one monarch in eastern North America. The state of the system on a given day was the location and life stage of the monarch. The output of the model was the probability that the monarch was at a particular location and in a given life stage for all combinations of location and life stage. This probability equals the expected proportion of the monarch population in each location and life stage.

The Monte Carlo model differs from an individual-based simulation model because it simulates a sample of individuals rather than all individuals in the population. Individuals are sampled with replacement. The sample size may be smaller or larger than the population size and is selected to obtain the desired standard errors in the model outputs. Because each sampled individual is simulated independently, interactions such as competition cannot be included. The model does not estimate the size of the population on each day—

only the proportion of the population that is in each state.

Migration and oviposition

To represent migration, eggs were distributed among representative study sites. The number of eggs allocated to each site on a given day was proportional to ($\propto$) the "favorableness" of the site for oviposition on that day, that is,

$$n \propto s_{\text{clim}} s_{\text{col}},$$

where n is the number of eggs allocated to the site, and s_{clim} and s_{col} are the climatic and colonization favorableness of the site, respectively. Eggs from a given female may be allocated to different sites, and all sites in the eastern United States were equally accessible to all butterflies. Climatic favorableness was calculated according to the observation of Cockrell and colleagues (1993) that temperatures in the Gulf States become too hot for larvae after mid-June, that is,

$$s_{\text{clim}} = \begin{cases} 0 \text{ if } l < 30^\circ \text{ south and } t > 15 \text{ June} \\ 1 \text{ otherwise,} \end{cases}$$

where l is the latitude of the site and t is the date. Colonization favorableness was calculated according to whether the first individuals or the "main cohort" had arrived at the site, that is,

$$s_{\text{col}} = \begin{cases} 0 \text{ if } t < t_{\text{first}} \\ 1 \text{ if } t > t_{\text{main}} \\ (t - t_{\text{first}})/(t_{\text{main}} - t_{\text{first}}) \text{ otherwise,} \end{cases}$$

where t_{first} and t_{main} are the arrival days of the first individuals and main cohort, respectively. The arrival days were calculated according to the regression equations of Cockrell and colleagues (1993):

$$t_{\text{first}} = t_0 + 4.85l - 138, \text{ and } t_{\text{main}} = t_0 + 4.48l - 111,$$

where t_0 is 15 March and l is latitude.

Study sites were the weather stations east of the Rocky Mountains in the weather data set. The stations were reasonably evenly distributed across the United States and therefore provided a suitably representative set of sites.

Development

Development of the immature life stages was estimated with a "linear over threshold" model using the parameters of Zalucki (1982; see figure 26.1). For immatures, these were a lower threshold of 11.5°C and a requirement of 337 day-degrees to complete development (figure 26.1). At temperatures above 29°C the development rate was set to that for 29°C. Development rate was not reduced at higher temperatures. Development accumulated with a 1-h time step using hourly temperatures extracted from sine curves fitted to daily maxima and minima.

To simulate variation among individuals, development rates were randomly varied according to a normal distribution with a standard deviation of 5%. Figure 26.2, derived from unpublished development data for monarchs described by Zalucki (1982), shows the variation in development time within each stage. The average standard deviation in development time among temperatures and life stages for those insects was 5.8%.

Egg maturation was modeled according to the fecundity curve of Zalucki (1981a):

$$E = 0.0019 d^{1.9} e^{-0.0114d},$$

where E is the number of eggs/female/day and d is the development time in day-degrees above 11.5°C since emergence.

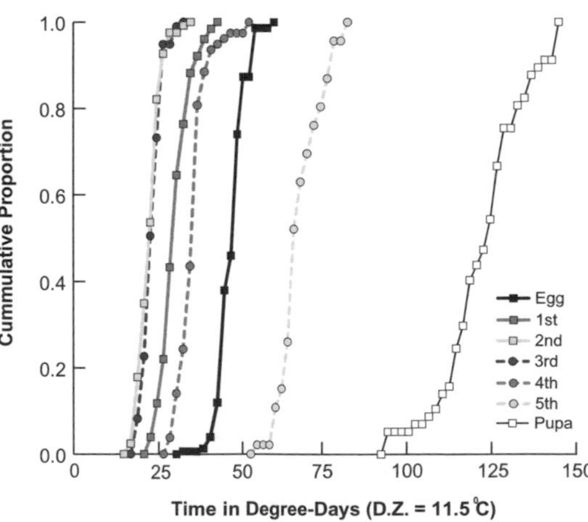

Figure 26.2. Variation in immature monarch development time in each stage, plotted as cumulative proportion completing development to the next stage against time in degree-days above a development threshold (D.Z.) of 11.5°C in that stage.

Generations and demographics

The first sample of mature eggs simulated in the model was from spring migrants from Mexico. This sample was evenly distributed from 21 March to 30 April, based on reported arrival times and female life span. The above sequence was run on this initial sample, then repeated four times, with the input sample of mature eggs being derived from the butterflies arising from the previous iteration. The outcome of this procedure was similar to that of a model in which each spring migrant laid one egg, which developed into one butterfly, which laid one egg, and so on. However, here each female laid on average one egg owing to the pooling and sampling of mature eggs at the start of each iteration. Since we modeled monarch development, we could use the proportion of individuals in each life stage to represent the population age structure.

Weather data and representative sites

Simulations were run on daily and long-term weather data. Daily data were extracted from the Daily Historical Climate Data Network data set (National Oceanic and Atmospheric Administration, 19 March 1998). The data set comprises temperature and rainfall values for 187 weather stations distributed across the contiguous United States. These data are quality controlled, the stations are relatively evenly distributed, and the stations were selected to be unbiased by local microclimatic effects. Less than 2% of records were missing from the data set in the period used in this analysis.

RESULTS

Model validation

Estimates of the spatial and temporal demography of the monarch population were validated against survey data for immature monarchs presented in Cockrell et al. 1993. Model estimates of the average age of monarchs at a site were significantly correlated with the average age calculated from the survey data ($r^2 = 0.12$, $n = 90$, $p < 0.001$). The correlation remained significant when the analysis was restricted to sites at which eggs or larvae were present in both survey and model data ($r^2 = 0.09$, $n = 56$, $p < 0.05$). To test for general bias related to location and time, latitude and day of the year were added to both regression models. Neither variable explained significant additional variance.

Temporal and spatial phenology in the eastern United States

With long-term average temperature data and model parameters set to their normal values, all life stages were predicted to be continuously present in substantial numbers from May onward (figure 26.3). There were troughs in the proportion of the population in the larval stage in mid-May and mid-July and peaks in late April and early May, mid-June, and mid-August.

Overlap between generations was substantial even in the absence of variation in spring migrant oviposition time (figure 26.3). When oviposition is confined to 1 day (5 April), the overlap between generations is entirely due to variations in development time (due to variations among sites in temperature and among individuals in development rate) and egg maturation rate. Monarch phenology was sensitive to spring migrant oviposition time. The times of the July trough and August peak moved almost the same number of days as shifts in the spring migrant oviposition period.

Variation among years in the proportion of simulated monarchs that were larvae was greatest early in the season. From 1985 to 1994 the average time of the July trough was 18 July (range, 14 to 24 July; standard deviation [SD], 3.6 days). The average time of the August peak was 16 August (range, 7 to 26

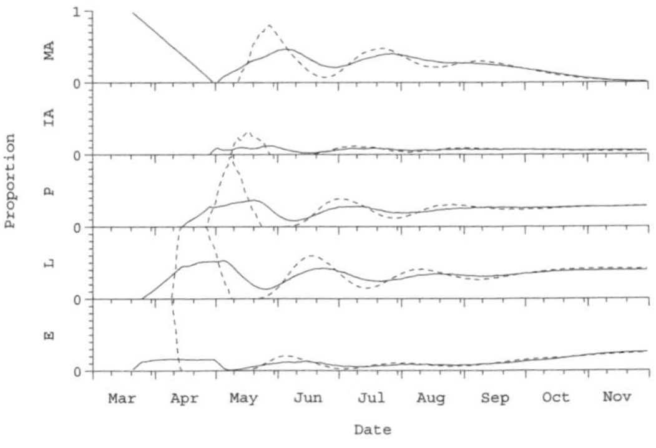

Figure 26.3. The simulated proportion of eastern U.S. monarchs in each life stage for two scenarios for spring migrant oviposition period: 21 March to 30 April (solid line) and 5 April (dashed line). E, egg; L, larva; P, pupa; IA, immature adult; MA, mature adult.

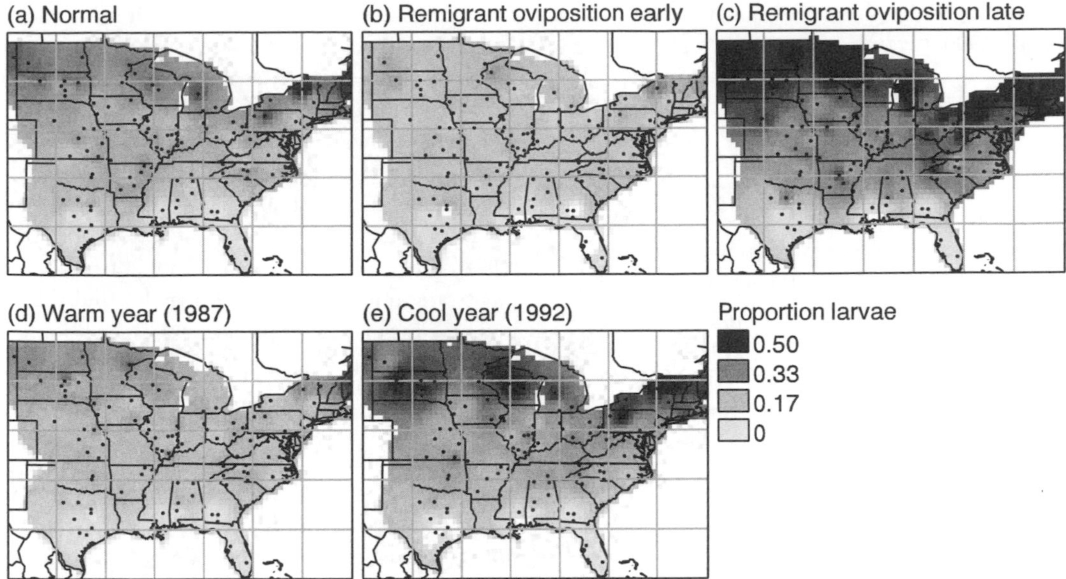

Figure 26.4. Spatial phenology of monarchs in North America shown as the proportion of the population in the larval stage on 11 July for (a) a normal year, (b) an early migration, (c) a late migration, (d) a warmer than average year (1987), and (e) a cooler than average year (1992). Dots on the maps represent weather stations.

August; SD, 5.4 days). The average proportion of monarchs that were larvae from 11 to 31 July was 0.26 (range, 0.22 to 0.29; SD, 0.02).

Monarch spatial phenology was sensitive to spring migrant oviposition time and variation in climate among years. For example, climatic variation caused the proportion of monarchs in the northern part of their range that were larvae in mid-July to be lower and higher than normal in 1987 and 1992, respectively (figure 26.4). Attempts to relate the monarch population that might be exposed to seasonal risks, such as transgenic pollen, will need to take this variation into account.

Large-scale fluctuation in abundance

Climate can have dramatic effects on the timing and spatial synchrony of a species, influencing the exposure of various life history stages to various mortality risks (above). The abundance of monarchs across a landscape level will be determined by factors that influence immature and adult survival and oviposition. While many factors may be important, climate and the distribution and abundance of host plants will be key factors for any insect herbivore.

Immature survival

As is common in Lepidoptera (Zalucki et al. 2002), monarch larvae have a high but variable mortality, particularly between the egg and established second instar (Zalucki and Kitching 1982a; Borkin 1990; Oberhauser et al. 2001; Prysby and Oberhauser, this volume; Prysby, this volume). The high mortality in the immature stages, particularly first instars, is related to many factors, including the milkweed defenses of cardiac glycosides embedded in a quick-setting latex glue, leaf hairs, and toughness (Zalucki and Brower 1992; Zalucki and Malcolm 1999; Zalucki et al. 2001a, 2001b). Some of the variation in mortality among sites is related to the size of milkweed patches, with higher mortality rates in large patches than on single isolated plants or small patches (Zalucki and Kitching 1982a). These differences may relate to an abundance of local predators; for example, parasitism rates from tachinid flies are higher in large patches than in isolated plants (Zalucki 1981b). The local distribution and abundance of milkweed may influence how well larvae locate plants—in theory this should be easier where hosts are locally abundant. Larvae move extensively among plants after about the third instar (Borkin 1990; pers. observ.).

Adult reproduction

Monarchs have a relatively long-lived adult stage, approximately 530 day-degrees. Breeding-generation females begin laying eggs about 45 day-degrees after eclosion. Egg laying peaks after about 200 day-degrees but continues throughout the adult stage. If a female survives about half her potential adult life, she will lay about 400 eggs, assuming milkweed plants are not limiting. Zalucki (1981a) showed that age and current weather conditions (rain, overcast conditions, temperature) have a dramatic effect on monarch egg production and laying. Daily temperature not only influences the rate of aging but also the rate of egg maturation. More dramatic is the effect of rain and overcast condition (Zalucki 1981a; figure 26.5). Under variable conditions, lifetime oviposition can be reduced by about 25%. These conditions may prevent flight and hence the ability to locate hosts. Monarchs cannot make up for the shortfalls in egg laying on subsequent suitable days (Zalucki 1981a). Consequently, we can expect large-scale weather events such as extensive rain or prolonged cool, cloudy conditions to dramatically reduce egg laying.

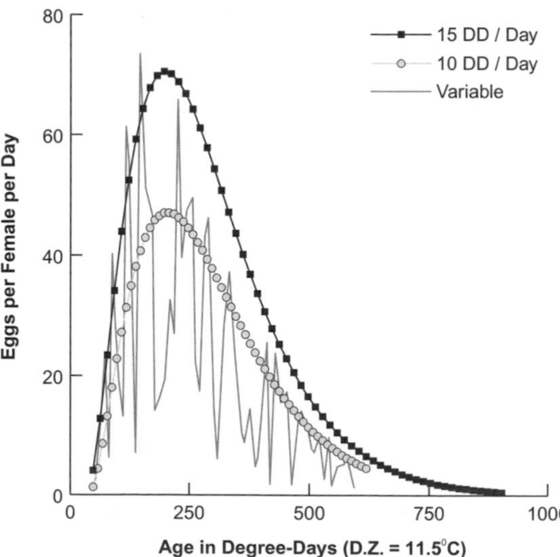

Figure 26.5. Simulated reproduction of monarchs for cool (10 day-degree [DD]/day), warm (15 DD/day), and variable conditions (see Zalucki 1981a).

Other factors can influence reproduction, such as the availability of adult food sources. These too will vary both spatially and seasonally. Areas with few nectar sources or widely distributed nectar sources should have lower potential reproduction.

The local abundance and distribution of milkweed influence potential reproduction (Zalucki and Kitching 1982b; Zalucki 1983; Zalucki and Suzuki 1987). When milkweed is rare and scattered, fewer plants are found by searching females, and full egg potential may not be realized.

Host plant abundance and distribution

The distribution and abundance of milkweed hosts at a landscape level will have a dramatic influence on monarch abundance. Even when they are not migrating, monarch adults do not stay confined to a single patch of milkweeds (Zalucki and Kitching 1985). Patch edges do not constitute a "barrier" to reproductive females (Ries and Debinski 2001), and a population covers much more than a local patch (Bull et al. 1985; Zalucki 1993). Zalucki (1983) simulated lifetime oviposition across a landscape made up of milkweed patches and scattered plants. The average birth to death distance of a nonmigrating female was about 11 to 16 km, depending on behavior between milkweed patches and on interpatch space. This is the average spatial scale at which environmental processes may influence the abundance of monarchs.

Host plant resource distribution should influence the survival of early-stage immatures, the survival of larvae when moving among plants, and levels of parasitism. Effects might also be expected on realized adult fecundity. Basically, as milkweed becomes less abundant and more widely scattered, we would expect monarch abundance to decline.

A number of factors may influence the abundance and distribution of milkweed. Agriculture can have a dramatic positive or negative influence, through land clearing, fallowing, plowing, and herbicide use. Climate can also affect the abundance and quality of milkweed by influencing the timing of germination and suitability of a season for plant growth. A warm, early spring might favor milkweed germination and regrowth from root stock, while a sudden cold snap or late-winter snowstorm could dramatically reduce milkweed abundance for migrating monarchs.

Modeling the influence of climate

Climate has a pervasive influence on insect populations, both directly and indirectly. Apart from the year-to-year variation in development and spatial phenology, climate can directly affect female reproduction and survival of immature stages. Consequently, we would expect considerable year-to-year variation in monarch abundance due to differences in climatic conditions. Historically, we know that there has been much annual variation in monarch abundance. In a comprehensive review, Brower (1995) listed years in which southward-migrating monarchs were in such abundance that they attracted extensive comment among scientists, naturalists, and the media. We do not yet understand what conditions may have been associated with such population events. More recent systematic collection of larval abundance data and adult-sighting records also indicates wide variation in monarch abundance among years (Prysby and Oberhauser, this volume; Howard and Davis, this volume). To determine whether anthropogenic factors have long-term detrimental impacts on species abundance, we need a null model that takes into account the influence of climate on year-to-year variation in abundance.

Zalucki and Rochester (1999) presented a model for the seasonal spatial distribution of monarchs in Australia and North America. That model was based on an analysis, using CLIMEX software (Sutherst and Maywald 1985), of the seasonal distribution of monarchs in Australia. CLIMEX enables the prediction of average seasonal (monthly) values for the ecoclimatic index for any locality. The ecoclimatic index is a relative measures that summarizes the climatic suitability of a site, combining the influence of temperature and moisture on potential population growth rates with various measures of climate stress (heat, aridity, cold, etc.). The model gave a reasonable prediction of the seasonal distribution of breeding-generation monarchs in eastern North America (figure 26.6). The spring distribution in the southern U.S. states was predicted, as was the summer range and absence of monarchs from certain spring areas. The model also predicted breeding in the southern areas in autumn, which has been subsequently borne out (Prysby and Oberhauser, this volume; W. Calvert, pers. comm.), and along the Gulf Coast in winter in some years if milkweed is provided.

We have calculated the seasonal ecoclimatic index for the southeast Queensland area (figure 26.7). Summer and autumn are about equally suitable, winter is generally much less so, and conditions pick up in the spring. Also shown is the average abundance of monarchs on a relative scale based on adult sampling over 2 years (Zalucki et al. 1993). CLIMEX prediction and adult abundance are similar except in autumn when monarchs are less abundant than expected. We attribute this to high levels of parasitism by tachinid flies in late summer and early autumn (Zalucki 1981b).

We extend this prediction of temporal suitability among years for southeast Queensland (figure 26.8). Obviously not all years are equally suited to monarchs, and we expect a good deal of variation in abundance. Unfortunately, we do not have the long-term data to test this prediction. Similar predictions could be made for North America.

DISCUSSION: LESSONS FOR NORTH AMERICA

Climate has an important influence on the distribution and abundance of insects. Apart from development and phenology, climate will influence the vital processes of reproduction and survival. Monarch phenology is relatively easy to model, and one of the salient predictions is that there will be large differences in the timing of abundance of different stages across years and space. The mechanisms responsible are likely to be the timing of spring migration from overwintering sites in Mexico and differences among years in temperature. This makes simple statements about the likely exposure of monarch life stages to seasonal risk factors, such as Bt pollen, problematic. The proportion exposed will vary between years and locations (see also Oberhauser et al. 2001).

Large-scale weather events are likely to have a major impact on abundance by directly influencing reproduction. Cool, overcast weather reduces egg production and the conditions suitable for flight and egg laying. The shortfall is not made up on subsequent suitable days. Extreme temperature may influence the survival of immatures and adults. Temperatures consistently above 33°C to 35°C are not suitable to monarchs and may account for their absence from southern U.S. states after spring (Malcolm et al. 1987; Zalucki and Rochester 1999).

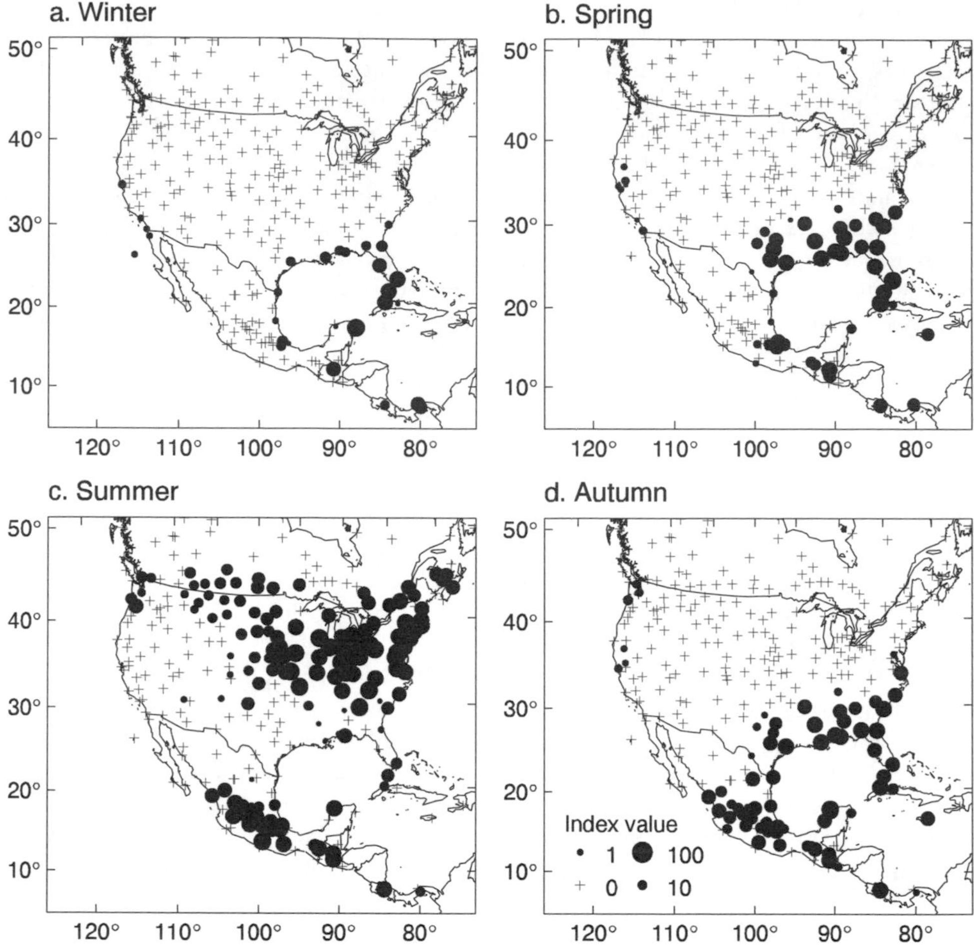

Figure 26.6. Predicted seasonal distribution of monarchs in North America based on a CLIMEX model for monarchs developed from Australian data (see Zalucki and Rochester 1999 for details). Locations marked with a cross have indices of zero, and the sizes of the solid circles represent relative abundances based on climatic conditions.

Climate can also influence basic requirements such as the availability of host plants and adult nectar resources.

The distribution and abundance of milkweed influence reproduction and the survival of immature monarchs. Breeding females range widely even when not migrating (Zalucki 1983, 1993), and if distances between patches are large, the patches are small, and individual plants in the interpatch space are rare, then female fecundity may be reduced. Patch size and distribution may also influence the survival of immature stages by influencing exposure to natural enemies and the success of larval movement among plants. Mapping the distribution of milkweed resources across the North American breeding range for monarchs is an essential first step to understanding their abundance at a landscape level (see also Zalucki et al. 1981), and we suggest that monarch-monitoring programs should assess local milkweed abundance.

Our simple CLIMEX analysis of the seasonal geographic distribution of monarchs in Australia predicted the influence of climate on spatial and temporal abundance; it is essential that such models be tested using large-scale monitoring data. Models can provide powerful tools for assessing long-term trends in changes in abundance that may be due to anthropogenic changes in the monarch's habitat.

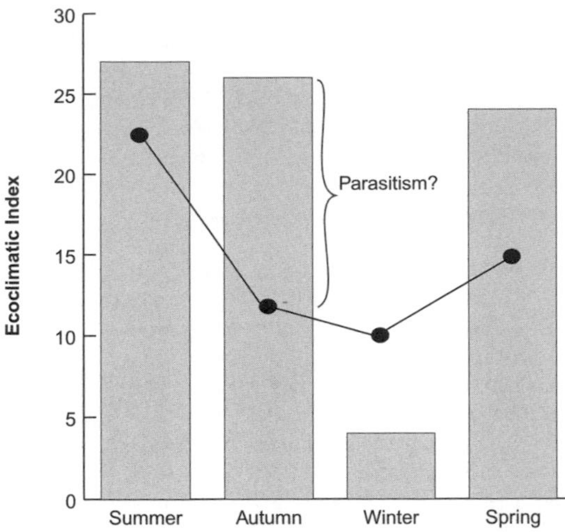

Figure 26.7. Seasonal ecoclimatic index (climatic suitability of a location) for monarchs in southeast Queensland (bars) and observed relative seasonal variation in monarch abundance (circles connected by line) (data taken from Zalucki et al. 1993).

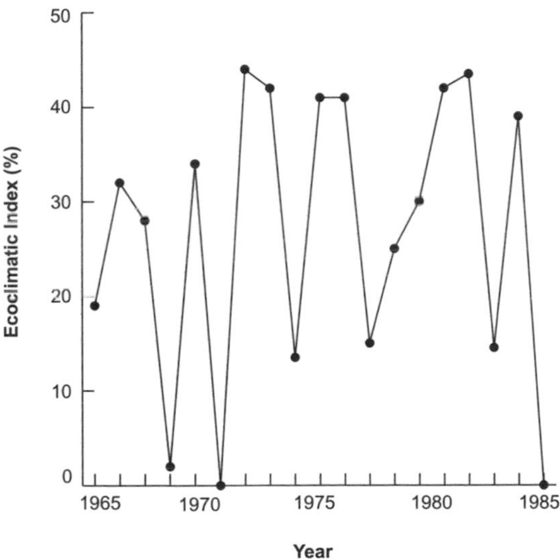

Figure 26.8. Variation in ecoclimatic index (climatic suitability of a location) for monarchs in southeast Queensland across years 1965 to 1986 based on climatic data for Amberley (lat 27°36′S, long 152°42′E).

Acknowledgments

We thank the U.S. Fish and Wildlife Service (in a grant to O. R. Taylor and K. Oberhauser) for support toward attending the Lawrence meeting. The bioclimatic analysis was supported by Australian Research Council (ARC) Large Grant A19937166. The phenology simulation analysis was supported by the ARC grant and funding from World Wildlife Fund Canada.

References

Borkin, S. S. 1990. Notes of shifting distribution patterns and survival of immature *Danaus plexippus* (Lepidoptera: Danaidae) on the food plant *Asclepias syriaca.* Gt. Lakes Entomol. 15:199–206.

Brower, L. P. 1995. Understanding and misunderstanding the migration of the monarch butterfly (Nymphalidae) in North America: 1857–1995. J. Lepid. Soc. 49:304–85.

Bull, C. M., M. P. Zalucki, Y. Suzuki, D. Mackay, and R. L. Kitching. 1985. An experimental investigation of resource use by female monarch butterflies, *Danaus plexippus* (L.). Aust. J. Ecol. 10:391–98.

Cockrell, B. J., S. B. Malcolm, and L. P. Brower. 1993. Time, temperature, and latitudinal constraints on the annual recolonization of eastern North America by the monarch butterfly. In S. B. Malcolm and M. P. Zalucki, eds., Biology and conservation of the monarch butterfly, pp. 233–51. Los Angeles: Natural History Museum of Los Angeles County.

Dingle, H., M. P. Zalucki, and W. A. Rochester. 1999. Season specific directional movement in migratory Australian butterflies. Aust. J. Entomol. 38:323–29.

James, D. G. 1979. Observations on two overwintering clusters of *Danaus plexippus* (L.) (Lepidoptera: Nymphalidae) in the Sydney area during 1978. Aust. Entomol. Mag. 5:81–85.

James, D. G. 1993. Migration biology of the monarch butterfly in Australia. In S. B. Malcolm and M. P. Zalucki, eds., Biology and conservation of the monarch butterfly, pp. 189–200. Los Angeles: Natural History Museum of Los Angeles County.

Jesse, L. C. H., and J. J. Obrycki. 2000. Field deposition of Bt transgenic corn pollen: lethal effects on the monarch butterfly. Oecologia 125:241–48.

Kitching, R. L., and E. Scheermeyer. 1993. The comparative biology and ecology of the Australian Danaines. In S. B. Malcolm and M. P. Zalucki, eds., Biology and conservation of the monarch butterfly, pp. 165–75. Los Angeles: Natural History Museum of Los Angeles County.

Losey, J. E., L. S. Rayor, and M. E. Carter. 1999. Transgenic pollen harms monarch larvae. Nature 399:214.

Malcolm, S. B., B. J. Cockrell, and L. P. Brower. 1987. Monarch butterfly voltinism: effects of temperature constraints at different latitudes. Oikos 49:77–82.

Malcolm, S. B., and M. P. Zalucki, eds. 1993. Biology and conservation of the monarch butterfly. Los Angeles: Natural History Museum of Los Angeles County.

Oberhauser, K. S., M. D. Prysby, H. R. Mattila, D. E. Stanley-Horn, M. K. Sears, G. Dively, E. Olson, J. M. Pleasants, Wai-Ki F. Lam, and R. L. Hellmich. 2001. Temporal and spatial overlap between monarch larvae and corn pollen. Proc. Natl. Acad. Sci. USA 98:11913–18.

Ries, L., and M. Debinski. 2001. Butterfly responses to habitat edges in the highly fragmented prairies of Central Iowa. J. Anim. Ecol. 70:840–52.

Rochester, W. A., and M. P. Zalucki. 2000. Variation in the phenology of monarch butterflies in North America: estimates from Monte Carlo simulation analysis. Final report. World Wildlife Fund Canada.

Shephard, J. M., J. M. Hughes, and M. P. Zalucki. 2002. Genetic differentiation between Australian and North American populations of the monarch butterfly *Danaus plexippus* (L.) (Lepidoptera: Nymphalidae): an exploration using allozyme electrophoresis. Biol. J. Linn. Soc. 75:437–52.

Sutherst, R. W., and G. F. Maywald. 1985. A computerised system for matching climates in ecology. Agric. Ecosyst. Environ. 13:281–99.

Woodson, R. E. 1954. The North American species of *Asclepias* L. Ann. Mo. Bot. Gard. 41:1–211.

Zalucki, M. P. 1981a. The effects of age and weather on egg laying in *Danaus plexippus* L. (Lepidoptera: Danaidae). Res. Popul. Ecol. 23:318–27.

Zalucki, M. P. 1981b. Temporal and spatial variation of parasitism in *Danaus plexippus* (L.) (Lepidoptera: Nymphalidae, Danaidae). Aust. Entomol. Mag. 8:3–9.

Zalucki, M. P. 1982. Temperature and rate of development in two species of *Danaus*, *D. plexippus* and *D. chrysippus*. J. Aust. Entomol. Soc. 21:241–46.

Zalucki, M. P. 1983. Modelling egg laying in the monarch butterfly, *Danaus plexippus* L. Res. Popul. Ecol. 25:353–65.

Zalucki, M. P. 1986. The monarch butterfly. In R. L. Kitching, ed., The ecology of exotic plants and animals in Australia. Brisbane: Jacaranda-Wiley.

Zalucki, M. P. 1993. Sex around the milkweed patch—the significance of patches of host plants in monarch reproduction. In S. B. Malcolm and M. P. Zalucki, eds., Biology and conservation of the monarch butterfly, pp. 40–76. Los Angeles: Natural History Museum of Los Angeles County.

Zalucki, M. P., and L. P. Brower. 1992. Survival of first instar larvae of *Danaus plexippus* L. in relation to cardiac glycoside and latex content of *Asclepias humistrata*. Chemoecology 3:81–93.

Zalucki, M. P., L. P. Brower, and A. Alonso-Mejía. 2001a. Detrimental effects of latex and cardiac glycosides on survival and growth of first instar *Danaus plexippus* feeding on the sandhill milkweed *Asclepias humistrata*. Ecol. Entomol. 26:212–24.

Zalucki, M. P., A. Chandica, and R. L. Kitching. 1981. Quantifying the distribution and abundance of an animal's resource using aerial photography. Oecologia 50:176–83.

Zalucki, M. P., A. R. Clarke, and S. B. Malcolm. 2002. Ecology and behavior of first instar larval Lepidoptera. Annu. Rev. Entomol. 47:361–93.

Zalucki, M. P., J. M. Hughes, J. M. Arthur, and P. A. Carter. 1993. Temporal variation at four loci in a continuously breeding population of *Danaus plexippus*. Heredity 70:205–13.

Zalucki, M. P., and R. L. Kitching. 1982a. Temporal and spatial variation of mortality in field population of *Danaus plexippus* and *D. chrysippus* L. larvae (Lepidoptera: Nymphalidae). Oecologia 53:201–7.

Zalucki, M. P., and R. L. Kitching. 1982b. Movement pattern in *Danaus plexippus* L. Behavior 80:174–98.

Zalucki, M. P., and R. L. Kitching. 1985. The dynamics of adult *Danaus plexippus* L. around patches of its host plant *Asclepias* spp. J. Lepid. Soc. 38:209–19.

Zalucki, M. P., and S. B. Malcolm. 1999. Plant latex and first-instar monarch larval growth and survival on three North American milkweed species. J. Chem. Ecol. 25:1827–42.

Zalucki, M. P., S. B. Malcolm, T. D. Paine, C. C. Hanlon, L. P. Brower, and A. R. Clarke. 2001b. It's the first bites that count: survival of first-instar monarchs on milkweeds. Austr. Ecol. 26:547–55.

Zalucki, M. P., and W. A. Rochester. 1999. Estimating the effect of climate on the distribution and abundance of the monarch butterfly, *Danaus plexippus* (L.): a tale of two continents. In J. Hoth, L. Merino, K. Oberhauser, I. Pisantry, S. Price, and T. Wilkinson, eds., The 1997 North American Conference on the Monarch Butterfly, pp. 150–63. Montreal: Commission for Environmental Cooperation.

Zalucki, M. P., and Y. Suzuki. 1987. Milkweed patch quality, adult population structure and egg laying in *Danaus plexippus* (Lepidoptera: Nymphalidae). J. Lepid. Soc. 41:13–22.

27

Simulating the Development and Migration of the Monarch Butterfly

Johannes J. Feddema, Jason Shields, Orley R. Taylor, and David Bennett

INTRODUCTION

A major issue in contemporary ecology is the extent to which organisms might be influenced by anthropogenic effects such as habitat fragmentation and climate change. In the case of the monarch butterfly, these concerns extend to protection of the overwintering sites in Mexico, transgenic crops, and agricultural practices. Monarchs, which are being monitored at the overwintering sites and by several citizen science programs, provide us with the opportunity to determine the extent to which one species is influenced by physical and anthropogenic factors. To make such distinctions, we need to develop models that effectively predict the timing of monarch migration and population size. Such models can also be used to assess the potential effects of climate change on the population dynamics of monarchs.

The annual migration of monarchs from their wide-ranging summer breeding grounds to relatively few concentrated overwintering areas is unmatched in other species (Brower 1995). These overwintering populations assemble individuals from widespread regions, and thus reflect the impacts of the weather, climate, vegetation dynamics, and human actions integrated over an entire continent (see Rochester and Zalucki, this volume). Here, we describe a model designed to simulate the timing and abundance of monarchs in their summer breeding range. This model is based on fundamental assumptions about monarch behavior in relation to climate conditions. We also consider how the model can be improved by accommodating additional climate factors and vegetation parameters. The ultimate goal is to simulate natural monarch behavior, accounting for impacts of natural factors such as climate, weather, and vegetation, in order to isolate the aggregated impacts of human actions. A secondary motivation is to develop a theoretical framework within which theories of monarch behavior, such as alternative theories concerning the factors that govern the initiation and pace of the spring and fall migrations, can be tested.

The model allows users to input parameter values that affect the population dynamics of monarchs, and is structured to provide considerable flexibility to users as they test different assumptions about monarch-climate relationships. The current version estimates the approximate number of generations of monarch butterflies produced during each summer season, as well as the timing and movement of the migrations. Model results can then be compared to observed statistics on spring arrival times in the United States, and estimates of overwintering colony sizes in Mexico.

MODEL STRUCTURE AND OVERVIEW

The structure of the model (figure 27.1) is based on a grid for which the user defines a resolution scale. The current model simulates a single annual migration cycle for the area within the contiguous United States east of the Rocky Mountains. The grid system is calculated based on input coordinates of the study area and a user-defined average daily travel distance of a monarch butterfly. Once a spring

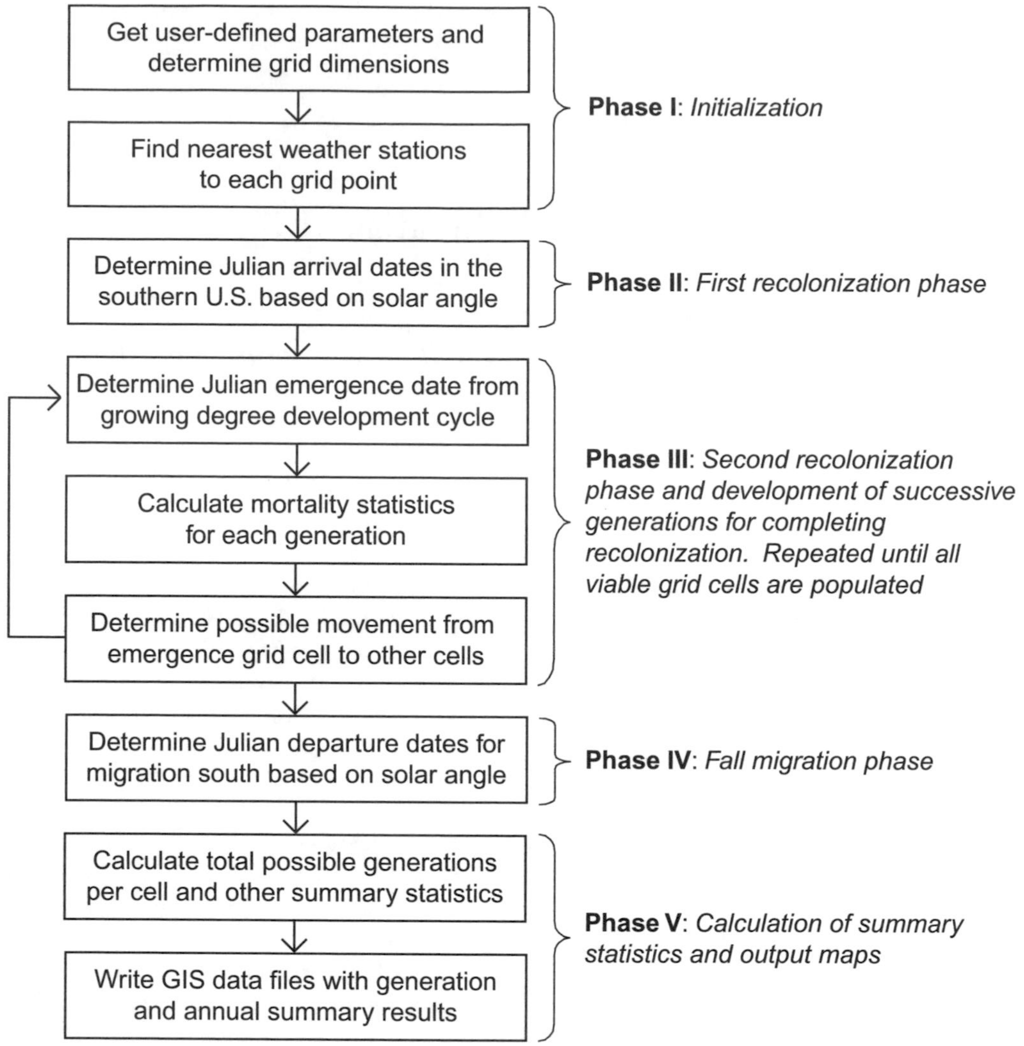

Figure 27.1. Overview of the model layout.

migration sequence is initiated, it continues until all grid cells are populated by monarch butterflies or until it is impeded by natural factors. When all grid cells with climate conditions compatible with monarch survival and development have been populated, a number of calculations are made to estimate the number of generations and the total seasonal monarch production at each grid cell. Estimates are also made of the number of nonreproductive monarchs that initiate the return migration in the fall.

We assume that the rate and pattern of recolonization is a function of sun angle, reproductive and development rates, and travel speed. The core of the model is based on the development cycle work of Zalucki (1982) and Cockrell and colleagues (1993), and uses growing degree-days to track the development of the monarch's life cycle from egg to adult eclosion. In addition, we use solar angle, derived from latitude and time of year, to control the timing of the spring and fall migrations. Solar angle is correlated with monarch arrival at different latitudes (D. L. Gibo and O. R. Taylor, pers. comm.). The user defines average daily travel distance during the spring migration phase, and the model assumes that movement is equally likely in all directions and equidistant from the cell where a butterfly emerges after the development cycle. Once one monarch reaches a

Table 27.1. Model input parameters

Parameter	Description/function of the parameter	Typical values
year	Year of simulation (only one year at a time)	1993–1999
xlatll	Latitude coordinate for the lower-left corner of the study area	30°N
xlonll	Longitude coordinate for the lower-left corner of the study area	100°W
xlatur	Latitude coordinate for the upper-right corner of the study area	49°N
xlonur	Longitude coordinate for the upper-right corner of the study area	70°W
gdist	Daily maximum rate of travel for monarchs (in miles)	50 miles
pmig	Northernmost latitude reached by recolonizing migrants from Mexico	38°N
sola	Solar altitude angle that signifies the arrival for the recolonizing generation of monarchs	58°
solr	First solar altitude angle in the pair that brackets the period of fall migration back to Mexico	60°
sole	Second solar altitude angle in a pair that brackets the period of fall migration back to Mexico	52°
growdd	Total number of degree-days required for an egg to pass through all stages of development and emerge as an adult	351.88°C
baset	Developmental zero, or base temperature used in the growing degree calculation	11.5°C
thgdd	Temperature above which each additional degree reported for the daily high adds only one half of a degree toward growing degree accumulation (T_{low} in equations 2 and 4)	30°C
tngdd	Temperature above which each additional degree reported for the daily high results in no additional accumulation of degree-days (T_{high} in equation 4)	35°C
ngeggs	Number of days eggs are deposited in a cell south of *pmig*, i.e., the duration of the migration wave through a grid cell	14 days
mdays	Number of days of the mating stage before newly emerging adult butterflies begin laying eggs	5 days
mmdays	Number of day equivalents butterflies travel during their mating stage (*mdays*)	5 days
edays	Number of days that migrating monarchs lay eggs (including *mdays*)	24 days
tml	Daily high temperature above which some mortality occurs for developing monarchs	38°C
mtml	Amount of mortality, in percent, that occurs with the incidence of *tml* on a given day	2%
tmh	Daily high temperature, above *tml*, at which additional mortality occurs	41°C
mtmh	Amount of mortality, in percent, that occurs with the incidence of *tmh* on a given day	4%
ntml	Number of consecutive days above *tmh* that result in additional mortality	3 days
mntml	Amount of additional mortality, in percent, that results with *ntml*	4%
tmmin	Daily low temperature that results in 100% mortality for developing monarchs	−3.33°C

Note: Parameters determined by the user at the outset of the model run. Parameter names are as used in the model code, and typical values are the values used for simulations in this chapter.

grid cell, it is assumed occupied until the fall migration is initiated from that cell.

To make the model as flexible as possible, a number of input variables are asked of the user at the beginning of the simulation (table 27.1). For each simulation, 21 output files are generated that include information on arrival and departure dates for each grid cell; emergence dates and mortality statistics for each generation produced; estimates of the total number of generations and associated mortalities produced at each grid cell; and the number of generations produced and associated mortalities for the nonreproductive southward migrant population, defined as the emerging monarchs produced during the days occurring between two user-defined solar angles. If requested, 2 files are created to store daily emergence and mortality data during the entire migration process for each day monarch butterflies are present in the study area. These files can be used to create animations of the migration. All the output grid files are in the ESRI ASCII grid format.

MODEL IMPLEMENTATION

The model is structured to simulate the following migration phases: recolonization of the eastern United States by monarchs from their overwintering grounds in Mexico, development cycles of successive generations of monarchs in the United States, and the fall migration back to Mexico. Here we describe the model setup and implementation for each of these phases, and review the calculation of monarch development summary statistics for each grid cell.

Phase I: Model initialization and data organization

To execute the model, users first determine the year of interest, the study area of interest, and the grid resolution to be used for the model run. After entering the year of interest (from 1993 to 1999, the only years for which data are presently available), the user specifies the size of the study area by entering the lower-left and upper-right latitude and longitude coordinates. The user also defines an assumed average daily travel distance of a monarch butterfly during the migration phase (*gdist*). For computational efficiency, this parameter, which is assumed to be 50 miles in the results presented here, defines the distance between grid cells (Zalucki 1983).

The second initialization step, and most computationally intensive portion of the model, involves the reading in and linking of the temperature data to each grid cell. Daily minimum and maximum temperature data are read in for 4672 Cooperative Observers Network (COOP) weather stations in U.S. states east of the Rocky Mountains. These data were obtained from the cooperative temperature data set from the National Climate Data Center (2001) and cover the years 1993 to 1999. These years were selected because they are the only years for which comparable observed monarch arrival dates exist, and because the volume of data precludes easy compilation of additional years of data. While this data set is rich with respect to spatial density, data are frequently missing. To overcome this limitation and avoid interpolations based on different stations within a development cycle, the model identifies and stores the location of the nearest 30 stations to each grid cell. When temperature data are needed to simulate a development cycle within a grid cell, the station nearest to that cell is checked for a complete time series of daily data for the duration of that development cycle. If there are no missing data, the development cycle is calculated. If data are missing, the program searches outward in stepwise fashion until the closest station with a complete temperature record is found. After this initialization phase, simulation begins.

Phase II: Recolonization of the eastern United States from Mexico

The successive brood strategy (Malcolm et al. 1993; Cockrell et al. 1993) drives migration in the current version of the model. This strategy assumes that return migrants lay eggs in the southern United States and successive generations recolonize the regions farther north. The model currently prohibits returning butterflies from migrating north of a user-defined latitude (*pmig*). Their arrival at grid cells below this limit is determined by a user-defined solar angle (*sola*), following the theory proposed by D. L. Gibo and O. R. Taylor (pers. comm.). The actual arrival date is calculated from the solar angle and the latitude of the center of each grid cell in the following manner (Oke 1987):

$$(1) \quad j = N \times \frac{\arccos(soldec/-23.45)}{360} - 10,$$

where j = Julian arrival date, N is the number of days in a particular year, and solar declination (*soldec*) is defined as the difference between the latitude of the grid location and the zenith angle derived from *sola*. By default this creates latitudinal bands of arrival dates across the southern portion of the study area, since the dates are strictly determined by the latitude location of a grid cell. Once monarch butterflies recolonize a grid cell, the next phase of the model is initiated.

Phase III: Monarch development cycle

Monarchs are assumed to begin laying eggs on the day they arrive in a particular grid cell. Duration of the egg-laying period (in days) in the southern portion of the study area is determined by the user (*ngeggs*). This parameter represents the length of time that monarchs migrate through a grid cell. In the results presented here, we assume that the migration lasts for 14 days. The model then begins calculating the development cycle in each grid cell where monarchs are present. To simulate the time of development from egg to butterfly, we use a slightly modified version of the growing degree model developed by Zalucki (1982). Zalucki (1982) determined that 351.88°C growing degree-days (*growdd*) above a developmental zero of 11.5°C (*baset*) was required for development of a butterfly from the egg stage.

We modified Zalucki's approach in our calculations of growing degree-days and also implemented a methodology for estimating climate-related mortality statistics during a development cycle within a grid cell. First, in a simplification of the method used by Zalucki (1982), the value for growing degree-days is determined from the difference between the average daily temperature and the developmental zero temperature (*baset*):

$$(2) \quad \mathrm{DD} = [(T_{max} + T_{min})/2] - baset,$$

where DD is the daily value for growing degree-days, T_{max} is the daily maximum temperature, and T_{min} is the daily minimum temperature. Second, the potential retarding effect of excessive temperatures on development rates is simulated. This modification is based on the findings by Zalucki (1982) and from our own observations (pers. observ.). This approach requires the user to define two temperature parameters that bound monarch development rates at high temperatures. If the maximum temperature reported for a given day lies between these two limiting temperatures, the following formula is used to calculate degree-days:

(3) $T_{adj} = (T_{max} - \text{thgdd})/2 + \text{thgdd}$,

where T_{adj} is the new adjusted high temperature and *thgdd* is the user-defined lower bounding temperature. If the maximum reported daily temperature for a given day exceeds the highest bounding temperature (*tngdd*), the following formula is used to calculate the new adjusted high temperature (T_{adj}):

(4) $T_{adj} = (\text{tngdd} - \text{thgdd})/2 + \text{thgdd}$.

T_{adj} is then substituted for T_{max} in equation 2.

The model also addresses mortality. While many factors contribute to monarch mortality, we will isolate only mortality related to temperature thresholds to begin understanding the relationship between climate and population dynamics. Zalucki (1982), Cockrell and colleagues (1993), and O. R. Taylor (pers. observ.) suggest that certain temperature thresholds, both high and low, can be fatal to developing monarchs. The occurrence of a hard freeze, as defined by the user (*tmmin*, less than –3.33°C in this study), results in 100% mortality for all developing immature monarchs within a grid cell. The user inputs high temperature thresholds and related percentages of mortality. Two threshold temperatures may be specified; the lower high temperature mortality threshold is set by the parameter *tml* (38°C in this study). If the high temperature for the day surpasses this threshold, it will result in a user-specified percentage mortality (*mtml*, 2% in this study). Similarly, a second threshold may be set in the parameter *tmh* (41°C in this study), and if high temperatures surpass this higher threshold, mortality will be increased to a percentage set by *mtmh* (4% in this study). A final threshold for mortality is based on the duration of excessively hot temperatures. If daily temperatures exceed *tml* for *ntml* days (3 days in this study), then an additional *mntml* percentage (4% in this study) for mortality is recorded during the development cycle. Mortality statistics are accumulated and recorded as a total mortality associated with the current development cycle in a cell. Although these mortalities are calculated, tracked, and reported, they do not yet affect the calculation of the total number of generations produced in a cell because of the uncertainty about the temperature thresholds and percentage of the population affected.

Once individual monarchs accumulate the required number of degree-days, the emergence day is recorded for the grid cell, as well as the combined possible mortality associated with both high and low temperature thresholds. The new adults begin to move throughout the migration range and recolonize cells not yet reached by previous generations of monarchs. In its current form, the movement phase is simply implemented and not very realistic. Since the model only needs to know when grid cells are first occupied, all movement takes place at the rate associated with migration. It is assumed that butterflies can move equally well in all directions from their cell of origin, at the distance of one cell per day (i.e., the user-specified *gdist*). It is further assumed that monarchs cannot lay eggs until they mature reproductively. The user specifies the typical number of days required for this to occur (*mdays*) and the maximum possible distance of travel that can occur during those days in units of number of travel days during this period (*mmdays* = 5 days in this study). For example, if *mdays* is set to 5 and *mmdays* to 3, butterflies can travel up to three grid cells in distance during the 5 days required to reach sexual maturity. The total distance a butterfly can travel is determined by its functional lifetime. This is determined by the user and represents the last day (*edays*, 24 days in this study), from the emergence date, on which a butterfly can lay eggs. Emerging butterflies can thus move equidistant in all directions to colonize all cells covered within a distance of *edays* – *mdays* + *mmdays* cells from the cell of origin. If a cell has not been previously occupied, then an arrival date is recorded. Once occupied, the cell is assumed occupied until the fall migration is initiated. This cycle repeats itself until all cells in the study area are occupied, or until the fall migration has been initiated.

Phase IV: Fall migration back to Mexico

The initiation and duration of the fall migration back to Mexico is determined by the solar elevation angles at a grid cell (determined from equation 1 and user inputs), based on observations by D. L. Gibo and O. R. Taylor (pers. comm.). The fall migration period is initiated by a user-specified solar angle (*solr*) and ends on another user-defined solar angle (*sole*). This period occurs earlier and lasts longer for more northerly grid cells. The assumption is that butterflies that emerge during this period are in reproductive diapause and will migrate to Mexico. The total number of cohorts produced is based on the assumption that one cohort begins development for each day after the first monarch arrives at the grid cell. Butterflies that emerge after the date specified by *sole* are assumed not to migrate successfully and are not included in summary calculations for that cell.

Phase V: Summary calculations

Once all calculations for each generation are complete, the program calculates summary information. First, the spring arrival date and initial and last days of the fall migration are recorded as output maps for each grid cell. Second, the model calculates the total possible number of generations that can be produced in each cell, truncated to a whole number. It also calculates the total number of monarch cohorts produced. This calculation is based on the assumption that one new cohort of butterflies starts developing each day that monarchs are present in a grid cell. Since mortality is tracked during the development cycle of each cohort, the mortality for all the cohorts developed is also calculated. Similarly, the total number of cohorts that form the fall migration (i.e., that emerge during the return migration period) is summed and reported along with a percentage for mortality.

MODEL RESULTS

Our description of model results uses the parameter settings shown in table 27.1. Shields (2001) provides a more detailed evaluation of the model results and validation. Comparison statistics are illustrated for differences in arrival date, predicted mortality for offspring of return migrants (spring), and the predicted number of cohorts (generations) participating in the fall migration (figure 27.2). To illustrate the possible range of differences between simulated results, comparisons are not always between 2 successive years. Arrival times of monarchs can differ markedly from year to year as illustrated in a comparison of Julian arrival dates for 1993 and 1998 (figure 27.2a). Even though there is little difference in the arrival times of the first wave of monarchs returning from Mexico, year-to-year temperature differences cause variations in the time needed to complete the development cycle of their offspring, resulting in significant differences in predicted arrival times north of the 38th parallel (*pmig*). Similarly, mortality maps for the development cycle of the second generation are shown for 1994 and 1998 (figure 27.2b). This generation is geographically limited to sites south of 38° north latitude in the model. In some cases 100% mortality in a few cells is caused by freezing weather occurring after the 14-day egg-laying period. Under these circumstances the model stops all development at those cells. Clearly, such events can have a large influence on monarch population dynamics (see also Rochester and Zalucki, this volume). Part of the patchiness in the results can be attributed to microclimatic influences on individual temperature stations used in the study.

There are also significant differences in the number of fall migrant generations produced from year to year (figure 27.2c), as illustrated by comparing estimates for 1993 and 1994. Two factors appear to control the variation in the number of cohorts that emerge during the return migration window. First, the window varies from 20 days in duration near 38° north latitude to 26 days in the northern regions of the study area. This explains the higher values in the northern areas. In addition, these values are influenced by temperature conditions that precede the migration window. If development is slow and suddenly accelerates just prior to the return period, many generations can emerge on the same day. Conversely, low growing day-degree accumulation during the window period results in few migrant generations being produced.

Simulated estimates of the maximum number of generations that could be produced based on temperature constraints only for 1993 to 1999 also show large variations from year to year (figure 27.3). This

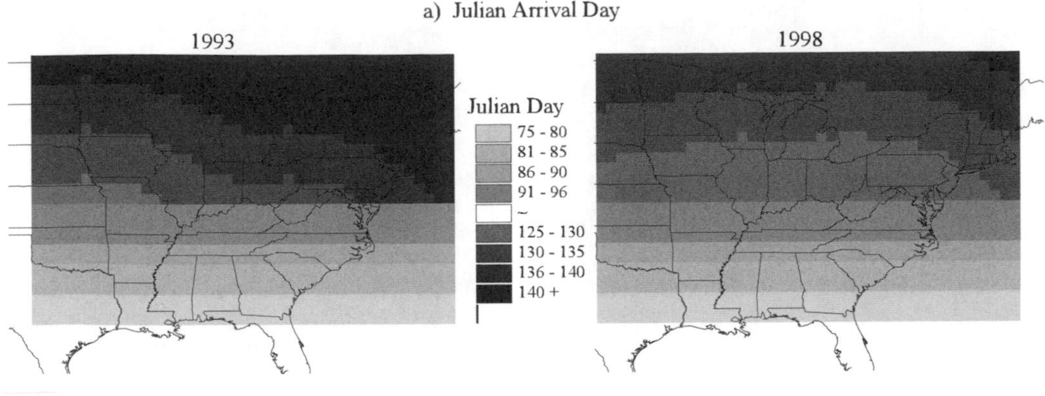

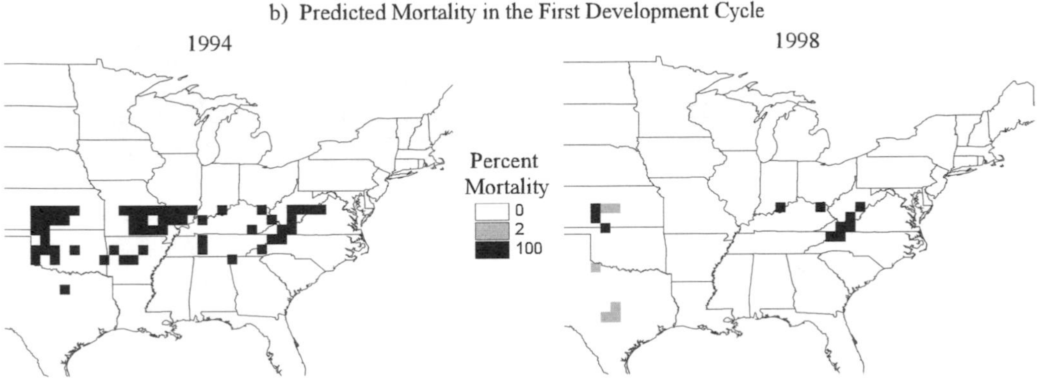

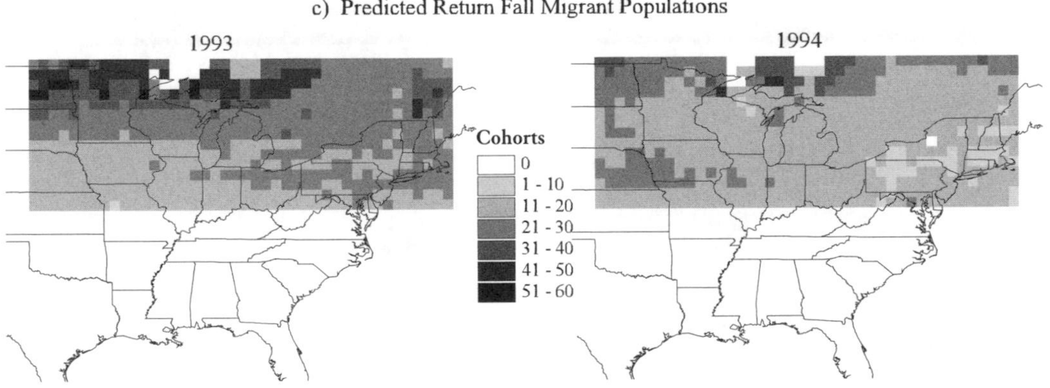

Figure 27.2. Comparisons of (a) arrival times between 1993 and 1998, (b) mortality during development for the second generation between 1994 and 1998, and (c) estimated total number of cohorts participating in the fall migration between 1993 and 1994.

statistic is based on the number of back-to-back development cycles possible in a grid cell. Although the entire study area is shown in the figures, only the cells producing return migrants (above 38° north latitude) are considered to contribute to the fall migration. Years 1993 and 1996 had a reduced capacity for monarch production, while 1998 was a favorable year, with larger than normal areas of the eastern United States capable of producing three or four monarch generations. These numbers reflect

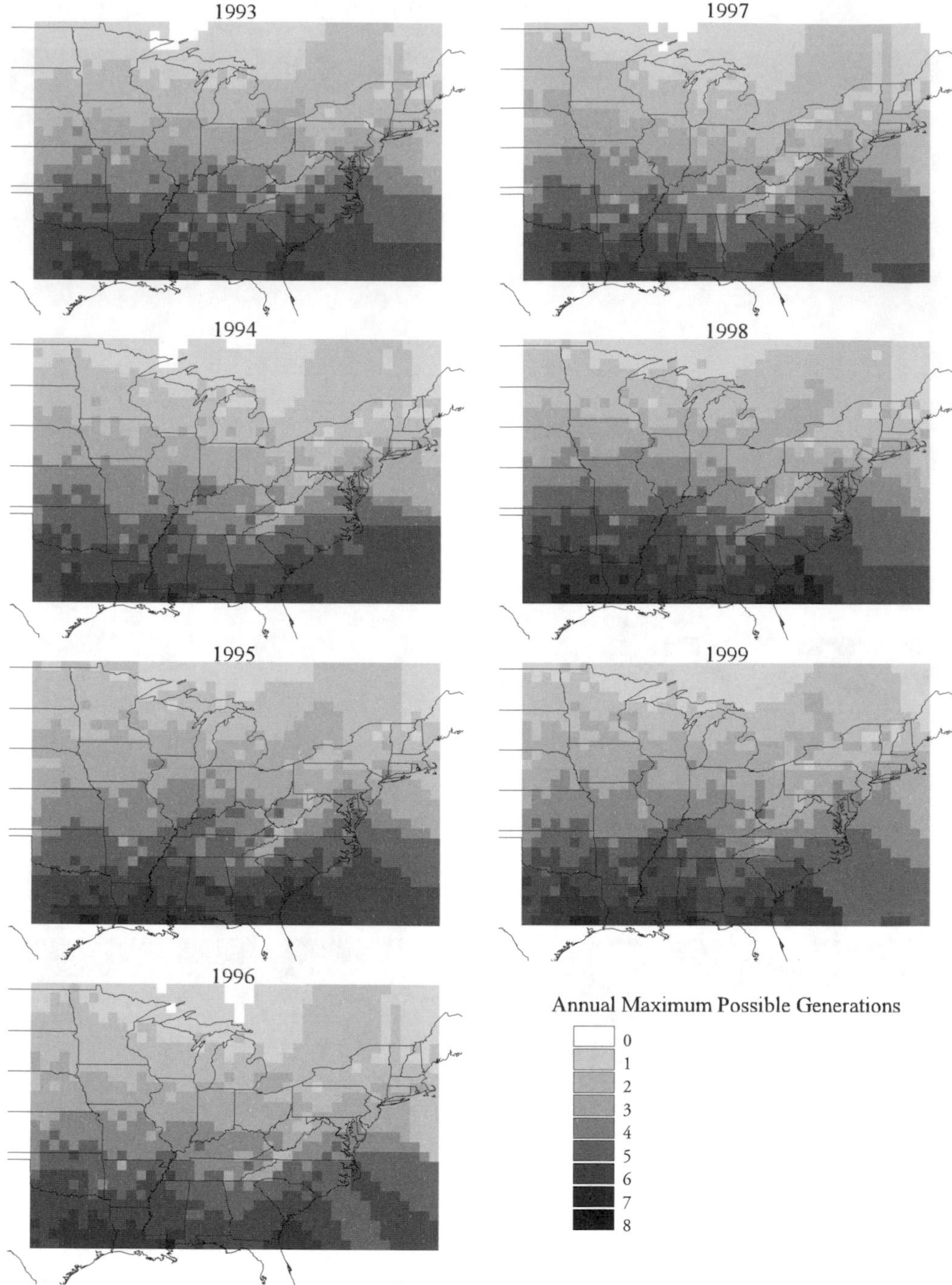

Figure 27.3. Comparison of total number of generations produced for the years 1993 to 1999.

the great potential for annual variation in monarch production, and could provide insight to the fluctuation of overwintering population estimates. Overall these estimates agree reasonably well with estimates from Cockrell and colleagues (1993), although they estimated three generations per year at St. Croix, Wisconsin, while we typically produce only one or two generations for the same location.

MODEL VALIDATION

Model validation is particularly difficult because relatively few observations are available that match the statistics produced by the model. First, and most importantly, Journey North data can be used to validate the timing of the recolonization phases of the model (Journey North 2001). The second data set is based on estimates of the volume of overwintering butterflies in Mexico. Each of these data sets tests different aspects of the migration and the model's predictive abilities. These data sets are the only data available for model validation, but since they were not originally intended for this purpose, their use requires caution when matching observations to model results.

A comparison of first-arrival data from Journey North to the closest grid-cell arrival dates for the years from 1995 to 1999 suggests that our results are reasonable (table 27.2). Comparative statistics reported here include the mean absolute error (MAE) between observed and simulated arrival times, the root mean square error (RMSE) between the observed and simulated arrival dates, systematic and unsystematic components of the RMSE, and R^2 (for a more complete description of the statistics, see Willmott et al. 1985). The MAE statistic provides the most direct measure of the model's performance, showing the average number of days the model arrival simulations differ from observed arrival dates. On average, model simulations differ from observations by about 10 to 17 days using the raw Journey North data. However, some of the observed error in the MAE statistics can be attributed to factors other than model error. When evaluating the data, we noted that many reports of first sightings have significant variations in quality. For example, in some cases within a single grid cell there are two or more observations of first sightings that differ by more than 30 days. To illustrate the effect of this type of problem on model validation, we have included a set of statistics for 1998 (edited 1998) where all obviously poor-quality sightings were removed from the data set. The model performs much better when compared to this edited data set, with model arrival dates differing from observed arrival dates by about 10 days. The relative number of recorded observations for a year, and the spatial coverage of the data, may provide further problems in calculating these statistics. These issues will need to be addressed when using this database for model validation in the future.

Components of the RMSE statistic provide additional useful information about model performance. The systematic RMSE component measures the difference between the regression line of the observed and predicted observations, while the unsystematic RMSE measures the random error about the regression line of the predicted observations. Most of the observed differences between the observed and modeled data are in the systematic RMSE. This suggests that the model systematically differs from observed migration patterns, and therefore significant model improvements should be possible. The

Table 27.2. Model validation statistics

Year of simulation	No. of validation observations	MAE (days)	RMSE	RMSEs	RMSEu	R^2
1995	138	13.24	15.96	15.34	4.41	0.63
1996	117	17.51	22.83	19.84	11.28	0.54
1997	287	11.21	15.53	13.13	8.29	0.68
1998	241	14.22	20.37	16.70	11.66	0.52
1999	281	9.56	12.61	9.77	7.97	0.83
Edited 1998	218	10.62	14.01	12.09	7.07	0.73

Note: First observation statistics from Journey North data (Journey North 2001). Model parameter settings are shown in table 27.1. MAE, mean absolute error; RMSE, root mean square error; RMSEs, RMSE systematic; RMSEu, RMSE unsystematic.

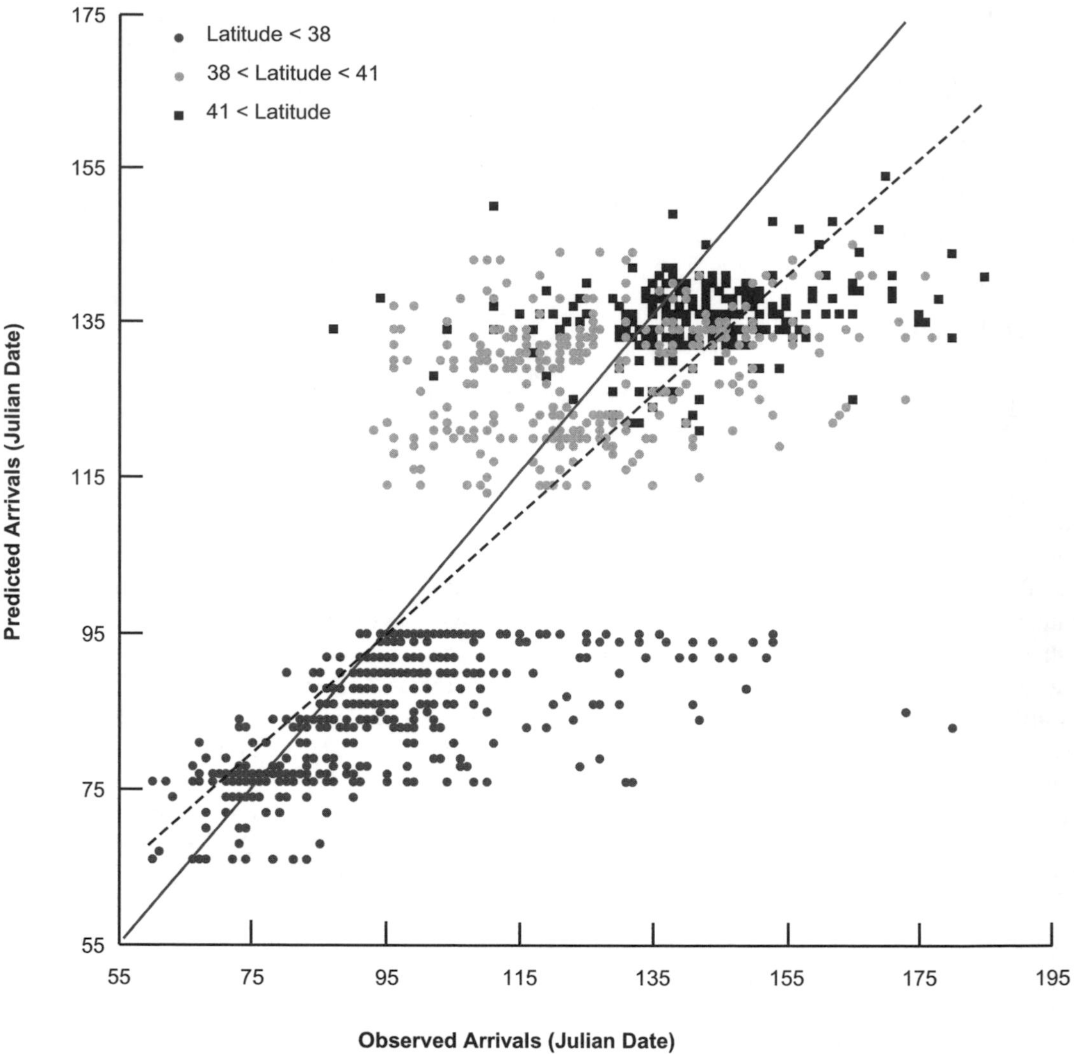

Figure 27.4. Plot of observed versus predicted arrival dates for the years 1995 to 1999 (observed data from Journey North 2001). Each observation in every grid is included on the graph.

correlation coefficient (R^2) shows the years in which observed and predicted values were most similar.

A plot of all observed arrival times from Journey North (2001) against first modeled arrival times in the corresponding grid cell reveals several model shortcomings (figure 27.4). The model shows a gap in the Julian arrival date from Julian day 95 to Julian day 114. This is because of the *pmig* restriction in the model, which allows only the second generation of butterflies to migrate north of this line. In actuality, many recolonizing butterflies continue beyond this arbitrary division. The additional time required for the second generation to develop and migrate north causes overestimates of arrival dates immediately north of 38° north latitude. Below 38° north, model arrival dates correlate well with the first-observed arrival dates in the field; however, for any given grid cell there are a large portion of much later observed arrivals. These late observations create a significant problem for model validation purposes and influence the validation statistics. The model appears to simulate the leading edge of arrival times, as expected.

Model performance is relatively poor immediately north of 38° north latitude, where the model cuts off migrating individuals from the first genera-

Table 27.3. Comparison of monarch production estimates

	Total area (ha) covered by colonies (following winter)	Model results		
		Total no. of cohorts produced[a]	Total possible no. of generations[a]	Total no. of return cohorts produced[a]
Year				
1993	6.23	40,590	1,263	14,367
1994	7.81	41,324	1,315	10,584
1995	12.61	48,214	1,511	12,602
1996	20.97	39,529	1,252	14,119
1997	5.77	39,528	1,208	10,602
1998	5.56	45,754	1,461	13,558
1999	9.05	46,541	1,490	11,226
Correlation coefficient vs. total area covered (ha)		−0.10	−0.06	0.36
p value at 95% confidence level		0.83	0.89	0.43

Note: Updated overwintering population estimates from Serrano and Alvarez (1998). Model parameter settings are shown in table 27.1. There are no significant relationships between model predictions and the number of hectares occupied by colonies.

[a] Sum of all grid cells north of 38° north latitude.

tion, especially for the leading edge of the observed migration. Above 41° north, reached by relatively few returning migrants, the model seems to improve again, although it still appears to predict arrival times about 15 days behind the leading edge of observed arrivals. This suggests that either the development time or travel rate of the second generation could be improved. This difference is reflected in the separation of the regression line and the 1 : 1 line on the graph.

We compared the relative numbers of monarchs produced in the model to estimates of the number of overwintering butterflies from 1993 to 1999 (updated from Serrano and Alvarez 1998). We used three measures of butterfly production in this analysis, integrated for all grid cells north of 38° north: (1) the total number of cohorts produced over the entire breeding season, based on the assumption that one cohort begins development each day after a grid cell is populated in the spring; (2) a summation of the total number of generations possible in each grid cell, based on the assumption that one generation must be completed before a second can begin; and (3) the total number of cohorts produced between the dates set for the beginning and end of the fall migration period. Each of these results is compared to the number of hectares and trees covered by overwintering monarchs (table 27.3).

None of the relationships are significant. There is a positive correlation between the number of return cohorts produced and the area occupied by the overwintering colonies, although this correlation is far from statistically significant ($p = 0.43$). This could indicate that conditions during the fall migration, and perhaps other factors such as predation, might be more important for determining overwintering populations than total monarch production during the summer period (see also Prysby and Oberhauser, this volume). Further study, including information about the origin of overwintering monarchs (e.g., Wassenaar and Hobson 1998), is required to obtain a better understanding between these relationships.

DISCUSSION

A number of improvements are needed to make the model useful for evaluating the impact of climate and human actions on the population dynamics of monarchs. Nevertheless, the results suggest that the natural dynamics of the population could be simulated reasonably well. In addition, further verification is needed to evaluate the model's performance in relation to specific climate events. We propose a number of modifications to address these issues and those raised above:

1. Change from using temperature data from the nearest station to using interpolated temperature values at grid cells.
2. Use a water balance model or satellite-derived normalized difference vegetation index (NDVI) as a surrogate for milkweed conditions to assess food resources and consider land-cover information.

3. Use wind speed measurements or storm data to create a vector-based movement model for migration.
4. Use mortality statistics to control migration rates and survival. Additional factors, such as the influence of daylength and temperature on egg laying, can also be included to improve this model.
5. Verify the development model (Zalucki 1982) with field observations of development in relation to measured temperatures.
6. Allow for alternative hypotheses regarding migration initiation, for example, the concept of a gradual change (rotation) in the movement direction of monarchs through the breeding season (Brower 1996).
7. Add a simulation that incorporates mortality during the fall migration, the overwintering period, and the return migration.

These improvements should help to overcome some of the systematic errors observed in the current model. Once these have been completed, evaluations of human land-cover change can also be introduced to assess the impacts of humans on monarch population dynamics.

Acknowledgments

We wish to thank Elizabeth Howard of Journey North and the Journey North organization for their generous contribution of the data used to validate this model. We also thank the National Climate Data Center for the use of and assistance in compiling the climate data.

References

Brower, L. P. 1995. Understanding and misunderstanding the migration of the monarch butterfly (Nymphalidae) in North America: 1857–1995. J. Lepid. Soc. 46:304–85.

Brower, L. P. 1996. Monarch butterfly orientation: missing pieces of a magnificent puzzle. J. Exp. Biol. 199:93–103.

Cockrell, B. J., S. B. Malcolm, and L. P. Brower. 1993. Time, temperature, and latitudinal constraints in the annual recolonization of eastern North America by the monarch butterfly. In S. B. Malcolm and M. P. Zalucki, eds., Biology and conservation of the monarch butterfly, pp. 233–51. Los Angeles: Natural History Museum of Los Angeles County.

Journey North. 2001. http://www.learner.org/jnorth/. Accessed 7 June 2001.

Malcolm, S. B., B. J. Cockrell, and L. P. Brower. 1993. Spring recolonization of eastern North America by the monarch butterfly: successive brood of single sweep migration? In S. B. Malcolm and M. P. Zalucki, eds., Biology and conservation of the monarch butterfly, pp. 253–67. Los Angeles: Natural History Museum of Los Angeles County.

National Climate Data Center. 2001. http://lwf.ncdc.noaa.gov/oa/ncdc.html. Accessed 12 Feb 2001.

Oke, T. R. 1987. Boundary layer climates. 2nd ed. London: Methuen.

Serrano, E. G., and X. M. Alvarez. 1999. Monitoreo de las colonias de mariposa monarca en sus sitios de invernacion de Mexico. In North American Conference on the Monarch Butterfly. Commission for Environmental Cooperation, ed. J. Hoth et al. Montreal, Quebec. pp. 177–82.

Shields, J. 2001. Simulating the migration and development of the monarch butterfly (*Danaus plexippus*). Master's thesis, University of Kansas, Lawrence.

Wassenaar, L. I., and K. A. Hobson. 1998. Natal origins of migratory monarch butterflies at wintering colonies in Mexico: new isotopic evidence. Proc. Natl. Acad. Sci. USA 95:154–39.

Willmott, C. J., S. G. Ackleson, R. E. Davis, J. J. Feddema, K. M. Klink, D. R. Legates, J. O'Donnell, and C. M. Rowe. 1985. Statistics for the evaluation and comparison of models. J. Geophys. Res. 90:8995–9005.

Zalucki, M. P. 1982. Temperature and rate of development in *Danaus plexippus* L. and *D. chrysippus* L. (Lepidoptera: Nymphalidae). J. Aust. Entomol. Soc. 21:241–46.

Zalucki, M. P. 1983. Simulation of movement and egglaying in *Danaus plexippus* (Lepidoptera: Nymphalidae). Res. Popul. Ecol. 25:353–65.

Contributors

Sonia M. Altizer
Department of Environmental Studies
Emory University
Atlanta, Georgia

Blanca Xiomara Mora Alvarez
Monarch Butterfly Biosphere Reserve
Angangeuo, Michoacán, Mexico

David Bennett
Department of Geography
University of Iowa
Iowa City, Iowa

Jane Borland
Lamar High School
Arlington, Texas

Walter Bremer
Landscape Architecture Department
California Polytechnic State University
San Luis Obispo, California

Lincoln P. Brower
Department of Biology
Sweet Briar College
Sweet Briar, Virginia

William H. Calvert
Austin, Texas

Thomas William Crumpton III
Baylor University
Waco, Texas

Andrew K. Davis
Department of Environmental Studies
Emory University
Atlanta, Georgia

Johannes J. Feddema
Department of Geography
University of Kansas
Lawrence, Kansas

Concha Fernandez del Rey
Breck School
Minneapolis, Minnesota

Dan Feuerstein
Department of Architecture and Environmental Design
California Polytechnic State University
San Luis Obispo, California

Miguel Franco
School of Biological Sciences
University of Plymouth
Plymouth, England

Dennis Frey
Biological Sciences Department
California Polytechnic State University
San Luis Obispo, California

Eligio García-Serrano
Monarch Butterfly Biosphere Reserve
Zitacuaro, Michoacan, Mexico.

Mark S. Garland
New Jersey Audubon Society
Cape May Bird Observatory, Northwood Center
Cape May, New Jersey

Kari A. Geurts
Department of Forest Resources
University of Minnesota
St. Paul, Minnesota

Liz Goehring
Ridge 2000 Program
Pennsylvania State University
University Park, Pennsylvania

Tammi Hoevenaar
Department of Biological Sciences
Western Michigan University
Kalamazoo, Michigan

Elizabeth Howard
Journey North
Minneapolis, Minnesota

Laura C. H. Jesse
Department of Entomology
Iowa State University
Ames, Iowa

Carol C. Johnson
John Jay High School
San Antonio, Texas

Andrés F. Keiman
Departamento de Ecología Evolutiva
Instituto de Ecología
México, DF, Mexico

David R. Kust
Breck School
Minneapolis, Minnesota

Katherine R. Kust
Woodland Elementary School
Brooklyn Park, Minnesota

Kingston L. H. Leong
Biological Sciences Department
California Polytechnic State University
San Luis Obispo, California

Stephen B. Malcolm
Department of Biological Sciences
Western Michigan University
Kalamazoo, Michigan

Jacob Miller
Breck School
Minneapolis, Minnesota

Monica Missrie
Department of Conservation Biology
University of Minnesota
St. Paul, Minnesota

Karen S. Oberhauser
Department of Fisheries, Wildlife, and Conservation Biology
University of Minnesota
St. Paul, Minnesota

John J. Obrycki
Department of Entomology
Iowa State University
Ames, Iowa

Karen Pape
Breck School
Minneapolis, Minnesota

Sandra M. Perez
Biology Department
University of Texas at El Paso
El Paso, Texas

Michelle D. Prysby
Great Smoky Mountains Institute at Tremont
Great Smoky Mountains National Park
Townsend, Tennessee

Linda S. Rayor
Department of Entomology
Cornell University
Ithaca, New York

Eduardo Rendón Salinas
Instituto de Ecología
Universidad Nacional Autónoma de México
México DF, Mexico

Jaime Lobato Reyes
Monarch Butterfly Biosphere Reserve
Angangeuo, Michoacán, Mexico

Wayne A. Rochester
Department of Zoology and Entomology, School of Life Sciences
University of Queensland
Brisbane, Australia

Walter H. Sakai
Department of Biology
Santa Monica College
Santa Monica, California

Andrew Schaffner
Statistics Department
California Polytechnic State University
San Luis Obispo, California

Jason Shields
Department of Geography
University of Kansas
Lawrence, Kansas

Michelle J. Solensky
Department of Ecology, Evolution and Behavior
University of Minnesota
St. Paul, Minnesota

Orley R. "Chip" Taylor
Monarch Watch, Entomology Program
University of Kansas
Lawrence, Kansas

Markisha Thomas
John Jay High School
San Antonio, Texas

Gwen Yoshimura
School of Earth Sciences
Stanford University
Standford, California

Myron P. Zalucki
Department of Zoology and Entomology, School of Life Sciences
University of Queensland
Brisbane, Australia

Index